Symbol of Authority

Symbol of Authority

The British District Officer in Africa

Anthony Kirk-Greene

I.B. TAURIS

LONDON · NEW YORK

Published in 2006 by I.B.Tauris & Co. Ltd
6 Salem Road, London W2 4BU
175 Fifth Avenue, New York, NY 10010
www.ibtauris.com

In the United States of America and Canada distributed by Palgrave
Macmillan, a division of St Martin's Press, 175 Fifth Avenue, New York,
NY 10010

International Library of Colonial History 1

ISBN: 1 85043 452 2
EAN: 978 1 85043 452 8

A full CIP record for this book is available from the British Library
A full CIP record for this book is available from the Library of
Congress

Library of Congress catalog card: available

Typeset in Palatino Linotype by A. & D. Worthington, Newmarket
Printed and bound in Great Britain by TJ International Ltd, Padstow

Contents

List of Illustrations

Foreword

At the time, it was never easy to describe one's job as a District Officer, particularly at home, when on leave, to somebody whose only encounter with public servants had been in the local council offices. With even the ending of empire now a fading memory, the extraordinary breadth and endless generality of the job not only beggar belief but invite scorn from the minutely specialized technocrats of the twenty-first century. The context in which a District Officer often performed his duties is equally difficult to take on board. People still know what it is like to work very long hours and to be on constant call, but few experience those conditions, day in day out, on their own, without radio or telephone, as much as 50 or more miles from the nearest colleague or, indeed, commonplace amenity such as a doctor or a store. In the wet season, moreover, colleagues and amenities might be accessible only on foot. The District Officer may have lived elaborately, even lavishly, by the standards of those whom he administered, but, by the standards of his contemporaries in the United Kingdom, his living conditions were usually elementary and unlikely to be envied.

It would, however, be hard to find another job, then or now, that gave responsibility and satisfaction in equal measure at so early an age, or a lifestyle that was as rich in enjoyment as it was rewarding in fulfilment. Few regretted embarking upon what its principal recruiter called 'one of the most many-sided and exacting careers in the world'. Many have excelled in second careers, but these have also been second best, unable to compete with the regard and affection in which all District Officers held their first careers.

There were District Officers throughout the British Empire but the greatest number were always in Africa, and it was in Africa that their role, if not the tasks they performed, became most clearly defined. Anthony Kirk-Greene, the acknowledged historian of the Colonial Service, has written two institutional histories, *On Crown Service* (1999) and *Britain's Imperial Administrators, 1858–1966* (2000), which set the scene in which District Officers worked. In *Symbol of Authority* he puts flesh on the bones of his previous work by drawing upon the memoirs of District Officers in former British Africa. He has selected memoirs covering the period from 1932 to 1966, the final years of an African empire, much of which had been established less than a century before. He provides an overview of the surprising range of tasks that District Officers undertook and the wide variety of everyday duties not only from colony to colony but also from district to district.

What made the job of District Officer in Africa special? There is, after all, nothing unique about administration. Administrators make things happen and see that they continue to happen. They are the oil in the engines of the world. From the beginnings of recorded history, empires great and small have come and gone: empire is not unique. Africa, however, can claim uniqueness. It is rare for those who now belong to other continents not to be swiftly seduced by the sight, the sound and the smell of the continent to which all humanity owes its genesis. Enveloped by its immensity but touched by the intimacy of its warmth, perhaps we experience a subconscious sense of coming home.

Certainly a sense of belonging, of representing the interests of the peoples of one's district, fighting for them when necessary, of being – what sounds so ridiculous today – 'their father and their mother', as one was frequently and without embarrassment addressed, were at the heart of the totality of commitment that characterized the District Officer. One had much to give but also much to learn. That tempered the built-in paternalism because one's ability to function, as well as one's safety, depended on mutual trust, a trust almost always strengthened on both sides by affection. It was this direct, close and unusually easy association with the people at every level of every activity, rather than status, that distinguished administrators most clearly from their Colonial Service colleagues in other professions. Administrators then lacked, as they still lack in most spheres, the clearly defined role and professional ethos of, say, doctor, engineer, forester, magistrate or teacher, all of whom had commitments to their professions and often enjoyed membership of professional institutions that guided their behaviour and restrained their approach. When independence came, they could continue with their chosen career elsewhere. The District Officer could still administer but had to do so in a very different setting.

Most of the time, formal policy impinged gently on the District Officer. He rarely had to impose policies from above. The essence of his approach was to manage from below within a modest framework of well-established law. There was immense scope for freedom of action and for initiative. Much of what he did would forever remain unknown except to those immediately involved. Being allowed to get on with it and being expected to maintain law and order by mere presence are probably what mainly distinguished the District Officer in British Africa from his counterparts in the French, German, Spanish and Portuguese colonies. These tended to be more constrained by central policies and to be more closely identified as the arm of central government.

Attending the Devonshire Course at Oxford University, I was among a group of cadets destined for West Africa who were addressed by Dr Francis Ibiam, a Nigerian doctor working in a mission hospital, a leading nationalist and later to become governor of Eastern Nigeria. He defined our role as stewardship. Forget about the history, of which there was more than one view, that had got us where we were. The District Officer was a fact of colonial life, doing a job that had to be done. But he was transitory. The people he administered trusted him to look after their best interests until they were again able to look after themselves, and they expected him to trust them. I have never forgotten what was the most inspiring hour of the year-long course. I have never found a better word to epitomize what we were about – stewardship.

Memory is always selective, and the mellowing of age may endow the mundane with romance, but I like to think that there was something, beyond the expected categories of school and university, in the formation of the generation administering the last days of empire that helped equip us to understand and to accept our stewardship: we had grown up in the shadow of the First World War. Our fathers and uncles had fought in that war but, for the most part, never spoke of it, such were its horrors, as is better known now than then. Their very silence had its influence. Our social conscience had been aroused by reading Dickens, on the bookshelves of every household of our youth, and sharpened by the Great Depression, the effects of which were felt in most homes. We were part of the Second World War, whether in the services or still as schoolboys. We knew things had to change. We recognized that the world order would never again be the same, that the empire must come to an end. We were well tuned to match the hour. One day, perhaps, history will recognize the part this played in ensuring that, in the main, the end of colonial rule and the coming of independence were achieved peacefully and hopefully. Of course, we made plenty of mistakes and we shared all the usual human failings, but perhaps our greatest fault was to join with those to whom we transferred power in a conspiracy of optimism. Our expectations and theirs, 50 years ago, were too high.

In *Symbol of Authority* Anthony Kirk-Greene, with wide experience of academic research, the sympathy of an insider and with a unique knowledge of autobiographical sources, has drawn upon the stories of many individuals who as District Officers in British colonial Africa exercised such enormous power and influence over a period of history not much longer than the average lifetime. In an easily accessible single volume and with great skill he provides the reader with all the evidence needed upon which to draw his or her own conclusions about a set of men whose job and whose like will never be seen again.

John Smith
District Officer, Northern Nigeria, 1951–70
Governor, Gilbert and Ellice Islands, 1973–78
(Dulverton, December 2003)

Abbreviations

ADC	Assistant District Commissioner/Aide de Camp
ADO	Assistant District Officer
BECM	British Empire and Commonwealth Museum
CAS	Colonial Administrative Service
CO	Colonial Office
CRH	Catering Rest-House
CRO	Commonwealth Relations Office
CS	Colonial Service
CSAB	Colonial Service Appointments Board
DC	District Commissioner
DO	District Officer
DSO	Distinguished Service Order
FCO	Foreign and Commonwealth Office
GH	Government House
GRA	Government Reservation Area
HCT	High Commission Territories
HE	His Excellency
HMG	Her/His Majesty's Government
HMOCS	Her Majesty's Overseas Civil Service

HQ	Headquarters
ICS	Indian Civil Service
LG	Local Government
LSE	London School of Economics
MC	Military Cross
NA	Native Administration/Native Authority
NFD	Northern Frontier District (Kenya)
NGO	Non-Governmental Organization
NT	Native Treasury
OAG	Officer Administering the Government
OCRP	Oxford Colonial Records Project
ODRP	Oxford Development Records Project
OSPA	Overseas Service Pensioners' Association
OSRB	Overseas Service Resettlement Bureau
PA	Provincial Administration
PC	Provincial Commissioner
PRO	Public Record Office
PS	Private Secretary
PWD	Public Works Department
RHL	Rhodes House Library
SDO	Senior District Officer
SOAS	School of Oriental and African Studies
SPS	Sudan Political Service
TANU	Tanganyikan African National Union
TAS	Tropical African Service
VSO	Voluntary Service Overseas
WAO	Woman Administrative Officer
WOPS	Widows and Orphans Pension Scheme

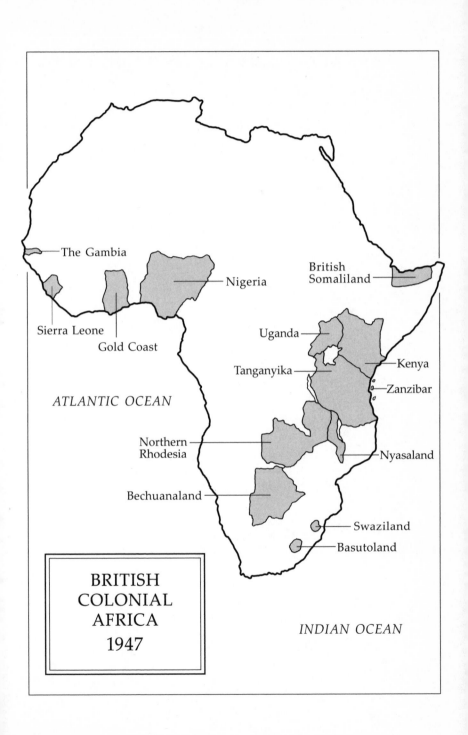

The Gambia

Sierra Leone

Gold Coast

Nigeria

British Somaliland

Uganda

Tanganyika

Kenya

Zanzibar

ATLANTIC OCEAN

Northern Rhodesia

Nyasaland

Bechuanaland

Swaziland

Basutoland

BRITISH COLONIAL AFRICA 1947

INDIAN OCEAN

Introduction

This is a socio-historical study of members of the Colonial Administrative Service whose careers were as District Officers in Africa between 1932 and 1966. It considers who they were in socio-educational terms and how they were recruited and trained, what they did in both their work and their leisure, the impact on them of the transfer of power and what happened to them when they returned to Britain prematurely retired in search of a second career during the decolonizing decade of 1957–68.

As such, it constitutes a lone-standing text. At the same time, it sets out to complement and expand on the two primary studies of the Colonial Service which have appeared in the last five years. My *On Crown Service* (1999) was an institutional history of the whole Colonial Service, not of the Colonial Administrative Service alone. My *Britain's Imperial Administrators* (2000) was a study of not only the Colonial Administrative Service in South East Asia and the Pacific as well as Africa, but also of the quite separate Indian Civil Service and the Sudan Political Service. Both histories were largely based on official documentation. This new study, on the other hand, is conceptualized as a collective portrait of the generic colonial administrator or District Officer in Africa, and is designed to put a human face on the two preceding histories, being drawn essentially from personal memoirs. The first two volumes set the stage and outlined the plot; the third focuses on the actors. In this attempt to bring the District Officer in Africa alive, the approach owes a debt of intellectual gratitude to Philip Mason, who 50 years ago brilliantly memorialized 'The Men Who Ruled India' and composed the telling epitaph: 'The hero is a thousand men, not a service nor a system but a thousand individuals, each different from the next.'[1] In its emphasis on personal memoirs as testimony, the present study also acknowledges the approach so effectively invoked by Charles Allen in his eye-witness trilogy of some of the surviving actors of empire a quarter of a century ago.[2]

The structure of the present book might be described in terms echoing that of the autobiographical volumes of Leonard Woolf, a colonial administrator in Ceylon almost 100 years ago, with his *Sowing* and *Growing*: 'Becoming', 'Being' and 'Beyond'. After delineating the context of the Colonial Administrative Service in time, place and policies in the opening chapter, Chapter 2 analyses the influences which so often inclined a young man in his early 20s to dream of a career in the Colonial Service: home and family connections as well as school and university, and, from 1939, war service or National Service. It also looks at the successive stages of application, interviews and probationary appointment. The process culminated in nomination to a postgraduate Colonial Service training course at Oxford, Cambridge or London University. This is examined in Chapter 3 and its value assessed in retrospect by some of those who attended the course. The chapter closes with a look at the necessary, and today quaintly dated, world of tropical outfitting.

Having now *become* a member of the prestigious Colonial Administrative Service, the cadet's identity story develops in Part II into what it was like to *be* one. Leading on from Chapter 4 – the initiatory experience of the voyage out, the journey to and arrival at one's first *boma* or up-country station, of being introduced to one's seniors and meeting one's colleagues, and of at last settling down to learning the job by doing it – Chapters 5, 6 and 7 depict in detail the vast range of work and responsibility that made up the District Officer's life, whether it was in station, in the central Secretariat, or – so often the joy of the moment and later the highlight of post-colonial memories – out 'on tour'. Chapter 8 concerns the opportunities for recreation in the District Officer's life, as critical to his mental as to his physical well being, while Chapter 9 reflects on a too often neglected yet extremely important approach to understanding what it meant to have a career as a District Officer, namely the woman's viewpoint on marrying into the Colonial Administrative Service.

Part III considers the last years of the District Officer in Africa, with Chapter 10 centred on the impact of politics, localization and decolonization on the changing nature of his work as well as on his future prospects, including the schemes for early retirement and compensation for loss of career. It also examines the kinds of employment taken up back in Britain by former District Officers, now retired early. The final chapter looks back at the life and work of District Officers, how they and others see the image in retrospect, and how former District Officers have kept in touch with one another.

Still on structure, the choice of the dates covered in this history requires an explanation. One possibility was to confine it to a post-Second World War study, say from 1946 when the Colonial Service experienced a vast expansion of staff, soon followed by a sharp policy re-orientation away from the classic indirect rule through local government and 'development' to the transfer of power – now to be sooner rather than later. Another option was to go back to 1926, when the Colonial Service introduced at Oxford and Cambridge a formal year-long postgraduate training programme for its administrative probationers. Yet another alternative was to go back to the end of the First World War, even though the work of the first generation of District Officers in Africa has already been soundly covered by Lewis Gann and Peter Duignan.[3] While the Colonial Service can trace its history back to 1837, when the first set of Colonial Regulations was issued, up to 1930 there was literally no such entity as the Colonial Service. Instead, each territory had its own civil service, for instance the Nigerian Civil Service, the Ugandan Civil Service, etc., with the Eastern Cadet Service recruiting staff for Ceylon, Malaya and Hong Kong. The eventual choice settled on 1932, the year in which the Colonial Administrative Service was established, incorporating all the hitherto separate territorial administrative services. Such a starting date allows inclusion in the text of the memoirs of District Officers who, joining in the 1930s, were filling the influential senior posts at the time that the large post-Second World War generation of administrative cadets arrived in Africa, between 1946 and 1951. As to the cut-off date, no such problem presented itself. Granted that the 14 African territories became independent not simultaneously but at different dates between 1957 (Gold Coast) and 1968 (Swaziland), the natural choice was 1966, the year in which the Colonial Office finally closed down. This represents far more of an 'end' than the reformulation of the Colonial Service into Her Majesty's Overseas Civil Service in 1954.

Throughout the text the term District Officer (DO) has been used to refer to the colonial field administrator, the successor, if you like, of the archetypal 'Sanders of the River' whose influence, whether through novel or film, was to prove so prominent in arousing the imagination of many a potential DO. While in most of the African territories outside Nigeria the colonial administrator was generally known as the District Commissioner (DC), with the appellation DO sometimes referring to a junior rank, the use of 'District Officer' as the pan-African generic term for the colonial administrator below the rank of Provincial Commissioner or Resident as the recognized representative of the government in the districts has most recently been confirmed by its adoption in the composite Service memoir of the DC in the Ugandan Administration, with its subtitle of 'Recollections of District Officers'.[4] The present study does not extend upwards to the Provincial Commissioner or Resident, or to the Governor. It is centred on the persona of the DO regardless of whether his rank at the time was Senior DO/DC, DO/DC, Assistant DO/DC, or cadet. In Africa, DO constituted an across-the-board and immediate identity, neither rank-specific nor territory-specific, simply the symbol of authority.

It may seem bold to try to subsume the life and work of the DO in 14 separate and sometimes uncontiguous African colonial territories into the conceptual identity of *the* DO. Yet, as any DO who visited or was transferred to another African territory was quick to recognize, there existed (minutiae apart) a sufficient degree of fundamental similarity, shared idiom and common ethos for the incomer not to feel like an extra-terrestrial alien or once more in his life be an utterly bemused tyro. African administration and its practitioners enjoyed as palpable a measure of similarity and continuity as they had of recognized procedural differences. Yet by depending here so deliberately on personal experience, the risk of the DO from Nyasaland declaring that 'it was never like that' when he reads the account of a DO's life in Nigeria is minimized. Nevertheless, I wish to apologize in advance for any occasions where I may have misunderstood a passage from a memoir and may have caused dismay in the locally experienced readers.

Finally, a word of explanation on the corpus of material from which the bulk of this history is derived. The sources are preponderantly and purposely the memoirs of DOs who served in Africa between 1932 and 1966, published (over 100) or unpublished (more that 50). To this archive there can now be added the shorter autobiographical contributions of a further 200 or so DOs which have appeared in the composite Service memoirs from Uganda, Eastern Nigeria, Kenya and Northern Nigeria in the past few years. My use of 'memoir' is here taken to include not only this standard autobiographical material but also the unique written reminiscences and reflections from another 300 one-time DOs in Africa, who, as members of the Overseas Service Pensioners' Association, responded to my research questionnaire in 2001/2, together with the extensive verbatim recollections presented in the symposium 'The Colonial Administrator in the Age of Decolonization' held at St Antony's College, Oxford, in 1978. The evidence is thus derived from an archive of 'memoirs' or written contributions from more than 500 DOs who served in Africa between 1932 and 1966. I have deliberately restricted my research to memoirs as thus defined, eschewing letters and diaries and the oral history interviews undertaken by the projects based at Rhodes House Library, Oxford, in 1970–72 and, currently, at the British Empire and Commonwealth Museum at Bristol. The reason for this decision is a qualitative as well as a quantitative one. The memoir, the conference paper and the written testimony in a research project is, in each case, a disciplined and carefully reconstructed document, a crafted account of what the author coherently recollects and how he or she, in considered retrospect, wishes the events to be recorded and read. The typical diary, on the other hand, is frequently and fundamentally a chronological record of events, instantaneous in composition, often in foreshortened form, essentially serving as a reminder and a resource for subsequent reference – which may, one day, form the basis of a disciplined memoir or a reflective autobiography. As for letters home to parents, spouses or children, they often tend to omit things that 'Mum would rather not read about' or 'Dad would not be interested in', with the accent, by their very nature, on the ephemeral or the immediate or the banal, or simply domestic items and the family. As for Colonial Service oral inter-

views, experience has proved that unless these are professionally prepared by those reasonably intimate with the work of the
interviewed and its context and are able to raise questions and
probe beyond the light observation or amusing anecdote, they
do not always manage to generate as much reliable substance as
that derived from the 'memoir' as defined here. Accordingly, for
all the potential value of diaries and letters and interviews, I have
concentrated exclusively on the memoir for this study of the identity and the image, projected as well as perceived, of the District
Officer in Africa. I believe the memoir to be the most authentic,
the most sustained and the most compelling of all the personal
sources available. It is in the memoir that we find the record of
a life lived at once carefully recalled and reflected on, and not
just spontaneously remembered. The Colonial Service memoir is
more than a secondary source: it can constitute a primary source
to a degree that the oral interview, the diary and the letter cannot
always match.

There remains one more matter: the pleasant task of acknowledgements. First and foremost my thanks go to all District Officers
who served in Africa since 1932 for their 'memoirs', unpublished
(in public deposit or on personal loan) or published either in solo
book form or as autobiographical contributions to composite
Service volumes of memoirs. All these memoirs form the basis
of this book and their reading has given me huge intellectual
reward and pleasure over the past three years. All are listed in
the bibliography of sources cited. A similar acknowledgement
is due to the large group of ex-colonial administrators who, as
members of OSPA, last year took part in the research project
'Towards a Retrospective Record of the Colonial Service', and
whose contributions of mini-essays now form an archive in their
own right, yielding data and opinions of major worth to Colonial
Service historians. Once again, the names of those quoted verbatim appear in the list of source materials at the end of this book.
I leave it to the deductive powers of readers to identify that 'one
DO in Northern Nigeria has recalled how ...', who from time to
time is quoted in these pages anonymously. The staff of Rhodes
House Library, with its unparalleled collection of Colonial Service manuscript memoirs, have displayed their customary knowledge and courtesy. My thanks are also due to the Warden and
Fellows of St Antony's College, Oxford, for their hospitality and
encouragement during the past 37 years, and to Marie Ruiz for

her heroic typing from my wayward handwriting. In particular, I thank John Smith for kindly agreeing to contribute the Foreword to this study of a career which he, too, knows so intimately and has written about so well. I also wish to express my appreciation of the warmth of the support shown by my commissioning editor, Dr Lester Crook, of the dedication of Kate Sherratt, and of the editorial and indexing skills of David and Alison Worthington. Finally, the measure of my gratitude to my wife is beyond expression.

Anthony Kirk-Greene
Oxford, December 2003

PART I. STEPPING STONES

CHAPTER 1

The Colonial Administrative Service: Chronology and Context

The bureaucratic organization of what was called 'the British Empire' up to 1939 has been a matter of obfuscation for post-imperial generations, Britons and others alike. To start the unravelling of the imperial vocabulary, the concept of the British Empire first needs to be broken down into the autonomous Dominions (Canada, Australia, New Zealand, South Africa) and the Dependent Empire. The latter, in turn, was divided into the Indian Empire and the Colonial Empire. In 1947 the first was dissolved and the second was restyled the Colonial Territories. Each unit came under the jurisdiction of a separate office in London, each with its own responsible minister: the Secretary of State for India, the Secretary of State for the Colonies, and, from 1947, the Secretary of State for Commonwealth Relations when the Dominions Office was hived off from the Colonial Office (CO). The Foreign Office remained responsible for relations with non-Commonwealth countries and non-colonial foreign affairs, again under its own minister. There was in Whitehall no overarching ministry or department of external affairs, nor, despite a series of internal inquiries during the last half-century of the Colonial Office's existence, was there any amalgamation of or regular cross-posting between the Colonial Service and the Colonial Office staffs in the way that was a standard feature of the

1

Foreign Office. Each was separately recruited, assigned and paid. Nevertheless after 1930 a separate division was established in the Colonial Office with direct responsibility for its Colonial Service. By 1950 this had grown into three departments (recruitment and training; appointments, transfer and promotions; discipline and pensions) overseeing the management of the Colonial Service.

At the end of the Second World War the CO was responsible for 37 territories, variously bearing the legal status of colony, protectorate, mandate or territory, including what the CO officially described as 'a number of islands and rocks throughout the world ... not included in any colony. Many of these have no permanent inhabitants but are leased for guano collection or for coconut planting.'[1] The colonial territories were spread over the seas across the world, from the Atlantic to the Pacific and from the Mediterranean and the Caribbean to the Indian Ocean and the Antarctic. By far the largest group to be staffed were the African territories, 14 in all from 1952 when the CO declared the local civil services of the three South African High Commission Territories to be henceforward inter-changeable with Colonial Service personnel.[2] Of the rest, four were in West Africa, five in East Africa, and two in Central Africa.

Although the history of the Colonial Service can be traced back to 1837, when Colonial Regulations were first issued, it was not until the end of the nineteenth century that the number of civil servants appointed on anything like permanent and pensionable terms justified public recognition of the Colonial Service as one of the Crown services. In 1899 the Colonial Service comprised 434 higher administrative officers (approximately 100 of whom belonged to the self-contained Eastern Cadet Service administering Ceylon, Malaya and Hong Kong), 310 legal officers, 447 medical officers, and 300 classified as 'other', giving a total of about 1,500. Among the possibilities considered at the turn of the century for the future shape and direction of the Colonial Service, now facing the challenge of finding officials to staff the new Crown territories in Africa, was either amalgamation with the Colonial Office personnel or integration with the Indian Civil Service to form a new British Empire civil service. A third option, advanced a few years later, was the creation of a separate Tropical African Service, along the lines of the West African Medical Service formed in 1902. In the event none of these options was proceeded with. Technically it remained incorrect, other than for the Colonial Audit Service, to talk in terms of 'the Colonial Service' until the 1930s. Each territorial government had its own establishment, so that officers described themselves as being in the Nigerian, Nyasaland, Gold Coast etc. civil services. To quote a perplexed secretary of state in 1927: 'Strictly speaking, there is no Colonial Empire and no such thing as a Colonial Service. I deal in this office with some twenty-six different governments, each entirely separate from the rest. Each has its own Administrative Service ... and other technical services, its own scale of pay, its own pensions.'[3]

The creation of the Colonial Service did not come about until 1930, when it was agreed to unify all the territorial civil services into a single Colonial Service (CS). Officers would now be eligible for transfer on promotion whenever a vacancy occurred in any other territory, though local discretion continued over promotion, rates of pay and leave conditions. Of the 20 CS branches progressively unified by 1949,[4] the first was the new Colonial Administrative Service (CAS), in 1932.

The 14 African territories in which District Officers operated during the period covered in this history, along with their size and population (1947) and the dates of their take-over by the Crown and of their independence are as follows:

Territory	Area (sq. miles)	Population	Crown Rule	Independence
WEST AFRICA				
Gambia	4,132	250,000	1843	1965
Gold Coast	91,843	4,095,000	1874	1957
Nigeria	372,674	22,000,000	1900	1960
Sierra Leone	27,925	1,800,000	1808	1961
EAST AFRICA				
British Somaliland	68,000	700,000	1884	1960
Kenya	224,960	4,200,000	1895	1963
Tanganyika	362,688	5,650,000	1920	1961
Uganda	93,981	4,000,000	1893	1962

Zanzibar	1,020	250,000	1890	1963
CENTRAL AFRICA				
Northern Rhodesia	287,640	1,660,000	1924	1964
Nyasaland	47,949	2,230,000	1891	1964
HIGH COMMISSION TERRITORIES				
Basutoland	11,716	556,000	1868	1966
Bechuana-land	275,000	294,000	1885	1966
Swaziland	6,704	184,000	1902	1968

(Source: Based on *The Colonial Empire*, Cmd. 7433, 1948)

The DO cadres of the African services had begun to expand at the beginning of the twentieth century, with the need to substitute government officers for the chartered company staff that had hitherto been responsible for such territories as most of Nigeria, and for Uganda, Kenya, Nyasaland, and in due course Northern Rhodesia. By the outbreak of the First World War there were 538 officers in the district administrations of British Tropical Africa, distributed thus:[5]

Gambia	4	East Africa Protectorate	117
Sierra Leone	29	Uganda	52
Gold Coast	44	Nyasaland	40
Nigeria	252		

A quarter of a century later, after both a world war and a world slump, the number of Colonial Administrative Service officers posted to Africa had more than doubled to 1,223 in 1937, distributed thus:[6]

West Africa		East Africa		Central/ Southern Africa	
Gambia	11	Kenya	164	N. Rhodesia	109
Sierra Leone	40	Tanganyika	185	Nyasaland	51
Gold Coast	91	Uganda	83	Basutoland	32
Nigeria	386	Zanzibar	20	Bechuanaland	20
		Somaliland	16	Swaziland	15
Totals	**528**		**468**		**227**

In terms of spread, Africa traditionally accounted for approximately three-quarters of the District Officer posts in the whole CAS. At its manpower peaks of 1947 and 1957, the regional proportions were 38 per cent and 31 per cent serving in West Africa respectively and 39 per cent and 44 per cent in East and Central Africa.[7]

The administration of each African territory was divided into a number of provinces, each in the charge of a senior administrator of the rank of Provincial Commissioner or, in Nigeria, Resident. In the largest colonies, a number of provinces might be grouped under a Chief Commissioner or a Lieutenant-Governor, for example Ashanti and the Northern Territories in the Gold Coast or the Northern, Western and Eastern Provinces of Nigeria. Each province would be divided into several districts, typically three or four, each under a DO, who in rank might be either a [Senior] District Commissioner/Officer (SDO) or an Assistant District Commissioner/Officer (ADO). The group rank of cadet was given to administrative officers who were on their first tour and who had not yet passed the examinations to be confirmed as ADO. It is these DO ranks that form the generic District Officer of this study.

In the early days of African administration they were sometimes known as Travelling Commissioners or Native Commissioners, and, as a group, Political Officers, this being indicative of their primary responsibility. Later Administrative Officers or the Provincial Administration became the group norm. In the capital, the Secretariat was usually staffed by DOs (temporarily labelled [Senior] Assistant Secretary), seconded from the provin-

cial administration to work under the Chief (in a protectorate)
or Colonial (in a colony) Secretary, the governor's principal staff
officer. The advent of, first, a policy of accelerated development
after 1947, and then of a ministerial system of government in the
run-up to independence, introduced a large number of additional
headquarter posts, most of which were held by DOs. In Kenya
there also existed the subordinate rank of District Assistant and,
during the Mau Mau uprising of the 1950s, the rank of Emergency
or Home Guard DO. These, however, were locally recruited and
not CO appointments,

Before considering the work of the DO, it will be helpful to
outline the development of the CAS, whose creation in 1932
marks the beginning of the period covered in this book. The
year 1930 was a landmark one for the Colonial Service in two
ways. Firstly, it brought about, as we have seen, the approval
of a unified CAS. Secondly, it saw the publication of the important Warren Fisher Committee report,[8] described by a senior CO
official as 'the Magna Carta of the Colonial Service'.[9] Its terms
of reference were to enquire into the existing system of appointment in the CO and in the Colonial Services (note the plural).
Where the report impinged most acutely and far-reachingly
on the DO cadre was in its recommendations on the method
of recruitment and appointment. Despite its acknowledgement
that overall the CS had clearly benefited from a system of selection that emphasized the importance of personal qualities (those
elusive desiderata of 'character', 'initiative', and 'leadership') over
the intellectual ones demanded by the sort of examination used
for the Indian Civil, the Eastern Cadet, the Home Civil and the
Diplomatic Services, the Warren Fisher Committee expressed its
firm opinion that recruitment primarily based on an officially
recognized system of patronage could no longer be justified.
While there was no evidence that injustice had taken place, the
potential for abuse when the interviewing and the recommendations lay in the hands of the secretary of state's unestablished
private office staff (openly designated as Patronage Secretaries)
was too great for the system to be allowed to continue.[10] Hence-
forth recruitment would lie in the hands of permanent CO civil
servants; an established post of Director of Recruitment would be
created in the CO; and the final decision to appoint or not would
be the responsibility of the Civil Service Commissioners. All this,
it was recognized, would open the post of, *inter alios*, DO to a new

quality of applicant and, as the CO now anticipated, place the CAS, in the public mind, on the same level of respect and career prestige as the Indian Civil Service (ICS).

Among the benefits derived from these two linked reforms – the unification of the CAS and the new system of appointment – came a widening of the horizon, intellectual and territorial, of the DO. No longer was a DO confined to the territory of his initial posting for the whole of his career – unless, that is, he had been picked out as potential gubernatorial material and tried out in another colony as the colonial or financial secretary or as governor of a small Caribbean island. After 1932, inter-territorial transfers could now take place at the DO level. For example, a small colony like the Gambia turned to Nigeria, with its large DO cadre, for mid-seniority staff. Furthermore, the CO initiated its own scheme of secondment, whereby a recently joined assistant principal might spend a year in a colony doing the work of an ADO. At the same time 'beachcombing', as the practice came to be known, was inaugurated, whereby a DO could be seconded to the CO for two years and vice versa. In contrast to some of the outward beachcombers who excitedly began to wonder whether they had chosen wisely in making the CO rather than the CS their career, there is no record of any inward beachcomber having such regrets. Another opening up process was the agreement in the mid-1930s by the CO to nominate one or two of its CAS recruits as DOs in the High Commission Territories, properly still the Whitehall jurisdiction of the Dominions Office.

The CAS, fundamentally a service to itself, was to receive two more injections of talent from outside at the end of the Second World War. One was the acceptance of a small number of ICS officers in 1947–48, who opted to continue as colonial administrators mostly (by choice) in Malaya but a few in Africa. This transfer also included several from the Burmese Frontier Service, with again some becoming DOs in Africa. The second was very much an intra-African affair. With the abolition of the Sudan Political Service imminent, in 1955 an astute Northern Nigerian government wrote a letter to *The Times*, inviting prematurely retired DOs to transfer to Northern Nigeria.[11] Others went to Uganda, again a neighbouring country.

In the same context of looking to the outside, notice must be taken of the deliberate and steady recruitment into the CAS between the wars, and even more vigorously after 1945, of people who were born in the Dominions. The CO's Dominions Selection Scheme started in Canada in 1923,[12] and was later extended to the other Dominions. Between 1923 and 1941 over 300 Dominions men joined the Colonial Service, with 100 from South Africa, 94 from Canada, 63 from New Zealand and 47 from Australia.[13] Many from the last two went to the Pacific territories, but a lot served as DOs in Africa. At least two New Zealanders and one South African became colonial governors. Immediately after the Second World War the CO reserved a number of DO posts in Kenya and Central Africa for Australians. Among the 155 Dominion appointments made between 1945 and 1955, eight of the DOs were Canadians. There were also at least eight Australian DOs in Nigeria. One of the first Australians to be posted to Nigeria was W.R. Crocker, who left early and published a bitter memoir on the quality of the senior administrators in the Northern Provinces.[14] By contrast, the memoirs of two post-war Canadian DOs in Tanganyika and Uganda paint a rosier picture for all concerned.[15]

There are firm grounds for describing the appointment of R.D. Furse to the new post of Director of Colonial Service Recruitment as a CS milestone in its own right. Furse had joined the secretary of state's patronage staff in 1910 and, apart from war service, continued there until 1930, by which time he was Private Secretary (Appointments). He remained in the new post of Director until 1948 (and as Adviser till 1950). His influence on the selection and calibre of DOs over the period 1920–50 cannot be exaggerated; suffice to say that by common consent, including that of the colonial governors whose staff he kept supplied with his – and often their – ideal of 'the best of British youth', Furse earned recognition as 'the father of the modern Colonial Service'. Another milestone, the policy proposals for the post-war organization and training of the Colonial Service, in which Furse played an important drafting role, particularly the CAS, will be considered in Chapter 3.

This leaves a final milestone: the abolition of the Colonial Service as a career in 1954 and its replacement by a non-permanent and non-pensionable Her Majesty's Overseas Civil Service (HMOCS), wherein the CAS was subsumed and its title converted to the Administrative Branch of HMOCS. A memorable CS postscript came in 1999 when, following the handback in 1997 to China of Hong Kong, the last dependent territory to be staffed by a substantial number of HMOCS officers, a special service of

Sir Ralph Furse, 'father of the modern Colonial Service'

remembrance for the CS was held in Westminster Abbey in the presence of HM the Queen. The Colonial Office itself had already closed in 1966, after merging first with the Commonwealth Relations Office (CRO) and then together into the renamed Foreign and Commonwealth Office (FCO) in 1968. The day of the District Officer in Africa was now past history.

With the chronology of the CAS now in place, we may turn to the policy context in which the DO operated. The principal objectives of colonial policy, as it impinged on the DO, are best illustrated in a succession of defining moments rather than by searching for a single, all-embracing and unchanging policy applicable from start to finish. To begin with, administrative policy – in so far as it was formulated at all and not just as a reaction to an international situation or as a pre-emptive occupation – was little more than the basic task of maintaining (often just creating) law and order. In the event, this was to remain an indispensable requirement of colonial rule right to the end, for even in the concluding era of planned infrastructural development and self-government it was as valid an objective as it had been 50 years earlier: without law and order there could be no development and no constitutional advance to independence. It was a lesson that the new nations were also quick to learn. Once Crown rule was secure, it was possible, with revenue accruing, to turn to planning improvements, however tentatively, in local administration, agricultural practice, cash crops, public transportation and health. For the African colonies, established at the turn of the century, the outbreak of the First World War (some of it fought in campaigns in West and East Africa) put a brake on any progress in social development policies. No sooner had things begun to regain an equilibrium in the mid-1920s than the metropole and colonies alike were engulfed in the slump of 1929 and its economic aftermath. Again history tragically repeated itself, for no sooner had the world begun to recover from the depression of the 1930s than the calamitous interruption of another world war occurred. Sadly, Africa was once more involved in and affected by it. In every colony, then, the first four decades of colonial rule after occupation were characterized by a fits-and-starts policy of development, regularly halted by a world disaster (1914, 1930, 1939). What forcibly strikes the student of inter-war colonial administration reading the memoirs of the DOs is the paucity of funds available to initiate and sustain plans for rural development, whether infractructural, economic, social or political. Progress had perforce to yield to prudence.

That, of course, was all high policy. The focus here is what it all meant when it percolated to the DO in the field and what his role was in policy execution. In outline, administrative policy in Africa can be broadly divided into periods, each one arguably generating its own need for a differing kind of recruitment criteria in the selection of the DO. For much of the period up to 1914 the DO was, as his memoirs amply reveal,[16] emphatically a loner, necessarily self-reliant and self-confident, often a law unto himself. Edgar Wallace was not far wrong in his image of Sanders of the River, whose voice when he spoke as Keeper of the King's Peace was 'bleak and cold ... the quality of an ice-cold razor' as he reminded recalcitrant chiefs that he was 'a man quick to kill, and no respecter of kings or chiefs'.[17] Many of the early DOs had seen service in the Boer War. Others had worked as administrators under the outgoing chartered companies across Africa, their experience often of real value to the incoming Crown government. A few had been adventurers, keen to go on enjoying the opportunity to breathe freely in Africa's open spaces and, now and again, sinisterly proud of their self-qualification of 'knowing how to handle Africans'. There was just time for the next cohort, the increasingly graduate intakes from 1909 onwards who had undergone a short course of training at the Imperial Institute in London, to begin to make their mark on the CO cadre before war broke out.

'After 1920 new needs called for new breeds. New men were required who had brains in their heads as well as fire in their bellies.'[18] The ex-army officer was heavily recruited into the DO cadres between 1919 and 1924, when preference was given in recruiting for government posts to those who had served in the war. The African territorial *Staff Lists* for the period are full of ADOs holding military rank, often decorated with a Military Cross to boot. There was a tendency, relatively unknown among the post-1945 generation of cadet, to carry one's rank into the Colonial Service – indeed into Civvy Street too. One rather critical DO observed on his arrival in Nigeria in 1933 that out of a dozen senior colleagues in the provincial administration no fewer than four were captains: 'it was more distinguished locally to be plain "Mr" '.[19]

The second wave of graduate DOs began to come into the Service in the mid-1920s, marked – not necessarily for the good in the eyes of some of their seniors – by the fact that on graduation they had undertaken a year's professional Tropical Administrative Service course at Oxford or Cambridge. It was this fourth cohort in our suggested periodization of DO recruitment, the Oxbridge (and in due course Scottish and municipal university) graduate, who from c.1925 to c.1960 established the CAS norm. Those who, following the 1919 pattern, went straight from war service into the CAS in 1946 without a degree and sometimes without the CS training course, were for the most part able to demonstrate that had the war not intervened they would most likely have gone to the university. It is this 'graduate' entry between 1930 and 1960 that comprises the bulk of the DOs whose memoirs have contributed to this history.

A recognizable consensus existed among latter-day senior administrators and top CO officials that in terms of quality and ability the cream of the CO intakes was discernible in two cohorts: first, the post-slump mid-1930s, when jobs were at a premium in Britain and the new CS training courses were attracting many of the best graduates, many of whom might have applied for the ICS had the constitutional advance and political climate on the sub-continent not threatened the likelihood of a full career in India; second, the ex-servicemen intakes of 1946–51, already full of achievement and quickly making their mark, many of them with experience of serving with African or Indian troops. For both groups, the final decade of colonial rule in Africa was to offer fresh challenges as they faced up to the successive policy stages of local government reform, development programmes, the introduction of ministerial government and the transfer of power. If 'fire in their bellies' had often been a feature, at times almost a qualification, of the founding DOs, from 1930 intellectual competence and personal empathy were prize attributes in the final model of the DO in Africa.

An influential colonial policy that inspired the 1920s might be described as 'the mandate ethos'. Although technically the League of Nations mandate was, in British colonial Africa, applicable only to the ex-German colonies, the principle behind it was of far wider application and attention. Its moral motivation was the belief that 'the well-being and development of peoples not yet able to stand by themselves form a sacred trust of civilization'.[20] Such a declaration came close to what the average DO probably thought of as his primary duty: to protect the oppressed, to ensure justice and to promote the well being of the people. Maybe, if pressed on the time perspective of the mandate's proviso about 'until people could stand on their own feet', he would in the inter-war years have replied, in all honesty as he looked round his miserably underdeveloped district and thought of his educationally disadvantaged Native Administration staff, 'Clearly not in my lifetime, unlikely before the end of the century.' The biggest brake on progress, human as well as physical, in colonial Africa during the inter-war period was the palpable lack of funds. It was not until the British government changed its policy and introduced the Colonial Development and Welfare Acts of 1942 and 1945, demonstrating that it was at last ready to grant money to the African governments rather than go on expecting them to raise the money locally for every new building or road and every extra doctor or teacher, that the colonial administration at last had real money to spend and the DO could at last begin to realize some of his and his predecessors' cherished plans for 'improvement'.

In the context of how colonial policy most impinged on the DO, the theory of indirect rule was to exercise in practical terms as much influence on his *modus operandi* as the moral message of the mandate ethos. Evolving from Lugard's Nigerian experience promulgated in his *Political Memoranda* and publicized in his *Dual Mandate*, and then refined by Sir Donald Cameron before being replaced as the pre-eminent administrative policy by that of local government in 1947,[21] indirect rule was the principal context in which the DO in Africa learned and practised his work. The essence of indirect rule lay in the relationship between the DO and the chief. The DO did not rule; the DO advised, the chief ruled, and the DO administered through the chief and his Native Administration. Through this gradualistic approach, Lugard believed, 'the regeneration of Nigeria [would be enabled] through its own governing class and its own indigenous institutions'.[22] In the homeland of indirect rule – the emirates of Northern Nigeria – its praxis at times assumed an almost sacrosanct air, to the extent that one senior officer bluntly warned his DOs that 'as regards qualifications for promotion and passing efficiency bars I put first the question whether an officer is imbued with the true spirit of indirect rule, and make my recommendations accordingly.'[23] About this time, too, an outstanding DO (he subsequently became a governor) received a severe reprimand from his Resident for having exceeded his authority and given orders directly instead of through the Sultan's representative, thereby earning an entry on his confidential report that he was never again to serve in an emirate.[24] As late as 1938 a top CO official was equally forthright about the awesome pedestal on which indirect rule was placed, impressing on the young DO entrant that 'It is to the furtherance of this policy that a man entering the Colonial Administrative Service may expect to be asked to dedicate himself.'[25] The new intake of post-war DOs were to find indirect rule, in the frustrated words of one of them, 'not so much a policy as a necessity, and over the years we turned the necessity into a virtue'.[26]

In the end, as two classic articles on the changing face of African administration argued,[27] indirect rule became out of date, a static policy and one irrelevant (even positively damaging) to the secretary of state's 1947 vision of the development of a modern system of local, representative and conciliar government as the indispensable prelude to self-government and independence. This new policy of 'African Local Government', which was to dominate the direction of field administration in the African territories for the next decade was, he warned, not to be interpreted narrowly. It embraced political issues, financial questions, judicial affairs and economic matters. Yet even with this sea-change in administration there was to be no shift in recognizing who would be responsible for the implementation of the new policy: 'The principal instrument for putting into effect the policy of African local government', the defining despatch concluded, 'is the District Commissioner. ... I regard it as of fundamental importance that DOs should be given the widest possible latitude within the general framework of policy to press on with the development of local government in their district and that full scope should be given for the exercise of individual energy and initiative.'[28]

For all the shift in the nature of his responsibilities, the DO was to be as irreplaceable in the final decade of colonial administration in Africa as he had been for the previous half-century. Now he would increasingly be expected to handle constitutional and political challenges and initiate developmental innovations which he had been neither trained for nor alerted to. The fact that he so often succeeded is a tribute to those fundamental qualities in which the DO in Africa, drawing on a tradition of learning from his seniors and predecessors, had long displayed as he set out to implement whatever policy or project was expected of him: determination, versatility and belief in the worthwhileness of the job. Who such motivated men were and where in Britain they were most likely to be found is the subject of the next chapter.

CHAPTER 2

Towards a Colonial Service Career

A major feature of interest in the study of the sociology of the Crown professional services is the weighting of motivation. Why, up to about 1960, did a young man, nearly always a graduate, choose to join the armed forces, the Diplomatic Service, the Home, Indian or Sudan Civil Services or the Colonial Service? What motivated him? What were the influences to which he was exposed and how decisive were they? Did he really 'choose', or was he partially pre-conditioned by his upbringing, education, family or friends? The question is no longer so relevant towards the end of the twentieth century, by which time graduates were offered (or sought) less of a career and more of a job, often – and preferably, for one reason or another – the short-term employment opportunity with scope soon to move across rather than the dedicated career structure of staying on and moving up. Nevertheless career motivation remains a matter of keen interest and key importance for understanding entry into the Colonial Administrative Service. It also happens to be one of the few unexplored wildernesses in the study of the Colonial Services. For the majority of historians, sociologists and many autobiographers, the story starts with the appointment and arrival *en poste* rather than with why and how this became the chosen career. In examining the so far largely ignored matter of motivation we distinguish between influences and opportunities.

In keeping with other Crown services, notably the army, the

existence of a family tradition was often a major force in motivation. The Colonial Service, which had not developed into a sizeable and recognized career opportunity until the beginning of
the twentieth century, lacked the far longer generational links of
many British families to India. It was not unknown for CAS candidates in the 1930s to 1950s to be able to point to Indian connections going back 100 years. Yet by the 1950s a substantial number
of family links had also developed within the Colonial Service,
notably among the DO cadre. Extreme, perhaps, but not unique
was the Brackenbury family. E.A. Brackenbury served as a DO
in Nigeria from 1905 to 1927. His nephew, A.F. Abell, was a DO,
also in Nigeria, from 1929 to 1950, when he was appointed Governor of Sarawak, his sister having meanwhile married another DO
in Nigeria, B.St.G. Thwaites. E.A. Brackenbury's son, B.H., then
served as a DO in Nigeria from 1946 to 1958.[1]

'My family believed in service overseas,' wrote F.A. Peet.[2] One
of his grandfathers had been a conservator of forests in Burma and
the other a high-court judge in Bombay; his father served in the
Indian Army and he himself was born in India. R. Barlow-Poole
reckoned that, with his family connections abroad and his own
war service overseas, 'motivation may have been in my genes'.
For G.C. Guy, it was a case of his war-service in India generating
'a fascination with the achievements of the British Raj'. Labelling
himself 'a strong traditionalist, I suppose', J.A.R. Forster pointed
to a father in the Sudan and a missionary mother, so that he 'grew
up knowing that we were doing a good thing in Africa'. J.N.E.
Watson looked back to a wide family occupational spread, among
them a legislator in the West Indies, a clergyman in Australia
and two civilians in India. J. Hennessy recalled how 'my grand-
mother would regale me with tales of my ancestors' exploits in
India and in the wars on the N.W. Frontier', where he was to end
up during the war: the die was surely cast. R. Brayne, a post-war
DO in Tanganyika, traced a widespread empire family network,
including a father in the ICS, uncles in Ceylon, Burma and Kenya
and a great-uncle in Nigeria – none other than Lugard.[3] It could
be argued that family connections were strongly encouraged by
Sir Ralph Furse at the CO, who in a confidential memorandum on
the art, as he saw it, of recruiting DOs, listed among his selection
criteria the Edwardian value-laden bonus of 'coming of stock that
has proved its worth, generation by generation, in the professions
or in the public service'.[4] Hence the special label he designed for

flagging application files from the sons of those who had been in the Colonial Service, 's/o F' ('son of father'). Among twentieth-century African governors alone, the 's/o F' paradigm was at work in the families of Sir Horace Byatt, two of whose sons became DOs in Nigeria and Nyasaland respectively; Sir John Waddington, whose son followed him to Northern Rhodesia; Sir Gerald Creasy, whose son also served (albeit only for a short while) in the Gold Coast; and Sir Edward Twining, one of whose sons understandably declared that 'Pretty nearly as far back as I can remember, say from the age of eight, I intended to join the Colonial Service – I considered no other career option.' As for the governors of Nigeria, there were no fewer than four instances of a governor's son becoming a DO. These included the sons of Sir Bernard Bourdillon (one to Palestine and one to Nigeria); of Sir Frank Baddeley and Sir John Patterson (both to Nigeria); and of Sir John Macpherson (to Tanganyika and then Hong Kong).[5] The list could be extended by looking at the sons of non-African governors or by taking the data back before the 1920s.

Although most of the DOs in our period, starting in the 1930s, were too young to see their sons enter the CAS by the late 1950s, the list of post-First World War DOs whose sons joined as a DO in the immediate post-Second World War years is larger than has been generally recognized. Examples of this 's/o DO' category include, from Tanganyika, the sons of J. Allen, H.H. McLeery and J.J. Tawney, all provincial commissioners who followed their fathers into the provincial administration, while P.J. Cator and H.G. Jelf, both DOs in Northern Nigeria, came from fathers in the Malayan Civil Service. Now and again one comes across not one but two 's/o Fs'. Among brothers serving as DOs were E.F.G. and M. Haig and again M. and R. Varvill in Nigeria, as well as the Byatt and Bourdillon brothers noted above. Brothers-in-law were also to be found among DOs, such as N.F. Cooke and M. Milne in Nigeria, and S.S. Richardson and L. McNeil, who together came as DOs from the Sudan to Nigeria. Of course not every DO's father encouraged his son to think of becoming a DO. In the 1950s H.J.B. Allen's father threatened that if he joined the CAS he would be cut off without a shilling, 'in the unlikely event that he still had one!'

Nor was the family influence on contemplating a CAS career always that of the direct family, whether grandparents, parents, uncles or cousins. It also stretched to friends of the family who, often living in the same town (for example, the popular ex-imperial retirement towns of Tunbridge Wells, Cheltenham, Eastbourne and Folkestone, or the warmer South-West) or else belonging to the same London club or same local bridge club, enjoyed nothing more than reminiscing with former colleagues about the Raj or showing their friends' offspring African artefacts they had brought home.

While fathers' occupation was far wider than the 's/o F' circle, it is clear that in the case of most (but not all) DOs recruited from the 1930s it could be typically classified as belonging to the middle class. 'We were mostly,' calculated K.G. Bradley, a notable writer on the CAS and himself a DO in Northern Rhodesia, 'the younger sons of the professional, middle class.'[6] The leading American historian of the CAS, Robert Heussler, got it wrong, through a flawed understanding of the nuances of the British class system, when he described the DO cadres as being largely English country gentlemen, including the aristocracy.[7] Very few were the Hon. This or Sir Something That, Bt. A more accurate term would, for some, have been the landed gentry, a categorization which also allowed for the measure of truth in the lighter-hearted description of DOs as 'the squirearchy', a label perhaps reflecting their paternalistic attitude of mind more than landowning antecedents. Heussler's thesis, subsequently developed in his classic study *Yesterday's Rulers*, was first propounded in an article published in 1961. The central argument ran: 'The Colonial Office appointments staff assumed that only upper-class families were likely to provide their sons with the qualities appropriate to service in the colonies.'[8] In Nile Gardiner's demolition of the social parameters of the Heussler theory, which he argues was based on personal discussions but lacked any statistical foundation, he has demonstrated that it is inconsistent with the biographical evidence available.[9]

Potentially – and in many actual cases of career choice – both school and university can be extremely influential forces. In the event, they appear perhaps to have been less direct in the choice of a CAS career than with other professions, for instance the army, the church, medicine, law, etc. With regard to school, apart from the shared customary formative experience of self-discipline, leadership and responsibility as a house or school prefect or as a team captain, the distribution of public schools attended by subsequent DOs reveals that, unlike Wellington for the army and earlier Haileybury for the Indian services, there was no single school that primarily catered as a feeder school for the CAS. Nor did any school operate a 'Colonial Service' class, in the same way as before the war many provided an 'Army class' for those aiming at a military career. True, certain schools such as Winchester and Cheltenham, and above all Marlborough, could point to a positive number of their alumni in the CAS, but what impresses in this connection is just how many schools could count a proportion of their pupils among the DOs. Over the 30 years of DO recruitment between 1926 and 1956, 15 public schools provided between 21 and 40 DOs, while between 10 and 20 came from another ten, among them three Scottish schools and one in Northern Ireland.[10] As D.G.P. Taylor wrote about his school, 'although Clifton was a school which had regularly supplied servants of the Empire, no notion for preparing for "bearing the white man's burden" ever featured in my education at school, or for that matter at Clare College subsequently.'[11] But what was a major moulding influence, however unconsciously at the time, on the making of potential DOs, was the self-discipline and self-reliance nurtured in the typical boarding school. This meant, as A. Forrest subsequently perceived, that 'they were accustomed to looking after themselves and accepting as normal some very spartan conditions'.[12] Although the CO did arrange for an occasional lecture on the CS as a career to be given to schools, often by a DO on leave, the school catchment area was by and large too young and too undecided (other than for those with parental colonial experience) to be thinking seriously in terms of a career before the – in those days – predictable next step, of going to the university with three more years before having seriously to consider what one was going to do.

When it comes to university as an influence, there is more evidence of an effect and a little more of a calculated appeal. Unlike most professions, the CAS was not interested in what subject a prospective candidate had read: provided he had obtained 'a good honours degree', i.e. hopefully higher than a Third, that was all that mattered intellectually. An analysis of the enhanced 1945–46 intake of DOs shows that out of the 160 entrants with a degree, 10 per cent had gained a First, 20 per cent a Third and 19 per cent a Pass![13] Though what might be called 'the myth of the modest Third' as the norm for DOs has, like most myths, an element of truth in it, what may surprise social analysts is how many Firsts

the CAS could count among its ranks, just as the Sudan Political
Service, with its unconcealed emphasis on athletic achievements
(best of all a Blue) could at the same time count 32 Firsts among its
total of 270 graduate DOs between 1899 and 1952 (and 93 Blues to
boot!).[14] DOs whose records have been accessed[15] show that they
graduated in agriculture, anthropology, chemistry, theology and
natural sciences, as well as history, classics, English and modern
languages. Surprisingly, perhaps, neither economics nor politics
was *de rigueur*, let alone that cornerstone of the DO's work and
his very title, public administration, still hard to find as a degree
course in Britain before the 1950s. It was precisely this indifference to any subject linkage that appealed to D.G.P. Taylor: 'I found
the job attractive because it was not specialised.' History was a
useful all-rounder's subject, though it might well be medieval
or ancient and in no way necessarily imperial history. A breakdown of the 300 or so responses received from retired DOs who
contributed to the 1983–86 HMOCS Data Project shows that, for
the post-1930 cohorts, modern history was substantially (27 per
cent) the preferred degree subject, followed by classics in second
place and modern languages and law in equal third place.[16]

Before the 1960s only the occasional university lecturer had,
outside the specialist teaching of African and Oriental languages
at SOAS, any experience of the CAS, though DOs remember the
knowledgeable and infectious enthusiasm of teachers like W.M.
Macmillan at St Andrew's, R. Steele in the Oxford school of geography and R.E. Robinson's lectures on 'The Expansion of Empire'
at Cambridge.[17] At Oxford, of course, from the 1930s Margery
Perham was looked on as almost a CAS institution herself, and
in recognition of her authoritative reputation she was in 1939
appointed Reader in Colonial Administration. At the same time,
back at the CO, Furse was too shrewd an operator (and too fond
of the conviviality of guest nights at high table) not to involve
carefully selected dons as what he called his 'talent scouts', whom
he encouraged to look out for likely DO material and point undergraduates towards the CS as a career. Those at Oxford included
J. Masterman, O. Stallybrass, P. Landon, S. Douglas Veale (Registrar) and, above all in the memory of DOs, Kenneth Bell. In this
targeting of the 'likely lads', the University Appointments Board
could often play an important role in guiding third-year enquir-
ers towards the CAS as a career. However, at Oxford M.C. Atkinson (later a DO in Nigeria), who had been unsuccessful in his

bid to join, was not amused by being offered the London North Eastern Railway or Coca-Cola after explaining to the Board his wish for a job offering travel. T.R.W. Longmore was far luckier at Cambridge. In his final year he had an interview with the very effective recruiter at the University Appointments Board, Major Guy, who, after considering the points made by Longmore on a postcard about what he was looking for in a career, replied 'I think that the Colonial Service might suit you.' The Cambridge Board recommendation was repeated when I.W.D. Peterson, still in his first year, told them he would be looking for a job abroad 'with variety in my work'. T.G. Brierly was in search of similar job satisfaction: 'I decided to join the Colonial Service because I wanted to see the world.' T. Lawrence's motives were even more exuberant, joining (like others) 'largely for romantic reasons – travel and wide open spaces and strange people'. Back in the 1930s J.H.D. Stapleton took a strictly realistic view: 'I liked the sound of it – and jobs were scarce then.' Twenty years later D.L. Mathews was yet more laconic: 'One has to do something, after all.' A more direct, though not necessarily profound, influence came from the existence of the CAS training course in the university from 1926, which meant that undergraduates would meet CAS probationers through the colleges' sporting and social life. There was also the periodic visit of a former undergraduate or school friend to his old college on his first leave home from Africa or, as in R.J. Graham's case, meeting an enthusiastic DO on the advanced training course who was also coaching the college VIII. It is not hard to imagine what such encounters could mean in the way of career interest arousal from stories told at the college or Colonial Service club bar. In the 1930s too, the publication in *The Times* of the names and colleges of candidates who had gained admission into the CAS brought added prestige to the DO career.[18]

There remains one area which co-existed with all three of the influences discussed so far: family, school and university. This is the influence of books and magazines read by adolescents and young men in the 1930s, often reinforced by the African adventure films enjoyed at the local cinemas. Numerous DOs have testified how their imagination was fired by reading Rudyard Kipling, G.A. Henty, H. Rider Haggard and John Buchan, or *The Boys' Own Paper* (launched in 1897).[19] Fiction aside, it is K.G. Bradley's memoir *Diary of a District Officer* that many DOs acknowledge as their prime career inspiration. A later generation of DOs have attributed their interest in the life of a DO to reading Sir Arthur Grimble's autobiographical *A Pattern of Islands* and, for the African enthusiast, Gerald Hanley's novel *The Consul at Sunset*. But above all it was *Sanders of the River*, both the series of Edgar Wallace novels and Alexander Korda's 1935 film, that unchallengedly topped the list as the defining career influence. As late as 1951, when J. Lewis-Barned was posted to Tanganyika, the London *Sunday Express* carried two columns under the heading 'Sanders of the River: Still the Best Job for a British Boy'.[20]

The Second World War introduced two new and weighty influences on why many a young man turned his thoughts to life as a DO. Arguably unparalleled in its impact, one was war service, often with the King's African Rifles (KAR), the Royal West African Frontier Force (RWAFF) or the Indian Army. The fact that the last-named kind of applicant often served not only with but under Indian officers brought added value in the eyes of the CO interviewers. This experience of service with African or Indian troops not only generated an interest in the countries and their people but also a liking for working with them, leading to a positive wish to continue the contact. Furse's recruitment staff were already one step ahead in the field, with a special team led by P. Renison, later Governor of Kenya, sent out from London to Delhi, Simla and Cairo to interview and pre-select officers awaiting demobilization. They were also able to attract a number of officers who had been selected for the ICS in 1946 but who, when recruitment closed, found themselves out of a job and welcomed the alternative of a career in the CAS.[21] An analysis of the expanded first post-war CAS intake of 566 DOs shows 99 per cent with war service, a third of whom had served with Indian or African troops. No fewer than 193 out of the 560 had won military awards, including over 50 MCs. More than 5 per cent had been prisoners of war.[22]

It was to be a similar experience a few years later, when National Service replaced war service. Again it was to KAR and RWAFF units that young officers were frequently attached, many of them then planning to return to Africa in the CAS. To quote R.A. Campbell, 'I took to African life as a subaltern commanding African troops in Kenya and Uganda, and wished to return after university.' D. Lambert recorded that, having done his National Service in Kenya in 1954 during the Mau Mau emergency, 'I so liked the country and the people that when my National Service was finished I returned to England and was determined to find a job which would take me back', while remarkably, according to C. Minter, no fewer than ten National Service officers from the 23rd (Kenya) battalion joined the CAS, eight becoming DOs in Kenya and two in Tanganyika.[23] What must be made clear is that this imperative for life as a DO came from the fact that military service, wartime or national, had been with Indian or African troops, and not from a period of disciplined service life *per se.* 'After four years in the British army,' B. Loach declared, 'I was looking for a stimulating, outdoor, unconventional life-style, with the prospect of adventure.' It was the same for R.F. Bendy, even though he came from an army family and had never thought about any other career. 'After the war I became somewhat disillusioned with the army as a career and my thoughts turned to "Sanders" which I had read as a boy.'

We may now turn, after influences, to the second aspect of career motivation, that is to say the opportunities offered and the attractions advertised or perceived. One such attraction was in fact at its most pervasive at the very end of the Second World War, and although this was a one-off peacetime rather than a wartime perception it deserves to be set beside the ex-war influences set out above. This factor has not been widely recognized or remembered in the literature, though recent research has revealed how strongly it was felt at the time. This was the shocked reaction, after war years often of adventure and overseas travel, to returning to the dreary, dank and still rationed (in clothes and fuel as well as food) milieu of Britain in 1946–47. Dismay engendered a strong belief that a return to Civvy Street in a climate of such grim austerity was not the kind of future to be accepted. A better life had to be found. Typical is the evidence of one who had never heard of the Colonial Service before he applied, E. Fox: 'but getting out of the misery of post-war Britain sounded good'. It was a sentiment echoed by W.J. Warrell-Bowring: 'After being stationed abroad during and after the war, life in Europe threatened to be dull and restricted in opportunity.' Cadets of the period have commented ecstatically on the relief of enjoying the relatively high standard of living on board ship as they sailed from Liverpool, Southampton or Tilbury, leaving behind the grim reality of post-war Britain. 'The most surprising thing on board,' recalled A.T. Clark when he set sail for Lagos in M.V. *Accra* in 1949, was the daily round of morning tea in bed, a large breakfast, beef tea (replaced by ice cream as the tropics were reached), lunch, afternoon tea, dinner, and finally sandwiches at 10pm. What impressed him most was 'the perfect whiteness of the bread: rationed UK had forgotten what it used to look like'.[24] In the final analysis, of course, Africa offered one bounty that Britain never could: a warm climate. All in all, it is little wonder that the post-war itchy-feet syndrome loomed large in the CAS applications of 1946–48.

If much of this was a negative motive, a form of escapism, there were plenty of more positive ones at work among the 1945–55 graduates who realized they had finally come face to face with the question of 'What do I want to do?' or, perhaps for the not so well qualified, 'What can I do?' Fortunately, as D. Connelly pointed out, jobs were readily available in 1946, as they were again in the 1950s when he left university. It may not always be easy for contemporary graduates to appreciate how vigorous in the minds of many young people were the twin determinants of a sense of duty and a desire for Crown service. 'To do something for King/Queen and country' was in 1944 enough for K.V. Arrowsmith to turn to the CAS, while 'service and duty' was the crisp explanation of R.A. Hill's decision to join in the same year. For J.E. Blunden the motivation was equally simple: 'to serve the British Crown'. J.S. Duthie was 'brought up to believe that the British empire was essentially a beneficial institution, a beacon of progress, touched by greatness. Hence my decision to aim for imperial service.' D. Savill prefaced his memoir of his career in Nigeria with a full reminder of 'how much all sections of the British Empire were part of everyone's lives and thoughts up until the mid-1950s. ... In a sense, the Empire was taken for granted by us all.'[25] So often too was the concomitant intention to join its Colonial Service. Such motives are no longer in fashion, but for a long time they were genuine and strong enough for countless young men to seek their realization in the CAS. To be a DO was a respected and sought-after job among graduates. Its attractive qualities were cogently advanced by the career advisers of the university appointments boards. The CO let it be quietly known, too, on its talent-spotters' grapevine, that in order to maintain the quality of its DOs it was the policy in the recruitment division to leave a DO vacancy empty rather than fill it with an applicant who was not up to standard. Quality was not be sacrificed for quantity; known competition enhanced the status of the job.

Assessing the evidence from nearly 600 DOs who joined the CAS between 1920 and 1960, Gardiner has calculated that family tradition accounted for a quarter of those motivated to join the CAS, war-service one-fifth, and 'an interesting job' or 'service to the Empire' one-tenth each. The proportion declaring another 20 motives ranged from 8 per cent 'to help others', through 'outdoor life' and 'responsibility' at 6 per cent each, to 'literature and cinema' at 2 per cent, 'responsibility' at 2 per cent and 'religious motives' at 1 per cent. A further 6 per cent had miscellaneous motives.[26] Further consideration may be given to the explanations of motivation.

Among the perceived most positive attractions of becoming a DO was the opportunity to exercise above-average responsibility at an early age, and certainly far beyond anything that could be anticipated in a job in the UK. Such was M.H. Shaw's motivation: 'I joined because I was looking for an exciting job overseas which would give me early responsibility.' J.R. Smith was attracted by the prospect of having 'freedom of action and responsibility very early in my career'. It was the same for R.B.S. Purdy: 'I wanted an active, adventurous, outdoor life, with plenty of responsibility at an early age.' F. Ashworth's assessment of the prospects was different: 'When one is in possession of the ordinary degree of B.A. and one is disinclined to teach and one's ambition to be the Greatest Geographer in the World is firmly squashed by academics and one would like to marry one's Best Beloved, one is given furiously to think. The outcome of these thoughts and pursuant action emerged as two alternatives: Postal Controller Grade III or a Colonial Service career.'[27] The secretary of state himself emphasized the opportunity for early responsibility at a tea-party he famously gave in Downing Street on 26 June 1940 to a score of new ADOs. They had been selected for appointment before the outbreak of the war, but after a shortened course had been sent for military training. Now he had delicately to reassure them that, despite their wish to go forward with their comrades into action, the decision of the CO to secure their early release for immediate posting to the colonies was indeed where their duty and patriotism lay. He pointed out to them 'it may well be that sooner or later your Government will assign you to military service with the local forces', and urged them all 'not to think of military service in your colony as in any sense a "second line" of Service. It may at any time become the front line.' 'It is the considered view of H.M.G.,' Lord Lloyd concluded, to the assembled cadets, 'that it is your duty to take up the job for which you have been selected and trained. I want you to regard this as a definite instruction from His Majesty's Government.'[28]

To be in independent charge (just what that meant was unlikely to have been clear at the time to the young graduate) of a district on average the size of a small English county, and soon maybe the size of Yorkshire or Wales, was exciting, even if it might be too early to grasp what one would be doing there. Promotion prospects appeared to be reasonable, at least clearer than they were in industry or business at home. A pension was a comfort, though at the age of 21 or so it was too far away in the distant and unimaginable mist of being in one's 50s. What was to be avoided at all costs – C.A.K. Cullimore's 'horror of horrors' – was the prospect of a 'safe' job in the city, commuting by the 7.58 up to Waterloo and rushing for the 5.58 back after a day of predictable and humdrum office work. 'I did not want to be working behind a desk all day' was J.H.F. Bown's motive for applying to be a DO. 'The prospect of working in clean air and wide open spaces,' confessed D.E. Nicoll-Griffith, 'wearing shorts and open-necked shirts, was decidedly more attractive than that of city rush and commuter trains.' One decision was already clear in J. Brock's mind: 'while at university I resolved not to pursue a sedentary career'. B.L. Jacobs applied to the CS because he 'was disappointed with the prospect of a career in insurance in the UK'; F. Kennedy thought the CS 'promised to be more exciting than a career in accountancy', in which he had spent two years before the war; and B.A.F. Read felt that at the end of five years in an oil company he was 'bogged down in the London head office'. For J.H. Smith it was the wish for 'an exciting life, an outdoor life, inspired by Arctic explorers, Baden-Powell and other heroes of my youth as well as by many afternoons glued to the dioramas in the Imperial Institute'. Routine was out, adventure was in, and the life of a DO was on. As for being a school teacher or going into publishing, commonly sought-after occupations in the 1940s and 1950s by arts graduates who had not read for the professions, D. Brown summed up his preferred career thus: 'of all the opportunities open to university graduates in the late 1940s, the CAS offered the most interesting opportunities: variety, responsibility, status, reasonable pay and a touch of romance.' As for the Home Civil Service, life in Whitehall came uncompromisingly into the category of 'routine' and 'commuting', evils to be avoided at all costs. The Diplomatic Service up to 1950 still expected its members to have a certain amount of private means, another countervailing requirement on top of the demanding exams and the gruelling 'house party' interviewing process. Clearly the Colonial Service was the overseas service par excellence. While nobody expected to get rich in it, the starting salary was higher than in most graduate jobs in Britain. Furthermore, the CO advised, the standard of living was 'generally higher than in the UK'.[29]

What in retrospect is remarkable about how the putative DO envisaged his job is the minimal thought he gave to what he was going to be doing. In T.G. Askwith's opinion, after many years as a DO, 'most of us had very little idea of what we were in for'.[30] Brought up on the impression that the main pre-occupation of DOs was 'to quell tribal disturbances and adjudicate in boundary disorders in a lordly fashion', he found on reaching Kenya that his expectations were at least 20 years out of date.[31] K. Blackburne conceded that he had 'no starry-eyed visions of service to humanity, nor of changing the face of the world; and the Colonial Service course of those days [1930s] was not designed to those ends'.[32] Joining in the middle of the war, A.G. Eyre had 'only a hazy idea of improving life for Audu in the bush'. B.F. Eberlie was no better prepared: 'I had little idea of what lay ahead, but that never worried me. It merely added to the kind of this new life before me.' W.L. Bell was just as untutored in his expectations: 'Didn't know – was assured Devonshire Course would enlighten but wasn't sent on one.' Equally in the dark were T.R.W. Longmore, 'On joining my ideas were hazy and probably naïve', and M.R. Harris, 'I had little or no idea of what I was meant to be doing.' D.D. Yonge was at least concise in the literary origin of what he thought he was going to be doing. 'Not a clue, beyond *Sanders of the River.*' Posted to Kenya in the troubled year of 1954, J. Dalzell envisaged a no less exciting job: 'I thought I would be doing a certain amount of paperwork, but mainly chasing the Mau Mau terrorists.'

For a DO not coming to Africa until 1956 (the year before the Gold Coast's independence), like D. Glendenning, it was easier to envisage his job as 'to guide the people of N. Rhodesia towards self-government at some time in the future'; or, in the mind of G.W.S. Bowry, 'I knew we were expected to administer in the widest and most general sense, in particular the administration

of justice and finances, in an even-handed and impartial manner
... all in preparation for the giving of independence.' The generation of mid-1950s recruits was aware of the need, in J.R. Smith's
words, 'to administer in a way which developed a cadre of local
staff', an objective for the most part outside the conceptualization
of DOs recruited in the 1940s. Nevertheless one of the post-war
recruits to the Gold Coast, C.G.C. Rawlins, acknowledged that he
was warned on appointment in 1946 that 'I would be going out to
Africa to work myself out of a job, i.e. to prepare the country for
independence.' J.H. Smith was another appointee with a forward
view, believing in 1950 that his job would be to help decolonize
Africa, following the example of India. He gave himself 'a certain
five years, a probable ten and a lucky fifteen'. D. Frost, going out
to Northern Rhodesia in 1947, found that any thoughts about
'bringing in evolutionary change were quickly modulated after
comments of "we must maintain standards" or "the African is not
yet ready", along with the unstated belief of "not in my time" '. In
Tanganyika in 1948 R. Brayne reckoned that 'we knew we were
working towards independence but did not think it would come
in our time'. In 1950 neither R. Short nor J.C.A. Mousley had much
of a problem in deciding what the DO's job was going to be in
Northern Rhodesia: for the former, 'Kenneth Bradley's *Diary of a
District Officer* was an excellent guide'; and, for the latter, 'I was
attracted by the life, particularly as described by Bradley's book
... the one single event which triggered the process.' Precisely
the same source for trying to grasp what the job was about is
found in J. Hennessy's recollection of taking up his appointment
in Basutoland in 1948. A latter-day cadet, D.L. Mathews, had kept
up with the post-Bradley literature, hoping that his job in Tanganyika in 1956 would offer '*Pattern of Islands* stuff – on dry land'. To
T. Gavaghan, who went to Kenya in 1944, the specification of his
job appeared to rest on the assumption that its practitioners were
'versed in the commonly held social, ethical and Christian moral
values called for in carrying the "white man's burden" of Empire.
Most were also reared in the less conformist qualities of ambition, idealism, adventure, physical courage and self-reliance.'[33]
J. Ashridge's simple post-war expectation was that he would be
expected to 'run the place in an orderly fashion'. Recruited in 1951,
A.E. MacRobert could recall no guidance at all from the CO as to
what the job of DO would entail and was left to derive what he
could from reading Hailey's weighty 1,600-page *African Survey*.

Perhaps G.M. Hector's description of the cumulative effect of the amalgam of the multiple influences to which many aspirant DOs had been exposed offers a valid summary of motivation: 'Both school and university combined with my family background to develop my attitude and personal philosophy towards a career abroad, but neither prepared me for my future positions. My wartime experience [KAR] did that.'[34]

While we have so far largely reflected what DOs thought – or did not think – their job would be at the time of joining, an examination of their retrospective views about the identity of the new job as recalled in retirement also carries validity. Sometimes it is a common echo, at others it conveys a difference in emphasis. There was space for a 'do-good' (used here in a strictly neutral sense) input into the image and the opportunity; to quote J. Lennard, an opportunity for 'helping others to help themselves – trite maybe, but in reality simply a continuation of being a school prefect, scoutmaster, and Sandhurst cadet'. There was always room in the CAS for the idealistic and the compassionate. In an idiom more commonly heard among the VSO and NGO volunteers 50 years later, D. Glendenning acknowledged that he joined 'because I wanted to do some good. I though I might be able to influence events in the colonies in some small way.' Both J.H. Banforth and his wife were 'practising Christians, and we felt that we could contribute to improving the life of the people in the colonies by providing knowledge, integrity and standards'. At the end of his time as a student E.N. Scott was not sure he had ' the vocation to ordination', and his college chaplain, a former missionary in Tanganyika, pointed him towards the job of a DO. For J. Brock it was enough that the job of a DO was to provide 'a stable, just, uncorrupt and efficient form of government', a basic administrative sentiment shared by P.O. Bowcock's belief (in 1955, though it could have been valid in 1935 or 1925) in 'keeping the peace and improving the condition of the people', and R.T. Kerslake's pre-war reflection on the objective of his job as 'the maintenance of Pax Britannica, the elimination of corruption or reduction of corruption, and more justice to the "underdogs" '. It was an uncomplicated belief, 'to ensure peace and stability under my charge and to see that justice prevailed', as P.H.M. Vischer felt and as G.C. Guy had in mind: 'justice, fair treatment, and the curtailment of abuse'. P.N. Mawhood was more down to earth. His opinion was that, 'despite a certain idealism connected with "giving the poor a leg up", many administrators – even the nicest ones – were semi-consciously attracted by the personal power in the DO's job', and he was adamant that in applying for the CAS 'I did *not* meditate on whether I would be "doing good" or any such thing.' While a number of pre-war DOs were the sons of clergymen, this background was less noticeable among the post-war entry, although in his study Gardiner rightly concludes that 'religious values and up-bringing undoubtedly played a very important role in shaping attitudes towards public service, combining to create a powerful Christian sense of "fair play" '.[35]

Looking back, E.B.S. Alton was confident that in 1951 his mission was 'to help in broad terms, to "run the country", including law and order and Lugard-like development through Native Authorities and Chiefs'. D. Barton had hoped to 'provide thoughtful, humane and fair administration at the district level' and for K.J. Barnes it had always been a matter of 'keeping the peace and promoting development', while for D.O. Savill the expectation had, in retrospect, been 'to raise local standards of living and to introduce the democratic process, always in a benign way'. The old idea of empire was still alive in 1949, for Savill also saw his mission as being to 'safeguard British political and economic interests', just as J. Brock's aim included 'maintaining the good name of Britain overseas'. At the same time, Savill severely qualified his empire enthusiasm. 'Having visited parts of the "great" British Empire during the war, and been appalled and ashamed of what I had seen, I decided that something needed to be done to reclaim whatever vestiges of its virtues should remain.' K.P. Shaw 'considered the British Empire, despite its faults, to be a major influence for peace and prosperity in the world'. For P.A.P. Robertson, sailing to Tanganyika just before the war, it was 'natural to want to spread British influence over less fortunate people'. By 1950 the implications of the secretary of state's 1947 Local Government despatch had become clear to DOs in Africa as well as to new cadets. 'We knew what we had to do,' noted D. Brown. 'Development was the in-word ... eventually a civil service that would replace us.' A latter-day entrant like J.C. Lawley, who became a DO in Northern Rhodesia in 1960, could in retrospect also deploy a modern vocabulary to express his expectations: 'Training towards self-government, prosperity, justice, rural development, good governance and eventual independence.' To round off, there is much to be said for endorsing the transitional view expressed by C.W.B. Costeloe, who spent his career in the Gold Coast: 'Initially [1944] I saw myself only as a hands-on administrator, concerned with the smooth running of the district. It was only in my later years that I saw myself as a trainer.'

The two principal surveys drawn on here,[36] involving nearly 500 former DOs and inviting them to look back on their motivation, both reinforce what may now be looked on as standard influences and aspirations but also reveal several less anticipated ones. Overall the data from DOs questioned in 1983–86 indicate that a quarter attributed their motivation to a family tradition of service overseas and a third to wartime service in India or Africa or the Far East, particularly citing the experience of working with African or Indian troops. This could include a working knowledge of the language, though R.F. Roper, who had served with Nyasa troops in the KAR, maintained that his posting to Uganda came about through a mistake in the CO typing pool of 'Luganda' for 'Cinyanja'. To this statistical summary of major areas of influence one might add J.R. Johnson's more prosaic hunch that 'Perhaps, too, it was the appeal of a life in the open spaces of a continent as opposed to a crowded island.'[37]

Recent research into the attractions of working abroad has introduced a new dimension to imperial motivation. This is Ronald Hyam's hypothesis that the imperative of young Britons seeking a career overseas can be interpreted as an adventure in, even a search for, sexual opportunities often denied by society at home. For Hyam, 'sexual dynamics crucially underpinned the whole operation of British empire and victorious expansion', concluding that 'without sexual opportunities which imperial systems provided, the long-term administration and exploitation of tropical territories, in 19th-century conditions, might well have been impossible.'[38] His argument is complemented by another proposition, that sexual attitudes and activities impacted on the lives of the ruling elite as well as the subjects of Empire. While Hyam's focus is on an imperial era well before that of the present study, and is associated with the resurrection of the confidential memorandum on concubinage addressed to Colonial Service staff by the secretary of state in 1909 (the Crewe Circulars A and B),[39] post-colonial literature has, as part of the deconstruction of colonialism, since directed its attention to such studies as masculinity and empire in imperial fiction (Chistopher Lane's *The Ruling*

Passion) and also in imperial fact, narrated by the imperial elite (Anton Gill's *Ruling Passions: Sex, Race and Empire*). Suffice it to say that the principal progenitor of this new 'sex and empire' school, Ronald Hyam, himself acknowledges at the very outset of his theory that 'it would indeed be nonsense to suggest that more than a minority of men initially went overseas to find sexual satisfaction'.[40] There, in the context of this book, we may leave it, other than to note the ballad popular among DOs at some club bars in Nigeria, known as 'ADO Bende', a parody on Kipling's 'And I learned about women from her'.[41]

Despite the fact that salary considerations rarely feature in the look-backs on motivation, the CAS conditions of service call for notice in this profile of why young men turned to the life of a DO as their career choice. What follows relates to the terms and conditions of service current in 1952.[42] This was at the end of the employment reshuffle of post-war Britain, when jobs fluctuated between being first plentiful and then scarcer, and at the moment when recruitment was reaching its peak, with the CO appointing some 1,500 DOs within seven years (750 in 1946 and 1947).

Under the 'cost of living', the would-be DO was presented with a sort of outline balance sheet comparing his position with that which he could expect in Britain. The superior standard of living in the colonies (sic) meant that he could expect expenses to be 'relatively high'. Against this could be set lower taxation, lower rentals and in most cases no rates. A following paragraph on the advantages of 'living off the country' was calculated to excite in the likely DO what was soon to become a strong preference for the up-country life in the bush rather than at headquarters. Rent was charged on the quarters provided at a rate not exceeding 10 per cent of salary, and the accommodation was furnished by the government, although in Tanganyika after the war J.A. Golding found he was expected to pay a further 5 per cent for the Public Works Department furniture.[43] In the case of housing designated 'not up to standard' (often labelled as temporary accommodation and frequently found in bush stations) or where official accommodation either did not exist or had to be shared, the rent was reduced. An officer was not allowed to retain his housing when he was on leave. Another compulsory deduction, about 4–5 per cent, was the contribution to a Widows and Orphans Pension Scheme (WOPS), payable whether an officer was married or not. A DO was eligible for a pension once he had completed ten years' service, but not if he voluntarily resigned his appointment. The normal pension rate was one six-hundredth of his final pensionable emoluments (i.e. excluding *ad hoc* allowances) for each completed month of service.

Applicants for the CAS were required to be under 30 years of age and preferably under 26. No one could be appointed who would not have reached the age of 21 on taking up an overseas appointment. In practice this meant that the usual minimum entry age for a DO was nearer 22, taking into account the year spent on the training course after graduation. Inevitably in the immediate post-war years the average age on entry was several years higher. The normal retirement age was 55, but in West Africa an optional retirement age of 45 was introduced at the end of the Second World War. The option was exercisable by either the officer or, to the consternation of many older DOs, by the government. Life assurance was strongly recommended, but it was a private matter and involved no government participation. J.H. Smith noted that one of his 'abiding memories of his year at Oxford before sailing to Nigeria was warding off the salesmen ready to quote terms for "the White Man's Grave" '.[44]

The leave allowance was generous, always on full salary. In West Africa, where the climatic conditions were recognized as harsher than elsewhere in Africa, the ratio was one week's leave for every month of service, with an 18-month tour as the norm for officers appointed after 1945 and 12–15 months for those with over ten years' service. 'For the first year of a tour,' noted J.S. Lawson of his experience in the Gold Coast, 'one remained at roughly the same level of energy and efficiency, but for the next six months, or until the end of the tour, there was a steady decline in both. In particular, once one's leave date had been fixed, there was a tendency to "mark time", and not to start any programme or project that one would not be there to finish.'[45] In Kenya, where the climate was generally benign, the length of tour was up to four years, followed by leave calculated at 4½ days per month of tour for officers serving in 'healthy stations' or at 5½ for those posted to unhealthy districts. In Tanganyika, Uganda and Central Africa the tour was from two to three years, with five days' leave earned for each month of service. In the three High Commission Territories, also with a comparably enviable climate and with the least attractive ratio of home leave, a DO could expect to serve a tour of three to four years, earning only 1½ months' leave for each

year of service – for a long time many members of the administration were South African citizens. The days spent on the voyage
home to and from leave, about two to three weeks for British DOs
in Africa, were counted as part of their tour of duty and not as
leave. R. Wainwright had no leave from Kenya between 1939 and
1946, and could barely add up the accumulated leave owed him.[46]
In Lagos W.F.H. Newington was obliged during the war to do a
30-month tour, at the end of which he had to fly home through
the USA via the Gambia, Brazil and Bermuda, culminating in a
two-and-a-half-week delay in New York before embarking on a
troopship to Glasgow – none of which came out of his leave allowance.[47] By the mid-1950s (earlier in Tanganyika) African governments required their DOs to fly both ways by air (first-class), for
which withdrawal of the sea voyage concession they were paid a
compensating sum of £15 each way. Most African governments
made provision for a short period of 'local leave' (i.e., at the DO's
expense) each year, to travel outside his area or outside his territory. The introduction of regular air travel in the 1950s meant that
an enterprising DO might fly – at his own expense, *bien entendu*
– to Europe for a few days' 'local' leave.

Salary rates tended to vary according to the year of recruitment. Furthermore the post-war years brought several influential salary reviews to the African territories. One of the earliest
alterations was to abolish the separate 'expatriation pay' paid
to British DOs in West Africa (about £150 on top of the starting
salary of £450 in 1950 and by 1952 ranging between £180 and £350
according to rank) and to incorporate it into a single salary scale,
payable to British and African staff alike. There was an efficiency
bar, usually at the end of about 20 years of annual increments.
Beyond this so-called 'long grade' came the considerably higher-
paid superscale and staff grades. Every DO was entitled to expect
to reach the top of the long grade, but beyond that it was strictly a
matter of promotion on perceived merit. For example, in Nigeria
in the early 1950s a DO's salary was from £750 to £1,560, rising by
regular increments over 18 years. In Sierra Leone the figures were
£660 for three years, then rising annually from £690 to £1,300. In
retrospect the DO was arguably neither overpaid nor badly paid.
A bachelor DO posted to an outstation could, drawing all his
allowances (bush, horse or car mileage, travelling, etc.), probably
expect to have saved a little money by the end of his tour. Where
the financial discontent lay was over the often impossible task of

keeping a family, and likely two homes because of the demands of children's schooling in the UK.

Besides the forces of motivation, opportunity and career conditions and prospects leading a young man towards committing himself to the CAS, there remains another influence to which he could expose himself once he felt he was really keen on becoming a DO. This was the image of the DO and his work purposely projected by the CO. We have already taken note of the effect of the 'Sanders of the River' paradigm, leading to the 'almost heroic image' of the DO in Africa.[48] But the by-now serious job-seeker was likely to want more than this image to move on from fiction to fact and discover an authentic description of the identity of the DO in Africa, his life and work. Here the CO literature was of prime importance. W.L. Bell went so far as to maintain that in his ultimate choice of career 'he was seduced by skilful Colonial Office recruitment literature'. So too was T.F. Bolter who, reading between the lines of his future father-in-law's questions about his prospects and realizing that what he really meant was whether on demobilization Bolter was going to be able to afford to maintain a wife, hurried back to the RAF mess library to peruse the careers pamphlets distributed by the CO in order to grab the mind of those shortly on their way to Civvy Street.

The CO's basic recruitment literature was its *Appointments in Her Majesty's Colonial Service*, regularly updated.[49] However, what seems to have been more influential (and far more fun to read) than leaflets on 'Information as to the Cost of Living in the Colonial Empire' or *The Colonial Territories: Report of the Secretary of State to Parliament*[50] was the mainstream literature written by K.G. Bradley. He had worked as a DO in Northern Rhodesia in the 1930s and, as we have seen, written an eminently readable book about it, *The Diary of a District Officer*. Unfortunately this appeared in the middle of the war, when there was a moratorium on CAS recruitment. A shrewdly timed reprint in 1947, just when the CO was faced with more than 500 DO vacancies for filling as rapidly as possible, immediately attracted an audience. As the proconsular giant Lord Hailey wrote in his foreword, 'a narrative of this kind serves better than any formal record to illustrate the work such an officer does and the place he fills in the life of the people'.[51] Its portrait of 'Sanders' 40 years on as a recruitment influence was unparalleled. The CO quickly moved to enlist the able pen of Bradley, as a follow-up to its own Sir Charles Jeffries' illustrated *Partners for Progress* (1949), subtitled 'The Men and Women of the Colonial Service', to write yet another recruitment booklet. Published in 1950 as *The Colonial Service as a Career* and again carrying many photographs of the Service at work, its purpose was as clear as it proved to be convincing. 'I have written this little book for a very special public and for a very special purpose ... those young people who are thinking of making their careers in the Colonial Service.'[52] Chapters included 'A Career in the Colonial Service', 'The Qualities Required', 'Life in the Colonial Service', and 'Work in the Colonial Service', all presented in just 60 pages of text. Seldom can a Crown Service have initiated such a felicitous piece of recruitment propaganda. By happy coincidence (choice or opportunity), Bradley's wife Emily published a notable companion volume in the same year, *Dearest Priscilla*, subtitled 'Letters to the Wife of a Colonial Civil Servant'.

With all these influences, often from childhood and all the way to graduation, brought to bear on him, the young man who had more and more been thinking about making his career as a DO was now ready to take the next step in realizing his ambition. It was time to move from thinking, talking and reading to doing. The moment had come to apply.

Reference has already been made to the dissolution of the naked patronage system in Colonial Service appointments, with its practice of instinctive, subjective and immediate (yet often virtually final) snap-judgements based on the impression – and the word was officially commended as an integral part of the process – conveyed by the applicant and its replacement after 1930 by a regulated process culminating in the appearance of the short-listed candidates before a final CSAB (Colonial Service Appointments Board) under the aegis of the Civil Service Commissioners. The key document in this selection process was the form known in the CO as the P/1, originally standing for Patronage but after 1930 for Personnel. This was obtained from the CO, but a prospective candidate was warned that he 'must himself apply in writing for an application form'. Application forms were not, it seems, automatically despatched by the CO. A. Forward noted how his request in 1954 elicited a reply requesting brief particulars of his qualifications and experience, so that the signatory could 'advise me as to whether any useful purpose would be served by inviting me to complete a formal application for appointment'.[53] Because vacancies were usually filled at a CASB meeting held in the summer, soon after the publication of applicants' final examination results, application forms were expected to reach the Director of Recruitment between 1 January and 30 April. It was then that the intense process of personal investigation got under way.

An applicant had to nominate three referees who were invited to submit a report, careful and specific, on his qualities. Typically the referees would include his housemaster or another master who had known him well at school, and his college tutor. The family doctor or bank manager was sometimes nominated. After the war, a likely referee would be the ex-serviceman's commanding officer. Candidates were sternly warned that 'attempts to influence the Secretary of State's selection through Members of Parliament or other persons who are not personally well acquainted with the applicant are useless'.[54] Significantly the CO added that a testimonial from such a source would be 'regarded as indicating that the applicant himself does not consider his qualifications sufficiently good to justify his appointment on his own merits'. The CO's policy was one of competitive selection without a competitive examination. Although testimonials cannot today be consulted in the PRO, a few have here and there come to light. The following testimonial (dates altered) may be taken as representative of the genre:

> XYZ was known to me whilst he was a pupil at the school from 1943 to 1949. As his House-master I had many opportunities of assessing his character and ability. I found him well-poised, a reliable and conscientious worker, tolerant and thoughtful. Though not conspicuous on the games field he was a keen and loyal member of his House and gave generously of his time and effort in furthering House activities. As a senior boy he showed a measured firmness in carrying out the disciplinary tasks allotted to him. During his last year at school he carried out the duties as Cadet Corps Under Officer with keenness and efficiency. His example was a valuable asset to both School and House.[55]

Besides their frank comments on the applicant, these testimonials sometimes also offer an unconscious insight into what the referee thought a DO was all about: for example, 'lacks personal charm … would probably be an efficient but unpopular colonial official', 'heart definitely better than head', 'looks the type', 'I think he is the kind of man who would do well in an emergency', 'useful man to have in a tight corner'.[56]

Candidates were allowed to name three colonies where they would like to serve, although the CO made it clear that there was no guarantee that they would be granted any of them. By the early 1950s the recruitment literature specified that most of the DO vacancies were in Africa. Of these only a few vacancies existed in the High Commission Territories. A few posts were available in the Western Pacific, and now and again a vacancy occurred in Aden, Cyprus or Mauritius, though these might be filled on secondment by a serving officer. 'There are *never* any Administration vacancies for overseas candidates on first appointment,' the advice concluded, 'in the West Indies, Bahamas, Bermuda, the Falklands, Gibraltar, Malta, St. Helena and the Seychelles.'[57] East Africa was very much the top African choice. Kenya appealed to many because of its dramatic scenery and abundant wildlife, but put others off because of the problems associated with settler politics. Uganda enjoyed a reputation as 'The Pearl of Africa'. Tanganyika seemed to some like lots of wide open spaces and still plenty of real bush touring. West Africa's reputation as 'The White Man's Grave' had not entirely dissipated, though in contrast to the Coast's mangrove swamps and dense forests the Northern Provinces of Nigeria offered plenty of open orchard bush, park-land, horse-trekking and the chance to play polo. Family considerations sometimes played a part in the candidate's choice of territory, e.g. that of a post in the Pacific 'so as to be as far away as possible from my mother-in-law', or, again, 'in order to get away from my dominant Irish mother, who had a harsh and robust Catholicism'.[58] But in the end it was where the vacancies were that governed the final appointment.

If the testimonials, along with any follow-up letters seeking elucidation or elaboration on points unclear to the CO, showed that here was a candidate who deserved to move on to the next stage, he would be invited to present himself at the CO for a preliminary interview. This was no formality and might last up to an hour. It was undertaken by a member of the recruiting staff, in a friendly and relaxing *tête-à-tête* atmosphere (the rule of Procedure No. 1 was 'be human'),[59] allowing the interviewer to follow up matters of interest or probe gaps that had caught his eye – positive as well as question-mark ones – and to seek elaboration on any of the testimonials. In the case of S. Hitchcock, who was interviewed for a post in Nyasaland, 'the only topics highlighted in his memory were the various systems used in contract bridge and the novels of Jane Austen'.[60] The interview gave the candidate the opportunity to ask questions on matters on which he wanted more information, such as the climate and health conditions, likely length of tour, or, if he were married (or hoped soon to be), how long before he might expect to be able to have his wife join him. Sometimes there might be a second interview, carried out by a different member of the recruiting staff. In due course all the documentation, notes and reports would be assembled to form what was known as a candidate's Submission. Basically this was an outline evaluation of the candidate as assessed by the CO, ending in a recommendation to the secretary of state. If this was positive, the Submission closed with the minute '? appoint'. In that case, the final stage would be a summons from the CO to appear before the CSAB.

The most vivid description and rationalization of what the CO was looking for in its DOs in the period 1930–48 is that given by the Director of Recruitment himself, supplemented by a confidential CO document on the art of interviewing, the *Appointments Handbook*. A crucial appendix in the latter contains enough material for one to compose a portrait of what the ideal candidate might hopefully look like in the eyes of the CO's interviewers, contributing to the compilation of the Submission.[61] Emphasis was laid on 'character and personal fitness'. Physical appearance was also important, including 'colouring, build, movement, poise, speech and gesture'. The interviewer was to have in mind 'the truism that weakness of various kinds may lurk in a flabby lip or in averted eyes, just as single-mindedness and purpose are consciously reflected in a steady gaze and firm set of mouth and jaw'. Great store was to be set by the qualities of 'presence', 'balance', 'background', and of 'leadership', all somewhat Edwardian attributes and virtues more tenable and identifiable in the 1930s and 1940s than today. 'Intuition, which must be the guiding principle,' the *Handbook* concluded, 'is a faculty that cannot be translated into words.' Though not actually written by Furse, the *Handbook* is an undoubted distillation of the Fursian version of how to interview for the CAS and how to identify the *beau idéal* of the DO. In Furse's own memoirs, a whole chapter is given over to what he calls 'Our System'.[62] Apart from aptitude ('the man must fit the vacancy you choose him for') a major consideration was how the DO would stand up to local scrutiny as he came into 'close daily contact' with the population, 'whose power of

sizing up a man intuitively is notoriously accurate'.[63] Tempera-
ment and imaginative sympathy joined the long list of desiderata
which Furse was convinced could never be tested 'by any form
of written examination yet invented'. It might be said that Furse
emphasized qualities more than qualifications, preferring evaluation over quantification. He has been criticized for instituting
a system of selection that was 'elitist and intuitive' with values
that were 'reactionary more than conservative',[64] and for relegat-
ing intellectual excellence to second place behind character in
his search for what Bradley described as 'likely young men from
the universities with a liberal education who would make good,
sensible and sympathetic administrators ... those qualities which
the rough character-building of a boarding school and then
the broad training of the mind provided by the older universities combined to foster.'[65] Content with a second-class honours
degree, Furse left superior intellect to the ICS. Bradley went so far
as to declare that Furse once told him that 'men of brains should
be slaves – slaves of the men of character'.[66] It has been claimed
that Furse's vision of the ideal DO was a candidate who had been
a house prefect as well as captain of the XI at school or college.[67]
If this was acceptable and quite workable for the 1930s, after
1948 colonial policy required – and the CO insisted on – greater
emphasis on the mental dexterity of the new DO cadres.

The final CSAB was a much more formal and potentially
intimidating affair than the 'be human' one-to-one preliminary
interviews held in the CO. It was chaired by the First Civil Service
Commissioner. Behind a long table would be up to a dozen people,
retired colonial governors, leaders of business or industry, maybe
a trade union official and possibly a DO on leave. Members of the
CS Division in the CO were on hand. The Director of Recruitment favoured a seat at the end. The Submissions had been read
by members in advance and were ready to hand for reference or
enquiry. Close attention would, after the candidate had left, be
paid to the DO's opinion, fundamentally on whether he would
like to have the candidate serving with him or not. Marks were
awarded out of 300 ('an exceptionally good all-round candidate'),
with 240 the minimum pass mark and anything below 200 'well
below standard'. By 1948, if not before, a leading question was
what class of degree the candidate had obtained, especially if
– as often happened – the Tripos or Schools lists had appeared
after the initial interviews had taken place. Unlike modern job

interviews, when an applicant is expected to have done a lot of homework on his potential employer's field of operation, candidates have sometimes related how they were privately advised not to show too much knowledge of imperial history and colonial policy (other than an intelligent grasp of geography) and above all should avoid giving the impression that they already knew all the answers to colonial problems. By the 1950s, however, any such reticence was seemingly dropped and more DOs recall 'a difficult innings and being bowled a few awkward googlies'.[68]

With the CSAB often sitting in July or August, the CO needed to let a candidate know of their decision no later than the beginning of September so that they could secure a place for him at Oxford, Cambridge or London on the CS training course starting in October. Projecting the image of a good employer, the CO was prompt to compile its list of successful CSAB candidates and to inform each of them that, subject to a successful examination by the CO physician, the secretary of state was ready to offer him an appointment in a specified territory. This offer was customarily sent by telegram. To quote an actual telegram of 1953: 'Subject medical fitness and satisfactory degree result you have been accepted for colonial administrative service and allocated Nigeria stop you may be required to attend course commencing October stop formal offer follows.'[69] In a number of recorded cases, the telegram led to a hurried search in the family school atlas to find out exactly where Nyasaland or the Gold Coast was.

A telegraphic acceptance, a successful medical by the CO physician, a few weeks later the train to Oxbridge, and the applicant had at last got his feet on the ladder to a career as a DO. The candidate had become a probationer. The next step would be to become a cadet.

CHAPTER 3

Training for the Colonial Service

It was the large-scale expansion of Britain's empire in Africa at the beginning of the twentieth century that introduced the need for a degree of professionalization for colonial administrators, by giving some kind of pre-job training. Nigeria, Ashanti and the Northern Territories of the Gold Coast, Uganda, Kenya, Somaliland, Nyasaland and Zanzibar now all came under Crown rule. By the same token, the number of the DOs working in Africa by 1909 had more than doubled within the decade, to over 1,000 from the 400 of 1899. By the outbreak of the First World War more than 250 were assigned to Nigeria, nearly 120 to Kenya and almost 50 to the Gold Coast.[1] Coinciding with this expansion, the principal sources of recruitment for DOs, namely the transfer of officials from the now wound-down predecessor Chartered Companies and military men who had seen service in South Africa, were drying up. Aware of the ICS precedent, the CO turned to the universities for help in bringing this new career opportunity to the notice of undergraduates.

At the same time, it was accepted that this new breed of administrators, lacking the African experience which their predecessors had brought with them, would require some sort of orientation – hence the decision to initiate a training course in what tropical African civil service work was all about. The CO arranged for new DOs – and those on leave too – to attend a course lasting two (later raised to three) months, organized at the Imperial Institute in London three times a year. The instruction was thinly spread, with lectures on an unduly wide range of subjects such as colonial accounts, tropical economic products, criminal and Mohammedan law, hygiene and sanitation, surveying, ethnology and African languages, all in no more than 12 weeks. A.F.B. Bridges, one of 70 future administrators gathered at the Institute in 1921, recorded how 'the Tropical Hygiene lectures were given by a gloomy doctor who, after describing the symptoms of the many tropical diseases one could get, often gruesome, usually ended by saying that "the patient usually dies" '.[2] As for African languages, this turned out to be mostly about phonetics, taught, as Bridges recalled, by chanting in unison 'R-r-r-rump steak'. To A.C. Burns, a future governor, who also attended a course at the Institute, it was a complete waste of time but, as he caustically noted, 'it only lasted for a few weeks, and as much of it was taken in an officer's leave it was at least not official time that was being wasted'. He was to extend the same criticism to the subsequent Oxford and Cambridge courses, looking on them as 'an even worse waste of time, although a very pleasant one', his principal objection being that they were too theoretical and ignored training in 'the two essentials, unlimited patience and a real sympathy for the people among whom the young officer will work'.[3] But at least a start had been made.

Once the post-1919 crash programme for recruiting DOs had run its course, with 300 vacancies filled in three years (nearly all in Africa, as the Eastern DOs were still being recruited separately for service in Ceylon, Malaya and Hong Kong), R.D. Furse at the CO put into effect the next stage in his strategy to bring the CAS up to the high status enjoyed by the ICS in the public mind. In this his task was made easier by the perception among graduates, confirmed by the falling ICS recruitment figures, that the pace of constitutional advance and of localization timetables, together with the outbreaks of violence in Bengal and the Punjab, meant that the ICS career was no longer so attractive and maybe no longer viable as a career. Furse persuaded Oxford and Cambridge universities to complement their long-standing and successful training courses for ICS probationers[4] with a Tropical African Service course.

The Tropical African Service (TAS) course was opened in 1926 and lasted for two terms. It was raised to a full academic year in 1928. According to a member of the 1927 Oxford course, R.G. Syme, 'we were a wild and unruly lot', with a mixture of ex-servicemen and what he called 'ex-varsity men', and right from the start the Colonial Service club was known as a 'trouble spot'.[5] The TAS was renamed the CAS (Colonial Administrative Service) course in 1932, when the newly unified Colonial Service incorporated the hitherto separate Eastern Cadet Service. Unlike the courses at the Imperial Institute, the curriculum of the Oxbridge courses was to be, at the insistence of the two universities, primarily academic and not vocational. University and not CO staff were to give the lectures and to set and mark the exams. It was not until 1945 that it became the practice for the course supervisor to be a serving DO, on a two-year attachment. The courses continued until the war. In the event, those nominated to the 1939–40 course were allowed to complete it, though for those going to the Gold Coast it was reduced to two terms.[6]

A major advance in this training course was its extensive reform and rebranding as the Devonshire Course after 1946 (named after the Duke of Devonshire who had chaired the consultative committee of CO officials and academics). The impetus was a far-sighted and vigorous memorandum drafted by Furse, the DO's Director of Recruitment, in 1943.[7] Not all of his proposals found favour with the Devonshire Committee, notably his innovative idea of dividing a DO's training into three stages: a first course, structured along the lines of the former CAS course; a sandwich period of apprenticeship in a colony, lasting up to two years; and a second course back at the university immediately following the apprenticeship tour. The manpower crisis in the colonies caused by the virtual cessation of recruitment during the war together with war casualties among DOs who had joined up, and lengthy leave vacancies to be filled, all conspired against any colonial governor being willing to wait three or four years for his new cadets to start work. Nor was this all that Furse had in mind for the professionalization of the DO cadre. While the Second Course would be an integral part of the tiered pre-appointment and then pre-confirmation training course, opportunity should also be given, Furse argued, to selected officers (not restricted to high-flyers) to undertake an advanced course, between their eighth and 14th year of service. On this, they would make a special study, in depth, on a topic of their choosing subject to the approval of their own government. In the end this advanced course was revised into a year's sabbatical study leave and became the Second Devonshire Course. Together they were re-titled in the 1950s the Colonial Service (later still Overseas) Courses A and B.

Furse was opposed to the suggestion of a Colonial Service Staff College. He dismissed it as 'a sort of Colonial Camberley, whose graduates write "p.s.c." after their name and are regarded as superior'.[8] He went on to warn that a 'pemmican' nature of instruction was likely to be offered, while – and here lay a clinching argument – 'experienced administrators are equally terrified at the prospect of higher promotion in the Service being confined to men who have graduated in a theoretical course'. What was at stake, he concluded, was the need to train 'the whole man' rather than merely imparting professional knowledge: 'to fit him mentally, morally and physically for what, in the case at any rate of the Administrative Officer, is one of the most many-sided and exacting careers in the world'.[9]

Furse foresaw that the end of the war would usher in vast social change, necessitating the broadening of the basis of recruitment for DOs. 'New elements of the population will have to be fused into the living body of the Service.'[10] Hence, he concluded, the fundamental need for training. 'The more varied the elements from which the Service of the future is built up – and this applies to the locally recruited as well as to the externally recruited officers – the more important it would seem to start them on their career with the common background of a course of training, which they can take together and, in so doing, come to understand each other better.' What is not to be overlooked is the impact of Furse's imperative of modern colonial race relations on the work of the DO. The CAS, he elaborated, 'will have to deal with a new type of coloured man and must absorb and acclimatize a new type of white officer'. To bring this forward-looking thinking home, he compared the role and reputation of yesterday's DO with what would be expected from him tomorrow:

> In the past he has gone into the bush and produced a miracle. One effect of the miracle has been the emergence of the educated native ... to a great extent the future mouthpiece and leader of his people. ... By some means our white officers must learn to understand him, as they have understood his brothers in the bush villages; to sympathise and work with him, and to co-operate with him intelligently. Otherwise we are heading for trouble. Cannot training help here?[11]

Importantly, a special team made up of one representative from each of the three participant universities (Furse himself had hoped to see CS training managed by a team of universities, including, besides Oxford and Cambridge, SOAS, LSE, a Scottish university and maybe one of the newer ones) was given an opportunity to monitor and modify some of the Devonshire assumptions when it returned from a fact-finding mission to Nigeria in the Christmas vacation of 1945. This Nuffield Foundation mission was charged with reporting on whether, and if so how, the universities' conception of their role in the new Devonshire Course might be conditioned by their acquisition of first-hand knowledge of the Service on the ground and ensuring that 'the proposed courses seemed as attractive in that setting as they had in Whitehall'.[12] The principal addition they brought back was an awareness that the new style of DO would need to be capable of operating effectively in the Secretariat as well as retaining his proverbial competence in running a district. To understand the problems of central government, the DO must now be trained 'to master the art of administration from an office, the use of statistics, the secrets of delegating authority while retaining effective control of policy, the mysteries of public finance – in short everything that a member of the Home Civil Service begins to absorb from the very start'.[13] They also touched on a basic issue that was to become a common grouse among DOs (and their superiors) as they looked back on the course and lamented the lack of any guidance on how to run even the simplest of offices, 'to cope with office work, to set an office in order, and to put the clerks to their proper work'.[14]

By the time the Devonshire Courses opened, at Oxford, Cambridge and now the LSE, alterations had been accepted for the proposed First Course. The original scheme was for it to last for 18 months rather than an academic year, with two terms of eight weeks each followed by one of six weeks being spent at Oxford or Cambridge on the general section, and one term of language and the regional section being taken at London. Out of the 254 hours allocated to the general section, 88 were devoted to colonial history and economics, 56 to law and anthropology, 40 to agriculture and 16 to geography.[15] But as colonial governors and probationers, predominantly ex-servicemen, both began to chafe at such a protracted delay before the cadets got into the field, the First Devonshire was soon revised to consist of a single academic year at the nominated university, with language now offered at each university and no longer being taught exclusively at London. The allocation of probationer to university was governed by the territory of posting and hence the language taught, e.g. Swahili and East Africa to Oxford. For a while, Hausa was available at both Cambridge and Oxford.

However, it is important to note that not everyone joining the CAS in 1946 and 1947 (and obviously, none for 1945) was sent on the First Devonshire. Sometimes this was to their chagrin, sometimes to their relief. 'Thank God I didn't do it,' was the verdict of J.A. Jones, 'it sounds as if it were a complete waste of time.'[16] B.L. Jacobs took an amused view of missing out on the First Devonshire. 'Throughout my career I never participated in any course whatsoever,' he wrote, yet he ended up at Makerere University and the Institute of Development Studies at Sussex University as what he modestly called 'a minor authority' in training courses for post-colonial administrators from overseas.[17] It is clear that the CO urged those who had just come out of the forces (and at an age several years ahead of the peacetime average of 22) that not only was their arrival eagerly awaited in the territory but that in the long run they would be better off through a year's seniority and an extra year's experience on the job rather than by a year spent ('wasted'?) on an academic course. N. Goldie-Scot, for instance, was assured by the CO in 1947 that an immediate passage out would be far more advantageous than spending three years getting a degree. He took the view that in the long run he did not lose out: 'Provided one was put under a good DC, on-the-job training was a pretty comprehensive way to learn.'

A number of probationers attending the course at LSE reported the tough time they were given by their fellow non-CS students who jeered at their imperial pretensions and proposed that they should be banned from the school. R.E.N. Smith recalled that the colonial probationers at LSE were known 'derisively as the "White Masters"'. 'For "liberal" thinking,' commented an exasperated I. Brook, who attended the course after doing a tour in Nigeria, 'it seemed a curiously illiberal gesture.'[18] Another probationer who was upset by LSE radicalism was A. Stuart, destined for Uganda: 'The School as a whole threw itself passionately into the Mau Mau cause. A Kikuyu lecturer was wildly applauded when he compared Mau Mau to the coming together of the British people after Dunkirk.'[19] Nor was Brook all that impressed by the lecturer in colonial affairs, who spent a whole hour telling them how dreadful British administration in Nigeria was. On being asked at the end how she thought it might be improved, she snapped 'That is not my business, I am here to tell you the results.'[20]

R.J. Graham's letter of notification of a pre-Nigeria course was typical of those sent out by the CO during the post-war years. 'Before taking up your appointment you will be required to attend a university course, lasting one year, which is held concurrently at Oxford, Cambridge and London, beginning in October. Your name has been entered on the list for London [entered in ink].'[21] An accompanying memorandum gave him an outline of the course, details of allowances payable, and conditions of service. The last-named starkly spelled out that 'The Secretary of State may, at any time during the preliminary course of instruction, cancel your selection if you fail to complete the course successfully within the time allotted, or if he receives what, in his opinion, is an adverse report on your conduct or work while attending the course.' If his selection was cancelled, he was warned that he would be liable to refund the cost of his training and the allowances paid. It was a sanction applied on very few occasions on the First Devonshire. P. Mullins, who provided a detailed and largely critical account of the 'curate's-eggish' quality of the teaching at LSE, recorded that one member of the course was failed by the supervisor, 'totally without warning'.[22]

Nomination to the Devonshire Course carried a number of immediate personal – if not directly Service – advantages. First of all, one was paid to attend it – true a small allowance but still a start on the earning ladder. In 1947 this was £23 a month, but by the time G. Winstanley attended the course at LSE in 1953 en route to Bechuanaland the rate had been raised to 75 per cent of an ADO's salary – 'I was rather well off.'[23] This was not the only privilege to place the probationer above his fellow students. At Oxford and Cambridge he was absolved from the proctoral regulation that no-one *in statu pupillari* was allowed to own a car or garage it within two miles of the city centre. Furthermore, for last year's graduate back for a fourth year, there was, if he were athletically minded, yet one more chance to gain a hockey Blue or play in the Varsity match at Lords. In an era when the university authorities were seemingly less strict over dual registration, several probationers reported that they managed to find time to finish their degree course or enrol for a diploma course at the same time as attending the Devonshire Course. Vacations were still vacations for the probationer, although they now often involved an attachment to, for example, a local government council to learn something about a topic new to most of them but now destined to be central to the DO's work. As for those fortunate enough to be nominated to the 1946 first post-war course, there was, as R. Sadleir found, one additional bonus, 'an immediate Class B release on grounds of urgent national importance'.[24] The comfortable Oxford style of lectures in the graceful Rhodes House and 'reading on a rug under the great college [Wadham] copper beech' was rudely shattered when the course moved to London for its second stage by 'a roll call at the beginning of every lecture'.[25] For most probationers, R.A. Hill's judgement of the 1947–48 Devonshire Course at Cambridge rang true, 'pure delight, utter bliss', coming at the end of five years of war service. For D. Bates, attending the Oxford course in 1935–36, it had been a unique year of no worries: 'One had all the excitement of being at Oxford without having the pressure of an exam and one had all the joys of an Oxford which one had got to know without the constant worry of whether you would get a job at the end of it.'[26]

A focus for the probationers was the Colonial Service club at each university, an institution to which Furse attached great importance. This was of particular social value at Oxford and Cambridge because, as R. Wainwright observed, 'it helped us to get to know each other, separated as we were in different Colleges'.[27] At Oxford, the club, originally located above what was then a barber's shop on the corner of Cornmarket and the Broad before being moved in the early 1950s to 3 South Parks Road (symbolically adjacent to Rhodes House), was a real centre for the probationers. It boasted living-in accommodation for members, including DOs on leave, to whom it was advertised as 'a home from home'.[28] In post-war Cambridge the CS Club in Petty Curie was unfortunately situated above one of the wartime British Restaurants, but once one was up the often odiferous stairs the club room, bar, library, table tennis and billiards facilities were as good as those at Oxford – or so the Cantabs maintained. LSE had its CS club house in Bloomsbury. Visiting governors, DOs and others from the CS and CO were invited to talk at club evenings (the legendary Lugard was a frequent guest in the 1930s), and Cambridge went as far as to publish a *Colonial Service Magazine* in

1928. Each club had its own tie: the hartebeeste at Oxford, a lion for Cambridge and a golden palm for London. For many years a friendly feud existed between Cambridge and Oxford, when it became a matter of honour for the former, when it was Oxford's turn to host the biennial sporting fixture, to try and 'liberate' the original hartebeeste head from the supervisor's office and spirit it away on the coach back to Cambridge.

As to the value of the First Devonshire, a recent alumni survey[29] has revealed a good range of retrospective opinion without necessarily diminishing the sheer joy, as was often the case, of a year at (or back at) the university for those who had just come out of several years of active service. Against this must be set the impatience at having to wait so long before being able to get on with the job and earning a salary and the frank disappointment of some like J.H.D. Stapleton, who was on the 1935–36 course at Oxford and concluded that 'all my working life I realised how little I had been taught and of how little value it was', or R.T. Kerslake, whose anatomy of the pre-war course concluded with the realization that each day brought little more than a 'bewildering range of studies',[30] or, 15 years later, of J.H. Smith, who found it 'a pleasant interlude but of little training and even less academic value' and considered the standard of Oxford teaching well below that offered to undergraduates at UCL.[31] There is also the thought-provoking reflection of J.P.L. Scott, who declared that he could not recall any of his seniors in Sierra Leone 'ever seeming to rely on course-gained evidence to make a point'.

The subjects generally awarded the highest marks in retrospect by probationers were language and criminal law. Although a few complained that the language turned out not to be the one spoken in their first district, for the *linguae francae* like Swahili and Hausa the teaching was widely appreciated. At Oxford, for instance, passing the Swahili exam was equated with a pass in the written part of the compulsory language examination held in the territory before a cadet could be confirmed. At Cambridge, the Arabic exam sometimes taken on the advanced Devonshire Course (see below) was recognized in Northern Nigeria as the equivalent of the written Lower Standard Arabic and financially rewarded accordingly. According to M. Varvill,[32] only written Hausa was taught at Cambridge in the 1930s, but post-war probationers recall idyllic hours punting down the Cam, repeating the days of the week in Hausa and the numerals up to 100 along with their teacher, Malam Ladan, perched nervously on the bow. Islamic law was especially appreciated by those heading for terri- tories with a sizeable Muslim population. At post-war Cambridge the law tutorials from G. Lane regularly elicited respect, partly because of his plea, as remembered by J. Cooke, 'When you are sitting under your respective palm trees, gentlemen, handing out basic justice, try to remember what I have taught you,'[33] and partly because he went on to become Lord Chief Justice of England.

Field engineering and the principles of building did not fire the imagination of many, though keen cricketers remembered eagerly sunny afternoons when both they and their instructor, a retired army officer, lazed in the Parks on their field trip and concentrated on cricket rather than the compass. T. Harris was one of the few to find Colonel Tandy's instruction of use when, many years later, he had a problem with a cesspool in Dorset.[34] On the 1953–54 course at Oxford the field surveying instructor, F. Langland, who had been a DC in Tanganyika, endeared himself to D. Connelly by laying great stress on how to lay out a tennis court. For J. Russell, Langland's *Field Engineering* ranked as his bush DO's Bible.[35] Views on anthropology were heavily condi- tioned by who was teaching it: an authority on the headhunters of the Naga hills found it hard to hold the attention of probation- ers allocated to East or West Africa, whereas a lecturer who had field experience in Africa immediately created a captive audi- ence. For A. Stuart, the anthropology lectures at London given by 'a distinguished but decrepit feminist', were 'a disaster', with those on race relations by 'a pink-politicked clergyman [being] equally unreal'.[36] K. Addis, assigned to Nigeria, retained a differ- ent memory of how superbly his course lecturers instructed the probationers 'on how to surrender the Empire'![37] The teaching on anthropology also received a knock from an ex-Sudan DO in Northern Nigeria who had an eager Cambridge cadet posted to him, only too willing to put forward 'his own ready-made solutions to problems' picked up from the social anthropology lectures on his First Devonshire.[38] Agriculture also evoked a split reaction in retrospect, its evaluation as nearly useful being balanced by those DOs who thought it nearly useless. Health, which at Oxford before the war had included a visit to an opera- tion at the Radcliffe Hospital, leaving one probationer in a fainting fit on the floor[39] and another, G.L. Stephenson, disturbed at being 'shown how to help babies into the world',[40] no longer included

visits to a hospital under its post-war rubric. Also dropped was
map-reading, although an ADO in the 1930s thanked his stars
he had been taught how to carry out a compass traverse. His DO
told him that none of the hundreds of square miles of the district
had ever been mapped, so H.H. Marshall should 'get busy and do
something about it'.[41] By 1936, in the opinion of J. Morley, tropical hygiene and field surveying were 'a relic of the times, disap-
pearing but not yet gone for good, when departmental specialists
were few on the ground and a DO with the time and inclination
could carry out his own programme of minor public works'.[42]
Twenty years on, B. Nightingale, one of the last five Britons to
be appointed ADO in Northern Nigeria, recalled that among the
subjects taught in 1956–57 was, sensibly (and at last), car maintenance.[43] M. Varvill was not the only ADO to have wished that
instruction had been offered on hair-cutting for DOs in the bush
(a duty that many a cadet was commanded to perform on his up-
country DO), suggesting that the task could be eased by playing
The Barber of Seville on the gramophone.[44]

Colonial history was interesting, but a common complaint was
that it completely ignored recent social and nationalist history
and any study of the transfer of power. Many regretted that it was
too colonial. What they would like to have had were lectures on
the history, pre-colonial as well as constitutional and political, of
their assigned territory. Assigned to Northern Nigeria, K. Blackburne regretted the dearth of historical background, confess-
ing that he had never heard of Sir George Goldie.[45] By common
consent (and deep dissent from probationers assigned to the
Western Pacific), the First Devonshire was heavily weighted
towards instructing cadets assigned to Africa. They were easily
the majority on the post-war courses. So obvious was this bias
that on one course a probationer destined for the Western Pacific
is said to have leaped to his feet and cheered in excitement when
for the first time in nearly a whole term the Solomon Islands were
mentioned.

What was lamented above all was the absence of any instruction on Africa's current politics, the principal phenomenon that
the DO of the 1950s and 1960s would be engaged upon throughout his career. D.G.P. Taylor recalled the 1955–56 Cambridge
course not only for the strong support he received from the
supervisor, H.H. McLeery, after Taylor's critical report on his
'useless' local government attachment to Bristol City Council, but

also for the singular lack in the curriculum of 'any of the political aspects of colonial administration into which we were pitched immediately on arrival'. Even as late as 1954, official directives such as the Northern Nigerian government's *Duties of a District Officer* piously hoped that the DO could be safely insulated from politics.[46] Nevertheless, the fact that by the late 1950s there was a growing number of African officers on both the First and the Second Devonshire Courses, with an easy ability for the British probationers to meet them at the CS club as well as in the college bar and pub, meant that the progress and problems of politics and self-government soon became part of the British probationers' image of the DO's work. Many have commented how this welcome extension to the courses' membership partially compensated for the stark absence of any lectures in African nationalism and party politics.

Other gaps in their training identified by probationers as they looked back on the course were, in W. Bazley's case, how 'nothing had been said about how an up-country office was run',[47] or, back in 1935–36, in S. White's reflection as he contemplated his 'first files with distaste' on arrival in Northern Nigeria on his first tour: 'I had been taught many things … but nothing about files or offices',[48] or how to handle account books and ledgers, or how Native Administrations actually worked. More seriously, M. Milne had cause to regret, as a pre-war DO in Nigeria, another gap in his Cambridge training: the procedures to be followed in his office when, as deputy sheriff, he was called on to carry out an execution.[49] Perhaps most surprisingly of all, there was no hint in the curriculum of what was quickly becoming the academic discipline of public administration. Here were future administrators being trained in virtually everything but administration. 'It was not until the career colonial administrator was well past his sell-by date,' one commentator observed, 'that the value of the textbook, so long enshrined in public administration in the USA, was recognized in UK government training circles.'[50]

While it was clearly impossible, given a course of some 30–40 probationers destined for a dozen territories, to have lectures on the administrative and political specifics of each colony, more might have been done with small tutorial groups, maybe from a visit by a DO on leave, on topics of the day like 'Background to Mau Mau', 'Community Development in Uganda', 'Political Parties in the Gold Coast', etc. The overall evaluation of the Devonshire

Courses – and their principal fault – was compellingly hinted at by F. Kennedy, who attended the Second Course at London in 1952–53. 'Were we not trained for the problems of simple, rural societies, rather than for the hugely different economic and political problems of societies emerging into the modern world with all its complexity?' The American anthropologist H. Kuklick, in her detailed anatomy of the inter-war Gold Coast provincial administration, was of the opinion that the TAS course was also looked on as an opportunity to give probationers who needed it an extra layer of that 'social polish considered intrinsic in a commanding personality'.[51]

The course supervisor was an important player. Before the war he was a member of the university staff, a college tutor or someone from the Appointments Board, but from 1947 he was a serving DO selected by the CO and seconded for two years from his territorial government. By the 1960s he was more likely to be a PC, perhaps just retired. Among those who stood out in the memory of Devonshire Course probationers were H.H. McLeery (Tanganyika) and G. Gardner-Brown (Northern Rhodesia) at Cambridge; J.F. Cornes, L.C. Giles, H.P.W. Murray (all Nigeria) and E.G. Rowe (Kenya) at Oxford; and H.P. Elliott (Nigeria) at London (R.E. Wraith was not from the CAS). D. Nicoll-Griffith, who attended the Cambridge course in 1951, reckoned that J.W. Howard, a Kenya DC who spent only one year as a supervisor, was particularly successful because of his current DC's knowledge of what was going on in the field.

At the end of the academic year exams were held. Most probationers felt that, after what they had been through in Schools or Tripos finals, the course examinations were nothing to worry about. On the Devonshire Course the results were graded into Distinction, Merit, Pass and Fail. Before 1945 the CO used to hold a viva board after the exams, to quiz the candidates on their papers and then classify the results into Firsts, Seconds and Thirds. P. Dennis thought that one of the questions put to him might have come out of a Douglas Fairbanks film: 'What would you do if you were bitten by a mad dog in the desert many miles from any medical aid?' The answer probably did him more good than harm: 'Die, sir'.[52]

The training courses were not the only way in which serving officers kept in touch with the university. Before the war, Oxford, at the initiative of the redoubtable Margery Perham, organized a residential Summer School on colonial administration in 1937 and again in 1938. Out of the 155 CS members who attended the first, 118 came from Africa and 101 from the CAS. Two-thirds of the 1938 conference delegates were DOs. On both occasions Lugard gave the inaugural address.[53] After the war the focus shifted to Cambridge, where, under the aegis of the academic R.E. Robinson, from 1947 to 1972 the CO's African Studies Branch sponsored an annual Summer School on African Administration.[54] The experience and calibre of those invited, new breeds as well as the old guard, meant that, as Andrew Cohen at the CO intended, here was an invaluable interchange between the CO and the CS, especially from the generation of up-and-coming DOs. On occasion the conferences could be used as a CO sounding-box for new policy ideas. Linked to this opportunity for thinking aloud were two journals sponsored by the CO. The *Journal of African Administration* was started by the African Studies Branch in 1948, and the monthly *Corona* (1949–62) emerged as the CS house magazine.[55] Both were designed to help the new-look post-war CS 'shake off its alleged parochialism and broaden its horizons – intellectual as well as practical – by having a focus for the dissemination of knowledge and ideas and for the exchange of experience on colonial administration and development'.[56] There is no doubt that from 1948 onwards the serving DO had little lack of opportunity – indeed he was officially encouraged to make his views on policy heard. Nor was he slow to do so.

There is no need to dwell on the Second Devonshire in the same detail as the First. Also consisting of an academic year at one of the same universities (originally a much wider choice was envisaged, including institutions outside the UK), it was essentially a sabbatical year in which the DO could more or less do his own thing, focusing on theory rather than practice. His interaction with probationers on the First Course could be of mutual profit. It was not to be treated as a staff college course for high-flyers. Sometimes it was used for those recruited as soon as the war had ended and at once sent out to Africa without any training. Sometimes it could be used for a DO on compassionate family or health grounds. Only half of J. Russell's explanation of why he was sent on the Second Course in 1956, having been recruited as an emergency DO in Kenya, is likely true: 'I was regarded as suspect material for HM's Colonial Service, so they sent me off to Oxford University to be suitably brainwashed.'[57] Certainly he found it a 'severe shock'. Ideally it was felt that the course should come in a DO's eighth to fourteenth year of service. Furse had his own characteristically phrased view of what the Second or advanced course was for:

> to check, criticize and clarify the experience the cadet had gained; to counteract those 'bolshevist' tendencies which are said to be most common about the fifth to seventh year of service, by teaching him where he fits into the general scheme of colonial government and how to understand and co-operate with other departments and the Secretariat; to deflate his conceit if he thinks he knows too much; and to fortify his morale after any shocks which his idealism had received during his tour.[58]

Once again, the course seems to have provided at least as much enjoyment as education, though J.A. Golding's principal memory of Oxford, where he had elected to study local government, was of the difficulty of finding accommodation for his family. They ended up in smart Park Town, but it was nothing more than a loft above a garage. Fortunately he already had plenty of experience of living in the bush in Tanganyika.[59]

Reverting to the compulsory First Devonshire, during the probationer's final term his thoughts turned from lectures and exams to the real finale of his preparatory year. This was kitting out for his next move – to Africa. There were half a dozen outfitters who specialized in tropical outfitting, such as the Army and Navy Stores (its service dated back to 1871), F.P. Baker and Griffiths McAllister in London, and, strategically, Alkit in Cambridge and Walters the Tailor in Oxford. The last of these had opened in 1914 and proudly played on its connection with Britain's overseas civil servants and the Oxford name.[60] Catalogues of recommended clothing and equipment were available and today provide primary research material as well as a good (if sometimes disbelieving) read. 'Your Overseas Needs at a Glance' was the title of Walters' substantial brochure. That put out by the Army and Navy Stores in 1937 ran to over 1,200 pages of items and illustrations, and weighed 4lbs. The probationer's preliminary reading for this venture included such official CO literature as 'Conditions of Living' and 'Hints on the Preservation of Health in Tropical Africa'.

Up to 1939 the recommended tropical kit purchases on first appointment included items of food as well as lightweight clothing and house utensils and furnishings, since what was available to buy in Africa was minimal and mostly confined to stores in the capital. Even as late as 1950 a cadet headed for Nigeria was advised by one of his seniors there to be sure he brought with him enough marmalade, toilet rolls and saddle soap to last for 15 months, along with at least a year's supply of soda-siphon sparklets. Clothing would be measured, made and tried on, with a record kept by the tropical outfitters against a customer's subsequent re-order, often by mail from Africa. A lightweight linen suit was recommended for formal wear. 'Kampala, is it?' an apprentice clerk is said to have advised a customer. 'Very hot in Malaya, sir – better make it two palm beach suits'. A cadet was not entitled to wear the white CS uniform until he had been confirmed in his appointment as an ADO, usually after three years. When the time came for such a purchase, the full uniform, complete with Class IV gorgets, white gloves, dress helmet, ceremonial sword and gold bullion knot could set him back a further substantial sum.

Apart from the full camp kit of bed ('not the low camp bed, sir, the snakes find it too easy to get at you', A. Stuart remembered his outfitter warning him),[61] portable chair, table, washstand and a tin bath, the selection of clothes and household items was largely optional. Yet certain accessories carried a semi *de rigueur* aura: a mosquito net for sleeping under and, indispensable if ungainly, ankle-length mosquito boots for the evenings, a Tilley pressure lamp, maybe a wind-up portable gramophone with a selection of 78" records, and often, to the reputed embarrassment of cadets who brought their mother along in the hope of her helping out with the hefty bill, a portable lavatory seat.[62] A portable medicine chest was also strongly recommended, including such items as serums and permanganate crystals for snake bites. Spine-pads to protect the back of the neck from sun and cholera belts to prevent a chill on the stomach in the cool of dawn continued to feature in the recommended lists well into the 1930s. While a sporting rifle was quite commonly purchased, after the Second World War it was virtually unheard of (or forbidden) for a cadet to take out with him a revolver or other firearm, as at one time had been strongly recommended.

Provisions like tins of marmalade and strawberry jam (regularly and specifically named), Ideal milk, sausages, kippers and butter, 'and don't forget the tin-opener, sir' – the staples of life in

Britain became the luxuries of life in the bush – were packed in what were known as 'chop [food] boxes'. These were specially made, fitted with a hinged lid and padlock, and guaranteed to be within the approved weight limit for head porterage, 50–60lbs. Once emptied they could be used for numerous purposes both out on tour and in a bush house, as bedside tables or stools. R. Wainwright, who went to Kenya in 1935, calculated that he was faced with an outfitter's bill of £400, twice his expected salary.[63]

Once the final selection of what was really necessary – as opposed to 'very much recommended, sir' – had been made, the outfitters would pack the purchases into a number of large crates and despatch them to the docks for loading on to the ship in which a passage had been booked for the cadet by the Crown Agents.[64] The clothes were placed in zinc-lined airtight tin trunks, which could continue to be used in place of wardrobes where there was no such amenity in up-country housing. Personal items were packed in the ubiquitous and indispensable sheet-metal (tin) bath, complete with a detachable wicker basket lining. Small wonder that in Tanganyika in the early 1930s the government allowed a cadet up to 50 carriers to headload his baggage to his first station.[65] Back in England, the outfitters would be there at the dockside to call on their valued customer in his cabin, confirm the purchases now loaded on board and hand over the 'Not Wanted on Voyage' manifest. Just one thing remained, the question of settling the payment. Clearly the official outfit allowance of £60 (£30 for those posted to East Africa) was not going to be anything like enough, so a credit arrangement would be delicately negotiated and signed in the privacy of one's cabin before the clerk went back on shore. Many cadets opted for a regular deduction from their monthly salary, and by no means all cleared their outfitting debt before the end of their first tour. Furthermore it was quite usual for an ADO to write back to London or Oxford during his tour and ask for, to quote actual orders, 'two quiet ties of blue or brownish mixture, and one Oxford Nomads Rugby Football Club tie' or 'two more pairs of khaki shorts – but one inch longer'.

Tropical outfitters may have been motivated by profit, but their attentive and knowledgeable staff also proved of real assistance to the generally confused probationer as he tried to distinguish between a Bombay bowler, a white Minto pith helmet and a khaki Cawnpore sola topi, or weigh the relative merits of a Roorkhee or Rajah green canvas chair. Their care and courtesy were the basis of tropical outfitters' business, whether it was whispering to an urban Northern Nigerian cadet who had been invited to try a saddle for size that 'the horse will be going *that* way, sir', or the tactful letter to another whose sailing date was coming very close: 'If circumstances permit of a moderate further payment before departure, it would be very helpful to us, but if this is duly inconvenient the existing arrangements are accepted with the utmost willingness.' That there were outfitters and 'not-so-fitters' is to be expected. J.S. Lawson landed up in the hands of one of the less reliable firms, even though it was one sponsored by the Crown Agents. The gorget badges of rank they sold him as an ADO turned out to be those of a chief commissioner.[66] At the very least, they could spare the young administrator-to-be the embarrassment felt by William Boot at having bought 'a collaps-ible canoe, a jointed flag-staff and Union Jack ... and a cane for whacking snakes'.[67]

With his tropical kit stored on board and his credit arrange-ments satisfactorily concluded, the DO-to-be could leave his cabin, go up on deck and contemplate the receding Liver Building or Royal Albert Docks with the conventional mixture of excite-ment tinged with a quickly dismissed shadow of sadness. With his salary starting from the day of departure, even though at half rate until the day he disembarked in Takoradi, Lagos, Mombasa or Dar es Salaam and established his date of seniority in the serv-ice, his African journey had in all ways begun, or, as in many cases in the late 1940s, begun again: 'There I was,' wrote ex-serv-iceman K.V. Arrowsmith, 'four years older and again wearing my khaki drill (but shorn of its badges of rank). Formerly it had been India and Malaya. Now it was Eastern Nigeria.'[68] The probationer had at last become a cadet.

CHAPTER 4

First Tour

If the thrill of visiting the tropical outfitters and then finding all one's crates labelled and loaded on board ship was the final stage in what had been a whole year's preparation for becoming a DO, the experience of the voyage out indelibly signalled the opening weeks of one's actual career as a DO. In the retrospective CAS mind, it often lays claim to a special place. 'We were entering into a strange new existence,' reflected K. Blackburne as he excitedly headed for Nigeria in 1930, 'a life based on a mud hut with one or two rooms and a verandah, with mud and wattle walls, thatch from the leaves and fronds of palm trees over our heads, hard-mud floors under our feet. ... It would be a long time before we would again experience the things which we had taken for granted – water coming out of a tap, lights to be turned on by a switch ... .'[1] R. Terrell was by no means certain that he was doing the right thing. Being a DO was not his chosen career. He was going to Africa on secondment from the CO, unimpressed by the telephoned assurance from Lagos that the government would be delighted to have him with them for a couple of years. 'Since then I have been living in considerable tension,' he confessed. 'Fear, fear of being alone; fear of tropical neurasthenia; fear of sexual starvation; fear of my own incompetence; fear of my own weakness. Fear of collapse.'[2]

Those headed for West Africa sailed by the Elder Dempster line from Liverpool, leaving every other Wednesday. They could look forward to a two-week voyage if they were bound for Lagos, a few days less if their destination was Bathurst, Freetown, or Takoradi for Accra. The Union Castle and the British India Steamship Navigation lines were the standard way of reaching East and Central Africa. Sailing from Tilbury, and taking up to three weeks via the Suez Canal, East African cadets landed at Mombasa or, for Tanganyika, at Dar es Salaam. Those destined for Central Africa usually went on to Cape Town, before taking a four-day rail journey to the north. P. Mullins took five days to reach Limbe in Nyasaland, clocking up a rail journey of over 2,500 miles.[3] Flying out to Africa by seaplane from Southampton was an exciting alternative in the early post-war years, as Marjorie Lovett Smith found on being posted to Kampala in 1950.[4] J. Lewis-Barned heard that his ship, the *Llanstephen Castle*, was due to sail to Dar es Salaam via the Cape, a voyage of six weeks. Furthermore, the ship was on her last voyage before being scrapped. As it happened, the slow nature of the voyage allowed him to disembark at Cape Town and enterprisingly spend three weeks hitchhiking across South Africa before rejoining his ship, by now on time, at Lourenço Marques and reaching Dar es Salaam as scheduled.[5]

The cadet soon met on board those who had already completed one or two tours and was quickly introduced to the Service's palpable sense of *esprit de corps*. While the passengers naturally included many non-administration members of the CS as well as men and women from the private sector and, on the Union Castle line, a lot of tourists too, the cadet would be quickly taken up by his own kind, involving him in shipboard games and after-dinner entertainments as well as at the bar. There might be a colonial governor or one's future chief secretary on board, another reminder that a lifetime's career had indeed begun. For an enthusiastic cadet, the seal was set at dinner on the day after sailing, when he dared to open his tin trunk and wear for the first time his territorial cummerbund with a white shell jacket or 'bum freezer', that smart, comfortable alternative in the tropics to a white dinner jacket.

Just occasionally in the 1940s a first-tour cadet, urgently needed, was sent out by air, much to the consternation, as R.N. Barlow-Poole discovered in Northern Nigeria, of his Resident, who feared that he would be quite useless until his baggage – including all his household furnishings and indispensable camp kit – in due course arrived by sea.[6] As K.G. Bradley reflected,

'When we finally sail, not one of us has any clear idea of what our life is going to be like, and such imaginings as we have are so wrong that a few years afterwards we cannot remember what they were.'[7]

A long-lasting impression of what life was going to be like seems to have been planted in the minds of cadets by those fellow passengers (and their wives) who were already 'old coasters' or 'old hands'. One wife sailing to West Africa claimed that the absence of any books on the Coast in the ship's library was to prevent the newcomer forming a poor opinion of the place.[8] For all their teasing of the tyro, especially by 'old coasters' about the dangers of the White Man's Grave, 'partly as lessons but mainly to horrify us with the prospects ahead', as G. Sinclair narrated of his first voyage out to the Gold Coast,[9] and for all their telling of tall stories in the ship's bar (in the 'bachelor' days open from 7am, but no women allowed on deck before eight and none in the smoking room), it was nevertheless possible for the good listener to acquire real knowledge about many things, major as well as minor, which he had not had the opportunity or dared to ask about back at Oxford or Cambridge. For instance, folk talked about buying kerosene for the pressure lamp or the refrigerator, yet on the tropical outfitters' recommendation he had bought a paraffin lamp. Was it the same fuel? Did a bachelor really need so many domestic servants? What did they all do? Can one buy English newspapers in Africa? What is the correct dress on tour or in the *boma*? Just how do you address your DC if you don't want to be sent home by the next boat – Sir? Mr? Dick?

The West African convention was that one's provincial posting would be telegraphed up the Coast and displayed on the notice board some two or three days before landing in Takoradi or Lagos. Older hands might then mysteriously offer their prayers that 'Bad luck you've been posted to the "Cholera Belt"' or their wives solicitously remark 'Let's hope you have a luckier first tour than poor old Carlyle.' One Northern Nigerian cadet assigned to Yola was sympathetically consoled by his brother officers on board with 'Oh dear, a punishment station. What did you do wrong on the Cambridge course, old boy?' In each colony one or two stations had the reputation of being a 'punishment station', like Yola and Lokoja and Makurdi in the riverain provinces of Northern Nigeria, or, as R. Short was assured when assigned to Kasempa in Northern Rhodesia, 'Coming men, even then the bane of a Service whose ideal was a "band of brothers", did their best to avoid such a posting.'[10] In the event, the label 'punishment station' was often indignantly rejected by those who served there. Officers earmarked for Uganda and Kenya were generally met by the government coastal agent at Mombasa who would inform them of their postings. Sometimes they did not learn until they formally called on the chief secretary the day after disembarking. Arriving in Mombasa, O. Knowles quickly learned that there was indeed method behind the apparent illogicality of the Secretariat's postings. His batch of six cadets was greeted by the DO assistant to the chief native commissioner with the question 'Which of you chaps plays cricket?'[11] Gradually it became part of the procedure to notify cadets of their posting (at least the province) while they were still on the training course.

Disembarkation and the day or two spent before starting off up country en route for one's first station, as well as the journey itself, are generally remembered as part of the baptizing voyage out. Many looked on the rail or lorry journey with the continuing sense of novelty, probably tinged with a touch of anxiety or of blaséness according to their age and previous experience. Not so G.L. Aitchison, ex-Gurkha officer, who remembered how, on the completion of his reception in 'the nightmare' of the customs shed and the long railway journey northwards, 'by the time I reached Minna I wished to hell I had applied for the Gurkha regulars or back to Selwyn for Tripos Pt. II or a Dip. Ed. – anything but Nigeria.'[12] He stayed for 20 successful years. Exuberance could still overcome misgiving. As D.O. Savill stepped off the gangway at Apapa, he felt he was 'bursting with knowledge, ideals, good works and ineptitude', having just completed 15 months at Oxford and SOAS, 'the idyll of a lifetime'.[13] True, 'I still had a lot to learn, and even to understand,' but this was it, the start of a chosen career. Disembarking at Dar es Salaam, A. Sillery was accosted on the quay-side by a stranger who growled at him 'So you're just coming out? Well, don't forget I told you, it's not too late to turn back.'[14] R. Wainwright, coming ashore at Mombasa towards the end of the slump and depression years, encountered an equally unwelcome 'banner headline in the local press saying the country could not afford this influx of administrators and they should be sent straight home'.[15] They were not – but their salaries were cut by 13 per cent. To make matters worse, his first DC indulged in an 'endless stream of dirty stories', his next was 'both uninterested and lazy',[16] while the third was 'intellectually bright but "wet"', dominated by a wife who set out to bully the new ADO too.[17] Nor did G. Billing meet a cheerful start. Stopping off at Bulawayo on his way to Northern Rhodesia, a retired old colonial offered him his sympathy: 'This is a white man's country, but where you are going is called by us "The Black North".'[18]

Where the port of disembarkation was also the capital, the newly landed cadet might spend a day or two being introduced to colonial protocol before taking the train up-country. Emerging shaken from the customs shed, he would be met by an officer from the Secretariat, usually a DO on secondment from the provincial administration. An early call was made to the office of the colonial secretary,[19] where he was welcomed to the colony and had his posting confirmed (occasionally changed). The visitors' books of top officials had to be signed. This was kept in a small, sentry-like box at the gateway to the grounds of such dignitaries as the chief justice and the colonial secretary, and of course the governor. The advice given to ADOs was 'always call when people are out'. The signing of the book, announcing one's arrival, had replaced the elaborate pre-war protocol of leaving calling cards. In the case of important visitors coming into town, it also enabled an invitation to Government House for a drink. The book had to be signed again when one was proceeding on leave, this time with p.p.c. added, *pour prendre congé*. In D. Barton's opinion, the omission to tell probationers about this ritual was another failure in the training course.[20] J. Cooke found the ritual in Dar es Salaam 'rather stuffy and very conventional'[21]

If His Excellency (i.e. the governor) was in town and there was time before the boat train was due to depart, there was usually a reception for the new ADOs (no longer cadets, save in the Secretariat files). When J.H. Smith arrived in Lagos in 1951, the 'new look' governor, Sir John Macpherson, had decreed that all new ADOs should be given a three-day induction tour of the capital and Secretariat. His greatest culture shock was in having a meal with a DO of the old school, who did not dine before 11 o'clock and insisted on inducting the ADOs into the palm-oil chop ritual, 'testing the consistency of the pounded yam by tossing it up into the revolving ceiling fan. It failed, and to our dismay the table was cleared and the cook ordered to start again.'[22] The ADO might be billeted overnight on another DO, if possible from the same province to which he was going. In Lagos, I. Brook and another ADO were told they were to be the guests of the financial secretary. Then they learned that he had just been killed in an air crash but they were to stay in his house nevertheless. 'Death has come to meet us on the Coast,' mused a sombre Brook. Things then moved fast: a call on the chief secretary to be sworn in, drinks at Government House and dinner with another official, who had also invited a Resident who was on his way home after 30 years, on retirement leave, a heavy drinker who had just been snubbed by the governor and not invited to G.H. for the usual farewell meal. 'The experience made us thoughtful,' he noted, 'this was a harsh service we were joining.'[23]

The cadet's host would help him on how to open a bank account in the colony and perhaps on where to buy provisions for taking up-country. When C. Rowling and his wife arrived in Lagos in 1933 and learned of their posting to Kano 500 miles to the north, he hurried off to one of the few provision stores and ordered groceries for 18 months: 'It was simpler to buy in Lagos, as Government paid carriage on all loads on return from leave.'[24] He might also be helped by his host in the difficult matter of engaging one or two servants before travelling up-country. Here the importance of language was emphasized, the advantage emphatically lying with a servant whose own language was that of the area to which the ADO was going. Conversely, colonial lore could die hard. 'Don't ever take on a coast boy if you're going up-country' or 'Never employ a mission boy, he'll steal all your whisky'. Prospective servants came in a number of ways, sometimes bringing their previous references (books) with them, sometimes on the recommendation of an officer who had left, and often brought along by other servants. Once again, what Charles Allen calls the 'old colonial chestnuts' featured unkindly in expatriate folklore, à la 'I'm sure this boy will do you as well as he has done me', 'This cook leaves me on account of illness – mine, not his',[25] or, not mentioned in Allen's list, 'Give this man a berth – the wider the better'. To judge from DOs' memoirs, despite such tempestuous starts many domestic servants remained with their first employer throughout his service, and often in touch well after his retirement.

Most likely accompanied by at least one house servant, the ADO was now ready to head for his first station. Perhaps because the novelty was beginning to wear off, doubtless speeded up by the experiences of disembarkation and doing the rounds of the capital, perhaps because travelling hundreds of miles by train or lorry began to lose its attraction when set beside the more recent idyll of punting down the Cam or cycling up the High, or perhaps just because of a newly acquired sophistication, new arrivals have not elaborated in their memoirs on this initiatory journey through miles and miles of Africa to anything like the extent they recalled the voyage out. Yet in East Africa there was a far bigger chance of seeing wildlife from the train than there was in West Africa. True, in Nigeria one DO swore that he had spotted giraffe south of the Niger on his first rail journey, but as that was 20 years ago and he had since become a gin-and-bitters devotee his story was not taken seriously. Travelling the 700 miles from Lagos to Sokoto, J. Morley found it all 'an enclosed country, which revealed no pattern or purpose to the newcomer' until he reached the undulating orchard-bush of Sokoto.[26] With her previous experience of the Gold Coast before her husband was posted to Northern Rhodesia, Yvonne Fox was able to contrast her first impression of the lack of villages and markets with her memory of the densely populated West Africa. She recalled the scores of people always walking along the paths and roads.[27] For G.L. Stephenson on his train journey to the Northern Provinces of Nigeria, the countryside simply 'testified to the size of Africa, there seemed to be no end to the landscape. Its ceaseless repetition reminded me of the sea.'[28] Another cadet felt disappointment that, after the lectures on the strength of Nigeria's agriculture at Cambridge, he had not witnessed thousands of peasants busily tilling the soil with their hoes as the train crept northwards. For those who had served with African troops during the war, it was a pleasure mixed with pride to call out greetings to the market women selling food at the railway station, *sannu* or *jambo*. But in general this rail journey took second place to the lyrical description of their first view of Africa from on board ship, typified in D. Bates's breathless exclamation at sighting the harbour at Dar es Salaam: 'it was how one had imagined it to be', the realization of a dream.[29] As for J.B. Carson, his first view of Mombasa with blue sky and white sand exceeded anything that Hollywood could offer, 'unlike most things in my first tour'.[30] Unfortunately, P. Allison's first dreamy glance at Africa from the upper deck was brusquely shattered by a tap on the shoulder and a sharp female voice of warning to be careful of the sun, 'You're in the tropics now, young man.'[31]

It was customary for an ADO, sometimes a more senior officer, to meet the boat train when it arrived up country. This welcome could also have a much wider sense, as the residents' cooks were able to buy fresh food like butter and fish, and the luxury of ice, from the restaurant galley. T. Scrivenor's wife never forgot the excitement of their arrival at Tabora after three wearying days on the train: 'When a new recruit from home was expected, almost the whole station came down.'[32] Coming to join her husband, Mrs G. Shipp was less amused at her reception. The European community had decided that all the officials should mix themselves up so as to confuse her, with the DC taking the role of a very Cockney policeman, with a red nose and ready to offer her unlimited gins.[33] Once arrived, the cadet might go through the same kind of reception as he had encountered on disembarkation, with a formal call on the PC to sign the visitors' book, being introduced to future colleagues and perhaps adding a cook or a steward to his staff. G.D. Popplewell thanked his lucky stars for the foresight of his tropical outfitters who, pre-war, had pressed a supply of calling cards on him.[34] N.F. Cooke recalled how in Northern Nigeria just before the war he was instructed to leave two cards at every senior married couple's house but only one for those whose wives were not in the country or for bachelors.[35]

Sometimes the PC or Resident thought it was a good idea to keep the ADO in provincial HQ for a few days' induction into what the province was and what the provincial office's role was. At a loss what to do with one new cadet while the river was in flood and with no provincial kit-car to take him to his station 100 miles beyond the collapsed bridge, the Resident told him to sit quietly in the office and read all the historical files of the past half-century. None of this meant anything to the ADO, but two decades later it was the memory of a secret report he had read that led him to research and reconstruct the whole story.[36] P. Sanders also traced his scholar's inspiration to collect and translate the poems of King Moshoeshoe in Basutoland ten years later to his very first days as an ADO in Lesotho.[37] To keep G.D. Popplewell, just arrived in Tanganyika, occupied his PC gave him less exciting reading than that of those two cadets, namely a copy of the governor's recently written 'brown books' on the principles of native administration, 'the DO's Bible', to read from cover to cover over the weekend.[38] In reality, of course, neither party wished to prolong this marking time in provincial HQ, the PC because he had more pressing matters to attend to ('Have you got a horse? No, well get one' was the limit of K.P. Maddocks's first conversation with the Resident of Kano),[39] and the ADO because all he wanted was to get out to his district at last.

In contrast to the often low-key memories of the journey up-country and the passing through provincial HQ on the way to their district, such writers have frequently left a vivid account of reaching their first bush station and, most importantly and often unforgettably, meeting with their DO. Representative is J. Cooke's first glimpse of the *boma* at Biharamulo in 1951, at the end of a four-hour drive in a Land Rover:

> A long straight avenue flanked by gum trees led to the *boma*, the Swahili name for the district office. This was a squat, fortress-like building on a broad hill-top, built by the Germans some 50 years previously. Within 6 feet thick stone rubble walls were enclosed the DC's house, the government offices, post-office, court-room, stores and workshops. Some distance half way down the hill was the small hospital, and on the far side of the hill the houses of the agricultural officers and the settlement officer. That was the station.[40]

As for the other half of the newcomer equation – meeting one's DO – this made what often amounted to a lasting impression, be it for good or less so. The evidence in memoirs is extensive. Reaching his first station in the Gold Coast, R.G. Syme was told by his DO, so drunk that he was unable to stand, that 'he had never heard of me and didn't want to'.[41] When Syme plucked up courage next morning to ask him his name, the DO replied: 'My boy, have no illusions, this is a bloody awful country. The birds have no song, the flowers no smell, and the women no virtue – so don't be bloody starry-eyed.' Any inclination towards idealism I. Brook might have had when he arrived in Nigeria in 1946 was quickly dissipated when a senior DO offered him his administrative aphorism: 'When you see an injustice, let it go; when you see a gross injustice, try to do something about it.'[42] When new cadet D. Bates, reaching Bagamoyo after a long journey from Dar es Salaam by lorry surrounded by all the loads he had brought with him – tin bath, camp chair, boxes, a shot-gun – came to a halt outside 'a very unpretentious white building ... flying a rather tattered and forlorn Union Jack', he looked up the flight of steps. 'On top of it a tall, thin, angular figure stood, with crumpled white trousers and a white shirt, his face was long and lean and rather grey. "Well, here you are," he said. I didn't know what to say and I stood there probably looking rather foolish. "Well," he said, "I'm off for my evening walk." And off he went.'[43] Bates remembered also how his first DC had two hates: Christmas and what he used to call mechanical contrivances. So he always went out on safari at Christmas – on foot.[44] Also in pre-war Tanganyika, Z.E. Kingdon fared even worse, being greeted by his old-timer DC with 'Why must they send me a bloody cadet?', a welcome followed by 'You're no good to me without a motor bicycle, you might as well go away again.'[45] The DC Tarkwa to whom H. Brind was attached in 1951 was 'a larger than life Scottish bachelor with a hair-trigger temper and a rich vocabulary. As he went through the morning mail, each item would be greeted by some exclamation, the more irritating letters causing him to jump from his chair and shout to all within hearing range of the imbecility of the writer.'[46] At Eldoret, K.L. Hunter's DC received him with the observation that 'I was very young and would not be much of a companion to him as he was rather fond of his liquor.'[47] When J. Smyth met his first DO in Nigeria, 'we summed each other up without enthusiasm', for it was none other than that 'terribly pompous fellow who had lectured us one afternoon at the Colonial Service club in London.'[48] In Nigeria K.V. Arrowsmith was uncertain about his first Resident, until the latter promptly invited him to dinner and then, somewhat anxiously, enquired 'By the way, do you play hockey?'[49] Happily, he did. T. Mayhew took an instant dislike to his first DC's 'haughty and imperious manner', and the hostility increased when Mayhew found out that he considered himself too good at tennis to waste time playing with such an inferior player as his new ADO.[50]

But by the law of averages, many other ADOs found a far warmer welcome from their first DO, with that pre-war tendency to authoritarianism and downright rudeness mellowing into a display of basic manners and more humane post-wartime 'man management'. Posted to Kenya in 1946, P.D. McEntee remembered how his first DC and his wife went out of their way to 'break us in gently' and 'patiently started to teach us our job'.[51] His luck continued, for his next DC was R. Wainwright, 'one of nature's enthusiasts, with a devastating store of energy'.[52] In Tanganyika another 'ideal boss' was E.G. Rowe, 'the archetype of a DC', in J.A. Golding's estimation when he was posted to Mbulu in 1946, 'all that a reader of Edgar Wallace stories of Sanders of the River would expect. ... He would tell you what needed to be done and then let you get on with it, giving the impression that he had every confidence in your ability to carry it out. But you knew that you could approach him for advice should it be needed.'[53] An ADO in Northern Nigeria recalled his panic when his DO, departing on leave, asked him to write the annual report. When pressed on what he, only just arrived, should say, the reply came, 'Same as last year, add 10% for good measure – and don't forget to change the dates.'[54]

In between the off-putting and the encouraging DOs encountered by a first-tour ADO was a group who believed in a policy of 'more or less to ignore them and let them learn for themselves'.[55] After all, as R. Hennings summed up his own experience in both roles, 'New cadets are, at first, as much of a hindrance as a help to their superior officers.'[56] Such a laissez-faire attitude, while sometimes endorsed by ADOs who resented their DO continually peering over their shoulder and breathing down their neck, could be taken too far. Remembering his arrival in Nigeria, J.S. Smith realized that his DO 'was not worried about me. ... I had to learn my official duties as best I could. I was completely inexperienced and I had nobody to teach me anything.'[57] Sometimes, of course, though maybe more in retrospect than at the moment, such benign neglect could be a kind of hands-off tuition. This was certainly G.L. Stephenson's impression, long afterwards: 'There is nothing like being thrown in at the deep end of the pool to learn to swim,' though he was a little perplexed at the labels on the three file trays on the DO's desk: Very Important, Overdue, Extremely Necessary.[58] Another ADO found that his DO, a former Cambridge cricket Blue, had labelled the file trays 'In' and 'Out', with 'l.b.w.' in the middle. It is not hard to understand how the nature of one's arrival and welcome from the DO could colour one's impression of the career that lay ahead. The wonder is that so many forgave it while never forgetting it.

Two points, however, need to be borne in mind. In the inter-war period, many of the DOs had come straight from military service into the administration. Often they brought with them attitudes – as well as their wartime rank, frequently enhanced with an MC[59] – convinced that a new ADO needed to be disciplined as part of his modelling into a useful DO. ADOs coming out from 1927, after the Oxbridge course had been established, carried the extra potential for having their rough edges ironed out. One DC in Kenya was known for his 'cadet-baiting'. With a year's university training, more and more frequently preceded by a university degree, they represented all the intellectual advantages that their seniors had missed. An unspoken sense of 'so you think you know all the answers' clearly created some of the initial tensions. Writing of his senior officers, 'their pleasures were not ours', commented F.W. Carpenter on his early years in Nigeria in the 1930s.[60] They were not interested in sport (true, Carpenter was an international hockey player), only with endless reading in their bungalows. 'We hadn't learned to drink vast quantities of gin and whisky without feeling very ill, and we hadn't yet got into the habit of talking shop on every conceivable occasion.' The pattern was repeated after 1946, though with an interesting difference. By now it was the graduate ADOs of the 1930s who were in charge of districts when the new ADOs began to arrive. Many of the former had been refused permission to join up in 1940. Now it was the ADO who came in with war service, with campaign medals and military decorations, up to the DSO and DSC and, quite exceptionally, in Tanganyika two with the VC,[61] 'all excellent material and with the self-confidence acquired in their war service', in the estimate of the civil secretary in Kaduna in the 1950s.[62] The difference was made embarrassingly plain for all to see on full-dress occasions like Empire Day, when the un-medalled DO would take the salute flanked by his ADO with a chestful of medals. Newcomers to a hierarchy are quickly sensitive to tensions. Summing up the personality of his first DO in Uganda, W. Bazley sensed that 'he seemed to regret that he had missed both world wars and felt in consequence that he could not hold his head quite so high. ... Inwardly I think he was jealous of the younger ones, like myself, who had been privileged to wear our country's uniform.' Later the DO added that 'the trouble with you navy chaps is that you're not tough enough. You wear all sorts of medal ribbons on your uniform, but when it comes to a job you don't have what it takes.'[63] Nor did being older than the standard peacetime ADOs, and often married, make things any easier. The DC Kakamega reputedly greeted the arrival of his first post-war cadet with 'I suppose you are another ex-colonel with two children?' 'No,' replied the ADO, 'I'm a brigadier with three.'[64]

The second point to bear in mind is that many of those 'quarterdeck'-mannered DOs of the 1920s and 1930s consciously

adopted the role of being a 'character'. They are looked back to
with affection, and often with respect, by their long-suffering
ADOs (just now and again, a love–hate relationship). The lasting
loyalty evoked by such names to conjure with as 'The Laird', and
'Lenox' and 'Marmalade Joe' in the 1950s, and earlier the sten-
torian Commander C. and 'Rustybuckle', all from the Nigerian
pantheon but equally found in every colony,[65] is testimony to the
value of the 'character' in his often unwanted role of mentor. These
'characters' have passed into DC lore, often out-Sandering Sanders, and often into the local lexicon too, with pin-pointing nicknames and further tales of wonder attaching. It was, of course,
far easier to be a 'character' in the unhurried, unsophisticated
and uninterrupted days of one-man stations, with no roads and
well away from official visitors and urgent ('vulgar', in 'character'
idiom) reminders from HQ. Such was the territory of H. MacGiffin
in the Gold Coast, whose 'boisterous good humour and informal-
ity ... thoroughly unconventional in his dealings with the unedu-
cated Africans [who] obviously respected him, and although he
made them roar with laughter they roared with him and not at
him', quickly earned the admiration of his new ADO in 1950, P.
Mullins.[66] After the Second World War, with more office work to
do, more government staff to work with, better communications
and fewer one-man stations, the DO as 'character', other than the
memorable pre-war relics, began to die out. As I. Brook, a post-
war ADO in Western Nigeria, described his DO, 'he was a bush
DO. He did his job in the old avuncular tradition but he was an
anachronism in an age beginning to feel the Fabian influences
in the Colonial Office.'[67] With one exception his replacements
rarely got beyond recognition as minor eccentrics, taking their
pot-plants on trek or chasing flying insects with a butterfly net.
This was the 'kingdom' of Kenya's Northern Frontier (NFD), later
Province.

The NFD was an area, at least in the eyes of those who served
there, that could not help but breed 'characters', independently
minded DCs, forceful and unforgettable, generically classified as
'The Men with Sand in their Hair'. With the DC positively a 'character', personality rather than protocol made it quietly plain that
there was no room for a second 'character' in the station. It was V.
Glenday, who took over the NFD in 1929 after it had been under
military administration and when its HQ moved from Meru to
Isiolo, who was in C. Chenevix Trench's mind 'the frontier officer

par excellence, more admired than loving, approving only DCs in his own image, inhuman, dynamic, tireless and pitiless'.[68] Following Glenday was what has sometimes been called an apostolic succession of officers-in-charge of the NFD, all of them spectacular 'characters'. First came G. Reece, previously DC Mandera in the NFD (Mandera was the station of the ill-fated – and equally eccentric – H. Grant, the DO killed by the Maasai in 1946).[69] Every DO who served under 'Uncle Gerald' was aware that he maintained a spy system in each *boma*, reporting what his DOs were up to. Reece brought his own style of administration to the NFD and to his DOs. T. Gavaghan, who was posted to the NFD in 1946, ranked Reece among the 'Giants of Empire', with 'a formidable reputation and authority over-spilling the bounds of his unique realm. It was compounded of a potent blend of force of character, unswerving dedication, incisive knowledge, with a strong relish of eccentricity.'[70] Another of the supreme NFD 'characters' was R.G. Turnbull, who succeeded Reece in 1948. It is difficult for the outsider to assess whether the fond anecdotes were more startling, or simply more, about Turnbull or about Reece.[71] Glenday, Reece and Turnbull all had clear ideas on what constituted a real 'NFD wallah': 'He must be unmarried … he must work 14 hours a day while in the *boma* and be out on foot half the month (lorry safaris did not count). He must stand loneliness and rise to a convivial occasion. He must regard a posting to the NFD as a privilege, not a penance.'[72] Many of the young post-war DOs who served under them were equally quick to paint word-portraits of these larger-than-life, loved, last 'characters' of colonial Africa.[73]

Whether under a 'character' or a benign housemaster all over again, the new ADO quickly had to move on from his DO's greeting to the next instalment of his welcome, confronting his accommodation. In an outstation this would almost certainly be a 'temporary' quarter (those which lasted longer than the PWD's 'permanent' quarters, according to administrators' lore), with a thatched roof and a verandah wide and long enough to live on by day and at night to serve as a guest bedroom. A common form of bush housing was the three round beehives or rondavels, made of sun-dried mud bricks and a roof covered with a thatch of grass and palm leaves.[74] In compensation, the view from the verandah could often be unbelievably beautiful, built up a hillside to catch any breeze that might be going and looking towards a river or a distant range of hills. P. Mullins found his ADO's house at

Chiradzulu, near Blantyre, ideally situated for its outlook and garden.[75] Many of the houses allotted to post-war cadets had been built 25 or more years earlier, often by the DO himself. 'My predecessor who had built this house,' recalled P. Allison of his home in Onitsha, 'had spent nearly all the money in erecting a solid concrete platform, and hadn't got any left to do anything except put up an erection of bamboo poles on palm-leaf mats to keep the rain out.'[76] In Kenya, J. Russell found his house had a corrugated iron roof but no ceiling, which meant that it was very hot by day, but it did have a superior feature in its bath, raised on concrete blocks above the slab floor, served by a 44-gallon drum outside, known as a 'Tanganyika boiler'.[77] In both Lokoja and Bida, DOs in the mid-1950s were still happy (at least the historically minded ones were) occupying prefabricated bungalows shipped out by Lugard at the turn of the century.[78] Often DOs preferred such houses of character to the improved T3 houses built in the 1930s. Transferred to Ado in Western Nigeria in the 1950s and offered a brand new house, I. Brook 'chose to live in the old DO's house, a beautiful bush building made of mud, with wide verandahs and low-hanging leaves so that it was always cool in the hot season and dry in the rains. It commanded a sweeping view … the DO who built it, like all the early DOs, had a fine eye for the country.'[79]

Not that post-war DOs did not build their own accommodation. In 1947 P.D. McEntee, a cadet in Kenya, was distinctly surprised when his DC gave him £150, with instructions to go and build a house of his own design for a new DO and his wife who were expected in a month's time.[80] Later McEntee built on to his own house a rendered white-washed guest room for his mother-in-law's visit. In J. Cooke's case the incentive was even greater. Reaching his *boma* in 1951 and enquiring of his DC where he might be living, the DC pointed to some newly dug foundations and told him one of his first tasks would be to supervise the building of his own house – 'and the sooner I got on with it the sooner I would have my own place'.[81] When the governor of Tanganyika heard that the DO's house in a district he had recently visited had cost only £380, he is said to have wryly minuted, 'A monument to the efficiency of the Audit department.'[82] I.F. Macpherson's first house in Tanganyika was just about par for many an ADO in Africa of the early 1950s. 'We had no electricity or flushing water, and I had to use pressure lamps for light and wood for cook-

District Officer's house at Moyo, Uganda

ing. Toilets were down at the bottom of the garden and were a hole dug in the ground, with a small hut built over it.'[83] T. Gardner arrived in Northern Rhodesia in 1946, with his wife, having been warned they would have to live in a tent. In the event, they were allocated a house in Fort Jameson, quite good and basically furnished, except for the total absence of any cupboards or wardrobes. 'We soon learned how to construct these from the wooden boxes in which tins of paraffin were delivered.'[84] Somehow E.K. Lumley's compensation for having to live in a two-compartment (room was too grand a concept) wattle-and-daub hut in early Tanganyika could only have come from a British DO: the beautiful view over the rolling downs and the distant hills.[85] Twenty years later W. Bazley's first house in Uganda was nothing to write home about (or was it?). It had already been officially condemned as uninhabitable by the PWD. 'There was a massive ant-hill in the living room and a snake of moderate proportions in the roof.'[86] His DC, who seemed intent on teaching him what a new ADO should (or should not) expect, pointed to the building with the comment 'Well, that's Africa for you.'

In Kenya J.B. Carson was also delighted, this time by the house itself, a low white bungalow with three rooms and a bathroom to which water was delivered daily by ox-wagon.[87] What bothered H. Phillips when he reached Karonga in Nyasaland in 1951 was not that he was expected to share a large house with the bachelor DC but the design of the bath: 'A past incumbent had constructed out of cement a coffin-shaped arrangement sufficient to accommodate a normal-sized body, and with a substantial ledge to hold reading matter, bottle and glass.'[88] In Kitui T. Gavaghan's pleasure at the sight of his first Kenyan colonial bungalow, with steps up to a wide verandah, was spoiled by what he saw as he stepped inside: 'a red-oxide painted heat-cracking, rain-roaring corrugated roof, its ceiling lined with soft-board stained by acrid bat droppings'.[89] M. Longford was in seventh heaven when he moved to Lindi as DC. Formerly a provincial HQ, by 1961 it had been downgraded to a district. The upper floor of the old provincial office was the DC's quarters and the lower floor provided accommodation for guests, 22 rooms in all, 'a home far more splendid than [a DC's] status really justified'.[90] But size was not everything. Transferred at the end of his first six months in Nigeria, K.V. Arrowsmith found his new accommodation more like a cricket pavilion than a home. 'It was low and open to the four winds, and I was able to drive my Morris Minor inside and park it in the sitting room. Only the bedroom, washroom and store had four walls. These did not reach the roof and were topped with broken glass to discourage predatory visitors.'[91] T.G. Askwith was thrilled by the view from his first house in Kenya, but less so when his DC threw open the door and said 'We should be able to get you some furniture in a few weeks' time.'[92]

Along with the question in the new ADO's mind of where he was going to live went the related concerns of his domestic staff and his health. Typically an ADO would engage three or four servants. A steward and a cook were the domestic minimum, and each was likely to insist on an assistant. A syce (groom) was necessary if one used a horse for touring or for an evening ride, and for a larger compound or one laid out by an enthusiastic previous owner a gardener would be needed, at least to elaborate on the grass cutting normally carried out by a gang of prisoners from the local gaol. 'It's easy to know which house X occupies,' grumbled one Northern Nigerian Resident of his new ADO a few months after he had moved twice, 'just by looking at the garden.'

The bachelor DO was vulnerably dependent on his indoor domestic staff, and it was quickly – sometimes painfully – clear to the new ADO that it paid to choose well.

As for health, injections like TAB/tetanus and vaccination against yellow fever had been part of the ADO's pre-sailing requirements. Standard precautions, whether on tour or in town, included boiling the water before drinking by pouring it into the filter procured from his tropical outfitters; sleeping under a mosquito net, again brought out in his loads; and taking a regular anti-malaria dose of quinine before the advent of mepacrine in the Second World War and of paludrine after the war. It was a matter of domestic debate when one took the prophylactic pill, the key being to select a regular moment that one was least likely to miss whatever the day's programme. Some opted for it with the breakfast coffee, some with the early morning tea, some with the evening whisky. In stations like Argungu in Northern Nigeria the mosquitoes were so bad that the DO slept in a specially constructed 'mosquito cage'. Elsewhere mosquito boots offered good if inelegant protection once the sun had set but there was little to keep off the aggressive sand-fly. When T.G. Askwith went down with his first dose of malaria, he was recommended the standard treatment of every Kenyan pioneer: two tablets of quinine, two of aspirin and two sets of tennis repeated as often as possible. His DC had a different prescription. 'You know, the best thing would be a bit of foot safari – you can take it easy the first day, but you'll be fighting fit by the time you've done a week.'[93] The Second World War had already seen the end of the spine pad, and wartime experience had proved that Europeans would not suffer instant sunstroke if they exposed their head to the sun for more than ten seconds. It was perhaps the fear of snakes rather than their sighting that frightened the DO – and his wife – although snake encounters did take place, often when walking home at night in the rainy season or in the darkness of the *chui* or lavatory. Newcomers were warned always to shake their shoes before putting them on, for a scorpion bite was singularly painful. It is beyond argument that the greatest impact on the gloomy annual compilation of what the British government called the 'vital statistics of non-native officials', namely the death and invaliding rate of serving colonial civil officers, was brought about by the introduction of the domestic refrigerator as a soon-to-be standard item of furnishing. Where there was no electricity

(the majority of stations in the 1930s), it could operate on kerosene, with the fridge's legs standing on a liquid base so as to keep
predatory insects at bay. This amenity, now re-interpreted as a
necessity, affected both health and morale. For the DO in Africa,
it was arguably on a par with the discovery of quinine as an anti-
malaria drug. Food could at last be kept fresh – as well as drinks
kept cool.

With the new ADO having met his DO and now settled into
his house (such as it was), he was ready to turn to learning what
he was expected to do. For I.F. Macpherson, posted to Tanganyika's Lake Province in 1951, when he reached the *boma* it was a
case of 'only just' learning. Crossing the river he was greeted by
the DC ready to cross in the other direction. He explained that he
was leaving for a fortnight's conference and Macpherson would
have to look after the district on his own. 'The district's in that
direction,' he added as he said goodbye, pointing to the west,
'and here are the keys of the Treasury. Make sure you don't lose
them.'[94] The district office turned out to be another 80 miles away.
Sometimes a DO was glad to have a cadet posted to his district
so that he could either get on with the things that he liked doing
best but had hitherto had no time for, for instance his pet projects
of village sanitation or building a dam, or else hand over to the
new ADO the tasks which he did not like doing and looked on
as chores, for instance court work or checking the local treasury.
Going on tour might fall into either category, to be given to the
cadet so that the DO could stay comfortably and alone in station
or to be monopolized while he left all the office work to the ADO.
R. Terrell found himself saddled with the latter kind of superior.
'Here in Gombe I am managing to make myself useful, writing
draft letters or minutes for the DO which he would find it trouble-
some to do for himself.'[95]

As he settled down to work, two of the little worries that might
have exercised him on the journey were quickly cleared up. Up to
1945 (and sometimes beyond) there was every likelihood that the
DO would address the new ADO by his surname, while in a two-
man station there was little need for the ADO to use any name at
all when talking to his DO. N.F. Cooke had been in Nigeria only
six hours when, in 1938, the wife of a senior official took it upon
herself to warn him that 'cadets were so brash as to address an
ADO of seven years standing by his Christian name'.[96] A thawing
in formality came after 1945, though it was still taboo for DOs to

address their Resident or PC other than as 'sir'.

Another minor worry had been over just what to wear at work. The answer now became evident. Khaki shorts, stockings and a short-sleeved white or khaki shirt in the office, and white shirt, tie and either shorts or trousers in HQ. Bush jackets were out, as too reminiscent of uniform. A jacket was always kept to put on when calling on, or being called on, by a major chief and for sitting as a magistrate. A trilby or fedora hat was worn after the war by younger DOs but a pith helmet never. On tour a double terai now became a favourite headgear. Apart from the full-dress white uniform worn by those entitled to do so on ceremonial parades, Kenya was virtually the only colony that had anything approaching a uniform for its field officers, with badges and 'royal' buttons. The post-war DO dressed more for comfort than to display his office: a white face, as one of the new African ADOs in Nigeria once commented, was in itself a sort of uniform – the symbol of authority.

At work at last, it did not take long for the new ADO to realize that whatever the job was it bore little resemblance to anything he had been taught on the course. Within 48 hours of reaching Tarkwa, J.S. Lawson, 'wholly untrained in law', found himself sitting as a magistrate to hear 'sanitary cases', offences in breach of the health regulations.[97] A similar 'first plunge' awaited K.V. Arrowsmith when the DO, having shown him what was meant by reviewing a case, wished him luck and drove off the next day, leaving him to fend for himself.[98] Yet for many the prompt immersion into court work, so often the DO's priority for the training of his cadet, proved to be a most valuable initiation into learning his job. Memories and anecdotes of court work are abundant in DOs' written recollections, though they feature less in those of DOs working in an indirect rule system, where the greatest legal exposure was to reviewing cases from the Native Courts rather than sitting as a magistrate. There was also the problem of language, which the new ADO had of course begun to work on during his training. Hearing complaints – or more usually for the newly arrived cadet, listening to the DO hearing complaints – was a major feature of time spent in the district office, offering not only an accelerated acquaintanceship with the local language but also an unequalled insight into local life and customs.

Nearly every ADO was given, among his first assignments, responsibility for oversight of the prison and of the Native or

Local Government Treasury. In some cases this was purely supervisory, with an NA staff member in charge of keeping the account books and the cash. In others it could be exacting. There was also the Government Treasury to manage. 'My job,' J. Blair told of his first tour in pre-war Abeokuta, 'traditionally was that of local treasurer. It was a routine job, but it taught one government accounting procedures, meticulous accuracy and observance of the minutiae of regulations.'[99] Prison work was just as demanding. On the weekly visit the DO had to interview every new prisoner, satisfy himself that he understood and agreed to the court's sentence, inspect the prison for cleanliness, check the accounts and listen to complaints by the inmates or the warders. From time to time a grimmer duty came his way: the supervision of a judicial flogging or, rarely but revoltingly, that of an execution for which the accused's appeal to the governor had failed.[100] M.C. Atkinson was hugely relieved that he had missed a prison execution by two weeks, unlike his fellow DO M. Cruddas, who had had to carry out three executions in a single morning, with a regulation 30 minutes' break between each hanging.[101]

While the DO himself was legally responsible for the Government Treasury in district HQ and held the keys, the ADO would find himself heavily involved in the work. As a cadet in Tukuyu in 1951, every morning M. Longford 'checked the counterfoils of each revenue receipt and payment voucher issued the previous day. I then checked that the cash on hand in the strong-room tallied with the figure in the cash book, and signed a certificate to the effect that the accounts were in order.'[102] Where, as in the larger NAs, the ADO was designated 'ADO Finance', his role was as much one of training the Native Treasury staff as of auditing. Under indirect rule, of course, he could not authorize any expenditure. It certainly taught the new ADO the inner workings of the NA structure – where the money came from and on what it was spent. ADOs recall how they spent hours counting out tax paid in pennies or a specie remittance. Even in Nigeria in the 1950s, the *anini* (one tenth of a penny) was legal tender. 'It was depressing,' reflected T.G. Askwith on his first tour in Kenya, 'that after working for three years to gain a degree and a further year to learn the techniques of colonial administration, all that we were thought fit for was to write out little receipts, for small amounts of money hour after hour.'[103]

Then there was for the new ADO the fundamental task of

getting to know the NA office-holders and staff with whom one was in daily contact, and of course the chief. This was especially important with the emirs and major chiefs. It could be a very formal occasion, as W. Bazley discovered on his second day in Bunyoro.[104] Significantly it was he who was introduced to the Mukama, not the other way round. In the strict protocol of an emir's court, the ADO was taught that if he shook hands with the emir he must not then shake hands with any other official.[105] Looking back, DOs have commented on the remarkable courtesy and tolerance which emirs, sometimes with up to 40 years on the throne, displayed towards the 23-year-old cadet just down from university. As A. Forward noted on his introduction to the top officials of the Ankole Local Government, 'they must have seen a number of raw young ADCs come and go, but there was no doubt that their welcome was genuine.'[106]

The ADO also had to meet the other government officers on the station. In a small station this was easy: having met the DO, there was no one else. Stations with just a DO and an ADO were still common after 1945 and into the 1950s. But in a large *boma* there might be an agricultural officer, a police officer, an education officer, a medical officer and an engineer. All were Colonial Service officers. In provincial headquarters, where a full complement of professional officers could be expected, relationships were not always smooth between them and the DOs. Normally they worked well in an undefined way but, as P. Dennis discovered in the Gold Coast, 'a management lesson quickly learnt by a junior administrative officer was that if you asked you would get, but if you demanded you would almost certainly be confronted with difficulties.'[107] He was not to know that this issue of official relationships between the DOs and the technical departments had long exercised minds in Government House and generated a series of guidance circulars.[108] Apart from meeting in the various offices when occasion required, the usual way of getting to know one's colleagues was at the club (see Chapter 5) or by entertaining at home. Where there was no club, as P.H. Burkinshaw found on reaching his up-country station in Sierra Leone, where the community consisted of himself and the DC and his wife, other ways of self-entertainment rather than socializing had to be resorted to or, more likely, created. 'My evenings were spent playing tennis, learning the local Temne language, reading and listening to an HMG hand-wound gramophone reproducing

melodies from Chu Chin Chow, Carousel or of Noel Coward. ...
One strove to maintain an element of sanity.'[109]

But beyond all this orientation for a DO's life, the ADO was
impatient for that ultimate induction, going on his first 'tour' or
trek, known as *safari* in East Africa and *ulendo* in Central Africa.
This was what had inspired him from reading K.G. Bradley's *Diary
of a District Officer*. Here was the epitome of the kind of romantic
adventure for which he had joined: a line of porters with his camp
kit on their heads and he himself striding manfully in the lead,
a walking stick in hand, a pipe in his mouth and an Australian
bush hat on his head. Even if it was not going to be quite like that,
the imagery was enough to make him chafe at being kept in the
DO's office and long to be off on tour. Recalling his ADO years in
Nigeria in the 1930s M. Varvill stressed touring as 'the abiding,
inexhaustible topic of youthful administrators, each with his pet
theory of how to organize carriers, loads, horses etc'.[110] The whole
scenario of touring, the essence of a career as a DO, is considered
in Chapter 6. Here the subject is looked at from the angle of the
cadet's first tour, part of his learning process. 'The first safari on
one's own,' mused F.A. Peet in Kitui in 1949, 'can be a test for any
cadet.'[111]

What exactly did one do on safari? When K. Johnson put this
question to his DO in Katagum, he received the reply: 'Do? You
don't *do* anything. You are going to learn the language, to see
how the people live, and to get to know the country.'[112] There
was clearly a valid element of 'showing the flag' in touring. R.L.
Findlay in pre-war Nigeria went so far as to conclude that 'the
mere process of touring by the DO was valuable, quite apart from
whatever work he performed'.[113]

The best DOs would take the newcomer out on a short trek
with them as a guided tour (A. Forward in Uganda coined the
Oxbridge phrase of 'on safari pupillari').[114] This was R. Posnett's
experience on reaching his station in Uganda: a safari combining kit-car, bicycle and foot. Where there was no rest-house, he
and his DC pitched tents. At the end of it, the DC judged him
fit to be allowed out on the next by himself, encouraged by the
admonition that undoubtedly the best way to learn a language
was to be forced to use it in order to survive. 'After ten days on
tour with no English speaker,' Posnett concluded, 'I was able to
get by in Swahili.'[115] D. Barton was equally grateful to his first DC
in Tanganyika who took him out on safari and coached him in

the art of conducting public meetings. 'We sat around and talked, mostly of agriculture and land dynastic matters, this always a subject of consuming interest.'[116] On the other hand, the DO's remit to D.T.M. Birks in Northern Nigeria was concise but hardly illuminating to a cadet who had been in the country no more than ten days. 'My DO armed me with a list of strange duties to perform, including checking the Native Treasury and stimulating the planting of groundnuts, whatever these might mean.'[117] Some DOs, only too glad to let the enthusiastic ADO do the touring, passed on their experience in advice rather than action. 'Remember a tour should be a visit, not a visitation' was one such precept, given to an ADO in Northern Nigeria. R. Bere found a very civilized outlook in his first DC in Northern Rhodesia in 1930, who advised him constantly to act with 'humanity, humility and good humour. ... Always respect the dignity of Africans as people and their right to a culture of their own. At the same time we have to show what honest humane and decent government is all about.'[118] In the Gold Coast, J.S. Lawson's advice from his DC on how to handle a difficult village meeting was, 'If you're ever stuck, seek out the oldest person present, ask his or her advice, and act on it. However unpopular, it would be accepted, such is the African respect for age.'[119] Among the most memorable pieces of advice to the cadet was the administrative aphorism of W. Bazley's first DC in Uganda, the 'character' Amory: 'Do nothing and do it well.'[120]

Somewhat extraordinarily, at any rate by post-war standards, in 1936 G.L. Stephenson was despatched on a 68-day trek in his first weeks in Northern Nigeria. It was not long before his touring diary entry read: 'Am already tiring of tinned milk and strongly tasting water.' As it happened, he was obliged to return to provincial HQ early, when all his boxes of ten weeks' worth of provisions were swept away after one of the carriers had missed his footing while crossing a swollen river. He felt that returning from such as epic first trek was 'the end of one era and the start of a new one for me. I felt I had now met the real Africa and dared to think I had been accepted by it.'[121]

For much of the period up to 1939 the major task of going out on tour was to collect tax. Z. Kingdon never forgot 'the burden' of tax-collecting in Tanganyika in the 1930s, with weary hours spent in the chief's village, 'going through the tax register, calling in defaulters and deciding whether to put them to work on local road or building development schemes, or exempt them'.[122]

According to H. Franklin, his first DC alarmingly (and mislead-
ingly) told him that in Northern Rhodesia 'The only [duty] that
matters, if you want promotion, is tax-collection. The more tax
you collect the higher the Governor will rate you.'[123] On tour the
village meeting, or *baraza* in East Africa, remained a major forum
for the government, through its field agent the DO, to consult
with or explain to the people of the district what it was planning
to do: stop soil erosion by terracing, build a new road, open a
school, set up a council, raise tax, hold elections (a difficult explanation here, for in many areas 'selection' was as far as Western
democracy went), and of course listen to complaints, all the way
from baboons or elephants destroying the crops and cattle-raid-
ing by traditional enemies to the need for a health dispensary
and maybe the prize of a postal agency.[124]

For the many ADOs who had not been taken by their DO on
a short induction trek to see what it was about and how to do it,
or who received no more instruction than 'Go and show your
face in those hilltop hamlets', it was the sheer ignorance of what
exactly one did on trek that added to the mystery and excitement
of that first solo tour. J.S. Lawson did not feel enlightened when
his DC in the Gold Coast sent him off on tour at the end of his
first month in station with the brief to organize an expedition to
visit the remoter villages, 'to meet the chiefs and village headmen, to learn what help they required from government, to issue
gun licences and gunpowder permits [for hunting], and generally "to show the flag" '.[125] In 1951 in Northern Nigeria one cadet,
bearing in mind his wartime command in the Indian Army and
determined to be punctiliously pukka, informed the district head
on his first night out on his first trek that he would inspect the
local police unit at 6.30 the following morning. The constabulary
turned out in full force – all two of them. On his accident-prone
tour the same ADO let it be known that he would be visiting the
new primary school in the foothills in a week's time. When he
arrived he found that the pupils (all four of them) had fled to the
hills rather than encounter their first white man. J. Stacpoole, on
secondment from the CO to learn what DOs did, found himself
in a similar predicament when in Sierra Leone he arranged to
take the salute at the Boy Scouts' march past on St George's Day.
But because of a misunderstanding over the time of the march
past, 'I found myself returning the salute of one scoutmaster, five
boy scouts, and one cub.'[126] It did not take another cadet, I. Brook,

The District Officer holds a village meeting

long to experience his first village riot in Western Nigeria, which sent the Baptist missionaries into a panic. His DO's instructions were crisp and concise: 'Nip up there and see what the hell it's all about.'[127]

The safari was, of course, the supreme opportunity (sometimes the necessity) for the new ADO to start speaking Swahili or Hausa, Twi or Chinyanja, or whatever *lingua franca* had been taught on the Devonshire Course. It was probably the only way to have any conversation during two or three weeks, for the English capacity of the accompanying messengers and his own domestic staff was unlikely to be extensive and that of the local headmen and villagers even less. J.H. Clive found that his DC made carefully sure there was not a single English-speaker in the party when he sent him out on his first tour. 'I jolly well had to learn Swahili or bust.'[128] The expatriate may have often smiled at the not quite English prose of the local press, yet if only the DO had realized some of the howlers he perpetrated or the complete reversals of meaning politely heard and gallantly grasped by his peasant audiences he might have wondered all the more at his reception. Doubtless the linguistic *faux-pas* of some of them live on in tales told in the village.

Not every cadet found himself posted to a district, with its opportunities for touring. Now and again the PC or Resident needed to keep a cadet in provincial HQ, as what was widely known as ADO Office (ADO/O), though in Kenya it was Personal Assistant to the PC and in Tanganyika Staff Officer to the PC. On his first tour in Northern Nigeria M. Varvill was made ADO/O, the Resident telling him to teach himself how to type, even with two fingers, after the office closed. When Varvill proved to the Resident that he could type, he was told to type out a catalogue of the contents of the HQ library (it turned out to be a single bookcase) and the Resident would then let him know when he could go out to a district. 'I know how you feel,' he told Varvill, 'but one day you will bless me for insisting on typing' – and he did.[129] In K.V. Arrowsmith's case, while the other two cadets went off to districts, he was kept in Calabar, where 'I systematically rearranged the Resident's collection of maps and plans, I filed an accumulation of secret and confidential correspondence, and taught myself to type. As a result of sitting in the same office [as the Resident] I gleaned a lot of useful general knowledge and made the acquaintance of a wide cross-section of people.'[130] In some stations the Resident preferred to work in what R.T. Kerslake called in Katsina the 'Olympian detachment' of an office in his house, often to the frustration of the ADO/O and the messengers who had to make countless trips to the Residency on foot or bicycle.[131] H.P. Elliott found being ADO/O 'a dogsbody first job', with the Resident continually adding responsibilities to his schedule – 'I was constantly out of my depth.'[132] I. Brook calculated that he spent his first day in the Resident's office signing 874 Crown leases and 542 on the second. His account of the file on the whisky ration for the Catholic Mission on the third day is an unforgettable cameo in office 'administration', culminating in the quickly learned lesson that 'the thing to remember is that the Resident is God'.[133] Besides the job of keeping the station tidy, a highly unpopular job for the ADO/O was informing officers of the Resident's assignment of housing on the station. For an officer – yet more so his wife – to see that a better bungalow had been given to someone junior in the official *Staff List* was the cause of some sharp words in the provincial office. By custom, certain houses went with certain jobs (e.g. the DO's house, the doctor's bungalow), but when not only further professional officers but also those from newly created departments came along in the 'development' expansion of the late 1940s (co-operative, adult education, well-diggers, etc.), the allocation of housing became a real headache.

Sir Donald Cameron, who as governor of Tanganyika took a close interest in the training of new ADOs by their superiors, warned that 'there is sometimes too great a tendency to make a young cadet a kind of "bottle-washer" – at the beck and call of all the other administrative officers in the station, with the result that he often gets "messed about" and disheartened.'[134] In Uganda A. Forward was quickly aware that a new ADO was fair game. His DC ordered him to take charge of the local Ankole football team, despite his protest that he had never played soccer in his life, and organize a series of matches. Next he had to set up a committee to oversee the construction of a grandstand. Then he was told to organize a new bus service. Lastly he was reminded that historically it was the new ADO's responsibility to organize all the school children for the annual Empire Day parade.[135] As part of a cadet's training, learning to understand how the province operated as ADO/O was valuable, but it also made the eventual posting to a district sweeter still.

Whatever his jobs on his first tour, and however many they were, the alert ADO would probably take away with him the basic lesson in the art of administration in the final years of colonial Africa. As B. Nightingale summed it up in 1959 at the end of a dizzy series of assignments and no fewer than four district postings in his first tour in Northern Nigeria, 'As a trainee ADO it was my prime duty to learn as quickly as possible how to exert influence – one had little or no power – on the beneficial working at all levels of local councils and their staffs.'[136]

Few ADOs spent the whole of their first tour in the same district. Apart from some crisis brought on by a senior officer's sudden ill-health or a requisitioned transfer to the Secretariat necessitating a reshuffle in provincial postings, it was policy to move junior officers two or three times in their first tour so as to give them more experience and wider training. In Kenya, for instance, with a lengthy first tour, it was the practice to move a cadet every six months or so, so as to expose him to the very different needs and practices of administering such groups as the settled Kikuyu and Kamba, the lacustrine Luo, the coastal Swahili and Arabs, the nomadic Maasai and the pastoral peoples of the northern frontier. In Nigeria, where there was virtually no field interchange between the regions with their very different peoples and environment and where the first tour was only 18 months, less than half that of the Kenya cadet, an ADO in the northern region might expect to spend his first tour in a couple of divisions and his second in the same province, but after that he was almost certainly going to be posted to another and different kind of province, say a riverain and Christianizing one instead of a Muslim emirate one in the Sahelian belt. F. Ashcroft had the unusual experience of spending nearly ten years as a DO in Owerri province, but such longevity was rare.[137]

Before the war the deliberate training of new cadets was taken quite seriously by several colonial governments. For instance, a four-month language school was held in Eastern Nigeria (known as 'the crèche'); a six-week induction course in pre-war Northern Nigeria, revived in the 1960s at the Institute of Administration in Zaria; in Uganda a three-week course bringing all the cadets together; and in Kenya after six months of service, a three-week course in magistrates' and treasury work carried the bonus of letting the ADOs meet a few European girls – for some resulting in marriage.[138] Before the Oxbridge courses got into their stride, the Gold Coast practice was to assemble all the cadets on their arrival in Accra and to give them a six-week training course in governmental structure and functions, and to make a start on the language of the area to which they had now been assigned.[139] It is interesting to note how one of the proposals put to the CO for the post-war training of probationers in the UK was that this kind of provincial orientation should be part of the course but held at the higher educational colleges at Makerere or Achimota.[140]

The one malaise the ADO was unlikely to suffer from in his first tour was boredom. Writing of his pre-war days in Nigeria, V.K. Johnson declared that 'for a young cadet on his first tour it was a lonely life in his "Outpost of Empire", but as I had plenty to do and not enough time to do it in I was happy enough.'[141] Reading J. Pollok-Morris's account of the opening weeks of his first tour in Eastern Nigeria, one wonders how he managed to fit all his activities into a mere 18 months, especially when 'the evenings tended to be short and bedtime early'.[142] The work certainly fulfilled one of the aspirational criteria of every DO on applying – in no way could it be called a nine-to-five job. On the other hand, in district work Sunday was often 'indistinguishable from the other days of the week'[143] and Saturday was a standard working day until 1pm. 'Saturday I spent a quiet evening at the office,' wrote R. Hennings, 'checking the cash, signing vouchers, and drafting replies to letters.'[144] The concept of the weekend was not part of the DO's life, other than it being an opportunity to work in the office without any interruption. If Sunday lived up to its reputation as a day of rest, it was only because it allowed the DO to catch up with the rest of the week's work. M.W. Norris's first impression of his work at Kilwa was of long hours, from 8am to 7.30pm spent in the *boma* office or in the courtroom: 'there was little else to do'.[145]

Social life in the sense of cultural events like theatres and concerts or restaurants and pubs was non-existent, but in the sense of socializing there was plenty of home entertaining by way of dinner parties, progressively enhanced as time went on by a steady stream of official visitors. The ADO quickly learned that, like any frontier society, hospitality was part of the job, with all that that meant in terms of nuisances as well as bonuses. In accordance with the adage that the first thing the British did abroad was to found a club and build a golf course or racecourse, stations of any size beyond the one-man variety would have a club. This offered the ADO the opportunity to meet colleagues and, despite the tendency to talk shop, also to take his mind momentarily off his work.

In the unlikely event that the ADO on his first tour might soon begin to feel he had really arrived and was now on the career ladder, his DO might tactfully remind him that officially he was still a cadet on probation, and that he would not be gazetted to the permanent staff until he had been confirmed in his appointment. For this to happen, he would need, as well as a good report from his DC, to pass the compulsory government examinations. In most colonies these consisted, apart from language (both written and oral), of exams in the laws of the colony and a knowledge of General Orders, Colonial Regulations and Financial Instructions. So voluminous did changes and amendments become that Northern Nigeria, for instance, issued its own *Office Guide* to help DOs keep in touch with what the current regulations were. The 1932 edition consisted of 260 pages, with the index alone amounting to 27. In Kenya it was failure in the district office to paste the amendments into the laws of Kenya that caused C. Minter to fail his law exam at his first attempt.[146]

As bad as degree finals, one had to pass all six of the three-hour papers at one sitting. On the language side, the instruction on the training course was good enough after the war for a pass in Swahili there to count as a pass in the written part of the government's Lower Standard exam. The oral exam required further work for another year or so. In preparation for sitting his Higher Standard exam, remarkably at the end of his first tour, R. Sadleir read *King Solomon's Mines* and *1001 Nights* in Swahili, as well as 'solemnly learning every word in the entire Swahili dictionary'.[147] In Kenya also, cadets were required to pass the Higher Standard exam, despite the fact, as R. Wainwright ruefully observed, 'The purest Swahili was never heard in Kenya, being spoken only by a few in Zanzibar and on the coast of Tanganyika.'[148] P.D. McEntee failed the exam the first time because he could not list the Swahili names for all the different parts of a dhow.[149] In West Africa an ADO who did not pass his Lower Standard language exam would have his annual increment withheld. It was noticeable how few pre-war DOs in Nigeria managed to pass the examinations in the major *linguae francae* of Ibo or Yoruba. This was partly because of the well-known difficulty experienced by Europeans in learning a tonal language, and partly because right across Southern Nigeria, English – or a variant of it, 'pidgin' – was a widely spoken method of communication.[150] A one-off bonus was payable on passing an examination. In Kenya this was £20 for Higher Standard. In Hausa, the Intermediate Standard was progressively phased out after the war, and linguistically gifted DOs could enter for the Higher Standard Hausa after only seven years instead of having to wait ten before being eligible to apply. Some DOs preferred to learn a second, even a third, language up to Lower Standard rather than tackle the Higher Standard in the principal language.

If the confirmation exams were not something to be looked forward to as the end of the cadet's first tour drew near, there was one thing that was: home leave. Not that a cadet was likely to have reached the stage of some of his seniors, who impatiently calculated the number of days left of their tour by crossing off the calendar or anticipatedly counting the number of paludrine tablets left. Now and again the excitement of the voyage home could be spoiled. K.P. Maddocks was given the sadly not infrequent assignment on the West Coast voyage of having to look after an ADO who had had a nervous breakdown as a result of the isolated life he had had to endure. All went well until the ship docked at Plymouth, when the ADO threw himself overboard. One of the ship's crew dived in and rescued him. But it was not the happy homecoming hoped for by Maddocks.[151] Compulsory travel by air in the 1950s for those proceeding on and returning from leave instead of proceeding by sea at least opened the opportunity for a stop-over in a choice of attractive European capitals.

Looking back on his first tour as he sailed from Dar es Salaam in 1933, Z. Kingdon's chief impression was how many Africans lived in fear: fear of the unknown, of famine, wild animals, rival tribesmen, authority, and above all the witch-doctor.[152] Lord Tweedsmuir's thoughts on his first tour (and sadly his last) in Uganda were different. 'The first impact of Africa filled me, as it does almost everyone, with violent energy, coupled with a raging appetite and the facility to sleep like a dog. After six months this was to dwindle, and at the end of the first year the edge is off. … To the newcomer, nothing is too distant, nothing is too much effort, and there is nothing which is not worth seeing.'[153] Across in West Africa, H. Brind congratulated himself on having been posted to Enchi in the Gold Coast for his first tour, 'an ideal place in which to start a career. There was plenty of time not only to read the office files but also to prepare for the examinations on law, government regulations and a local language.'[154] When M.W. Norris ended his first tour in Tanganyika he reckoned that 'probably my greatest advance was in adjusting to Africa'. Having 'suppressed a tear' at leaving his first posting at the end of two years, he left the next one 'with less of a wrench, mostly I suspect because that "first district" emotion was passed'.[155] C. Chenevix Trench, 'an incurable romantic' and one of the few Indian Political Service officers to join the CAS after India's independence in 1947, knew within days of his posting to Kenya's legendary Northern Frontier District that this was where he wanted to spend many years. 'How can I manage to stay up here?' he asked his DC. 'Don't marry' came the answer (he had just done so), 'and walk.'[156] Thinking about how happy he had been on his first tour in Kenya, P. Johnson had one recollection sticking in his throat, 'being told by a bunch of elders on the Coast that they preferred the German administration to the British because the Germans were consistent bullies, not like the British who were so unpredictable'.[157] It was a comment familiar to DOs in Togoland and the Cameroons too.

While R.O. Hennings was one of those who could count among the blessings of his first tour the care with which his DCs had taught him his job,[158] C.A. Baker's memory was equally vivid if not quite so grateful. As his DC got into his car, leaving the *boma* in cadet Baker's care, he asked 'What am I supposed to do? "Build a bridge, old chap". So I asked where. He said, "Damn it, man, there must be a river round here somewhere." '[159] At the end of his first tour from Eastern Nigeria, M. Milne put practical considerations first, drawing up a summary of his domestic budget, which came to an expenditure of £223 in 1939, out of a salary of £400.[160] Doing the same sums for his first tour in 1954 in Bechuanaland, G. Winstanley's monthly pay of £23 had still allowed him to run a car, keep three servants, and enjoy the rare prize of a refrigerator.[161] As for A. Sillery, reviewing his first tour in pre-war Tanganyika, he switched into the spiritual mode, composing a heartfelt prayer: 'If there is such a thing as reincarnation, and with it a machine that will put us back to a time and place that we remember as happy, then I give to the Almighty notice that I want to be the DC Musoma.'[162] On the other side of Africa, an ADO so fell in love with his first station of Yola that he changed his will to request that if he died on duty anywhere in Northern Nigeria he should be buried there. Fortunately his passion for local history was never put to the test.

A hypothesis might be adopted that in the majority of cases cadets would go along with P.D. McEntee's feeling at the end of his first tour in Kenya: 'Embu was my first posting, and of all the many districts I served in later, it remains my first love.'[163] This generalization does not rule out the occasional ADO who suffered a disastrous first tour and never wanted to see the station again. On the whole, however, there is a case for developing the 'favourite station' argument along the lines of H. Phillips's conclusion at the end of his 20-year career in Nyasaland, allowing for the mix of adolescent adventure and the attractive luxury of a top job: 'On looking back, the most interesting and rewarding years for me were the first two and the last three.'[164]

K.G. Bradley was not alone, facing up to the review of a first tour and the anticipation of a first leave, in indulging in what might have been sympathetically if secretly shared by many first-tour ADOs, the manifestation of 'the White Cliffs of Dover' syndrome. 'At Southampton,' he wrote, 'we made the taxi driver stop outside the docks so that we could feast our eyes on a small square patch of municipal English grass. It was the first truly green grass we had seen for two and a half years.'[165]

CHAPTER 5

The Day's Work: In Station

F ew CAS memoirs pay much attention to how the ADO spent his first leave. Some go no further than chronicling family affairs, though most managed to exceed W.F.H. Newington's laconic 'Spent a quiet leave', noting that he still had some of his Cambridge debts to pay off and 'had little or no savings'.[1] Early weeks were generally spent in enjoying, consciously if unexpressed, the minor yet meaningful pleasures of life in Britain contrasted with life in Africa: the carefree filling of a glass of water from the tap, the implored absence of chicken from the home dining table after so many meals of scrawny birds, and, as in J. Morley's mind when he left behind his DO with his enthusiasm for sanitation schemes: 'plug-pulling is one of the recognized joys of the colonial newly home on leave in England'.[2] One ADO who had spent much of his tour trekking in the plains and mountains of the Northern Cameroons found himself looking across the Weald of Kent and on to the South Downs mentally calculating how many days it would take him to trek cross-country from one village to the next.

There were, of course, relatives to visit and college friends to look up and impress with vignettes of life as a DO. Quickly and quietly it became home, not abroad, that filled the day, with its programme of all the recreations that one had taken for granted as part of life yet which were totally unknown to the DO in Africa outside the capital cities: a meal in a restaurant, going to a concert or a theatre or just the cinema, reading recent leading novels or catching up with the latest musical, maybe just shopping in big stores rather than haggling in the market. There was also the long-dreamed-of holiday again in Europe, maybe skiing. One ADO in the 1950s, having enthusiastically told his DO that he was thinking about buying a property in the newly opening-up area called the Algarve, was seriously cautioned against it: 'All that sun and peasant poverty, too much like Africa, old boy.'

A first-tour ADO was unlikely to call on the CO (as with many seniors, too) and would be too junior to be invited to one of the CO's Cambridge Summer Schools. These might feature in later leaves, with perhaps a request from the Commonwealth Institute to lecture at some school or from the CO to sit in on a meeting of the Colonial Service Appointments Board in a neat reversal of what he had experienced some years previously. If it were midsummer, he might summon up courage to accept the invitation of another, more senior DO on leave to attend the annual dinner of the Corona Club, the social club of the Colonial Service, at the Connaught Rooms in London, where he could gaze with awe at the long top table of the bemedalled great and the good. Others had their hobby, newly acquired or earlier indulged in, to follow up: checking what books the Royal Commonwealth Society library might have about nineteenth-century travellers to the area where he had just spent the past year, or sailing or mountaineering. Yet four to six months is, in any job, an awfully long holiday. It is not surprising that many DOs began to look forward to their return, maybe to the same friends and job, more likely to a new station or a completely fresh assignment. A. Sillery was quite specific: 'Like all my friends in the Service, I was quite ready to go back to [Tanganyika] when the time came.'[3] From Nigeria, I. Brook expressed himself even more explicitly: 'As the first euphoria of being home fades, one finds oneself beginning to worry. What is happening in the Division? What has old Chief so-and-so been up to? How is the bridge across the creek getting on? What has happened over the land dispute? ... Your part of Africa has become part of you. You are hooked as surely as any drug addict.'[4] Soon it was time to check up on TAB and yellow fever inoculations and then start the prescribed dosage of paludrine two weeks before arrival in Africa. Maybe a quick visit to the tropical outfitters would help identify that essential item which one (or one's domestic staff) had so keenly felt the absence of last tour or discover some new item of equipment or clothing. Soon the Crown Agents would send notification of one's passage booked and the Secretariat of one's new posting. It would be good to get back.

With his return from his first leave, the ADO could feel that his foot was now firmly on the second rung of a career ladder in the CAS. Admittedly, in the case of those serving in West Africa, where the tour was only 18 months against twice that in East Africa, the shorter tour meant that he was not yet confirmed in his appointment, due at the end of three years' service subject to passing the necessary examinations and the earning of good reports from his seniors. On confirmation he would no longer technically be a cadet but would be gazetted as an Administrative Officer Class IV. In terms of local nomenclature, he had been referred to as an ADO/ADC right from the date of his first arrival in the colony, and his seniority in the territory's *Staff List* derived from that date. With a retirement age of 55, the prospect was potentially one of some 30 years as an administrative officer, in most cases within the same colony. Promotion to Class III, District Officer, came along in seven years or so. There was no guarantee of promotion to Class II, which high-flyers might reach in ten or 12 years but with a median of 15 to 18. The staff grade and the dizzy heights of a transfer to another territory on promotion, possibly as deputy colonial secretary and one day even governor, were unlikely to have featured in the ADO's mind as he returned at the end of his first leave and reflected on his new posting.

'While I was on my first tour,' M. Longford recalled as he returned to Tanganyika, 'I had formed a number of preconceived ideas about where I would like to be posted for my second tour.' He found himself assigned as Staff Officer to a provincial commissioner, 'the job which I wanted to avoid at all costs'.[5] On the West Coast, the short tour of 18 months meant that it was at least on the cards that the ADO could find himself re-posted to the same province, but unlikely to the same division. On the other hand, in the name of his 'training' as well as to meet the demands of juggling with leaves, vacancies and unforeseen emergencies or the sudden need for close administration in the wake of a widespread rural disturbance or maybe an urban riot, he might just as well find himself posted to another province, say a coastal, lakeside or riverain one instead of the desert-like or mountainous or dense-forest one he had known before.

If new ADOs needed to widen their experience of the differing contexts and conditions of provincial administration, seasoned DOs had to be prevented from becoming too identified with their district. When J.H. Clive was at last posted to settler-heavy Eldoret, after 20 years' service in other provinces, the chief native commissioner could still give priority to 'training', pointing out that in his own interest he ought to get some non-native experience under his belt.[6] R.O. Hennings was one who endorsed the intellectual and moral reinvigoration brought about by interludes of a posting to Kenya's 'Settled Areas', seeing things 'through the other end of the telescope'.[7] Exceptionally, M. Leonard, the DO at Nkata Bay in Nyasaland, with its reputation of being a querulous and difficult district, spent 'most of his working life in the one district', because he was looked on in Blantyre as 'the only man who could handle it'.[8] PCs and the Secretariat always had their eyes and ears open for reports of DOs who had gone 'bush happy' and were resisting all attempts to move them. The same DO remained in charge of Rufiji district from 1949 to 1961. It was generally believed within the Tanganyika administration that he had private means and whenever an attempt was made to transfer him he simply submitted his immediate resignation.[9] L. Whitehouse's career of 20 years as a DO in Maasailand was something of a record.[10] On the other hand, J.A. Golding lamented that in all his ten years in Tanganyika he had never once completed a full tour in one district.[11] In Northern Nigeria K.P. Maddocks commented on how unusual it was for him to have served ten years in the same province, the last seven of them consecutively, and even more so that out of his 17 years' service only one year had been spent in an emirate rather than a riverain province.[12] A gubernatorial minute on one old Nigerian file put another gloss on the once-hallowed precept of continuity in postings: 'This officer has for too long been the sole pebble on the beach of Katsina. It would be good for him to be transferred to where he would be but one amongst the other grains of sand on some southern river bed.'[13] In Kenya T. Gavaghan was sent to lacustrine Kakamega after two years up on the arid, sparsely populated northern frontier, so that he could 'put his law exam to good use in court there and experience a change of life among half a million peasant farmers and indigenous forests'.[14] R. Terrell, possibly strengthened by being a 'beachcomber in reverse', i.e. on secondment from the CO to Nigeria, actually approached the Kaduna Secretariat and set out his reasons why he should be sent to a different province on his second tour, among them his inability to continue living the celibate life of so small a station as Gombe and his need to learn about problems faced in administering non-Muslim areas.[15]

There is one further consideration in the question of the frequency and continuity of DO's postings. This somewhat silent view is revealed in M. Varvill's report of a conversation between emirs at the annual Northern Nigeria Chiefs' Conference. When one of them put the question whether any of his colleagues could tell him the best way to have an unpopular DO moved away, an emir replied 'You tell me how to keep a popular one.'[16] The definition of unpopularity might also extend to an ADO's relations with his senior officers. Here the classic published case is the career of W.R. Crocker, an Australian who was assigned to Northern Nigeria in 1930. He soon developed a very low opinion of his seniors, and was quickly posted round the provinces, including to the 'punishment' station of Makurdi. He soon resigned and two years later published extracts from his diary.[17] Fifteen years later, an irked SDO fired a warning shot across the bows of what he looked on as an uppity cadet, with the admonition 'Just remember what happened to Crocker'. Unfortunately the name then meant nothing to the ADO. The concept of a punishment station was prominent in every local administrators' lore, a posting for 'DCs who had blotted their copy-books', often cursed with an unhealthy climate.[18] 'We'll have to send him to Obubra,' a well-known punishment station 'for unwary or unfortunate' DOs, quipped the governor-general when the private secretary, R. Anderson, managed to singe HE's hand as he handed round the box of cigarettes at an official party.[19] In a painstaking and invaluable piece of research, Liebenow has traced the Tanganyikan service of the 26 DCs who were in charge of Newala from 1919 to 1962 and of the 28 in charge of Mikindani (later Mtwara) between 1917 and 1950, showing the length of time each spent as DC there, ranging from one month to six or seven years.[20] Lugard's magisterial dictum on continuity in the posting of DOs being of 'paramount and indeed vital importance' was everywhere as often breached as it was observed.[21]

And so, after this discussion of postings, back to the ADO returning from his first leave. Having met up with his steward and his cook, and any other of his domestic servants to whom he had paid a retainer during his leave, he told them the good/bad news of the province to which they had been assigned, collected his car (if he yet had one) from the PWD store and set off for his provincial HQ. There he would learn, he hoped, to which district he had been posted, unless of course the PC intended to keep him for a while in the provincial HQ office.

This chapter and the next two describe the kind of work and life that the DO could expect to experience over the next ten to 20 years. His growing seniority would bring a difference in the degree rather than the nature of his work. After all, the officer posted as in charge of a division might be in the rank of ADO, DO or SDO, while a Resident or PC was in many ways still a DC writ large. In the Secretariat, too, there were posts for the junior DO (now restyled Assistant Secretary) or the SDO and PC (called Senior Assistant Secretary and, once the ministerial system of government had been introduced, Deputy or Permanent Secretary), all on loan, as it were, from the provincial administration. Continuity, not in post but in work familiarity, was thus very much the career route of the DO in Africa, rather than having him branching out innovatively. It was not until the development policies of the late 1940s and the constitutional changes of the mid-1950s, introducing an elected ministerial system of government and thence self-government leading to independence, that the DO's job began markedly to change, not only in his field responsibilities but above all in the wide variety of jobs, specialist as well as administrative, that came his way. It would nevertheless be true to say that the DO of the 1950s could without difficulty still recognize in his role and responsibilities the work and life of the DO in the 1930s, however much the 1930s DO could not have imagined some of the work schedules of his 1950s counterparts. The work of the DO in Africa within our chosen period of 1932 to 1966 proved to be a classic case of change within continuity.

In locating this chapter in 'the station', it is necessary to be clear what in colonial Africa a station was. The term is principally used here, along with its East and Central African term *boma*, to distinguish between the work and life in a divisional HQ from, at one extreme, life in the one or two-man HQ where being out on trek was a major requirement and, at the other, life in the colony's teeming Secretariat in the capital. To an extent, the concept of station covers the provincial HQ too, which might also have two or three representatives from the private sector. But the real

focus is on the divisional HQ, staffed by the DO, perhaps with
one or two ADOs and maybe half a dozen government colleagues
from various professional departments. Some of these would be
married, thus expanding the size of the still small community.

In the provincial HQ, nearly every department would have its
representative: police and education, engineering and forestry,
veterinary science and agriculture, often a medical officer and a
nursing sister or a matron. Besides the Resident/PC there might
be a senior DO, one or two DOs, and several ADOs, especially
where the provincial HQ was also the site of a major divisional
HQ, as was often the case in the Nigerian emirates. Again, many
officers might be married, so that the government community
could number anything from a score to twice that number – a far
cry from the two-man station in which the ADO had likely spent
much of his first tour. A divisional HQ was the typical station
in the West African idiom, the generic *boma* of East and Central
Africa. However, as P. Mullins observed in Nyasaland, *boma* could
mean much more than the romantic ex-German fort-like building and its limited accommodation. In Chikwawa, which had
benefited from 'a flush of Federal money' in the 1950s, Mullins
occupied 'an immense, brand-new boma building on two floors,
with numerous offices, a court-room, garages and stores – it was
well over half the size of the Zomba Secretariat', along with a set
of new houses for all the departmental staff.[22]

In talking of the *boma* or divisional office, it is important to
rid oneself of the image of the local government office we know
today, complete with computer screens, fax machines, e-mail
facilities, the whole paraphernalia of modern dot coms. Right
into the 1950s a telephone was a rarity in the divisional office.
In Kenya it needed the Mau Mau emergency of the mid-1950s
to introduce radio communication into the provincial administration and enable the DC Embu to hold a version of 'morning
prayers' by calling up each of his DOs in turn.[23] In the divisional office everything was written in longhand, including all
the DO's drafts. In Bunyoro the clerks were so confused by the
DO's atrocious handwriting compounded by his passion for
Latin phrases (a language none of them had ever seen), that they
took to consulting his wife over deciphering the drafts.[24] One DO
calculated that a small divisional HQ in Eastern Nigeria handled
over 15,000 letters in a year, all to be dealt with by two DOs, one
of whom was often away on tour, and three clerks.[25] Some DOs'

enthusiasm for modern technology such as a dictaphone was dampened by the complaint from the Secretariat that a draft was being returned because of the reference to a promising new DO as having 'a rugger blue and a double thirst'.[26] Again, in Northern Nigeria another DO, keen to promote the work of the first generation of secretaries trained as palantypists (audio typists), only just saved his bacon when he spotted, as he was about to sign an impeccably typed letter to the governor, the would-be unctuous sentence 'we are almost grateful to Your Excellency for last week's visit'. At least one DO, however, went all the way in his attempt to overcome communications problems in Bechuanaland: J. Millard bought his own Tiger Moth for £180 and learned to fly.[27]

Letters would be typed (with ms. corrections) on a non-electric typewriter of uncertain vintage, with a carbon copy for retention in one of a series of numbered foolscap-size manilla (sometimes dark green or blue) file covers. The DO had his own small safe in which he kept secret files along with a variety of objects he did not know what to do with: anonymous letters, code books, confiscated gold dust, unclaimed war medals. Now and again a revolver or a half-empty whisky bottle was found by the DO taking over. The contents of the 'goat bag' might also be kept in the safe, that happy East African DOs' device for retaining against treasury audit unspent cash from unspent votes at the end of the financial year and using it for worthy purposes in the next, e.g. repairing buildings when there was no money left in the vote, Christmas recreations for the *boma* staff, sports enterprises, informers, etc.[28] 'It was,' noted J. Russell in Kenya, 'a term for funds collected from numerous improbable sources, which were difficult to explain and even more difficult to bring to account.'[29] In the 1950s papers were fastened together with pins, not staples or paper clips. When the six-monthly stationery supply ran out, as it frequently did, envelopes were recycled for new addressees and often thorns were plucked from the trees in the DO's garden and used instead of pins. Fifty years later it has not been unknown for retired DOs to bring their commendable (once critical) habit of husbanding office stationery home with them, hoarding old envelopes and scrap paper against the day when their study is once more bare.

The office staff could be almost as sparse as the contents of the stationery cupboard. That the office functioned at all was often a miracle, with constantly changing DOs, each of whom was likely to have either no or emphatically his own idea of what constituted best office procedure and sometimes, following the disappearance of a crucial file in transit between offices, being prompted into drafting for guidance his own 'Office Bible' for his preponderantly self-trained group of clerks. One clerk described the well-known DO in Kenya L. Whitehouse ('Wouse') as 'a real terror inside the office ... who would often hurry back to his office in an obvious fit of rage and quickly type out on his portable typewriter one of his many Office Standing Orders'.[30]

Government clerks, just like their DOs, had never been taught the principles of office management, but thanks to their devotion, honesty and tolerance and despite the whims of their DOs, they succeeded in running the *bòma* or divisional office. Many DOs would agree with P. Dennis, who in the Gold Coast 'was often surprised by what good memories many clerks had in turning up something from many months, or even years, earlier'.[31] In East Africa these clerks were predominantly Goans, admired and trusted by generations of DOs.[32] Others were Nyasas from Central Africa. In an educationally disadvantaged protectorate like Northern Nigeria, the clerical grade initially featured a fair proportion of Sierra Leoneans and Gold Coasters, gradually replaced from the 1950s by southern Nigerians and eventually by northerners. Outside Government House and the Secretariat, shorthand typists and personal assistants were practically unknown until after the war, though now and again a hard-pressed PC might manage to find funds to employ a shorthand-qualified wife of an officer in the station to undertake his confidential typing. Hence the greeting extended to one ADO by his Resident, regretting they had not taught him typing on the Cambridge course!

Vital to the running of the office, and to the DO's contacts with the villages when he was out on tour, were the government messengers. These were 'the group of khaki-tunicked, red-fezzed Africans, each wearing on his chest the brass emblem of "D.O." stamped upon it' who met T. Harris on his arrival at Korogwe in Tanganyika, and 'provided a knowledgeable, loyal and informative link between D.O. and the African public, by whom such messengers were normally respected and accepted as authoritative arms of the "Serikali"'.[33] In the office they did far more than carry files and gossip on the verandah outside. For R.T. Kerslake, they were 'the contented chaps, who helped to keep us all happy'.[34] The provincial office might have half a dozen messengers, fewer in a divisional office. They were purposely chosen from local men, who spoke several of the languages of the area with a fluency that could put any ADO with his honours degree in modern languages to silent shame. Many of them had already displayed their loyalty to the government by having served in the army or the police. In Northern Rhodesia, where virtually every DO showed huge admiration for them in his memoirs (R. Short dedicated his memoir 'To the District Messengers of Northern Rhodesia'),[35] they were described by one DC as 'guides, philosophers and friends', an acknowledgement of the indispensable link between the *boma* and the villages, 'with memories which were worth books of records and files'.[36] For R. Sadleir at Kahama, the head messenger Nassaro combined the qualities of sergeant-major and diplomat,[37] while a succession of DOs in Bornu mention in their memoirs the sterling work of M. Dungus. Up in the unique Northern Frontier District of Kenya, the work of the *dubas* (so-called because of their red turbans) or Tribal Police in keeping the administration in tip-top condition was applauded by all who served there. Another category of assistant in some divisions was the interpreter, principally used in court work but also of help to the DO round the office. To announce visitors to the DO, to marshal the daily queue of local complainants and often to serve as interpreter when neither party spoke the local language, to help the ADO count out a specie remittance of £100 in small denomination coins, and in the provincial office let the DO two doors down the verandah know that the Resident would like to see him – now!, were all part of the messengers' role in keeping the DO's office in top gear.

Mail was usually despatched to divisional offices from the provincial office by the mail lorry. While on tour the DO would receive mail by the hand of a government messenger. Even in the early 1950s DOs out on trek could recount tales of how they had received a letter by the Sanders-like forked stick, though that DC's apparently invaluable pigeon-service had long gone out of use (if it had ever existed in colonial Africa). The mail lorry was generally a commercial lorry contracted to the provincial office. Time was money. This meant that in some outstations the DO might have no more than a couple of hours in which to open the week's mail, sort out the contents and addressees, and, if he was really conscientious, set about replying to the Resident's urgent queries, all within the hour. In the provincial HQ where the mail from the outside world was delivered (and taken away) by air once a week, the station gathering at the airport's sole building could become a mini-social affair. However, if the pilot, a star batsman, was required to open the innings for Kano that weekend, the weekly service to Yola was likely to be cancelled! Thus telegrams remained right up to the end the preferred form of urgent communication. Each department had its own approved reference signature. 'Executive' or 'Political' was used by the Administration (in Northern Rhodesia one PC was fond of 'Provincer'), 'Schools' for Education and 'Trees' for Forestry, etc. One ADO spent hours searching the code book of departmental identities for a clue to the forthcoming visitor who had signed the telegram 'Cross Key', only eventually to hear the arrival's introduction, 'Hello, I'm Roger Crosskey'.

Not every district HQ had a post office. Based at Kilwa Masoko on the Tanganyikan coast, J.C. Cairns's description of the district office with its queue of those seeking help and the clerk's summary as he contemplated the crowd – 'the district office is like a well. But from a well people expect only water. From the district office people expect everything' – is a fine vignette.[38] If the DO was the eyes and ears of the government, then the messengers were surely the eyes and ears of the DO. 'I have known all the *Bwanas* [DOs]', the head messenger addressed the new DO in Mikindani, 'I have always been their friend. You must be strict. The people respect that. When a *Bwana* is not strict, the men laugh. He is not a lion, he is a goat, that one.'[39]

Two documents were of major significance amid all the clutter of correspondence files and the very miscellaneous contents of the confidential safe (of which the DO was the sole key-holder). One was of permanent importance, the other of ephemeral use. The first was the District Note Book (DNB), which the jokey humour of the NFD called 'The Noted Blokes' Book'. The DNBs were

the guide books of the DO to each of [his] districts, showing the village units, their history, size, tax collection figures over several years, and details of the village chiefs, whether the appointment is hereditary or not, and if not, if there is some traditional way of choosing the next one. Where the office is hereditary, there is a family tree of the ruling house, showing the holders in the past, the existing ones and possible successors. Their object is both to instruct new officers in taking over and to be the source of information when disputes arise.[40]

Given the frequency of postings among DOs and the urgency to be aware of the traditional procedures of selection in the event of the death of major office holders in the Native Administration, this regularly updated compilation was a local reference book of the first order. Because of its highly personal comments it was kept in the DO's safe. The second document, again invaluable for continuity to so many incoming DOs, was the handing-over notes which every DO was expected to leave for the guidance of his successor. It was essentially a summary report on everything that had been going on in the division, with special reference to current development projects as well as political events. The object was in no way to pre-empt or limit the initiative of the incoming DO, but to draw his attention to what the present situation was and to ongoing projects on which he might wish to keep a close eye as soon as possible.

DOs' offices also usually contained a number of government handbooks, such as the colony's laws and the various volumes of government regulations and financial instructions. Now and again a literary journal or book might also be on the shelf, an inscribed copy of a traveller's memoir about the district he had once visited or perhaps an out-of-print copy of a book on local flora or languages, even the rarity of a Portuguese–Swahili or German–Fulani dictionary. In Northern Nigeria most offices had a copy of the one-time 'DO's Bible', Lugard's *Political Memoranda*, the pages too brittle and the cover too white-ant ridden to risk opening it, despite the label advising the reader that 'the solution used in binding this book has been specially prepared in order to render the work impervious to the ravages of insects'. In Tanganyika the equivalent museum pieces were Sir Donald Cameron's valued 'little brown books' on native administration issued to every DO in the early 1930s.

With the district office scene set, it is time to look at its activities. Since the DO was the government's chief representative in his area, he had to be kept informed about everything that went on. Callers inevitably occupied a major part of the day. Answering letters and compiling reports and returns were other major responsibilities. After 1945, and seemingly more effectively in East and Central than in West Africa, a new policy was that of the

District Development Team, set up in many divisions, comprising the local departmental officers under the supposedly neutral chairmanship of the DO. In Nyasaland, for instance, the DO's district team in Chikawa included a police inspector, a doctor, two agricultural officers and one vet.[41] Berman takes a rather cynical view of these teams in Kenya, dismissing them as 'vehicles for the provincial administration to keep track of and exert control over the activities of the technical departments'.[42] During the Mau Mau uprising in Kenya, the DO would also find himself chairman of his District Emergency Committee, comprising police and army officers, set up to co-ordinate operations. Even outside such emergencies, most provincial headquarters maintained a regular Security Committee, of which the DO was a member. Where there were no departmental officers in the station, the DO retained, as he had done for the past 50 years, responsibility for all 'development'. This meant that in a division where the DO ran everything it was easy to spot the changing interests of the changing DOs. 'In one division it was all road construction,' wrote a pre-war DO in Western Nigeria, 'in another it might be schools, or infant health centres or dispensaries, or demonstration farms, or village industries or water supplies; in another the emphasis might be on the creation of a multiplicity of village courts, in another the erection of imposing public buildings or the creation of forest reserves, or sports grounds.'[43] In pre-war Northern Rhodesia the typical DO was described as 'able to do what he liked and to try his hand at anything. He was road-maker, bridge-builder, doctor, teacher, detective, policeman, magistrate, farmer, cattle-breeder and, if necessary, undertaker'.[44] For E.K. Lumley, a pre-war DO in Tanganyika, road building was 'always one of my administrative interests'.[45] It was his ambition to be the first person to drive a car into Kibondo, which he did! K.G. Bradley recalled that in Northern Rhodesia his 'passion for latrines' was unbridled until he heard how a colleague, subsequently touring in the district after Bradley, had at last persuaded the chief to build a row of latrines, but then found them totally unused. The chief explained, 'Of course we could not use them. Supposing someone came in the night and put medicine in my latrine? So why did we build them? The *Bwana* [DO] wanted them. He knows his own heart.'[46]

If the days of the all-doing single-handed DO had disappeared by 1945, his office schedule in no way reduced his responsibilities. K.V. Arrowsmith returned to Port Harcourt from leave to find that his schedule of ex-officio appointments in this thriving township included those of President of the Town Council, Chairman of the Catering Rest-House Management Committee, Registrar of Marriages, Secretary of the Liquor Licensing Board, Chairman of the Tax Appeal Committee, Chairman of the local branch of the Nigeria Ex-Servicemen's Welfare Association, Chairman of the Local Broadcasting Committee, and Assistant Food Commissioner.[47] R. Sadleir reckoned that as DO Handemi he wore at least 30 different 'hats', along with another dozen unofficial ones such as player/manager of the local football team.[48] Posted to Malindi, O. Knowles found out that apart from his 'ceremonial and entertainment functions as the sole representative of His Majesty … he was also a Gilbertian Pooh Bah', as well as being Keeper of the Lighthouse, Receiver of Wrecks, Chief Sanitary Officer, Keeper of Burial Grounds, and receiver of stolen ivory.[49] Office hours varied with both the climate and the need, in larger stations, to coincide with the habits of non-government institutions. A common pattern was along the lines of 7 to 9 in the morning (the coolest and least interrupted part of the day) and then, after home for breakfast, from 10 to 2 or 3pm. Many DOs returned to the office, unofficially (i.e. no callers) at 5pm for another uninterrupted hour or so until it was dark.

Nor, of course, were all his visitors to the office government or Native Administration officials. The DO's office was the focal point for those in the private sector too. A missionary might have a problem with the way his application for an education grant to the mission school had been handled, or maybe with a missionary of another faith who seemed to have his eye on converting a group of villagers by offering to open a primary school in an area where one already existed, though of a different faith. A trading company agent might be worried about the renewal of his store's certificate of occupancy, or a sisal plantation manager come to discuss the health of his workers. Relations with settlers and missionaries carried a risk for the DO, as J.A. Golding wisely bore in mind in Tanzania: 'Although I made a point of visiting estate owners regularly, I did not like to stay with them or with missionaries, for should land or labour disputes arise between them and the Africans, it was necessary not only to be quite unbiased but also to appear to be so.'[50] A buying agent might also want to find out from the DO why, despite the good harvest, farmers seemed reluctant to sell their produce.

Very much a post-war phenomenon was visitors from overseas. Air travel meant that Africa was readily accessible not only
to CO officials but also to ministers and MPs, in a way it had
never been before. None would dream of passing through without calling on the DO. K.P. Maddocks recorded in his memoir his
dismay, even disgust, at the limp visit by one of the CO's top men,
A. Cohen, in 1950.[51] Writers and journalists now came to Africa
to see for themselves, some of them more welcome than others. A
DO noted that he had been told to show round 'that arch trouble-
maker Mr Kingsley Martin of the *New Statesman*' and 'keep him
out of mischief if I could'.[52] Other fact-finding journalists who
wrote up their visits to Africa in intimate naming detail were
Negley Farson and John Gunther. There were informed travellers, too, like Elspeth Huxley and Alan Moorhead, and, in due
course, professors, often American, following in the footsteps of
pre-war visiting academics like Margery Perham and Lucy Mair.
Film crews also turned up in the DO's office, finding in colonial
Africa an ideal setting for films like *Where No Vultures Fly*, *The
African Queen*, *Mogambo* and *West of Zanzibar*, complete with Clark
Gable and Ava Gardner.

Where a small station lay beside a ferry on one of the busy
trans-provincial roads, the DO often took extreme measures to
protect his assumed hospitality from being exploited by those
who, he was suspiciously convinced, timed their crossing to coincide with a meal time or to take a couple of cold beers off him. P.
Johnston served under a possibly shell-shocked DO of the 1914–
18 vintage whose station lay on the Great North Road in Tanganyika and who worked out a timetable of meals which enabled
him to look an unexpected visitor straight in the eyes and say 'I'm
afraid we've just eaten, otherwise you would have been welcome
to join us.'[53] His breakfast was served at 6.45, lunch at 11.15, and
dinner at 6.30. From Tanganyika, too, came another illustration
of how DOs anywhere could react to visitors: 'I was pleased to
see the occasional visitor, provided he did not stay too long. After
two or three days I was quite happy to see him depart … visits
seemed to break the rhythm of existence.'[54] 'How lonely you must
be, stuck out in the blue,' friends of C. Chenevix Trench sympa-
thized when he was serving in Kenya's remote Northern Frontier
District. 'On the contrary,' he observed, 'our heaviest cross was
the constant stream of visitors.'[55]

In divisions where the Native Administration or local govern-

The District Officer in ceremonial uniform

ment HQ was situated, a large part of the DO's time would be set aside for meeting members of their staff. The day might start with a call by a senior officer-holder, to report on anything of note that had happened the previous day or that was on the programme for that day. A fairly regular visitor would be the treasurer, perhaps to discuss the query on tax which the DO had sent to him last week. The completion of the annual estimates or budget for the Native Administration was a major joint operation, lasting some weeks. For all his lack of accountancy training, the DO became a past-master in the art of drawing up budgets. The chief's representative might call in to discuss the DO's forthcoming tour to the districts beyond the river, or the supervisor of works to consult the DO about repairing a culvert on the dry-season road. Finally, the agenda for next week's council meeting would bring in a further series of callers.

The DO's office was traditionally the focus for complainants, that is to say anyone who needed help or felt aggrieved. If the hearing of complaints at times seemed time-consuming or wearisome, the facility it offered lay at the very heart of colonial district administration: the right of anyone to seek a hearing from or a redress through the DO.[56] It also enabled the DO to gain a unique insight into the mind and life of the peasantry, often learning more about where things were – or might soon be – going wrong than he could by any other means. If such conversations called for a sound grasp of the *lingua franca* as well as of the local culture, at the same time they afforded the DO an unparalleled opportunity to improve his knowledge of both. K.G. Bradley's insider's belief that complaints and court cases could teach the DO more about the people he was working with than any amount of administration[57] is supported by I. Brook's argument that if, as local officials might sometimes fear, 'the DOs knew too much of what went on, much of what they knew was as a result of their work in the Native Courts'.[58] Complaints or answering written petitions often seemed to be a chore, even a waste of time, yet at the end of the day the DO realized that they constituted the very foundation of district administration. It was a principle to be preserved at all costs. M.C. Atkinson pointed out from Western Nigeria, where answering petitions was a wearisome task, that 'the least of His Majesty's subjects had the right of petition up to the Throne itself'.[59] M.G. Power's definition of the DO's office as 'a mixture between a Citizen's Advice Bureau and a sorter out of little problems' has much to commend it.[60] Revealing also is the petitioner's letter addressed to K.V. Arrowsmith in Eastern Nigeria: 'To the Helper of the Helpless, the Honourable District Officer.'[61]

The DO in a station may have regularly spent a large part of a long day in his office, but two other responsibilities could take up much of any time left. The first was in a way the reverse side of his early morning callers to the office, namely his return visit to the Native Administration offices, to pursue points raised or new queries that had come his way from provincial HQ. There might be a talk with the *alkali* or Muslim judge about a court case just finished. Council meetings with the emir or chief tended to be held at regular times, but there were almost always matters to follow up with councillors on the implication or execution of items agreed in council. While the essence of the policy of indirect rule was that the DO advised and administered but never gave orders (it was the emir or chief who ruled), as the new local government system based on the UK model got under way after 1947 so the DO began to withdraw from his executive role, albeit obliged for a while to adopt a more direct line with some of the nascent elected councils and their budgets. In Tanganyika after the war, the appointment of professional magistrates in towns like Dodoma, and in some larger cities in East Africa a European town clerk, helped to ease the DO's burden of urban administration.

The second major preoccupation of the DO in a station was that of sitting in court, now that, having passed his law exam, he had been gazetted as a magistrate. Here the work of the DO in West Africa, above all in the Muslim emirates, was very different from that of his colleagues elsewhere. Because most of the original cases were heard in the Native Courts, the DO's role here was to renew cases in his administrative as much as his legal capacity. He sat as a magistrate only in townships, within the jurisdiction of the government and not the Native Administration Police. By contrast, the memoirs of DOs in districts where indirect rule was not practised are replete with recollections of their work in court, in original cases and in cases on appeal, at once an absorbing and instructive as well as major part of their work. Land disputes were unending in many divisions. Attempting to summarize the fundamental differences between the work of the DO in Northern and Southern Nigeria, M. Varvill declared that the latter spent his year in hearing 360 court cases, with a short bit of travelling by launch from and back to his bungalow, and did his job in English. The Northern DO, on the other hand, rode hundreds of miles on horseback each year, had no bungalow, and did his job in Hausa.[62] It was a common matter of debate among DOs whether a litigant could expect better justice from the DO acting as prosecutor as well as judge but with a deep knowledge of local culture and customs, or from a professional judge or magistrate whose local knowledge was limited but was culturally an outsider and hence more objective.[63] Derived from his experience as a DO in Tanganyika, J.A. Golding concluded that the tiered opportunities for justice, over even the most trivial of matters, with complaints listened to and petitions acted on by the DO in his office, cases heard in Native Courts and then reviewed by the DO, were 'one of the reasons why it was possible to administer large districts containing some hundreds of thousands of people, with a staff of one or two administrative officers and a dozen or so African policemen'. 'I always found,' he added, 'that provided an African litigant had a full and a fair hearing, he generally accepted the verdict even if it should not please him.'[64] In Swahili the DO was known as *Bwana Shauri*, the officer concerned with complaints and disputes. He was, in J. Cooke's estimate, 'a safety net'.[65]

M.C. Atkinson calculated that on the eve of the Second World War the average DO in the average station in Western Nigeria away from provincial HQ allocated the following proportions of his average 34 hours a week in the office, bearing in mind that 'the greatest part of his work was done outside the office': complaints and reviewing Native Court cases 15 per cent each; correspondence 10 per cent; tax collection matters, investigating crime, supervising the prison, constructing and inspecting roads and buildings, each 5 per cent; running the Government Treasury 3 per cent; and 17 per cent on visiting institutions whether government, Native Administration or mission.[66] By 1942, when he was in charge of Benin, the time spent on reviewing court cases rose to as much as a quarter of all his office duties. His average was 30–40 reviews a day, with a record of 55. 'I found this quite enough', but he adds that this was as nothing compared with DOs in Eastern Nigeria, 'for whom only a number above 100 was exceptional'.[67] Atkinson did wonder in retrospect 'how close to justice we got in our review of cases'.[68] An exasperated DO in Northern Rhodesia entertained no doubts about how he had to spend most of his office time: 'counting things (people, goats, prisoners, bags of grain, rifles and ammunition) – and then making lists of what one has counted'.[69]

In no way was all this office time the sum of the DO's work in station. In a one-man station like Potiskum, astride the main road from Jos and Kano to Maiduguri, the DO was 'expected to carry out spot checks on the post office and keep an eye on the catering rest house', a sort of small motel for those passing through, all the while bearing in mind that keeping a judicious eye on the Native Authority was his principal responsibility.[70] Responsibility for the Government Treasury took up a lot of time, apart from reconciling the daily accounts. When a delivery of specie was received, the coins had to be counted by hand (with the practised help of the government messengers): bags of money could not be weighed, as they might easily contain forged coins or small stones. It took G. Allen, a DO in pre-war Nigeria, and two clerks 14 days to count 1,200,000 pennies.[71] Then there might be some Board of Survey or of Inquiry to convene and to chair, to determine why there was a deficit of 77 iron rods in the PWD yard (necessitating laborious counting of the stockpiles of the commodity) or how the nursing sister's house had been burnt down when she was away on tour and no electric storm, as was claimed, had been reported by the Meteorology Department within 200 miles. The DO was responsible for the upkeep of so-called temporary buildings in the station and the rest-houses in bush. A disused prison block might, through the DO's creative accountancy, be converted into an elementary squash court. Where, as in Kenya, the DO had a 'goat bag' at his disposal, not only was it possible instantly to re-thatch a house whose roof had been blown off by a tornado but, according to G. Hampson, progressively to construct over the years an open squash court and a golf course.[72] In his responsibility for the upkeep of the station, a major source of labour was the gang of prisoners from the Native Administration gaol. It was not hard for the amenity-minded DO to put them on to cutting the lush grass so as to reduce the breeding of mosquitoes and then, in the name of such a laudable public health measure, to proceed with the laying out of a small golf course and insist on trim greens (often rightly known in Africa as browns).

In major stations above divisional HQ the DO was sometimes restyled Local Authority, responsible for the township areas that lay outside the jurisdiction of the Native Administration, reminiscent of the cantonment magistrate in colonial India. The allocation of housing on the station, with all its inherent bitterness and protest which threatened his popularity, was, as we have seen, also on his schedule. 'Nothing causes more bad feeling on a station than housing,' observed I. Brook. The DO in charge of the station acted on the Resident's behalf: 'the Resident is in charge of housing,' Brook accepted, 'he has an absolute right to put anyone anywhere he likes.'[73] The administration of urban centres, often artificial creations and non-traditional towns, was in a markedly different category than the DO and his office work, as was the *sui generis* administration of Northern Rhodesia's Copper Belt.

The final decade of colonial rule ushered in two events bringing a new and major responsibility for the DO in station. A major one was the conduct of national legislative council elections and all that went with them. First, the whole principle of electing, of one-man-one-vote, had to be explained to a population for whom this particular aspect of the democratic process was often foreign. Next came the division of the area into constituencies and wards. Then there was the selection of sites for voting booths and the provision of secret balloting, even though this could be negated in early elections where illiterate voters wanted help from the

DO on how to indicate the candidate of their choice. If the voter was often illiterate, he was never anything but street-wise when it came to weighing up politicians. There was also the preparation of ballot boxes, one for each candidate and all marked with the party's symbol to help the illiterate voter, together with the selection and training of returning officers. Of paramount importance were the DO's arrangements for the sealing and securing of the boxes, and then the supervision of the final count. Finally, of course, came the procedure for announcing the result. There were contingency security plans to finalize with the police, just as there had earlier been applications to the DO for the issuing of permits for party rallies. Not untypical was the experience of D. Nicoll-Griffith in Kenya in 1960, when he was told to organize the first general election in Fort Hall, a medium-sized district of 400,000 people and only a couple of years previously the centre of the Mau Mau uprising and the site of the grave of a DO who had been murdered at Gakuruwa by the terrorists. It took three weeks for four DOs to register 87,000 voters.[74] In Eastern Nigeria K. Addis remembered the first election arrangements – 'to be made by the DO: who else?' – and the DO's 'thick file containing a list of all the things that might go wrong', but in the event the DO thought it had turned out to be a low-key affair: 'no one shot, no one in prison for more than a week-end, nothing burned down and no one seriously hurt, no suavely reproachful lawyers, no ritual vituperation, no mention even in the newspapers'.[75] Just another routine job in the day of the DO. But let it not be forgotten that this responsibility for running a national election in his division, all the way from registration to result, was that of young men who, such being the strict rule of the British government about any involvement of Crown servants in politics, were disenfranchised at home and, given their age on joining the CAS, had in many cases never voted in a general election in the UK and might not know a ballot box from a polling booth.

The second major post-war impact in the work of the DO was the imposition of 'development' as the new mantra of colonial administration in the districts, and the advance – both concurrent and consequent – towards ministerial government at the centre. Development generated a huge expansion of 'special duties' involving the DO as the most likely person to hold the newly established posts. This was particularly in evidence at the centre, where new specialist posts sprang up in the Secretariat,

for instance as Senior Assistant Secretary Security, Director of
the Translation Bureau, Chief Information Officer, Commissioner
for Native Courts, and so on. The proliferation of new assignments percolated down to the provincial HQ too. Within six
months of learning the ropes in the *boma*, J.R. Johnson found
himself restyled DO Land Consolidation in Embu. In Northern
Nigeria an ADO found himself appointed by the Resident to be
in charge of a mass literacy campaign, possibly because of a fear
that the education department might give priority to professional
purity over popular palpable progress. The periodic census or
the responsibility for conducting elections at the provincial
level found the DO taking on another special duty within the
province, often finding that it could be an assignment of equal
excitement. The arrival of the triennial UN Trust Territory Visiting Missions in Tanganyika, the Cameroons and Togoland meant
that a DO had to be taken off his regular work, first to help draw
up the detailed report required by the Visiting Mission and then
likely to be seconded to them to accompany the government's
senior representative as ADC. 'One had to answer 247 questions,'
complained the DO charged with preparing the special report
for the visit of the 1949 Mission to the Cameroons, A.F. Bridges,
'some apparently composed by people who hadn't the slightest
knowledge of Africa'. It took him ten days to finish the report,
with another week compiling the statistical appendices.[76] In some
areas community development became the flavour of the month,
and the work of E.R. Chadwick in Eastern Nigeria achieved
wide recognition, culminating in the CO film *Daybreak in Udi*
(admittedly, a few disenchanted DOs renamed it *Dusk in Udi*).
In Tanganyika the Usumbara Development Scheme, essentially
a soil conservation and agricultural development project, deeply
involved the provincial administration. In Northern Nigeria C.
Hanson-Smith was ordered by his DO to spend nine months as
liaison officer with the nomadic Fulani to work out how they
might be integrated with the Native Administration (a spin-off
was his compilation of writing the first Western Fulfulde dictionary), while T.M.B. Sharp was sent to carry out a survey of the
potential for rice farming.[77]

   Wartime conditions had inevitably meant new jobs for the
DO, so he was not totally unprepared for the plethora of specialized work that subsequently came his way with the introduction
of 'development' in all its ramifications, as the new policy in 1947.

In wartime Nigeria, DOs were deployed on special campaigns to boost the growing of groundnuts in the north and palm oil production in the south, while others were sent to increase the number of men volunteering for the tin mines. Everywhere, of course, young men in the villages were encouraged to join the army. As a consequence, the pre-war practice of DOs regularly touring their districts largely lapsed. In the West African territories that bordered Vichy-controlled Francophone Africa, several senior DOs were seconded to the cloak-and-dagger Special Operations Executive (SOE), among them B.E. Sharwood-Smith, P.H.G. Scott and, in Greece, M.V. Backhouse.[78] It was from Lagos that W.F.H. Newington and A. Abell played a distinguished role in the SOE raid to board and seize the Italian ship *Duchesa Aosta* sheltering in Fernando Po.[79] In Tanganyika the German presence among the planters was a strong one, so that in the late months of 1939 DOs were 'constantly on the move, bringing in wanted Nazis and collecting firearms, radios and fuel dumps', wrote J. Millard, who had previously spent most of his time at Mbeya on safari, getting to know the German Mbozi coffee-planters and reporting on their political leanings.[80] Nor did the end of hostilities mean that the DO was able to return to his normal district administration. In Kenya W.H. Thompson found himself appointed Civil Re-absorption Officer to help with the re-employment of ex-servicemen, which led him into the provincial administration,[81] while M.J. Dent remembered how he had to distribute 2,000 medals to the ex-servicemen who had been awarded the Burma Star and the 1939–45 war medal.[82]

The emphasis on 'development', on community development and local government in the late 1940s, and the acceleration of 'politics' in the 1950s, all part of the run-up to self-government, never let the DO in charge of a division lose sight of his longstanding primary responsibility for the maintenance of law and order. That was always his badge of office, the foundation and the rationale of his being, the symbol of his authority, and the explanation of his office as being the first point of contact for anyone coming into his area and for knowing everything that was going on it. It was not unusual for this status of the DO on his station to lead to problems with some departmental officers who might well in terms of length of service be senior to him, but in no other respect. While the label of 'The Heaven Born' was more widely employed in the Raj than in the Colonial Service to describe the administration cadre, K.P. Maddocks, writing from nearly 30 years' experience in Nigeria, accepted that all too often the attaching label there before 1945 was 'the bloody Political'.[83] Quite simply, however gallingly at times, the DO *was* the government in his district. Not only did he, in J.B. Carson's judgement from Kenya, have 'to pave the way for the mandates of Government but he also had to see that they are carried out, a much more diffi-cult task, seeing that his efforts are judged by results'.[84] Such was the burden of his authority. To make this authority clear to all, the DO had the privilege of flying the Union flag on a tall flagpole in his garden, a status symbolically enhanced by its formal raising at sunrise and its lowering at sunset by a uniformed policemen accompanied by a bugler.

Formal occasions in a station came along rarely, but when they did they demanded a huge amount of organization by the DO, including the donning of his full-dress uniform, complete with sword and helmet. Empire Day was a regular event, every 24 May, and the DO had to devote the whole day to celebration, both parading and partying. Having taken the salute at a morn-ing parade of all the school children, he would likely spend the afternoon watching or refereeing or even taking part in a foot-ball match. In the evening he would be expected to give a drinks party for the station, followed by a select dinner party, at the end of which the sovereign's health would be drunk. Another annual event in the Muslim areas was the festival at the end of the month of fasting, when the DO would pay an official courtesy visit on the emir, likely mounted and wearing his uniform. Then there was Remembrance Day and more parading. An unseemly station *cause célèbre* erupted at Kilifi, when the judge took a short cut across the grass as the PC walked solemnly down the path, each bearing a wreath, and the judge sought to establish seniority by placing his wreath first.[85]

There were also one-off public celebrations for the DO to arrange and lead, for instance the VE Day week in May 1945 mark-ing the end of the war, colourfully re-enacted by the DO's wife at Mbeya, Mrs Kingdon – 'What a week to remember!', with the PC making the announcement of the end of hostilities an hour before Churchill's speech was broadcast.[86] Another likely once-in-a-life-time occasion was Coronation Day in 1953. When the day broke in Numan in Northern Nigeria the DO was already up and spent the morning helping the Sudan United Mission to clean up after a violent thunderstorm. The parade of school children had to be telescoped into the sports meeting, at which the DO, now out of uniform, was able (allowed?) to win a donkey race *à la* Blackpool sands. In the evening, pleading exhaustion rather than admitting to his fear of fireworks, he sent a valiant PWD pupil engineer across the river to set off the display.

The grandest, and most worrying, of these station occasions was a visit by His Excellency the Governor (HE). Most governors liked to get away from their duties in the capital, sometimes to see what their new bailiwick was like and now and again to revisit nostalgically the districts of their youth,[87] and always to get to know the staff in the field, senior PCs and junior DOs alike. Often his tour up-country would be built round the installation of a major chief or the opening of a new national institution. Anecdotes about HE's visits, the mishaps or narrow squeaks as much as the highlights, abound in DO's memoirs. J. Lewis-Barned recorded a typical day when HE visited Ufipa.[88] As far as the DO in his station was concerned, a basic convention for HE's visits applied. The DO always moved out of his house and the governor, his wife if she was accompanying him, and his immediate private staff moved in. To add to the accommodation problem, the PC would always accompany HE within his province and had to be put up too. The Government House protocol, of course, came too, complete with visitors' book and sentries. During J. Brayne-Baker's first experience of a gubernatorial visit in the Cameroons, his DO, a real old-timer set in his ways and fond of the bottle, warned him: 'Make sure that the guard doesn't sound the bugle every time His Honour goes into the garden to spend a penny.'[89] A subsidiary custom – but far from insignificant to the cash-strapped DO – was that HE brought with him on tour all the drink (tax-free for Government House) that was required for the dinners and receptions on the station which the DO had been instructed to arrange in the name of the governor. In Tanganyika Sir Edward Twining indulged in this convention to the full, according to the DO Iringa, T. Harris, who accompanied him on his safari. HE suddenly decided to double the number for whom the dinner table was set in the DO's house and then 'initiate a number of silly games to break the ice'.[90] T. Gavaghan was told by his DC to take care of Sir Evelyn Baring on tour in Kenya. 'I had been briefed to supply bland food, including marmalade without coarse rind to avoid upset to his amoebic liver, but Robertson's Golden Shred still required the teasing out of slivers of simulated peel at verandah breakfast.'[91]

In horse-happy Northern Nigeria, the Governor-General, Sir James Robertson, let it be known on one tour that he wished to be escorted by all the DOs, also in full uniform. One horse-shy DO in Bornu confided to his Resident that he could not trust himself to stay in the saddle if he were to join the glittering cavalcade en route to the emir's palace. To his surprise the Resident agreed to excuse him. To his chagrin, his name was omitted from those invited to lunch with HE at the Residency. On one occasion in Kenya, it was the governor rather than the DO who was surprised. Awaiting HE's arrival in an NFD district, the DC, M. North, a keen ornithologist, spotted a rare bird on the edge of the airstrip and hurried off to observe it more closely. He had still not returned when HE's plane landed.[92] For all the nostalgic wish of many governors to feel that on tour they were partially recapturing the happy memories of their own days in the bush, a governor like Sir Andrew Cohen, who had been brought up in the commuter mode of Whitehall rather than the safari one of Uganda, preferred, according to one of his DOs, to indulge in 'the most sybaritic of all safaris'. As A. Stuart explained, 'GH had two entirely distinct sets of safari equipment, each with its own lorry transport and presiding chefs, laundry-men, personal servants and latrine diggers.' When Cohen went on tour, 'these two entourages leap-frogged ahead of him,' with the alternate safari-camp already set up before the governor left his previous one.[93]

A good DO needed to know something about the visiting governor's leisure passions. When Sir Patrick Renison was touring Embu he told the DO, 'Wainwright, your future depends on my catching a fish this evening.' Next day he sent him a note: 'Your future is assured, I caught two.'[94] Another DO and his colleague, both of whom had played tennis with distinction for their Cambridge colleges, fixed up a game with the governor-general and his PS and planned to just lose. In the event they hardly managed to win a set! Governors as keen amateur botanists like Baring in Kenya, or ornithologists like Bourdillon in Nigeria, or walkers like Turnbull in Tanganyika, all had their leisure pastimes indulged on tour by DOs who played their cards right. The DC also had to act as interpreter for the governor's official addresses when the language was a major one. On one occasion in Tanganyika before the war, the DO faced a sudden crisis when the interpreter assigned to translate the governor's speech from Swahili, as translated by the DO from HE's English, into a lesser spoken language suddenly went missing. The DO quickly identified a suitable speaker whom he had sentenced to gaol the previous day, provided him with a change of clothes, put him on the platform and all went off without a hitch.[95] But things could go wrong, and often did. DOs across the continent would recognize the meaning of the DO Tabora's comment that 'Never have I seen so much relief expressed in any community as when HE left', or that of the Nigerian DO: 'The gubernatorial visit was, I suppose, a success. At any rate, nothing went disastrously wrong as far as the arrangements were concerned' – apart, that is, from the dozing trumpeter in the local band serenading the governor as he alighted from his Rolls Royce, not with the promised 'God Save the Queen' but with the opening notes of 'Come to the Cookhouse Door'.[96]

Yet even a visit to an up-country station by the governor could be outgunned – by a royal visit. Practically unknown in colonial Africa before 1950, except for the Prince of Wales's well-documented visit to West Africa in 1925, a visit from a senior member of the Royal Family, often the Queen herself, became an integral and often final part of a colony's progress towards independence. Single occasions that they were, they feature prominently in the memoirs of DOs fortunate enough to have been involved and maybe rewarded with a glimpse, a word, perhaps a decoration in the sovereign's own order after months and months of preparation. A royal visit earned many pages in the hosting governor's autobiography.[97] Reflecting their reduced proximity to such events, DOs' memoirs are briefer on the subject: a single (but valuable) page from T.H.R. Cashmore on the Queen Mother's visit to Narok,[98] C. Chenevix Trench's problem over accompanying four Turkana worthies to a garden party at Government House in Nairobi to meet Princess Elizabeth,[99] or J.H. Smith's account of marshalling the durbar so brilliantly staged at Kaduna before the Queen and the Duke of Edinburgh in 1956.[100]

The final point to be mentioned in this overview of the DO in station is more in the way of a function than a responsibility, not part of his office but still part of his social role in station life. This was the matter of the club, more likely to be found in a provincial HQ than in any but the larger divisional HQs. By and large the colonial club has, like the colonial administrator, received a bad name in the post-colonial literature, in particular because of its exclusive nature and the socially discriminatory effect of its membership policy. L. Whitehouse's account of the Aga Khan incident in pre-war Kakamega, when the Prince, the guest of the PC, was allowed by the committee (as DC, Whitehouse was ex-officio chairman) to use the golf course provided he did not enter the clubhouse, is telling enough to require no gloss.[101] However, there were clubs and clubs. Clubs in the capital were not the same institutions as those in up-country stations, and those in settler areas were again different from those in other administrative headquarters. The focus here is on the DO and the club in a smallish station, whether he was ex-officio chairman or just a member.

It was arguably an unwritten imperative of his position that the DO simply had to be a club member in the typical provincial or divisional HQ such as that at Bauchi in 1949, described by A.T. Clark as boasting 12 government officers and one wife, 'at the hub of a province half the size of Ceylon',[102] or that at Degema, 'low and squat, its corrugated iron roof and walls painted a drab green [and] no proper windows, just flaps which were held in an upright position by bamboos'.[103] The club offered not only a social meeting place for the expatriate community of the station, the sole alternative to drinks and dinner parties in each other's houses, and – like all clubs – the opportunity to talk shop, to sound out or smooth over a small matter of personality or policy. Above all, the club provided facilities for sport, that exercise so indispensable to healthier living in the tropics. Often too the club had a small library of discarded novels and old copies of *Country Life* and *Blackwoods*, so that the expatriate away from the socio-intellectual atmosphere of the large towns did not need to feel totally isolated from what was going on in the world of books and theatres back home. It was, of course, that very 'home from home' atmosphere that lay at the heart of some of the arguments about not opening membership to Africans, whose personal interests and social recreations would not in the main be the same as those of Europeans. It is interesting to find such a liberal, Fabian, anti-racist governor as Sir Andrew Cohen in Uganda defending the role the station club played in colonial life. 'Some compensations are needed,' he argued, 'for the restricted and rather petty life of a small up-country station, or even a larger colonial town. This partly takes the form of British tribal ceremonies, such as Caledonian gatherings and the like, Scottish dancing, and various forms of sport practised by the British. They are the lifelines of the British abroad to their life and habits back home.' He concluded, 'As one who has always done my best to break down social barriers, I should like to explain that after a long day's work people overseas want to relax in an atmosphere as far as possible reproducing what it is like at home in Britain.'[104]

Sport aside – and its secondary function as a social emollient could be a primary one in a DO's life on station – whether playing cricket with colleagues or tennis with African clerks at their club, the club was not always the DO's favourite gathering place. Indeed, apart from tennis and on some stations golf, the average station was too small to assemble a hockey or football XI, so that to indulge in any of these team sports the DO found that the best opportunity for recapturing his fast fading college skills was to play in the local secondary school or police team. When club doors began to be slowly inched open to admit African members, more and more of whom now held senior government service posts, it was generally the DO who took the initiative, often against colleagues' inclinations. If, as was often the case, once having overcome the hurdle of being elected to the club, many Africans found it was not to their taste and so rarely came along and preferred to socialize at home, at least one of their earlier myths about the club, particularly in headquarter stations, was allayed: contrary to rumour, postings, promotion and confidential reports were definitely not disposed of at the club bar. In terms of race relations, sadly it was too often a case in up-country stations that the club turned out to be a place where one mingled and mixed but did not always meet on equal terms. W. Bazley summed up the ambivalence commonly felt by many DOs towards the station club as the 1950s drew to a close: 'At best the club would organize the sporting and social life of the station, draw people together and allow them to exchange useful ideas. At worst it was a drinking den where bored misfits could complain endlessly of the heat, the lack of facilities and the bloody Africans.'[105]

The life of the DO in station probably filled a larger part of his career than did life in the bush and out on tour. Neither can be fully understood without its comparison with the other. For all the imbalance in proportion of work in station to work in the bush, it is often the case that when the DO thinks back in retirement on his work and life, it is the days out on tour rather than the months spent in his office in station that he tends to recall first and most vividly, and to which we turn in Chapter 6.

CHAPTER 6

The Day's Work: On Tour

L ord Tweedsmuir wrote of his short service as a pre-war DO
in Uganda: 'The life of an administrative officer falls into
two spheres. One sphere is the indoor work when he is at
District HQ. ... The other, and the more exhilarating, is when
he is to go on safari.'[1] Writing of Kenya at about the same time,
R.O. Hennings welcomed the complementarity: 'A week or two
on safari, followed by a spell at headquarters, this alternation
is characteristic of life in an African outstation and contributes
greatly to its charm: the open air, the tents, the rough tracks and
the jolting lorry contrasting with the office routine, the pleasant
bungalow, the tennis in the evening, and the glass and silver on
the dinner table.'[2] Not that it was only a matter of two or three
weeks spent on tour. One view of the mix-and-match interludes
was expressed by D. Barton in Tanganyika when he undertook
safaris of just two or three days in the 1950s. His evaluation
was that, while they were 'not perhaps cost-effective in terms of
achievement to time spent, they were almost invariably thera-
peutic and it was always a pleasure to escape the unremitting
pressure of the *boma*'.[3] The same sense of escape is detectable in
J. Stacpoole's consecutive comments on a 24-hour tour in Sierra
Leone in 1959: 'Out of the office, a blessed change'/'Back in the
office, nothing but frustrations.'[4]

Yet for all the distributional imbalance of the DO's total career
which, over an average of 20 years might not have seen much

more than 10 per cent to 15 per cent actually spent out on tour/
trek/safari/*ulendo* (earlier just 'bushwhacking'), it is those days
that dominate his recollection and reconstruction of what the life
of a DO was. A certain purism creeps into the memory of touring. It could of course be undertaken by foot or on horseback,
sometimes camel. But 'real' touring meant only one thing. 'By
safari,' declared C. Chenevix Trench, already indoctrinated into
the NFD ethos, 'I mean a foot safari. Swanning around in a vehicle does not count.'[5] The mystique extended to no self-respecting
DO in the NFD even using a Land Rover, for fear of the stigma of
decadence.

Lugard had laid down in his canonical *Political Memoranda*
that, while a proper equilibrium must be preserved between a
DO's judicial and executive duties, neither must undermine the
amount of time to be spent on district work. He quoted with
approval the Indian precept that 'the work done by a Political
Officer in his district, surrounded by his people, is greatly superior to the work done in the office surrounded by untrustwor-
thy officials.'[6] In the early days of administration in some areas
the Political Officers were designated Travelling Commissioners,
and as late as the 1950s several of the more remote and sparsely
populated areas, such as Adamawa in Northern Nigeria, had
posts recognized as Touring Officer Northern/Southern Area.
The Lugardian concept of the DO being on the move continued
to be imparted to new ADOs throughout the years, all the way
from A.C.G. Hastings' assertion in the 1920s that 'trekking is the
soul of life ... the essence of our work in Nigeria',[7] to R. Short's
description of Northern Rhodesia in the 1950s where 'PCs of the
old school considered "tours" the summit of felicity. An aura
surrounded Touring, and older officers would nod approvingly
if one had accomplished a large number of days "under canvas".'[8]
Only by touring, ran the pan-continental colonial lore, could the
DO learn the problems of his district and take the pulse of the
people. Only by getting away from the road, into the bush or
up into the hills, could the DO know his people and the people
know their DO. In Nigeria, where close touring had almost lapsed
during the war because of the shortage of staff, R.L. Findlay was
taught that 'the mere process of touring by DOs was of value,
quite apart from whatever work he performed'.[9] A neat analogy
was coined by M. Longford in Tanganyika, where he found that
'DOs travelled round their districts in order to promote good

government, just as hospital consultants go round the wards to see how their patients are getting on'.[10]

PCs called for a monthly return of how many days the DO had spent out of his station on tour. Before the war an ADO might be out on tour for two or three months at a time. Fortunately the government's expectation and the DO's anticipation coincided. 'I lived for touring, I always did,' was how J. Lewis-Barned took to this part of his duty in Tanganyika in the 1950s.[11] One felt one was in touch, on the spot, to a depth that hearing complaints in the office could never attain. 'It was mainly on safari,' recalled R. Brayne as he looked back on his career in Tanganyika in the 1950s, 'that one organized all the development, met the people, heard their problems, put across our policies, and generally kept our ears to the ground and found out what was going on.'[12] Camping out in the bush miles away from the public glare of the divisional office meant that one could pick up tales of discontent and rumours of impending trouble. Sometimes information was whispered to the DO by a justifiably frightened informant under cover of the darkness of the night. Posted to some of the finest touring country in Northern Nigeria, D.T.M. Birks was happy to spend three weeks out of every month in Tangale Waja, where they had not seen a DO for five years.[13] Another ADO in the same territory found himself in 1953 the first DO to visit a group of hill villages in the Mandara mountains since the late 1930s. In Kapenguria in Kenya, it was in the early 1950s still the custom for either the DC or his DO to be out on tour every Tuesday to Friday.[14] The touring returns for Karamoja in the mid-1950s showed that DOs were averaging 30 per cent of their time out on safari.[15] In Northern Rhodesia just before the war, the DC at Fort Jameson spent three weeks out of every month on tour, aiming to visit 1,100 villages every year.[16]

To revert to the lasting Lugardian principles, 'The primary object of travelling through the Province is that the Political Officer may show himself to the people and hear their complaints at first hand. ... By frequent touring, abuses are redressed before they become formidable ... and trust and confidence in Government are fostered.'[17] However, in designing the official form for reporting the touring statistics of his DOs, the economy-minded Lugard was conscious of the cost involved and required the DO to record the type of transport used and any special object for which the tour was undertaken. 'Travelling, it must be remembered, costs money, and is not undertaken for pleasure.'[18] If a well-run district was not solely a well-toured district, a bad district would almost certainly be viewed by provincial HQ as an under-toured district. H.P. Elliott noted how in Eastern Nigeria in the 1930s, 'if trouble started, usually fighting to establish claims for more land, the first question the Resident would ask of the DO of that area would be "How much touring have you done there?"'[19] Good district administration was defined as close administration. Fortunately, for most ADOs, to the accepted importance of touring could be added the benefits it brought to a young officer in his junior years. There was the opportunity to learn the language in a way and to a degree that no training course back in England could ever have done for him. For here he was, out for several weeks at a stretch, accompanied by a handful of messengers, visiting and talking to headmen and villagers, and in all probability with not one of the people he was spending the day with being able to speak more than a few words of English. Touring was the epitome of learning on the job. Then there was the sheer adventure of it, seeing and doing things which a year before, on the Backs or in the Parks, he had half-dreamed of as he read books like Bradley's *Diary of a District Officer*. Now he was indeed out-Sandering Sanders. And, just to double the cream in his coffee, here was a government paying a small allowance for every night he spent out of station on tour. Life was indeed good when on tour.

There were two principal kinds of touring. There was the routine tour of a general nature, basically showing the flag in the name of good district administration, and there was the touring undertaken with a specific objective in mind. On routine touring, the DO would often be found sitting at a table outside his tent or rest-house, with the Union flag prominently flying to indicate where he could be found, holding court, checking tax registers, listening to complaints, following up a promise or request made on his (or his predecessor's) last visit, and generally being seen and accessible before he moved on to another village the next day. The essence was, in J.M. Blair's definition from Western Nigeria, of the DO 'wandering around and enquiring into the state of the farms, the ravages of elephants or locusts, the weather, the health of the children, knowing and being known'.[20] In the 1930s it was not uncommon for an ADO to be sent out on a leisurely tour of 100 days or so. R. Terrell, speaking from an upbringing in the CO, was less lyrical in his assessment: 'Much touring was intended to achieve little more than an impression of goodwill and concern on our part.'[21] Even if post-war routine touring was likely to be counted in weeks rather than months, it was still welcomed by the DO as at least a break from the monotony and the pressure of office work in the station, 'to indulge in a little shooting, to inspect the material progress of the Division, and to renew contacts with the grass-roots'.[22]

In the second or specific kind of touring, the objective would be smaller yet sharper, and the tour itself could be shorter and less leisurely. Before the war, tax collecting was one such objective.[23] Another was locust campaigns. After the war, the collection of *jangali* or nomadic cattle tax continued in Northern Nigeria as a specific tour, but consultation increased too, for instance seeking villagers' views on proposed cotton-growing or ridge-terracing measures, the construction of a new market or a spur from the trunk road, or on how to prevent baboons or nomads' cattle from destroying their crops. In Western Nigeria, M.C. Atkinson's special tour was 'to assess the amount of compensation which would need to be paid for economic trees, mostly cocoa and kola, along the trace of what was to become the main motorway between Lagos and Accra'.[24] The *baraza* or village meeting was an ideal way to explain government policy, whether it was mass literacy, a rice- or cotton-growing campaign, or a fertilizer or health vaccination programme. Touring was also resorted to as an effective method for informing people about how novelties like a census or legislative elections were going to affect them.

Touring was not always the foot trek of popular imagery. The CO's examining doctor may have exaggerated when he discovered C. Minter's flat feet and warned him that 'my brief is only to accept men who'll be capable of walking 40 miles a day when they are 40 years old'.[25] It could be undertaken in a number of ways. Instead of the DO walking with a line of porters carrying his loads on their heads, in areas where there were no tsetse-flies he might tour on horseback. In areas of dense forest, such as the southern parts of Nigeria and the Gold Coast, a bicycle was used for touring. 'Bicycling along bush paths I find a much more enjoyable form of travelling than I imagined,' wrote J. Morley when he was transferred from horseback Sokoto to riverain Kabba.[26] A 'bicycle boy' might accompany the DO in case he preferred to walk rather than wobble and bump for parts of the trek. Once on tour in Eastern Nigeria, K.V. Arrowsmith and his wife preferred to sit on the carrier and be pedalled by two sturdy cyclists.[27] A motor-cycle was occasionally used in the 1930s, at least in Eastern Nigeria and Tanganyika. In river and creek country, touring was possible by barge or canoe, as P.H. Burkinshaw found in the Gambia on board *The Lady Blood* or the spanking new M.L. *Baddibu*.[28] East African coast touring could be by dhow. In semi-desert regions like Somaliland and Kenya's NFD, touring might be by camel. This beast averaged a slow 2½ mph. In Western Kenya R.O. Hennings undertook a four-week safari by donkey, with 12 pack donkeys carrying all the loads. Though they disliked the forest, what they feared most was the smell of elephant.[29] Where a railway cut through a province, a DO might undertake part of his tour by train, as P. Dennis sometimes did in the Tarkwa district of the Gold Coast, and then trek outwards from the station with carriers.[30] Embarking on a railway safari in Tanganyika, T. Harris struck lucky by being given the comparative luxury of the coach provided for the Permanent Way Inspectorate, hitched to a goods train.[31]

Progressively after the war, though often against strong opposition from their seniors convinced that it would be the end of 'real' bush touring, DOs were allowed to tour by kit-car or pickup, later by Land Rover and, as the roads improved, by saloon car. Tanganyika had already experimented with car safaris since the 1930s, using the box body Model A Ford. Loading the kit-car involved a necessary ritual. As W. Bazley described it in Uganda, 'the spare tyre would have to be accessible, heavy articles placed low down, and my rifle in its canvas case lodged behind the seats. Bedding would go on top and the very last thing to go in was a freshly baked loaf of bread.'[32] To this load, J.B. Carson added 'the usual quota of squawking fowls tucked away in odd corners ... an inevitable accompaniment of any safari'.[33] Many years earlier touring would be by hammock, at least for the DO's wife, while he strode manfully ahead. Spotting an old hammock in the office just as he was about to set off on trek in the Gold Coast in 1952, H. Brind hinted to the carriers that he would like to try it out on the walk to Dadiaso, 45 miles away. This met with 'a muttered reaction that modern DCs were heavier than of old'.[34]

Once the area, purpose and method of transport of the tour had been decided upon by the DO, he could proceed with the organization of its details. In districts where there was a Native Authority the DO would inform the chief of his itinerary. In cases of a surprise visit, this protocol had to be discreet: there was no point in a surprise audit of the local headman's tax records if he knew the DO was coming. In the Northern Nigerian emirates the DO had always to be accompanied by an emir's representative, and it was he and not the DO who passed on the latter's wishes as the emir's orders. On tour the DO would be accompanied by at least one government messenger and sometimes by a government police orderly or an escort from one of the variously named territorial local police forces. In West Africa it was rare for the DO to have an armed police escort unless he was out on a special mission, such as to investigate an armed affray or apprehend a murderer. 'Armed' requires a gloss. Yes, the two constables carried a .303 rifle, but out on tour the ammunition was kept by the DO in a locked iron cash box chained to his bed or to the tent pole at night, and issued by him only when he thought it necessary. The station clerk did not accompany the DO but stayed behind to man the office. J. Blair learned that his predecessor in Abeokuta had gone off on a two-month trek, leaving the strong-room door open, with £10,000 inside. On his return, not a penny was missing. When he upbraided the clerk for not closing the door, the latter explained that he thought his honesty was being tested, so he just told the police to be extra vigilant.[35] Out on tour in Tanganyika, E.K. Lumley was furious at receiving a sheaf of telegrams (it was on the eve of the Second World War) from a runner from HQ and having to trek several days back to the Kiberege *boma* because the code book was in his office safe.[36]

To round off the touring party, the DO would have his cook and steward with him and, if touring by horse, a syce too. He might, as we shall see in Chapter 9, be accompanied by his wife. The introduction of the saloon car for touring (as opposed to a kit-car or the station lorry) created a problem over just whom from his entourage the DO should take with him. As N.C. McClintock observed when he bought his new car to Fika, there was quite a queue of qualified priority passengers: two servants, his government messenger, a police orderly, and of course the emir's representative – and then his own loads, all competing for space in a Rover 75.[37] A part answer was a small trailer for all his loads, bouncing along behind the car.

Finally, of course, there were the carriers or porters. Because the DO on tour was going to spend each night away from the station in a village where there was no accommodation for him, he had to take with him his full camp kit and his touring loads. By kit-car or lorry these could be carried in the vehicle, but on a foot or horse tour all the loads had to be head-loaded. In some district HQs there was a group of professional carriers, always ready to accompany the DO on tour. Alternatively, carriers would be found in the market by the government messenger. The days of conscripted carriers, still known in the 1920s, were now a thing of the past, except possibly in cases of emergency like a locust plague or a flood. In north-western Kenya the DO's porters were changed at the boundary of each location, 'an equitable and comparatively simple method of porterage', according to J.B. Carson.[38] Still in Kenya, R.O. Hennings noted how, as soon as the first lot of porters handed over their loads, 'they set off home, many of them on the run and whooping like schoolboys let out of school'.[39] In the hilly area of Gwoza in Northern Nigeria, the town-bred carriers could not carry their loads up the steep inclines, so local youths would swoop down to barter with them and earn a few pence to carry the loads up the hill.[40] Each carrier was limited to carrying a maximum head load of 60lbs. The DO's camp kit was separated into manageable individual loads: camp bed, camp chair, wash-stand, and a zinc bath with a wicker basket inside into which clothes could be packed. Many DOs have told tales of how they were floated across a river in their tin bath (duly emptied); others have related how all their clothes were lost when the bath rolled over into a river in flood. Other head loads for the carriers included the cook's utensils, and food in the versatile 'chop' boxes which, along with all his camp kit, the DO had bought from his tropical outfitters many months ago.

T. Gardner described setting out on his first safari in Northern Rhodesia accompanied by an agricultural officer. Their kit comprised 'bicycles, tents, stores, tilley and hurricane lamps, boxes containing kitchen-ware, changes of clothing, food (apart from items we could get in the valley such as chickens, eggs, groundnuts, or fruits), chairs and tables, and a bath'.[41] They were allowed 22 carriers each. The work was popular and there was no lack of carriers. For his three-week foot trek in the Cameroons, K. Wareham had 14 separate loads, of which three were for tinned food, one for 'drink, whisky, soda siphon and cartridges', one for 'books, binoculars and personal kit', and one for money – mostly in pennies and threepenny bits for paying the carriers. The party comprised 42 carriers and their two headmen, one court clerk, one court messenger, one police constable and rifle, two cooks, one education officer and the DO.[42] The more experienced carriers were keen to carry 'important' loads, like the DO's radio (often the headman's perk, since it could be carried in the hand) or his shotgun (for shooting for the pot), the tilley lamp, and the office box, provided it did not have too many books in it. One DO recalled how his carriers went on strike when they saw the size of Bargery's *Hausa Dictionary* and demanded extra pay. Another perennial responsibility of the DO was making sure that enough food was brought by the villagers at each overnight halt for the carriers to buy.

While recreational reading was one of the delights of being out on tour, discretion leant towards the paperback rather than the hardback edition of such favourites as *War and Peace* or *The Decline and Fall of the Roman Empire*. F. Kennedy was relieved when his tour of Awgu in Eastern Nigeria turned out to be by the divisional lorry and not with carriers, and 'by the hiss of the tilley lamp and the smell of roasting beetles' he ploughed through Scott Moncrieff's 12-volume translation of *À la recherche du temps perdu*.[43]

Tents were clumsy in every way; they also required four extra carriers. For all their rustic romanticism they gradually faded out of the touring process. In Nyasaland, R.A. Dick noticed that the tent canvas, tent pegs and the iron cash box were left for the last carriers to arrive.[44] Unusual loads included those taken on tour by a DO in Northern Rhodesia, a chest of drawers and an aspidistra in a pot, 'to lend a homey touch to the rigours of camp life'.[45] More often than not, the caravan was completed by the DO's dog, the sole member of the party who had no loads to carry or to be carried.

Partisan debate took place among DOs on the best timetabling of being on tour. Here in M. Varvill's experience in Nigeria was 'the abiding, inexhaustible topic of youthful administrators', each with his pet theory of how to organize the party and plan the day.[46] The two hinge factors were the necessity for the carriers to be spared walking in the heat of the day and the need for some kind of accommodation at the next stop to be ready for the DO's arrival. Some DOs liked to send the cook ahead before dawn to find a site under a tree or on a hillock at about half-way and welcome him with breakfast round about 9 o'clock before proceeding on to the day's camp. One DO in Kenya was known for his colourful safari timetable of stopping punctually at 10 o'clock, wherever he was.

A camp table would be set up and a snow-white table cloth laid out, while the cook boiled the water for a cup of tea served from a superior china teapot, all under a coloured umbrella – 'a remarkable sight to behold in the hot, waterless bush country of Turkana', commented J. Russell as he recalled his own DC's comment that on safari 'any fool can be uncomfortable'.[47] A general consensus emerged that early to bed and very early to rise was the best policy, say bed no later than 9pm and then, after just a cup of coffee ('What an advertisement for Nescafé!,' thought one ADO, 'walking 10 miles before breakfast, all on one cup'), off on foot or horseback at 5am. The loads would all have been packed up the previous night after supper, other than the DO's camp bed, which would follow with one of his domestic staff and one porter after he left at five o'clock. The carriers would have set off before midnight.

Another issue was whether in the hot season the DO should trek through the night rather than by day. 'My seniors,' reported J.H. Smith from Kano in 1951, 'often spoke with nostalgia of the advantages of trekking by night.'[48] Intrigued, he tried it. 'Setting off at two in the light of a full moon and after a good sleep, I revelled in the ride,' in theory reaching his destination at 8am to find bath and breakfast waiting. As it turned out, his carriers did not catch up with him until midday. Smith's messengers had not liked the idea and arranged for the loads to be lost. He never tried a night trek again. One DO felt that the worst part of having a meal out on tour, apart from the excitement of eating dinner in the moonlight, was how quickly the whole thing was somehow over. At least the mail sent on by the office clerk could spin out the meal. It was, however, not unknown for a DO who had been away on tour for some weeks to develop an over-sensitivity to communications from his DC back at HQ, reading sharp criticism into a neutral comment or taking a sensible suggestion as a sign of his being guilty of an omission.

The DO tried to limit the distance of the day's journey. An average trek for the carriers was about 15 miles, depending on the nature of the terrain (bush or open plain, hills to climb or rivers to ford), but such was their cheerfulness, stamina and determination that they often covered far more. The DO was allowed to pay them extra money for what he estimated to be a 'double trek'. The swamps of Lake Chad were so infamous that regulations permitted two carriers for each load.[49] On a horse safari, the DO would often ride much further than the carriers walked because of his zigzgging to hamlets not on the shortest route, but such diversions – and a chance for a canter or a gallop rather than a steady trot – might have to yield to the knowledge that a reception committee, often musically accompanied, might well be waiting on the outskirts of the next village in the rising heat of the morning sun. To bypass a village in the area of the day's trek was frowned on, and somebody somewhere would be bound to take offence. For a horse safari, R. Chambers' ride of 65 miles in 12 hours over rough country in Kenya, accompanied by six dubas or tribal police, all arriving without a sore back or girth-gall, must surely be a candidate for any Guinness Book of Colonial Records. When D. Bates was setting out on tour in Tanganyika, he learned that there was a debate among ADOs whether one should walk at the front or the rear of one's line of porters. He decided not to consult his own caustic DC, fearing a reply along the lines of it didn't matter a damn where you walked, with the after-thought of 'if you had any sense you would walk in the opposite direction'.[50]

Accommodation on tour varied. The one thing never found was the superior dhak bungalow of India, furnished and often with a resident cook. In West Africa there was generally a rest-house in major villages, a locally constructed rondavel mud hut, with a caretaker nominally responsible for keeping the compound clean and free of bats and snakes (one DO found a leopard asleep inside when he opened the door) and for bringing water and firewood on the DO's arrival. He had a hard life, with visitors being both irregular and demanding. The 'Rest House Book', when finally produced for signature, could be an amusing anthology of memorable witticisms, as the seven years' entries in Amolatar rest-camp in Uganda reveal.[51] The average rest-house had no furniture, hence the need for the DO to bring everything with him. Mwinilunga in Northern Rhodesia was something of an exception. There it was the custom for the DO on tour to sleep on a *kadidi* bed made from a base of solid tree trunks built up to a framework on which a huge palliasse of grass was laid. This 'superbly comfortable edifice was warm and soft', in R. Short's judgement, being built up each night by the DO's carriers.[52] The seasoned DO would bring a portable lavatory seat with him on

The *boma* at Mwinilunga, Northern Rhodesia

tour, for the facility was at best a 'long drop' pit latrine some yards from the rest-house and at worst an open corner at the edge of the forest. On occasion an earth closet might be rigged up in, as J. Morley described it, 'what was fondly imagined to be the European style, though often more suitable for an acrobat'.[53]

When a tent was still in use, sleeping and living could be more comfortable, though sudden showers were just as disturbing as sleeping under a leaking thatched roof. The Robert Stevenson image of the romance of sleeping under a tropical starry sky was often shattered by mosquitoes or a sudden sand storm. Many DOs preferred to sleep outside rather than inside the rest-house, despite the threat of inquisitive hyaenas and snakes, but in East and Central Africa with the ever-present likelihood of wildlife, this was a less sensible option. A. Stuart's worries on safari in Uganda were not about the rest-house or the wildlife, but the tribal police guard posted to stand within a couple of feet of his bed beside the camp fire. Every time he turned over, the sentry presented arms, rattled the bolt of his rifle, and shouted out 'All correct – Sah!'[54]

There was plenty of work the DO could do by day in the village where he was camped, especially if there was something that he could officially inspect, such as the district head's office, a new village well, the Native Administration or mission primary school, and of course the local court records or the tax register. In villages well off the beaten track, the DO could find himself being begged for medicine, even if it was only the aspirin, elastoplast or Epsom Salts that he had with him. In the Gold Coast, DOs going out on tour were sometimes provided with a travelling medicine chest equipped with simple 'home' drugs. Among the problems frequently met with on tour in Eastern Nigeria were counterfeit coins and illicitly distilled gin.[55] In Uganda in the 1930s R. Bere found that 'the first job after greeting the chief would be to inspect the local grain reserve to which every householder had to contribute to assure adequate stocks in case of famine'.[56]

In settler areas a call on the family of a planter would be appropriate, or a courtesy call on the missionary if there was one in the area. A junior ADO was surprised to be invited to a meal by an American mission family and then hear the grace ad libbed by the prayer 'And please God, help the senior DO swear less'. Important was the local gathering in the late afternoon, when the DO would hold an informal meeting with all those who wanted to hear him, make a complaint, or, for some, just see what a DO looked like. Where the DO rarely toured, his visit was a 'must see' for local children anxious to know whether it was true that the European actually sat down to bathe and sat up at a table to eat with things already held in both hands. 'We ought to accept,' recorded R.F. Bendy, 'that in a bush village the arrival of the DO and his party was rather like the arrival of a touring music hall.'[57]

In an enlightening description of the conventional *baraza* of Uganda, B.L. Jacobs wrote that 'depending on the time of the year, the political climate, the strength of the local chief, and the reputation of the visiting administrator, these open meetings might be attended by up to a hundred people of both sexes and last up to four or five hours.'[58] In Kenya, camps were often sited near a large baraza tree. Of his *barazas* in north-east Uganda, J. Cleave wrote that 'typically I would urge that more children be sent to school and more cattle for inoculation (and more sold to the Cattle Buying schemes), and complain about tax delinquents and trespass in the closed grazing grounds'.[59]

Food could be a problem on tour. An experienced cook who had done it all before might alert his DO to the wisdom of visiting a certain village on a Tuesday, when there was a weekly market and hence the possibility of a cow or sheep being slaughtered. Otherwise it was frequently a case of chicken, chicken, chicken, if such a term was not too great a compliment to the scraggy, stringy bird served up on safari again and again. Touring among the Kara-majong, the diet was more likely to be goat galore – 'Shepherd's Pie made from goat and maize meal is really revolting,' J. Bras-nett never forgot.[60] The DO who would go out for a stroll before sunset and shoot a guinea-fowl or duck for the pot moved up one notch in everybody's estimation. When on tour in the Cameroons in the 1930s the young F.W. Carpenter thought it might be a good idea for himself and his domestic staff if he restricted himself to a simple meal in the evening, only to be sharply reminded by his class-conscious staff that 'only second-class officials' dispensed with a full meal on trek.[61] The *al fresco* sunset drink was a mile-stone pleasure for every DO on tour, lone though he be. Some preferred to remain 'dry' on tour, either for economic or give-it-a-break health reasons. 'Touring was not only great fun,' declared R. Wollocombe, 'but essential for economic reasons, as one was paid an allowance for spending nights away from the station'.[62] It was a boast of some DOs that they managed to live on their bush allowance (five shillings a day in Northern Nigeria in the 1950s, when their salary was about £600 per annum). Apart from locally bought food, there was nothing to spend money on while out in the bush. Government regulations were strict that no presents should be accepted from local officials, so the convention was that in order not to give offence the DO would tip the person who brought a chicken, eggs or some fruit from the chief the going rate for such items. The same practice was observed in station when a chief sent a small gift at Christmas or at some religious festi-val. At the end of his first tour in pre-war Tanganyika, A. Sillery calculated he had saved £101 (about a quarter of his salary), much of it from his bush living and touring allowances.[63]

DOs often found time to indulge in their hobby while they were out on tour. This might be reading (no wonder the CAS was so well read) or probing into some aspect of local culture and history. Or it could be linguistic research or – a popular pastime – bird-watching. For a mountaineer, East Africa was a pleasur-able challenge, as R. Posnett found in Uganda and J.G. Wallace in

Northern Nigeria, and as P. Wyn-Harris made the most of in Kenya
before making an attempt on Mount Everest in 1933. Yet it was the
late afternoon hours, say between 4.30 and sunset (always early in
the tropics), which could be the most rewarding time of day out
on tour. Strolling through the village the DO instantly became
part of the homely scene and learned at first hand how people
lived as they greeted him and invited him to share their meal.
Climbing up the small hill behind the village – an apparent urge
of every DO, in amazed local eyes, for pleasure and not because,
like the villagers, he had to – he might find himself pursued by a
troop of schoolchildren keen to try out their English. Talking to
them not only improved his command of the local language, it
also opened new vistas into the impact of modernity on an often
very cut-off village life. One DO always used to take with him
on tour a collection of English primers, as prizes for impromptu
competitions. Another collected all the old tennis balls from the
station club to hand out to the village children to play with. There
was of course always the sheer beauty of the sunsets or of full
moonlight, and the unbelievable restfulness of listening to 78rpm
records played on a wind-up gramophone (those blessed tropical outfitters' advice again!), guaranteed immediately to attract
an amazed audience outside the rest-house. Touring by road in
Kenya, one DO went further yet by taking along in the station
lorry a small projector and attaching it to the battery so as to show
films in the villages.

As a northern Kenyan DO summed it up, 'nothing can quite
compare with the utter peace of a night time in the desert,
particularly after a tiring drive followed by a good meal'.[64] Even
on a two-man safari (not always a winner), the golden loneliness of reflection and feeling at peace with the world could be
enlivened by conversation with a good companion, such as C.
Chenevix Trench found in the legendary R.G. Turnbull up in the
NFD, 'stretched out in a canvas chair, a whisky and water beside
him, witty, erudite and scandalous, he discussed anything in the
world, from Stravinsky to mountaineering, from camel-breed-
ing to Shakespeare'.[65] It was surely this type of description about
the evening joy of touring which had ignited the imagination of
the would-be DO back in Britain: 'It is the quiet which I love. ...
I am camped on a ridge tonight, and as the sun set I watched
the orange and green pattern of the tree-tops down below turn
slowly to red and purple. The night came swiftly and furtively,

The District Officer takes an evening stroll
in a mountain village

drawing over the forest a soft, secretive veil. Lion and leopard
were moving boldly under its protection.'[66]

Back in station at last, the saga of touring had to be wrapped
up. On the domestic side, there was the undoubted comfort of a
proper meal in a proper setting, and of a real hard bed instead of
a narrow, flexible, canvas camp bed. T.G. Askwith admitted, at
the end of a bone-breaking bicycle safari, that he was thankful to
get back to Kisii: 'a proper bath, clean clothes, a cool night, fresh
milk, bread untainted with insect repellent, and the prospect
of remaining in one place for more than one night, was bliss.'[67]
P.H. Burkinshaw went so far as to welcome his return to station
and an end to the exhaustion of trekking: 'It was sometimes
with a feeling of relief that the DO set off on the relaxing march
through the bush back to base.'[68] T. Gavaghan found, after three
weeks of camel safari, that even his mud-walled blockhouse in
Mandera 'seemed like a palace'.[69] On the personal side too, after
several weeks of one's own company and speaking and hearing
only the local language unless one had been fortunate enough to
have a wireless with batteries strong enough to pick up the BBC

overseas service, one sometimes appeared to others on the station to be suffering from an attack of extreme garrulity. K.G. Bradley remembered how, on returning to his station at the conclusion of his first solo safari, 'I slunk into Fort Jameson by an unfrequented path, terrified lest I should meet anyone. After only three weeks without seeing a white face or talking any English, the thought of having to lift my hat or to say good morning appalled me.'[70] One's domestic staff were even gladder to be home and see their families again. So too were the carriers. J.A. Golding commented on how, towards the end of one safari, he realized, when still two days away from the *boma*, the work was finished. He offered his porters two days' pay if they got back to the station in one day. 'They agreed with alacrity, although not many minutes before they had been complaining at the size and weight of some of the loads.'[71]

On the office side, there was a lot of work to be done in converting the tour into action. A list of items requiring the Native Administration's attention had to be sent to the chief's offices or along with a letter to those departmental officers who might/ought to be interested in matters brought to the DO's attention when on tour. Writing of Tanganyika, E.K. Lumley warned touring officers about 'the mistake of going through their districts issuing orders but not returning soon enough to see if they had been carried out'.[72] Then there was the District Note Book to be updated, that indispensable mix between an encyclopaedia, gazetteer and *Who's Who?* A copy of his touring notes had to be made for the eyes of his DC and PC These might come back later with comments in the margin. In his memoir J.H. Smith valuably included an extensive set of touring notes submitted between 1950 and 1952 when he was touring officer in Kano Division and later when he was touring officer in the neglected area of southern Zaria in 1954.[73] A sample touring report from Eastern Nigeria is that written by R. Somerset in 1952,[74] while a selection of such documents appears in Heussler's study of Tanganyikan field administration.[75] Finally the touring return had to be made up, of how many days spent where and why and by which kind of transport, and claims submitted to the treasury for the number of days' touring allowance due and for settling the imprest for the cash for the pay advanced to the carriers while out in the bush. Within a few days the memory of the safari would be overcome by current office problems, but very soon the DO was again looking forward to the next one. 'Give me life in the bush every time,' as J. Lewis-Barned put it in a hugely enthusiastic paean in praise of touring.[76]

For all the ecstatic memoirs re-echoed by DOs when they recall the days – and nights – out on tour, there existed an equally honest few who thoroughly disliked the upheaval and discomforts of having to leave their station and get out to the bush for a few days. For these, the arrival of an ADO desperately keen to get out on foot or horseback was the answer to the stay-at-home's prayer: 'See you in a fortnight, old chap, wish I could get out and join you, come and have a drink when you're back', leaving both parties more than satisfied with their lot. The truth was that a DO's work was neither all touring nor all office. It was not unusual for an ADO touring the valleys and the blue-hazed hilltops to dream, even pray, that this was how he would like it to be for the rest of his days, perpetually posted as Touring Officer Northern Area. This administrator's romantic vision has been identified as the Arcadian syndrome: the harking back to a seemingly ideal world of rural contentment, for the village-folk as well as for the DO, displayed by DOs who rejected the bustling vulgarity of bureaucratic administration and increasing political nationalism and saw themselves being nearer to the people and in the 'real Africa' when they were out in the bush.[77] Lord Tweedsmuir's reflection as he walked into the station at the end of his first foot safari is a memorial for many. 'To be twenty-two, to be strong, and to be in Africa. There was nothing else that the world had to offer that I would have changed for that life.'[78] It was touring that took a young man's fancy, captured his imagination and in later life conditioned his memory of a previous career. All this despite the fact that out of that career he likely never spent more than a tenth of it out on tour. In the final analysis, as Tweedsmuir indicated, touring was a young man's pleasure. It was youth that was its essence, the unrecognized factor in the self-created image of touring as the would-be perpetual paradise. As N.C. McClintock summed it up, 'the successful man was he who could keep the two in balance, who could satisfy the requirements of the office and yet make time … to be on tour'.[79]

Dream as he might, in his heart of hearts the young DO realized that he was not going to spend the rest of his career on a revolving carousel of weeks on tour and occasional periods in the station. He knew that before long the next step would willy-nilly

catch up with him. It was time for another move in the process
of professionalization. This could be a posting to the provincial
office or, *horribile dictu*, a transfer to the Secretariat. 'My career as
a Bush DO was at an end,' sighed S. White as he packed up on
being moved to Kaduna. 'At last that half-sexed desk-bound life
that I loathed had caught up with me.'[80]

CHAPTER 7

The Day's Work: The Secretariat

A colony's Secretariat was, in a way, one of its provincial headquarters writ large. Here, usually in the territory's capital city, a group of officers were posted, mostly drawn from the district administrations and departmental cadres. They worked under the immediate eye of the colonial (in a colony) or chief (in a protectorate or mandate) secretary and through him directly to the governor. The Secretariat was charged with the formulation, delegation and implementation of decisions on the political, administrative, economic and social processes of the colony. Where decisions on matters of high policy were initially taken in London by the Secretary of State for the Colonies, the Secretariat provided the link between Whitehall and the colony. J. Blair's concise description of the Nigerian Secretariat as 'the Chief Secretary's Office' in the early 1930s was sufficient for every African Secretariat up to the post-war introduction of ministerial government and the reorganization of the governor's Executive Council into a Cabinet under an elected prime minister, when the single Secretariat became many ministries. Until the 1950s the Secretariat was, in Blair's words, 'the nerve centre of the body politic, into which all information was sent and through which all the government instructions were issued'.[1]

In one or two large and ethno-geographically disparate territories such as Nigeria and the Gold Coast, regional Secretariats under a chief commissioner were established in addition to the central Secretariat: at Kaduna, Ibadan and later Enugu as well as Lagos, and at Kumasi and Tamale as well as Accra. Only in Uganda were Government House and the Secretariat situated outside the capital city, on the lake-shore at Entebbe a few miles out of Kampala, the commercial capital. A story used to circulate in Uganda that the American wife of the governor, Sir Charles Dundas, once opened her address to a large group of Europeans with the words, 'Ladies of Entebbe! Women of Kampala!'[2] The capital might of course move, taking the Secretariat with it, as was the case with the old governmental Zomba eventually to the economic centre of Blantyre in Nyasaland, or Livingstone to new Lusaka in Northern Rhodesia in the 1930s, or from Lokoja to Zungeru to Kaduna in the early years of the Northern Nigerian Protectorate. Further moves of the capital took place in the post- colonial period, for example from Lagos to Abuja in Nigeria, Blantyre to Lilongwe in Malawi, and Dar es Salaam to Dodoma in Tanzania.

From time to time inter-territorial Secretariats were set up, though, because of Britain's policy in Africa that each colony should go in its own administrative direction and proceed at its own pace, they had limited and clearly identified responsibilities. Examples of this kind of Secretariat were the pre-war East African Common Services Organization, later the East African High Commission; the West African Governors' Conference, significantly a wartime – and only a wartime – organization; and of course, in the 1950s, the controversial Central African Federation headquarters in Salisbury, not situated in a Colonial Office territory but drawing on colonial civil servants from two of its three countries. But in the daily Colonial Service idiom, the Secretariat was the headquarters of the colonial government, hence the personalization of the capital to indicate the origin of the central government directives, 'Accra wants ...', 'Nairobi requests ...', 'Lusaka reports ...'.

On one count, however, the analogy of the Secretariat being to the provincial administrators what the CO was to the territorial government, that is to say responsible for supervising the delivery of policy decisions and servicing staff, breaks down. Despite frequent internal inquiries and committees, the staff of the CO were never integrated into or interchangeable with the Colonial Service and so continued to be a distinct and separate civil service, in recruitment, appointment, terms of service and deployment, throughout the history of the CO. Secondments there may have been, both from and to the CO, for a couple of years under the practice known in the CO as 'beachcombing'. But those were attachments and in no way cross-postings. In each territory the DOs stoutly remained members of the provincial administration, and among their regular transfers within the colony was a probable posting to the Secretariat, always for junior officers with the likelihood of a return to field administration. Indeed, in the case of the DO, it was almost a matter of course that he should expect to spend two or three years in a Secretariat job at some stage of his career, probably in his junior years and possibly again when he had attained senior rank, whereas on the second, senior posting to the Secretariat many DOs, especially once the ministerial system was in force in the final decade of colonial rule, found that they were retained in the Secretariat far longer, often all the way to retirement without getting back to a province. On his posting to the Secretariat he was commonly wont to fume at his 'bad luck' or 'sentence' in accordance with the principle of Buggins' turn having caught up with him, but soon he was already planning his chances of getting back to the 'real' work of a DO, that which had prompted him to join the CAS in the first place.

Such a policy was not only a deliberate stage in the training of the DO and an important part in the government's formation of the all-round colonial administrator. It was also tacitly accepted by both parties that, looking ahead to the unexpressed nurturing of those who might go far, nobody should realistically expect promotion to the upper echelons of the Service unless he had had some Secretariat experience, and certainly not to the top posts of governor and chief or financial secretary. The exceptions to this promotion path were very few, a notable one being the appointment of B.E. Sharwood-Smith as governor of Northern Nigeria in 1954. A minor but meaningful argument in a DO's transfer to the Secretariat was that on his return to provincial administration at the end of his posting it would be useful to him to know how the HQ operated and to be able to put a face to the name at the bottom of a Secretariat circular or letter. In the quasi-autonomous regional services like Nigeria and the Gold Coast, where a northern DO might otherwise never meet his colleagues from the south, a Secretariat posting enabled them to get to know each other. Just a few DOs, in the 1930s more that the 1950s, adamantly refused to accept a posting to the Secretariat, preferring to offer their resignation instead. Often those were 'characters', whose reluctance was well understood by those responsible for postings.

If colonial administration and the work of the DO underwent a sea-change in its functions between the 1930s and the 1950s, even less recognizable to the pre-war DO would have been the image of the typical Secretariat in the final decade of colonial rule. Before the war and into the early 1950s the key Secretariat posts consisted, in so far as the DO was concerned, of the governor and a triumvirate of top officers, carrying portfolio titles along the lines of chief or colonial secretary, who would often act for the governor when HE was on leave, albeit with the official designation of Officer Administering the Government (OAG) and not as acting governor. In Kenya the post of Chief Native Commissioner (CNC), who was responsible for the whole of the provincial administration staff and was widely looked on as the DO's 'friend at court', remained without executive power until he was redesignated Minister for African Affairs in 1954. In territories where there were additionally regional Secretariats, the post next to the lieutenant-governor or chief commissioner might carry a geographical qualifier, e.g. Secretary Northern Territories, Secretary Southern/Northern Provinces. The argument advanced by Heussler about Kaduna in the 1930s is probably valid for other regional Secretariats. There the high command consisted of experienced provincial officers. 'If they were largely superior and were given deference accordingly, it was as senior members of the same club and not as an alien breed',[3] was often the mutual perception of field officers and Secretariat officials. The Secretariat also included the top departmental officers, for example the Chief Medical Officer and the Chief Education Officer, the Inspector-General of Police, and so on. Each secretary had under him a small number of DOs, temporarily restyled Senior or Principal Assistant Secretary or, for junior DOs, Assistant Secretary, during their posting to the Secretariat. The pre-war Secretariats were small, maybe no more than six to ten DOs on secondment. 'A Colonial Secretariat is not as a rule a large department,' wrote Jeffries in 1938.[4]

Yet that very element of being a small and tight-knit institution generated in DOs newly posted to the Secretariat a level of hostility. One such, T. Harris, was particularly harsh on the personnel of the Secretariat in Tanganyika, accusing some of them of 'selling themselves to the God "Bureau" in return for the creature comforts, such as they were, of Dar es Salaam', but conceding that they 'often brought a breath of Africa's unfresh air to the deliberations of those in whose veins flowed more ink … than the honest red blood of reality' and, if properly handled, could be turned into 'useful allies in the enemy camp rather than turncoat traitors to the Colonial Administrative Service in the field.'[5] In Tanganyika J.A. Golding, on learning of his posting to the Secretariat in 1949, was not slow to invoke the traditional picture of mutually dismissive rivalry: 'Those in Dar es Salaam were convinced that nothing would function without their guidance and instruction. Those of us serving up-country on the other hand were of the opinion that things would function more smoothly without them, and wished they would all pack up and go on leave.'[6] Taking up his new job in such a frame of mind, it is not surprising that he found the work 'dull and not to my liking … soul-destroying'.[7] J. Gutch was another to have a low opinion of the pre-war Secretariat, this time in Accra. 'Some of the older hands had served there for many years and one suspected them of being out of touch with things in the districts. They appeared to contribute little to discussion of problems apart from adding their initials to the minutes of others in the files.'[8] Looking with a jaundiced DO's eyes at the Secretariat elite gathered at a Government House party in 1946 when he was pondering on whether the time might not have come to resign from the Service, R.T. Kerslake felt that 'the new and rising power-holders' seemed to be distinguished by 'a preponderance of brash hard faces and loud voices with clothes to match'.[9]

The arrival of a ministerial system of government in the 1950s altered the functions and structure of the colonial Secretariat beyond recognition. Whitehall had come to Accra and all Secretariats east. Sophistication had at last reached the Secretariat. Each ministry was headed by a permanent secretary, with perhaps an under-secretary, and a pyramidal group of principal and senior assistant secretaries and a number of assistant secretaries. The initial appointment of Residents and PCs to the top post of permanent secretary caused much disquiet among the staff of the professional departments, with officials like the chief medical officer or the chief agricultural officer declining to accept orders from a permanent secretary ignorant of the professional aspects of the department. 'We were a thin upper layer of bureaucracy,' wrote P. Mullins in a critical judgement on the DOs staffing the Nyasaland Secretariat, 'imposed on perfectly competent medical, agricultural, forestry, public works and numerous other departments.'[10] From his experience of integrating the departments into a ministerial system in Lagos, J. O'Regan was left with the opinion that 'a DO was certainly no more likely to possess the qualities of administration required in a Ministry than a senior professional officer'.[11] Following the report by Sir Foley Newns in 1957 on the integration of departments within ministries which the Nigerian government had commissioned him to undertake while he was on leave in London,[12] and which was subsequently widely distributed among the emerging Commonwealth states, a compromise was reached whereby the permanent secretary, still a former DO and sometimes junior in length of service to the departmental head, would be balanced whenever a professional view was at stake by the new rank of directors (of public works, medical services, agriculture, etc.). The most influential post, generally combined with the title of head of the Civil Service, now became permanent secretary to the prime minister/president.

Since the made-over Secretariats now required a complement of a score or so of assistant secretaries, nearly all ADOs, the number of DOs compulsorily seconded from the provincial administration to work in the ministries quickly reduced the number available in the field. But this reinforcement of assistant secretaries in the ministries was not the only fresh demand on field DOs. The first generation of African ministers, many of them having started their career in the Native Administrations and Local Governments, tended to turn to the DO whom they had known and worked closely with as the person they now wanted as their private secretary, at least until such time as they could secure one of the newly trained African ADOs. Once more it was the provincial administration which became the principal loser of manpower. Alongside this expansion of administrative posts within the ministries went yet another call on the DO, beyond the Kenya story of a rapid transfer from Kisumu to Nairobi because the Secretariat XI desperately needed 'a middle-order bat who could bowl a bit'.[13] This was the creation of special duties posts, yet again primarily drawn from DOs. In the wake of accelerated development funds came a whole series of assignments on special duty. In few if any of these cases did the DO have any direct qualification, yet many acquitted themselves so well that their chosen field was to become the specialization they adopted when the time came for them to take early retirement from the CAS.

At the legislative level the newly elected Houses of Assembly and appointed Senates required Clerks to the Legislature, followed in due course by a Clerk (again a DO) to the Executive Council, later Secretary to the Cabinet. Public Service Commissions were established in the 1950s, replacing the bureaucratic Establishment Secretary's office, often with a DO as secretary or even chairman. The opening of new parastatals and other boards frequently looked to a DO to act as the secretary. Enhanced security awareness brought about the post of Senior Assistant Secretary (Security), a belated acceptance of what M. Milne had discovered when he was posted to the Enugu Secretariat in 1952 as, on paper, Asst. Sec. (Political Liaison), in reality Chief Intelligence Officer for the whole of Eastern Nigeria, responsible for producing 7,000-word Political Intelligence Notes (Regpins) every month and expected, in his words, 'to forecast disturbances before they occur'.[14] Whether there had been an embryo public relations officer or not before the war, it was wartime needs that brought about the growth of information departments. As the careers of such notable Information Officers as J. Moxon in the Gold Coast, T. Harris in Tanganyika, C.R. Niven in Nigeria and H. Franklin in Northern Rhodesia (of 'saucepan radio' fame) showed, most governments looked for a DO to appoint to the post and then recruit journalists and trained public relations personnel. The courts, too, beckoned to DOs with legal qualifications, many of them becoming on the eve of independence commissioner for or adviser on Native Courts. In Kenya T.G. Askwith was 'without any warning sent to have a go' at community development, first as principal of the Jeanes School at Kabete and then as Commissioner for Community Development.[15] This was the field in which E.R. Chadwick had made his name in Eastern Nigeria. In Kenya a DO was put in charge of the rehabilitation of detainees in the closing years of the Mau Mau rebellion. In Uganda in 1959 the troubles in the neighbouring Congo obliged the government to appoint a French-speaking DO as liaison officer. Twenty years earlier the same government needed to find a DO to take charge of refugee camps for thousands of Poles who had been deported by the Russians. In the Gold Coast the government had to appoint a Cocoa Rehabilitation Officer in 1948, while in Uganda F.R.J. Williams found himself posted as secretary to a new Agricultural Development Committee.[16] When local radio services added TV to their productions in Nigeria, it was two DOs who took charge, J.F. Wilkinson and M.C.A. Large; and – as it were – they never looked back professionally (both joined ITV/BBC). The titles of new central government posts created in the 1950s and the names of those selected to fill them could be continued, but the point has probably by now been made that it was, in nine cases out of ten, the DO cadre from which they were selected.

A DO might also suddenly find himself assigned to a special *ad hoc* duty. Many colonies had a long history of appointing DOs to be census officers, one of the most celebrated being C.K. Meek for the Nigerian census of 1931, setting him on a course that led him to become a professional anthropologist. Similarly, in the 1950s, chief and regional election supervisors were nearly always DOs. Major commissions of inquiry set up by the CO tended to ask for a local DO to act as secretary. When Lord Hailey embarked on his vast African Survey project in the mid-1930s he was given a DO as the mission's secretary, D.W. Malcolm from Tanganyika. Among the tasks that no DO had ever anticipated on his training course in Britain was the one that came the way of R. Posnett in 1962, 'the job of organizing the independence celebrations throughout Uganda', supported by another DO, B.L. Jacobs, all within six months and with a budget of £250,000.[17]

Diplomatic assignments could also come the way of a DO. In Kenya a DO might be seconded to act as consul to Ethiopia for border incidents, and from Nigeria the post of consul in Fernando Po, with its large population of Ibo workers, and sometimes that in Gabon, was fairly regularly filled by a DO. When W.L. Bell was seconded from Uganda to Washington for six months to work with the World Bank, he commented on the irony in the address: 'Washington DC – what became of Sanders?'[18]

It was, however, in the field of public service training and Africanization – that template for the final decade of colonial rule – that the DO was in conspicuous demand in every territory. Since 1946 the CO had made a point of carefully selecting an experienced DO, sometimes of PC rank, for secondment as supervisor of its training courses in Britain, for instance the popular and successful H.H. McCleery and E.G. Rowe, both, as it happened from Tanganyika. Now the scene shifted to Africa, where governors looked through their staff's personal files to find the best DOs to run the training programmes for African DOs in each colony's new institute of public administration.

The pioneer of these institutes in colonial Africa was that at Zaria, where the first course for training Africans to become DOs was opened in 1957, known as the Administrative Service Training Course. Warmly endorsed within the territory and commended as a model for others to follow by the international and former Ghanaian civil servant A.L. Adu, it was soon joined by similar ventures at Kenya's Kabete, Uganda's Nsamizi, Tanganyika's Mzumbe and Nyasaland's Mpemba, with in each case a carefully selected DO in charge of the course programme. In each case, too, the director of the institute was an experienced DO, and in many instances the institute became incorporated into the new national university. As an integral item in plans for Africanization, which at heart was aimed at replacing European civil servants with Africans, the DO paradoxically was in the lead in programmes to replace him. What is equally noticeable is how many of this latter-day cadre of DOs turned course supervisor were, in the passing of time, head-hunted by the centres for public administration opening in the UK in the 1960s, notably those at the universities of Manchester, Birmingham and Sussex, where together nearly two dozen former African DOs were taken on to the faculties. When the staff college principle was taken forward, initially in East Africa, it was once more to the DO that the institutions turned for teaching and supervising the programmes. Apart from public administration, a number of DOs were assigned to support the fledgling external affairs departments to get off the ground in time for independence and help train the new ranks of national diplomats.

In this overview of new opportunities for the DO to exercise his talents either in the new ministries or in the innumerable newly created posts of special duty, there was one DO post that had been part of a HQ secondment even before there was a physical Secretariat. This was the post of private secretary (PS) to the governor. Traditionally a post reserved for a young DO (the days were past when governors appointed their own relatives), the summons to become a member of the governor's personal staff could fill a DO with a mixture of awe and anxiety, which a posting to the Secretariat proper was unlikely to inspire in him. From a wide range of memoirs written by private secretaries, that of P.

Thirsk, who was called in from a district in Eastern Nigeria to be PS to the Governor-General of the Federation of Nigeria, Sir John Macpherson, admirably recounts the reversal in his lifestyle. His conclusions were that while 'some memories were apt to bring an uncomfortable blush to the cheek, most conjured up pleasant memories of long hours spent close to a governor distinguished for his common touch, great humanity, and sheer determination to do his best ... even at the expense of the somewhat rigid protocol which he tried not to let dominate his life', and that, while being at the centre of things had its undoubted attractions, 'the problems of coping with irate tribesmen or recalcitrant estimates were on the whole simpler and more straightforward than soothing the ruffled feathers of the few prominent wives whose dignity was always apt to be outraged by an unjustified idea of mistaken precedence at some function or other'.[19]

If few were called, fewer refused. One of them was the firm-minded T. Mayhew in Tanganyika, who somehow managed to deflect Sir Edward Twining's wish to have him as his PS with 'not the post-war life I wanted'.[20] A typical posting to Government House was for two or three years. Anything more might disrupt a DO's chances of a promotion post. Anything less might engender *schadenfreude* thought among his colleagues: 'What *has* he done?' R.J. Graham was exceptional in spending five years in GH Enugu, and J.H. Smith was unusual to have spent one tour in GH Kaduna as ADC and then, after a break, another as PS to a different governor. The PS had, of course, no responsibility for policy matters. That was the function of officers in the Secretariat. But files and papers coming up from the Secretariat were minuted to the PS GH and they passed under his eyes on their way to the governor and, just as revealingly, on their way back to the Secretariat with the governor's minutes written (or typed) in red, so the PS was entirely *au fait* with everything that was going on. It was not all that easy for a PS, being a junior DO yet being treated as one of the family. V.K. Johnson, who was PS to a bachelor governor in Eastern Nigeria, related how 'we were often alone at meals when neither of us spoke a single word'.[21] Several PSs commented (in retrospect, of course) how the common gubernatorial passion for playing bridge could turn GH evenings into a nightmare. A governor's wife sometimes overstepped the mark by treating a PS as if he were her PS. Fortunately the non-stop domestic responsibilities of GH were taken off the PS's shoulders by the ADC. A full governor (but not a lieutenant-governor or a chief commissioner) was entitled to an ADC to look after the ceremonial and the domestic side of GH. This was often another young DO, though as time went on it became an opportunity for a promising African police officer or subaltern to be tried out.

That becoming PS was a sign of recognition for an up-and-coming DO is beyond dispute, even if the occasional governor came to wonder how he had ever committed such a painful error of judgement. It is interesting to identify which PSs were the sons of governors and which, too, went on to become governors themselves; suffice to say that while many one-time private secretaries have countless tales of humour and of horror in their memoirs, forming a substantial collection of GH lore and of the image of their master, governors have courteously tended in their memoirs to comment on the punctiliousness and reliability rather than on any inadequacies in the conduct of one who was so close and crucial to HE's performance. Among the most forgiving was Sir William Clark of the High Commission Territories who, when his PS J. Millard apologized for a gross *faux-pas*, endearingly said: 'Thank you for your apology, which I appreciate, but remember one thing, young man, a private secretary is never wrong.'[22]

When it was time for the PS to return to provincial administration, he was by convention allowed to ask for the posting he would like. Many chose the remote touring area, beautiful country where peace and quiet reigned, far removed from the pomp and circumstance of the past few years in Government House. M. Longford was surprised (and his colleagues would have been shocked, had they learned) that when his time was up as PS, Sir Edward Twining asked him to compile, for his eyes only, candid pen-pictures of every unmarried DO in his second tour of service and, based on his personal knowledge of his contemporaries, to make his recommendation on who the next PS should be.[23] Obviously a young DO like the PS could not, despite having visited many of the provinces with the governor, know every DO personally. Yet he had one huge advantage. As PS, every DO's annual confidential report came through his hands before being passed to the governor. Thus he had a unique insight, incomplete but invaluable, of strengths and weaknesses and how a DO might fit in with HE's off-duty hobbies as well as his on-duty demands. H.P. Elliott admitted that, as PS to Sir Theodore Adams in Kaduna, among all his responsibilities that of typing HE's comments on to

the confidential files of all the Residents in the north was the one
he most enjoyed.[24] It was a convention of the annual confidential reporting procedure that only if the senior officer wrote an
adverse report and pointed to a weakness which could be reme-
died by the officer would the report be shown to him before it
went on to Government House.[25]

There was only one confidential report that did not pass
through the PS's hands. This was his own, which went direct to
the governor. M. Milne related how, when C.J. Mayne, the deputy
governor of Eastern Nigeria, moved into Government House
to act for Sir Clement Pleass while he was on leave, he and his
own deputy, P. Gunning, fell into a neat but friendly trap. After
a couple of gins they decided to have a peek at their confidential
reports in the safe. There was only a single page, a scribbled note
from Pleass saying 'Thought you would!'[26]

So back to the Secretariat proper. It would not be too much of
an exaggeration to say that the first thing the DO posted to what
H. Franklin labelled 'the holy Secretariat'[27] had to learn was how
to run an office. 'For the first time in my life,' wrote P. Sanders on
being posted to the Secretariat in Maseru, 'I had to come to terms
with files.'[28] P. Gordon's initial impression as he started work in
the old Secretariat in Nairobi – 'a square, squat building whose
sides, it was easy to imagine, were distended by the weight of
innumerable files crammed within' – was that, faced with an ever
increasing accumulation of files, 'the object was to shunt them
onto someone else at all speed'.[29] According to R. Wainwright,
when the Nairobi Secretariat building was burnt down, the DOs
in the field gleefully suspected sabotage by one of their number
(in fact, it was an accident caused by an electric kettle left on by
one of the tea ladies) and regretted that it was only the policy and
not the personal files that had been destroyed.[30] There was also
the novelty of the Whitehall tradition of minuting upwards to
get accustomed to. Comments on policy issues would start with
the most junior officer, who would express his view in a minute
to his superior. It was also the assistant secretary's responsibility
to make a first draft of a letter in reply to another. His superior
might revise it and then approve it for issue, or might in turn pass
it up the line to his superior for final approval. As K. Blackburne
observed of his initiation into Secretariat practice, he 'learned for
the first time the punctilio of official correspondence and the habit
of senior officers to correct almost any draft letter placed before

them'.[31] Every letter went out over the name of the permanent secretary, never over one's own name, though on purely routine matters an assistant secretary might be allowed to sign on behalf of ('p.p.') the top official.

Beyond the basic understanding of office organization and practice came the need to 'learn the language', to acquire and understand the Secretariat vocabulary, unheard of and unneeded in the *boma* or outstation office, where in any case there was generally no one else to minute files to. What did all those initials on correspondence and files mean – 'i.d.c.', 'f.y.i.', 'f.y.a.', and the sacrosanct 'BU' and 'KIV' (keep in view), the last-named an insurance against nothing else being heard of the matter ever again? What was the vital difference between 'n.f.a.' and 'PA' on the last page of a current file, a source of coals of fire being heaped on a new assistant secretary's head who unwittingly condemned the whole file instead of just the most recent letter received to being permanently 'put away'? As for mixing 'n.f.a.' with 'f.n.a.', DOs could be officially reproved for such Secretariat sabotage. Were the initials on a letter of complaint, 'l.s.d.l.', a fully integral Secretariat abbreviation, or was it just a humorous senior officer's way of indicating the wisdom of doing absolutely nothing, 'let sleeping dogs lie'? Certainly the governor of Tanganyika's laconic minute 'C.C.L.' had his Secretariat searching through their guides to office procedure until his PS eventually translated it as 'couldn't care less'.[32] Another story was said to be a chief secretary's defeating minute 'TINHAT', finally decoded as 'There is no hurry about this'. Acronyms and abbreviated titles of addressees within the Secretariat also had to be mastered. Different coloured flags pinned to files meant differing orders of priority, the most urgent being PQ (Parliamentary Question), in London rather than Lagos or Lusaka. In Nairobi the colour coding was red for urgent, blue for immediate and yellow for legislative council questions. As H. Walker observed when he was put to drafting answers to PQs, they 'required almost clairvoyant anticipation of likely supplementary questions'.[33] Colour also dominated the categories of files in the Entebbe Secretariat. Pale yellow file jackets were open files, kept by African clerks in the General Registry; confidential files were green, kept in the Security Registry; and secret files were blue. Top secret files, a very limited class, were orange.[34] In Zambia, on the other hand, the security files, kept in a special Secret Registry, were red. Then there was the matter of coloured

ink. Only the governor was allowed to minute or write in red ink
(a red ribbon was used for typescript). Green ink was restricted
to the audit department. Purple ink was the prerogative of the
attorney-general's office, though it might take longer for the new
DO to learn the traditional Secretariat secret that the best way to
'lose' a file from circulation was to minute it across to the attorney-general's office for an opinion.

'Morning prayers' were a new routine for the DO brought up
in district administration, the informal (no minutes taken) daily
meeting of the permanent secretary and his staff before office work
got under way. An early necessity of the new assistant secretary
was to acquaint himself with the structure, function and personnel (often recognized only by the initials of their office, DPW for
the Director of Public Works, CMO for the Chief Medical Officer,
etc.) of the professional departments within his and other ministries. A lesson in geography was another requirement, for with
the continually expanding Secretariat and consequent out-hous-
ing, the one-time Secretariat block soon overflowed into offices
spread around, with some buildings up to a mile away. Gone
were the pre-war days when along the verandah was as far as
one needed to walk to talk over a matter with a colleague. In West
Africa, Secretariat hours in the mid-1950s generally followed a 7.30
to 9.30 timetable before breakfast, when the offices were closed to
visitors and the office work could be quietly attended to. From
10.30 to 2.30 the routine was very much that of meetings, whether
scheduled committee ones or with callers. In the cooler climate of
East and Central Africa, the working hours could be from 7.30,
after breakfast, through to 12.30, returning after an hour's break
for lunch and staying till 4.30. This had the advantage of coinciding better with the standard hours of the private sector, which
found it inconvenient if the government offices closed for the day
at 2.30. In any event it was common for the DO to return to work
in the late afternoon and spend from 5 to 6.30 alone and undis-
turbed in his office, rather than playing tennis or golf. P. Gordon
soon learned that in the Nairobi Secretariat 'any officer creeping
out of the building before 7p.m. on weekdays or arriving after
9a.m. on Saturdays did so with a sense of guilt. On Sundays, it
was tacitly accepted, I suppose, that you had been to Communion
and breakfasted, so 10a.m. was acceptable for clocking in. Only a
dedicated few turned up on Sunday afternoons.'[35] One DO posted
to the Kaduna Secretariat was advised by a slightly cynical but

successful senior that 'there is, of course, no need at all to go back to your office after 5 o'clock or at the weekend, but if you do, make sure you park your car where everybody can spot it'.

Dressing in the Secretariat was far more formal than it had been on station. Long trousers, progressively no shorts ('too colonial'), became the fashion as elected ministers took up office. White shirts were *de rigueur* and no khaki bush-shirts. It was the practice always to keep a jacket in the office in case of being summoned by a minister. A tie was essential, 'the distinction', in D. Barton's opinion 'which separated the Secretariat sheep from the up-country goats'.[36] 'We were all in uniform,' was R. Sadleir's picture of the Dar es Salaam Secretariat officers in the 1950s, 'immaculately dressed with white shirts and shorts and white stockings, like the crew of a warship in tropical waters.'[37] Naturally the PS to the governor always had to dress up. In Dar es Salaam the ceremonial-conscious Sir Edward Twining told his new PS to have the best tailor in town make him a black tail-coat, with dark blue velvet lapels, light blue silk lining, and large gilt buttons with the insignia 'ER'.[38]

Seniority reared its head in the Secretariat hierarchy, not only through such mechanisms as who called whom 'sir' rather than by his Christian name, but also which level of officer was allowed to hang curtains in his windows or have a carpet on the floor. T.G. Askwith was struck how far the Whitehall insignia of rank had penetrated the Nairobi Secretariat: 'the carpet for the most senior with an armchair for the visitor; the rooms at the back overlooking and sharing the dust of the car park, with no mildewed law books and reports on the shelves, were allocated to the less exalted'.[39] Great was the rejoicing, it was said, in the new multistoreyed Lagos Secretariat when the senior officers took over the top two floors overlooking the Marina only to find, in due course, that the lifts to the upper floors failed for a sweltering week while the air-conditioning in the juniors' ground-floor offices continued to work like a dream.

H. Walker probably got the Secretariat right when he wrote that 'working to very senior officers was challenging and stimulating but also stressful',[40] all the more so when the DO knew well that he was unlikely to be there for more than a couple of tours. Familiar as the management procedures and ethos of business firms will be to many today, they were quite alien to the average DO transformed from his up-country station to the Secretariat.

The average reader today could probably have moved into a Secretariat post with infinitely greater ease of relocation and grasp of the mechanics than he could have taken on the functions of an ADO. To work in the Secretariat was not why DOs had joined the CAS. It is not surprising to find in their memoirs how little space is devoted to the minutiae of their work in the Secretariat when set beside the long accounts of time spent on tour and in station. Yet many DOs who did serve in the ministries from the mid-1950s accept that, even if such work did not feature prominently in their memoirs, in career terms and in the matter of feeling they were very much part of what was going on at the heart of politics, as colonial administration moved towards the excitement of self-government and Africanization, the post-war Secretariat experience was palpably more worthwhile, even more rewarding, than the image of such a purgatory posting had been in the eyes of pre-war DOs. For all the ritual chafing of the typical young DO on learning the 'bombshell' news of being posted to the Secretariat[41] and the institutionalized contempt for those there who, it was said, could not tell a safari from a salami and had forgotten the worth of the bush-and-boma work of the DO, the interest and involvement to be found in a Secretariat job during the final years of colonial administration are not to be denied. To the end, however, the Colonial Service held out against the argument for two separate services, one to man the Secretariat and one to staff the provincial administration, and opted for a system of regular interchange between central and district work, even if, as time went on, more and more officers found themselves moved into ministry and special-duty jobs.

Work aside, there were compensations for the DO transferred to the Secretariat. It was where power lay, and it was absorbing to see policy being made, even to contribute to the process. There were colleagues by the dozen to work with and to talk to, not the inevitable small circle of a small station or, in a two-man station, the same limited company day after day. The Secretariat presented a far greater intellectual challenge, in drafting and devilling, researching and summarizing, in a way unknown and uncalled for in a district office. The DO was now able – indeed obliged – to think deeply about and beyond his work, an opportunity that he frequently felt lacking in the pressure of routine administration up-country. That mental isolation in a district often commented on by DOs was turned on its head by the range of people, unofficials as well as officials, with whom he now came into frequent contact. Names became faces, faces became friends, and friends exchanged ideas. Working in the capital, whether London or Lagos, Edinburgh or Entebbe, could turn out to have as many compensations as it had drawbacks.

If the day's work of the DO posted to the Secretariat opened vistas and opportunities unknown in life in the district, these were as nothing when set beside the variety of social life now at his disposal, unimaginable in any *boma*. For a start, accommodation was likely to be more modern (even to the extent of a purpose-built government flat, unheard of in colonial Africa before 1945), with piped water, electricity, flushing toilets and a refrigerator now a basic provision. Few houses would have mud walls and thatched roofs, the symbol of bush life. If the junior officer was well cared for in his block of flats, the houses allocated to senior officers were generally large, comfortable and attractive. This is not to suggest that in the capital, just as in provincial HQ, there was no shortage of accommodation for the DO arriving on transfer. In the city there were clubs and meetings of societies actively interested in such things as local flora and fauna or culture or history. In the opinion of C.R. Niven, rich in Secretariat experience in his 30 years in Nigeria, 'in all good tropical capitals a botanical garden was a *sine qua non*.'[42] Unlike station life, where the club was the sole club, here clubs included the Polo or Gymkhana Club, the Yacht Club, the Nairobi, the Accra, etc.[43] A Swimming Club added to the recreational fare, and a posting to the Secretariat in Freetown, Accra, Lagos, or Dar es Salaam brought the additional pleasure of beaches and surf bathing, and the chance to go sailing at the weekend. Not only was there at least one cinema, there were probably occasional theatrical performances and an opportunity for indulging in amateur dramatics. Instead of being able to make up a tennis four if one were lucky in station, the Secretariat was a wonderful chance for the athletically minded DO at last to play the team games he had not enjoyed since coming down from the university, especially cricket and hockey. Here too might be the first golf course he had seen for years. And every colonial capital worth its name had a racecourse. Gradually restaurants came on the scene, both in hotels and as self-standing enterprises, perhaps imaginatively serving Chinese food, so that at last it was possible to talk about going out for a meal without meaning to a friend's house. In this cultural respect the settler areas of East and Central Africa were way ahead of West Africa. African cuisine was slow to make its mark, though in West Africa African nightclubs were active. Above all, unknown in the districts, there were shops – not the trading store of West Africa or the *duka* of East Africa, but real shops, like a butcher, a chemist, a bookshop, and post offices and banks in the plural. Imagine the joy of the DO's wife in actually being able to go out and have her hair done! D. Savill's uninhibited excitement at hearing that on returning from leave his posting would be to the Lagos Secretariat – 'I couldn't believe my ears' – is best understood in the context of it not only being promotion for him but 'it also meant some fun and normality' for his wife.[44]

Nevertheless, in the final analysis, however much many DOs determined to make the most of the posting and necessary experience of their Secretariat secondment, there stubbornly remained deep inside them the belief that this was not what they had joined the CAS for. Had it been a desk-job they wanted, would they not have applied to the Home Civil Service in the first instance and done it in comfort, pacing the cool corridors, rather than panting along the muggy verandahs of power? If the Secretariat progressively became what colonial administration was mainly all about in the 1960s, being an up-country DO still remained what the post-war cadet still dreamed of and wanted to be. The typical inner ambivalence of the DO was summed up by R.L. Findlay, who at the end of his service in Nigeria argued that, while the average DO would choose to be in charge of a division ('that, he would probably feel, was what he was really meant for'), there were many who, 'placing society and games or physical comforts high in their scale of values', would plump for the Secretariat option.[45] Reviewing his post-war spell in the Gold Coast before he left to join the Diplomatic Service, H. Brind had initially challenged 'the accepted belief that officers hated a stint in the Secretariat. ... Being healthy outdoor types, they preferred being with "their people" in the district than dealing with files in a city office', but by the time he finished his tour in the Accra Secretariat he was glad to return to district work, which he had left 'much against my will ... one had not joined the Colonial Service to sit in an office in the city.'[46] Against the trend, J.S. Champion frankly welcomed the chance of a re-posting to the Entebbe Secretariat, while it was his wife who was furious at having to leave the up-country station of Toro. But Champion, clearly on his way to a governorship, honestly (if in a minority) declared that out of all his postings in Uganda, the one he had enjoyed most was that of Acting Permanent Secretary in the Ministry of Health.[47]

Leaving the work attraction and job satisfaction to one side, it is to the social appeal and advantages of a Secretariat posting that one might pay more attention. Arriving in the Secretariat and being absorbed into its life, on and off duty, the newcomer DO quickly appreciated how different things were outside as well as inside the office. Gone – at least temporarily – were the days when the peak of the week's entertainment was perhaps dinner with the agricultural officer and his newly arrived wife, the woman education officer, and soil scientist visiting from provincial HQ; or the highlight of the month was either four and a half couples doing Scottish dancing at the club or a communal play reading, from shared, dog-eared texts, of *Macbeth* or, calling for no female parts, *Journey's End*. In the capital there were plenty of opportunities for amateur dramatics, and no longer was the WEO (Woman Education Officer) the only unattached female he might meet. The Secretariat was almost awash with single women, in Health and Education, as well as in the new post-war cadres of personal assistants, legal assistants and administrative assistants. 'As single girls of marriageable age,' noted D. Savill, 'they were much in demand socially and inevitably most soon married,'[48] often to a DO. The new phenomena of Red Cross and British Council representatives often turned out to be single women, a further bonus for the DO in the Secretariat. In the course of time, VSO and American Peace Corps volunteers began to appear on the social scene, often young women. Air travel in the 1950s meant that teenage daughters began to come out to join their parents in the holidays. 'We younger cadets,' recalled T.G. Askwith when he was posted to Nairobi, 'were constantly being entertained by the parents of unmarried daughters.'[49] Add the likely establishment of a university or an advanced education college with nearby a major library, and the proportion of unattached females soon began to lower the conventional disproportionate number of bachelor DOs. Here could be a powerful, if not much voiced, factor in the DO learning to look on the bright side of a posting to the Secretariat after all.

For the DO who in all sincerity regretted his time in the Secretariat because he lost touch with, and felt himself becoming estranged from, the 'ordinary African' of his up-country memory, with whom constant contact had been the daily thrust of his work, a valuable compensation was to hand. For the capital was the heartland of that newish phenomenon, one which the DO had barely encountered in the districts and rarely in any out-of-office context, namely the new African elite, still referred to in the 1950s literature as the 'educated African'. Serving in Accra before the war, J. Gutch was aware of the difficulties in trying to overcome the racial cleavage by giving 'mixed' parties.[50] But after the war Africanization of the civil service made it much easier for those who wanted to mix socially (still more among African males than with their womenfolk, especially in Muslim areas) to start such initiatives, for instance R. Sadleir's weekly teatime discussion group of young African civil servants in Dar es Salaam[51] or the Scrabble parties, boldly tried in Hausa or English, which met in the staff houses at Zaria's Institute of Administration, along with debating societies and cultural discussions which DOs helped to promote in several divisional HQ towns. Despite the number of Africans who, particularly from West Africa, had been trained in the UK and USA as lawyers, doctors and teachers, many of whom returned to reinforce the nationalist movements and become leading politicians, it was not until the DO found himself working alongside African civil servants on equal terms and in equal rank and living in the same part of the city that the social positions began to change gear, generally with mutual and lasting pleasure. Once again the more cosmopolitan nature of the capital as well as the larger numbers involved meant that it was a Secretariat posting that first enabled the DO to participate in such gatherings.

Whether the DO posted to the Secretariat decided to smile or sulk at his fate, from the point of view of those responsible for good administration there was no doubt that he would in the long run be a better DO for having learned at first hand how the central government worked and what its relations were with the provinces, right down to the district level. 'Some people,' P.D. McEntee mused on the typical DO's career, 'are definitely better at pushing files and not so good at practical field work.'[52] Until a DO had done a bit of both, neither the government nor he could tell where his forte lay. Experience of both was necessary to produce the best blend or single flavour. The good DO made certain that he consolidated the considerable advantages offered him in the complementary halves of his work towards his career development. One man's prose might be another's poetry.

With the DO's work done for the day, be it in station (Chapter 5), on tour (Chapter 6) or in the Secretariat (Chapter 7), it is relevant to give some consideration to what he did by way of relaxation from the burden of his duties at the end of the day. The DO's leisure hours could be as formative to the level of his performance as was the routine of his work.

CHAPTER 8

After the Day's Work

While the young cadet may well have had it dripped into him by his seniors on his first tour that 'a good DO is on duty 24 hours a day' and that 'the best DO is constantly accessible, by day or night, in the office or at his house', a state of such super-readiness was not predicated upon a regard for unbroken work. Saturday up to noon may have been an official working day for most of a DO's life and Sunday looked on as an opportunity to catch up with the rest of the week's work. Yet whatever the regular office hours were, the time from five o'clock to sunset – never a late hour in the tropics – and the quickly darkening evenings from 6.30 till bedtime, along with periods at the weekend, could legitimately be looked on as a likely break from the routine of scheduled work and as, unforeseen interruptions and self-imposed overtime apart, a time for leisure beyond the encompassing context of work. It is what the DO did after the day's work was done that is the focus of this chapter. 'Leisure' takes on a very different connotation when it relates to the lone DO in an outstation and to the bachelor DO in a small *boma* rather than to the lifestyle of the Whitehall civil servant who commutes 50 miles home to suburbia, with its regular menu of restaurants and theatres, cinemas and concerts, tennis and golf, and get-away weekends, all enabling the week's work and worries to be temporarily kept out of sight and mind.

It was precisely the capacity for self-sufficiency which was so purposely sought out by the CO in its preliminary evaluation of those applying to become a DO. CS lore is rich in its tales of the interest shown by interviewers in a candidate's athletic record, not because they expected him to play rugger on the Gold Coast or make up a rowing VIII on Lake Victoria, but as evidence of healthy and regular recreational activity as well, of course, as assumed leadership and respect-earning material. Emphasis was purposely placed on how the prospective DO might adjust to long hours of being alone, in station as well as when out on tour. How self-contained was he? How would he fill in his time when the office was closed for the day? How self-reliant was he? What were his hobbies? Was he robust enough in mind to live in, and with, loneliness, of being 'by himself' for hours at a time, day after day? Being a DO was going to be a sharply different context of living from that experienced by the typical applicant just graduated from the intense socialization of university or the camaraderie of the regimental mess. As E.K. Lumley was to find in inter-war Tanganyika, where in one of his up-country stations his sole recreation was to hit a tennis ball against the wall of his bungalow, 'in the lonely [sic] districts ... officers would serve spells of a year or even two years without speaking their own language except to themselves'.[1] A capacity to overcome was what the CO was looking for, not to survive physical danger but to avoid psychological decline. One of the most frank as well as most frightening admissions of the loneliness of the DO is found in the description by M. Milne of his first year in Southern Nigeria in 1938–39:

> Of all the adverse factors in an African colonial service career – climate, tropical diseases, absence from familiar cultural facilities, distance from family and friends, roughness of living conditions – the long spells I was forced to spend away on tour, away from my own kind, came to me as the greatest hardship of all. I was away on that tour for about three weeks and I experienced loneliness such as I'd never experienced before.[2]

There could be intellectual isolation as well as physical loneliness. 'Nguru was for me,' wrote R.T. Kerslake as he looked back on his posting to the sandy scrub of the Bornu sahel, 'a lonely place in spite of my meeting many people, because I had so little in common with them, and there was no one whom I could call a close friend.'[3] Quite unlike at home, where choice in making

friends was commonplace, a station of no more than half a dozen
government officers meant that it could be a matter of acquaintanceship rather than friendship, with people whom perhaps
one might not have met so intimately and so regularly in a job
in Britain – 'public *faute de mieux* rather than personal choice',
in the potentially explosive phrase of a DO's wife who shall not
be named. In the event, most DOs would prefer to endorse the
judgement of a DO in up-country Tanganyika, who maintained
that

> Paradoxically, I think its lack of amenities and its vulnerabilities
> were factors which helped to make Mahenge such a happy place. We
> all relied on each other for companionship and simple hospitality
> in each other's houses. We knew each other much better than was
> possible in larger stations, where people tended to form cliques and
> snobbery was rife. Everyone got to know everyone else, and even
> those who would probably not have become friends on a bigger
> station enjoyed each other's company.[4]

What impresses in post-colonial Britain is how many and how
close friendships made in small stations 40 to 50 years earlier
have continued.

The CO's focus on the potential DO's well being related to
his mental attitude as much as to his physical health. A candidate whose intellectual aptitude, character and administrative
competence were beyond doubt would be no good as a DO if he
could not handle the personal rigours of living up-country. His
performance might begin to crack if he found he was unable to
look after himself by creating his own ways of filling up his leisure
time. Living successfully in the bush was as much a matter of
mind as of physique. Introspective unhappiness and worry had
to be controlled no less than mosquitoes and malaria. Such a risk
was going to be amplified in conditions of palpable loneliness
and limited – on occasion minimal – living comforts, the whole
often exacerbated by the commonplace climate problems of heat
and humidity and an irritating insect life, let alone the phobia of
spiders and snakes from which many suffered. A sick officer, be
he mentally disenchanted or physically ill, was a casualty that
the CO was loath to risk. Nor were the facilities for treating a sick
DO in any way adequate. There were few doctors and few nurses,
maybe only a once-a-year visiting dentist. Up-country, the nearest hospital might be a day's journey away by car or, as was not

unusual in the 1950s, the nearest medical help up to a week away by horseback in those areas where there was as yet no road. The 'vital statistics' of those who had died in or been invalided out of the CAS in the early decades of the century remained a stark warning to the CO against appointing staff who might not be able to take the hardships, mental as well as physical, of life as a DO up-country. Hence the belief that a happy person who could take care of himself was on the way to remaining a healthy person.

In the life of the DO, such mental well being was inseparable from his ability to manage his leisure hours as well as those he successfully spent at work. 'I found that my cricket,' noted T. Harris, transferred to Dar es Salaam, 'was as effective an antidote to the cares and worries of state as trout fishing at Lushoto had been many years earlier.'[5] The DO often took his recreations seriously, and now and again his reputation in his hobby could lead to wider, even international, recognition. That his occupations at the end of the day's work were as important to him as what he had been doing for the rest of the day is apparent in the space devoted in composite Service memoirs to such themes as 'Off-Duty and Recreational Pursuits', 'Leisure Pursuits' and 'Fun and Games'.[6]

In the examination of the DO's art of relaxation after the day's work, an overriding distinction can usefully be made between the DO in the bush, usually when out on tour but still in the 1950s often in a one-man station, and the DO in station. If the opportunities for social recreation were limited in the latter, they may be said to have been virtually non-existent in the former. Hence his frequent recourse to walking round the village in the late afternoon, chatting to all and sundry and quickly learning the polite vernacular refusal to come and share the sunset meal. Climbing a near-by hill, often escorted by a crowd of schoolchildren, was another almost standard leisure activity indulged in by the DO on tour. Another might be to take one's gun and go shooting for guinea-fowl or francolin for the pot. Shooting game could also be a recreation for some DOs. Alternatively a DO might find the ultimate relaxation at the end of the day's tour in listening to records on his wind-up gramophone as he sat outside his tent. Occasionally it was possible to arrange a display of local dancing, or maybe witness one of the famous masquerade dances of Eastern Nigeria, or arrange a discussion of some cultural tradition. W. Stubbs used to take along a local story-teller in his touring entourage in Northern Rhodesia, and G. Sinclair found a performance of drumming the highlight of his touring in the Gold Coast.[7] Or the DO might be interested in asking some grey-beard to describe the coming of the Germans to the village or show him the site where their first DO had died and been buried, or narrate what happened on the day that the earth shook in the famous earthquake. There might even be ghost stories to swap, for several pre-1914 houses dating from the German occupation of the Togoland, the Cameroons and Tanganyika were said to be haunted. For many, early to bed was the prize relaxation when on tour. To take it further still, it could be argued that for the office-bound DO, getting out of the station on tour was in itself the sublime leisure activity. Exercise was the name of the game, often indulged in to an extent which might have troubled the CO interviewers.

In a small station, too, leisure activities might well resemble those enjoyed by the DO on tour, with perhaps a little more walk-ing round the station with his dog, a little fewer cultural gath-erings, and certainly no shooting for the pot within the station curtilage. Yet shooting and fishing by driving out of the station were often sports waiting for the keen hunting DO. 'In one way and another we have our relaxations,' A. Forward wrote about his posting to Bukedi. 'I have been fishing for trout on the northern slope of Mt. Elgon ... duck-shooting on Lake Lemwa ... and in the evenings I sometimes wander through the fields around Budraka looking for guinea fowl.'[8] Fishing was not always interpreted as a recreation by the locals. According to R.G. Syme, in one Gold Coast village the local people were so worried that their DO must be hungry when they saw him trying to catch fish that the next day the chief sent a string of girls to the rest-house, all bearing calabashes of fish on their heads.[9] A DO posted to a coastal station, like D. Bates at Bagamoyo, could enjoy a special bonus from the lone DO's traditional evening walk. 'In the evenings for exercise I used to walk along the strip of sand between the coconut palms and the sea,' though this idyll had to be timed so as to avoid his DC who often went for the same walk, 'not because he believed in exercise but because it made him feel, when he poured out his first whisky afterwards, as if he had enjoyed it. Walking, he once told me, took the place of soda.'[10]

Where the principal difference lay between recreation in the bush or a small station and that possible in a larger station was in the existence of hospitality by way of dinner parties in one another's houses, and the club. The dinner party, often the highlight of the week in station, was not the black-tie and embossed menu affair of Government House. It was the custom to invite others on the station to an evening at home, keeping the delicate social wheels well oiled and offering a pleasant relaxation. More likely than not, the guests would find the meal being served by their own servants waiting at table, on loan for the evening to one's hostess like some of the rather familiar crockery and cutlery. To quote I. Brook's impression of Western Nigeria, 'a small station is a very small place. There is no escape.'[11] Even if the club offered neutral ground, it was likely to be the same faces. Yet relaxation the dinner invitation nearly always was. Just occasionally a guest might be visiting the station from provincial HQ or beyond, bringing fresh news and ideas as well as the local gossip. As W. Bazley found in Uganda, 'one of the abiding problems in up-country Africa was the isolation and shortage of news'.[12]

For the studious DO, leisure hours could be welcomed as extra learning hours. The first-tour cadet, of course, had his compulsory examinations in law and government procedures to pass, and for him out-of-office hours provided a godsent opportunity. 'I had to spend most evenings studying for exams,' wrote J. Lewis-Barned of his time in Iringa, having given up bridge at the club after he had revoked when playing with the PC and his wife.[13] It is remarkable how many DOs, often prompted by the love of the court work they were doing, decided to read for the bar examinations during their time in Africa, and how many of them succeeded in such a dedicated objective, eating their dinners on leave and qualifying as a barrister while they were still a DO.

Sometimes a DO brought a hobby with him. Other times a hobby developed from within one of the interests of his work. A dedicated DO could soon find his hobby advancing from a pursuit to a passion. This was as true of outdoor hobbies, like gardening (A.T. Weatherhead's enthusiasm for rose-growing was famous throughout Northern Nigeria, despite the maxim that to plant roses was the surest way of being quickly transferred) or bird-watching or riding or hill-walking, as it was of those requiring books and copious note-taking, such as map-making or the study of local history or languages.

Frequently without a radio, and with a London newspaper reaching the station by airmail every two weeks or so (four to six weeks in the days before air communications), the DO quickly realized how isolated he was. Even his sense of calendar was unbalanced. 'This is the tempo,' wrote J.C. Cairns in Kilwa as he watched the rains give way to the cool season and then back to the small rains. 'The clock does not matter any more. The rains are what matter.'[14] In Numan Division, R.T. Kerslake tried to retain the newspaper reading schedule of his days in England. 'Breakfast on the verandah with Jocelyn, looking across the river Benue, was probably the pleasantest meal of the day, enhanced and prolonged to the full hour between 9 and 10 by *The Times* crossword of some two months' earlier date, tackled solemnly in correct sequence.'[15] For a weekly like *The Spectator* or *The Economist* to arrive a month late was not as disconcerting as to receive a daily newspaper weeks old, though many DOs had to adjust to skimming through the special Christmas magazines, complete with red-breasted robins and snowmen, crackers and carol singers, when with them it was nearer Easter than Yuletide and over 100° in the shade outside. As a result of being cut off from news in its standard sense, the DO could find himself becoming a very well-read person, possibly reading more novels in a year than he had ever read since his last school holidays. But even this recreation could be frustrating. To quote J.S. Smith in Nigeria, 'I spent a great many evenings alone, reading. This was a solitary sort of interest, since I found hardly anyone who cared to talk about books.'[16] A young ADO was luckier when he was posted to Bida, in Northern Nigeria, where his DO (whose bungalow was less than two minutes away) promptly had a telephone installed in the ADO's house, 'in case of emergency – of course – and to ask you about any *Times* crossword clue I can't manage or what you think of the latest Nevil Shute novel'.

What a club or a station meant for many DOs was, relaxed socializing apart, the opportunity to take part in sport. After all here was an interest to which, for whatever reason, the CO had consistently paid attention. Clubs were not as ubiquitous in Africa as the common perception of colonial society would have it. M.C. Atkinson recorded that only two of the seven stations in Western Nigeria to which he was posted between 1930 and 1949 had a club.[17] Here was a tennis court, possibly a golf course, for those to whom leisure time meant physical recreation. Furthermore a bigger station meant that it was likely to have a provincial school in it, with a chance to participate in a team game, such as hockey or cricket or football. For the DO to play games could be a bit of an obsession. In Northern Nigeria, polo was not only played to a high standard, but it also proved a first-class opportunity for the local elite and DOs to meet off duty, in the same way as fives was to follow in the aftermath of self-government (like golf in some other capitals), with the Premier a leading devotee. In Uganda W. Bazley committed the solecism of being seen by his DC carrying a pile of files out of the office at 5pm. 'Take those back to the office where they belong,' shouted the DC, 'and meet me at the tennis-court in half an hour.'[18] A.F. Bridges described the determined attempts to play outdoor games during Southern Nigeria's rainy season as 'a race every evening. One could see the rain-clouds somewhere over Benin as one changed, and it was a question whether one could get to the court and finish a game before the rain reached us'.[19] Unsurprisingly tennis rackets seldom lasted more than a few months. Five hundred miles further north, R.T. Kerslake took a more charitable view of the effect of the rainy season on recreation. 'When the rains came at last, Maiduguri seemed more bearable and it was cool enough to play tennis or squash.'[20]

Indoors, the club probably had a snooker table. A game of bridge was easily found, but there was no longer any reason for a DO to experience that nightmare of shame when, arriving as the fourth person on a small station, he had to admit that he did not know how to play bridge. Larger clubs, like those found in provincial HQs, widened the meaning of leisure considerably. Apart from more sports fixtures, evening activities could include Scottish dancing and Burns Night festivities. Moonlight picnics were popular recreations, as were 'progressive dinner parties', where each member provided one course at his house before the party moved on to the next house – and the next course. Most Residents and PCs ensured that their DOs came into HQ from their stations at Christmas. Following fashion down the years, ludo, mah-jong and Scrabble parties widened the number of guests who could enjoy an evening out with friends without the seriousness inherent in playing bridge, although in one station a group of young DOs once or twice unworthily wondered whether the DO's wife was not keeping a note of their weekly scores to help her husband compile their annual confidential reports. H. Phillips in Nyasaland and M. Fairlie in Swaziland were both able to indulge their passion for classical music by forming choral societies in the respective capitals.[21]

The fleshpots of the Secretariat have been set out in Chapter 7, including the enhanced opportunities for those sporting activities so dear to many DOs as well as the greater cultural leisure activities available in the capital. Inter-regional polo competitions and inter-colonial cricket matches, as well as race meetings, were among a colony's sporting fixtures in the capital.[22] To place Olympic oarsmen like T.G. Askwith in Kenya and DOs who had stroked the Cambridge boat like T.E. Letchworth in Northern Nigeria in a riverain posting was not always possible. On the other hand, DOs' lore in the north-east of Nigeria was rich in anecdotes about bullying Residents who sent out to the bush any DOs who declined to turn up for an evening on the polo field, followed by a rapid posting to a tsetse-ridden province where the noble sport could not be played.

While such sports were pre-eminently team games, there is one sporting pursuit that can be as much an individual as a team effort. This is mountaineering, a recreation in which the DO in Africa seems to have excelled. R.G. Turnbull, notable for his seven-league boots when he was PC up in Kenya's NFD, added to his reputation in Tanganyika as one who was never happier than when climbing mountains. Kenya gave P. Wyn-Harris, later to be a member of the 1933 Everest expedition, superb chances to improve his mountaineering techniques on Mount Kilimanjaro. He was the first to climb it since H. Mackinder 30 years earlier. In Uganda, both R. Posnett and A. Stuart were keen mountaineers, the former climbing the Portal Peaks of the Ruwenzori range and the latter, in a 'mood of melancholic male macho-mania' climbing the 12,000 Mount Elgon 'in a day to prove myself'.[23] In Uganda too was their mountaineering mentor, R. Bere, who as a DO climbed an astonishing number of African peaks between 1930 and 1960.[24] In Nigeria J.G. Wallace broke a long-standing local taboo by climbing Wase Rock, and R. Anderson climbed the three Obudu peaks, 'formidable by Nigerian standards, albeit hillocks by alpine norms'.[25] In the same region Mount Cameroon, West Africa's tallest peak, became an amateur's challenge for many DOs, including African ones on the Outward Bound courses at Man O'War Bay, as did Loitokitok on the north side of Mount Kilimanjaro.[26]

Most of the ways in which the DO spent his leisure hours after the day's work have so far taken the form of recreational and social relaxation, with the undertone of the imperative of good health in a climate where such a blessing did not come easily. But mental relaxation, in the necessary sense of the DO switching off from his 24-hour-a-day responsibilities, could also be derived from personal hobbies. Although stamp-collecting was cited by some candidates to explain what had aroused their interest in the CAS as a career, it was too cumbersome and the weather too unfriendly to make it an easy hobby to pursue while in Africa. Curiously perhaps, despite all the splendour of Africa's scenery (including the majesty of those very mountains discussed above) and the colourfulness of its peoples, fewer DOs than one might have imagined developed skills in drawing and painting. J.M. Blair was one of the few who did, at the age of 41 (why not, he asked himself, when Churchill had done the same at 40), 'using it as a Sunday refreshment after a hard week's work'.[27] More often than not, whether because of longer periods of uninterrupted time available to them or because of their more distanced eye on the landscape and the people, this art became the preserve of some DOs' wives, such as (in Nigeria alone) Caroline Sassoon, Rosemary Hollis and Patricia Morley, and in Tanganyika the wife of Z. Kingdon. Inevitably photography was a commonplace leisure activity, to the advantage of post-colonial museum collections. Comment has already been made on the huge amount of reading which DOs often had the time to undertake. R. Posnett reckoned that a box of books was a basic requirement of a safari kit.[28] On his first tour in Tanganyika G.D. Popplewell got through the whole of Charles Dickens, sent out to him by his parents,[29] while H.H. Marshall used to take out to Nigeria 50 new books each tour – 'how grateful I am to the Penguin Edition!'[30] On his first tour M. Milne averaged four hours a day reading novels in his lonely after-office hours.[31] The DO's reputation for being well read is manifest in the pan-African story about one DO who, angered by a nit-picking letter from his Resident, peppered his answer with a series of phrases from a dozen foreign languages, all taken from the multi-lingual label of an Angostura Bitters bottle. Another DO is said to have ended his furious minute to a self-styled intellectual PC with a punch-line row of Chinese characters copied from the Lyle's Golden Syrup advertisement, which he alleged was one of Confucius's maxims.

But what has been less noticed is the DO's literary accomplishments as a writer. Several DOs became novelists, the most celebrated being Joyce Cary, once a DO in Northern Nigeria, whose African novels contributed to his place in English literature. The novels by DOs like H. Best, I. Brook, K.A. Dobson, W. Fowler, A.C.G. Hastings and M. Kittermaster, to name but half a dozen, all have a place on any bookshelf of African novels. Even more prolific was the DO as a short-story writer, *Blackwood's Magazine* being a popular outlet for many of the best. Yet more numerous were DOs who loved to compose light verse. Sometimes doggerel, sometimes delightful, such verse was written by DOs for a number of reasons, often out of frustration with officialdom or in undergraduate-style amusement at the latest Secretariat circular. Now and again a DO published a collection of his verse, for instance K. Dewar and K.J. Bryant's *In Lightest Africa*, J.H.H. Rowland's *A Nosegay of Cacti*, and Luke Ubrative's (D. Savill) *Lyrics on Lagos*, or those included in M.C. Atkinson's three privately circulated *Nigerian Tales of the Colonial Era* volumes. Sometimes specimens turned up in the district office or tucked into some file. Several well-known poems became local ballads, such as the NFD 'DCs' Meeting, Isiolo 1946' from Kenya and the Nigerian song 'ADO Bende'. Here is an original and rewarding sidelight on the DO in Africa, which has still to be collected and evaluated.[32] Versification certainly ranked higher among the DO's leisure occupations than has hitherto been assumed.

For amateur anthropologists, linguists and historians (some of whom went on to earn professional recognition), the opportunities in the DO's work and the leisure hours that came his way offered an enviable researcher's bonus. Most territories could count on their official library shelves' historical accounts of the founding of the colony compiled by DOs of that era. Many of these were looked to as standard works of reference before African history began to become professionalized in the universities during the 1950s, often derived from a mixture of official sources and contemporary oral history. As many of their successors found, there was never any lack of source material to be uncovered and explored by the intellectually inquisitive DO: carbon manuscript copies of official reports from the DO in days before the office typewriter was in use, narrated folklore and proverbs, law and custom from the records of Native Courts, dance and ceremonial rituals, and language data unlimited. The well-known anthropologists G.I. Jones and C.K. Meek from Nigeria and J.H.M. Beattie from Uganda had all started their careers as DOs. Two other

Northern Nigerian DOs, B.E.B. Fagg and H. Sassoon, went on to make a name for themselves in the world of museums, while in Uganda E.C. Lanning so developed his research that he was elected a Fellow of the Society of Antiquaries. Realizing that his degree in medieval history was not going to be of immediate use in Tanganyika, M.W. Norris switched his leisure interest into Makonde art and carving, and put on an exhibition for the governor's visit to Newala.[33] In several territories DOs played a prominent part in helping to establish and contributing to what grew into respected academic journals in the 1930s, for example *Tanganyika Notes and Records*, *The Uganda Journal*, *The Nigerian Field*. A search of international journals like *Africa* (the International African Institute) and the *Journal of the Royal African Society* reveals how frequently contributions were accepted from DOs. After the war, the CO tapped into this proclivity of the DO to research and write by promoting two professional journals written largely by CS officers, *Corona*, the house magazine of the Colonial Service, and the *Journal of African Administration*, the house journal of the CO's African Studies Branch. If the pre-war DO at times felt he was intellectually starved, his post-war successor could easily find himself exposed to the happy buffet-like style of 'eat as much as you like' as his knowledge gained in the field was steadily sought after by those professionally engaged in the new discipline of the study of Africa, in the USA as well as the UK. The emergence of African Studies in the universities, both in Britain and the USA in the 1960s and in the new African universities, coinciding with the ending of the CAS as a career, meant that a number of DOs who retired early were able to build on their first-hand knowledge of Africa and become academics in their 'second' career.

Nor at the end of the day did the DO have to resort to exercise or intellectual occupations to give him the break from his work that he needed. Manual or practical hobbies could be as relaxing – for some, even more so – than the doggedly intellectual ones. Besides his sports prowess, R. Wainwright was known all over Kenya for his consuming interest in and gift for carpentry. He took out with him a complete set of carpentry tools and made all his own furniture. Later on he built a circular table out of 52 different Kenyan woods supplied by the forestry department and offered it to the Coryndon Museum in Nairobi.[34] Carpentry was also a hobby of J. Cooke in Lushoto, who was said to have specialized in coffee-tables. Inevitably the British DO found solace and relaxation in keeping a pet, frequently a dog but also a whole range of local fauna, including monkeys, duikers, and even a zebra, a cheetah and a baby leopard. From the Gold Coast, A.C. Russell went further still and sent 'ten consignments of live-stock' to Edinburgh Zoo between 1946 and 1957, containing one baboon, one chimpanzee, eight monkeys, and 50 birds.[35] His wife did not approve of his trying to collect snakes. They were mostly collected, under his guidance, by road labourers in his employ. One DO cricketing enthusiast, deprived of any hopes of a team in his small station, found relaxed consolation in tuning in to the BBC and keeping the scorebook for every ball of every Test match. Amateur mechanics were a godsend in any station, and the DO who could repair anything from a radio to a refrigerator rarely lacked for social invitations. Gardening was another hobby which offered plenty of scope though not always equalled by success. Finding his tumbledown bungalow in Ankpa in a state of complete neglect, J. Morley, with the help of prison labour and seeds sent out from home, set about transforming the garden over the next six months. So triumphant was the make-over that, with true DO realism, Morley feared that 'if my time is up here I should not be in the least surprised!'[36] A keen horticulturist ADO was known for taking all his pot-plants out on tour, carried by a line of porters, and another amazed his carriers and impressed his DO by his dexterity with a butterfly net in the bush.

Beyond the fact that the ability to relax at squash, requiring no opponent or team-mate, was an ideal recreation in a one-man station, actually building a squash court or laying out a golf course could also bring as much relaxation as eventually playing the game, as R. Posnett found in Silimani and J. Ransom learned in Handeni. Part of the latter's pleasure may have derived from his personal triumph in securing a grant to build the squash court by his innocent telegram to the High Court in Dar es Salaam: 'Please send £50 urgently required for court'.[37] At Mbarara the DO closed the gaol and converted it into a spacious open-air squash court. In Bauchi the cricketing enthusiast R.H. Wright set about beating ant-hills into a cricket pitch and turning out bats and wickets in the PWD workshop, though for the sake of both the pitch and the equipment only a tennis-ball was used.[38] Another cricketing DO, J.S. Smith, took a cricket ball on tour and then spent hours fashioning bats and stumps from the heavy forest trees so that he could organize his carriers into a team. All bowled under-arm, of course, the l.b.w. rule was ignored, and the score was kept by dropping stones into a tin. 'The last rule was that I retired after three balls.'[39]

Few DOs were bold enough, given the threat of constant re-posting and of a climate cruel to its tuning, to bring out a piano, but music-lovers made the most of their gramophone and at least one brought out a guitar as companion on lonely evenings. In Northern Nigeria a group of DOs combined their guitar (also a favourite leisure pursuit of J.K.R. Thorp in Kenya) and their voices into a madrigal group, while in Eastern Nigeria W.F.H. Newington recognized that his new ADO was going far (it was K. Blackburne, a future colonial governor) when he revealed that his hobbies were motor mechanics and playing the saxophone.[40] Yet statistically it would appear that for the average DO on an average station, always supposing such mediums could be found, his most regular form of leisure after the office closed and before the evening's drinks or dinner party was taking exercise, be it a sport or simply walking round the station. J.R. Bird's catalogue of all the sporting opportunities he was able to enjoy in his 20 years in Northern Nigeria, culminating in his launching a motor-club, with gymkhanas and moto-crosses,[41] is a telling testimony to the value set by DOs on recreation as the best way to relax after the day's work. And the point of that relaxation was of course to help him keep fit in a climate and conditions which did not immediately lend themselves to a state of either physical health or psychological poise. In the minatory words of the official *Nigerian Handbook* (1955 edition), 'The tendency to "slack" is great and, if indulged in, is apt to lend to nostalgia, tedium, isolation and over-indulgence in alcohol. The remedy for all that is vigorous exercise.'[42]

If the possibility of a breakdown in health never disappeared from the list of problems generated by the DO's work and quality of life, to the extent that throughout his career he was likely to continue to have his health (and even more that of his family) at the back if not often in the forefront of his mind, it must be made clear that conditions for the post-1930, and even more so for the post-1950, entry were immeasurably better than those faced by their predecessors. One DO of the 1930s recorded the irony of the reply from the Dar es Salaam Secretariat to his suggestion that the station at Kiberege should be moved back to its original more salubrious site. It was not, he was told, government policy to station its DOs in healthy places.[43] As relative as that comparison must be, the difference was nonetheless a real one. Two main reasons can be put forward to explain improvement.

In the first place there was the advance of anti-malarial drugs. Quinine had saved the life of many a DO, yet the dreaded blackwater fever from which so many of the deaths in pre-1920 West Africa occurred could sometimes be due to quinine over-dosing. A.C. Russell recorded his consternation when, catching malaria yet again on his sixth tour in the Gold Coast, the medical officer frankly told him that 'as I was having it so often, it was only a matter of time before I caught blackwater fever, which was almost always fatal'.[44] This was as late as 1940. The wartime mepacrine simplified the daily taking of an anti-malarial prophylactic, and when the paludrine pill became the preferred medicine in the late 1940s, as simple and as without side effects as taking a daily Vitamin C pill back in England, the main problem now facing the DO was to decide which moment of the day he was least likely to forget to take it. Yet in many areas the mosquito net remained essential in station as well as on tour.

In the second place, though arguably of at least equal importance as the curbing of malarial infection, was the progressive improvement in the standard of housing. Tile roofing rather than thatch, brick or concrete walls rather than mud, were a start. In many ways the turning point came with the arrival of the refrigerator in the mid-1930s and its distribution to DOs as a now standard item in the PWD furnished accommodation. For many years to come it could not be run off electricity up-country, but ran instead on kerosene. At last food could be kept safely for more than a day, free from rapid putrescence and, if one was lucky (unlike H. Mitchell in Sierra Leone), from pullulating ants, provided the refrigerators legs stood in water.[45] An iced beer, too, was no longer an hallucination. From over 30 years' experience in Nigeria and a sharp student of its history, C.R. Niven awarded the kerosene-powered fridge 'the invention that made the greatest difference to life in the tropics, after quinine'.[46] When electricity was installed, a healthier lifestyle became even more possible, with a piped water supply instead of water drawn from a well, and flushing toilets. Yet in Nigeria not even Government House had air-conditioning installed until the Queen's visit in 1956. By the mid-1950s it was goodbye to the moody but beloved pressure lamp, as it was too to the spine pad and the sola topi. Nothing brought home to the DO of the 1950s the long way he had come from the 1920s more cogently than a visit to the station cemetery to read the list of his predecessors who were buried there, a hundred times more likely to have died from illness than to have been killed in the course of duty.

In any consideration of the importance attaching to the maintenance of good health through the opportunities for recreation and relaxation after the stresses and pressures of the DO's daily life and work, the analyst must return to the biggest restorative of all: home leave, anything up to six months at a time, and the added bonus of the voyage there and back. Now and then the DO might spend a week or two of his leave in London's Hospital for Tropical Diseases, but in most cases simply being at home on leave was the best treatment any doctor could prescribe. For the bachelor DO, such a long leave was an opportunity to meet girls and unmarried women, both at a premium back in his upcountry station. As he departed on leave, J. Gutch, bachelor after several tours in the Gold Coast and one in Palestine, and now aged 33, reflected that it was time he got married. 'Leave in England would amount to little more than four months – a limited time in which to find the right partner and get engaged and married to her. So I had written ahead to two possible partners whom I had known in the past.'[47] In Northern Nigeria, the Resident's wife told one of her husband's young DOs off to Cambridge to attend the Second Devonshire Course to 'forget all that academic work, this is your chance to find a wife'.

Heather Dalton rationalized her study of the Colonial Service in the 1980s by pointing out how in DOs' memoirs 'there appeared to be little recognition of the part played by the wives or interest in their activities. ... Family and social life seemed sparsely recorded.'[48] It is to the DO's wife that we shall now turn, for too long the missing factor in DOs' memoirs.

CHAPTER 9

Through Female Eyes

On an epic journey across Africa from coast to coast shortly before the outbreak of the war, the writer Negley Farson, accompanied by his wife (gratefully acknowledged in the contemporary idiom of praise as 'better than any man') made the following note on 'success' in the Colonial Service as told to him in Uganda. The reflections were prompted by Farson's mentioning a fat-kneed DO in Kenya, a former Cambridge Blue, whom he described to his host as looking as if he were continuously suffering from sex starvation. 'Aye,' mused his Scottish host, 'either wanting a woman or trying to get rid of one. That's the trouble with a lot of the sahibs out here, but you can't rise in the Service unless you're regarded as SOUND. Evidence of being that is to have a wife to show that you're not after somebody else's wife.'[1] Writing 60 years later, from his memories of Northern Nigeria in the 1950s, A.T. Clark summed up his assessment of 'the DO and his wife' scenario in these terms: 'Colonial officials had to exercise patience before higher authority would allow their spouses to join them, and conflicting feelings might be aroused over sending weaker sexes or lonely singletons to hardship stations.'[2] One of the most rewarding breakthroughs in the literature on the DO in Africa did not come about until many years after that career was over. It was not until the 1980s that the post-modernist discipline of gender studies brought its focus to bear on what had hitherto been generically termed 'the life of the colonial wife'.

For most of its existence the DO cadres had been thought of in terms of an essentially – almost exclusively – British male institution. The life, including the climate, was generally looked on as, to quote the colleague's reception of a DO who brought his wife to Nigeria in 1925, 'Mrs Niven, this is no place for a White Woman.'[3] The CAS Britishness had begun to be diluted in the 1920s by its recruitment of a number of DOs from the Dominions. But the transformation of the fundamental male image of the CS did not take place to any marked extent until after the war. Up to then women members of the Colonial Service had been virtually confined to the Colonial Nursing Service, the Colonial Medical Service and the Education Service. How encouraging the postwar expansion figures were is shown by the recruitment figures for these three services. Between 1922 and 1943, only 83 women were offered posts in the Education Service and 72 in the Medical Service. The figures were far better for the Colonial Nursing Service, with its long history of service in Africa right back to the turn of the century (there were two nursing sisters at Lokoja, in Nigeria, in 1902), with over 2,000 nurses being recruited between the wars.[4] From 1942 to 1952, a further 1,400 nurses and over 600 female education officers were appointed.

The end of the war brought another stage in the catching-up process, when not only were women recruited as personal assistants for service in Africa,[5] but also became eligible for appointment to the Administrative Service. The scheme was announced in 1944, in a recruitment pamphlet headed 'Appointments of Women Administrative Posts in the Colonies', and was duly cautious over the fact that this new departure would be very much an experiment. To begin with, the new posts were styled assistant colonial secretary, later changed to woman assistant secretary, both titles emphasizing the Secretariat nature of the job and hence discounting any likelihood of an assignment to the provincial administration. The title also made it clear that the post carried none of the authority inherent in the office of DO, for the CO did not wish to arouse any African reaction against women exercising authority vis-à-vis the Native Administrations. The first two women administrative officers were posted to the Gambia, Mair Evans and Margaret Burness, both of them having been in temporary posts in the Home Civil Service. Out of the 1945 intake nine went to Tanganyika. Nearly 80 such women were posted to eight of the African territories between 1944 and

1960, as many as half going to Tanganyika and another 25 to Nigeria. In Tanganyika Joyce Sugar is believed to have been the first female DO,[6] and in Nigeria Margaret Stubbs was the first woman administrative officer posted to a province.[7] It goes without saying that many WAOs and PAs married DOs.

For all the importance of the work of women in the Colonial Service, the established parameters of the present study require the concentration of the spotlight on, as it were, the women who married into the CAS, the wives of the DOs whose identity and image form the focus of this book. Despite the valuable but very occasional memoir by a DO's wife written before 1950, such as the classic contributions by Constance Larymore of Northern Nigeria in the 1900s and by Laura Boyle of the Gold Coast in the 1920s,[8] accounts (let alone adequate acknowledgement) of the role they played in the work of their DO husbands, besides the revelation of their own reflections, reactions and lives, went unnoticed and untold for too long. To quote the opinion of one of the 1980s' pioneers of the need to study 'the tales of colonial women', to use her own subtitle, 'in marrying into the Service a woman married a job, a way of life, a privilege, and a deprivation'.[9] The DO's wife was, to place her in the influential conceptualization of the feminist scholars of the 1980s, 'an incorporated wife', 'that condition of wifehood in a range of settings [army, police, Oxbridge colleges and African colonies] where the social character ascribed to a woman is an intimate function of her husband's occupational identity and culture'.[10] In other words Helen Sellar was not so much Helen Sellar as Mrs DO. This image of invisibility received a further correction, once again in the same influential decade for the righting of the record of 'the colonial wife', the 1980s, in the publication of Helen Callaway's influential study of European women in colonial Nigeria, in which she analysed the restrictions on women's lives as wives dependent on their husbands' rank within the imperial culture and then deleted from the subsequent memoirs.[11] In the event, and perhaps still unknown to the mould-breaking feminist CS researchers of the 1980s, what surprises the researcher 20 years on is the quantity and the quality of memoirs written by DOs' wives, most of which are still unpublished but many of them quoted throughout this book as primary data, along with the increasing number of DOs' wives' memoirs now being published. As one of the still unpublished memoir writers, Diana Bridges, lamented of her time in Nigeria in the early

1930s, 'for years I wondered why my Resident's wife (or for that matter any Resident's wife in S. Nigeria) had never written a book successor to Constance Larymore's'.[12]

Further evidence of the secondary place so wrongly allocated to memoirs by DOs' wives is seen in the fact that some of those now published were actually written many years earlier but then put aside, for instance Noël Rowling's recollections of Nigeria in the 1930s and 1940s, which did not appear until 1982, and Laura Boyle's account of the Gold Coast in the 1920s, not published until 1968. An examination of the contents of *Corona*, the Colonial Service's house journal (1949–62), suggests that the magazine encouraged many wives to try their hand at writing articles about their life in the colonies. Fortunately the new generation of DO memoirs was at least getting as far as a nod in the right direction by chapter titles such as 'The Part Played by Women in Tanganyika', with its premise that 'no account of life in the East African Colonies would be complete without mention being made of the part played by wives and single women', and 'The Helpmeets and Their Appendages'.[13] Recent additions to the genre of DO memoirs have now and again tended towards over-domesticity, but many have, of course, started life being written for the families who would otherwise never have known what it was like to be a DO – even what a DO was.

It is helpful to contextualize the position of the DO's wife in Africa. To begin with, there were markedly fewer married men in their 20s than there would be in other comparable hierarchical institutions, such as big business, universities and the Home Civil Service. While statistics have not been computed, a glance at any territorial *Staff List* at once reveals the preponderance of bachelors among DOs, both in their first five years of service and, especially before 1950, even into their 30s and 40s. The official attitude of the CO and of the respective governments was, in short, to discourage administrative officers from being married while they were still ADOs (say up to seven years' service) and positively to prevent them from getting married as cadets, i.e. in their first three years. As late as 1952 the CO policy, while superficially that of encouraging officers to have their wives and children with them, was qualified by warnings that 'where restrictions exist, they are imposed largely in the interests of the officer himself', 'lack of suitable accommodation for a married man', and that 'the need for extensive travelling in undeveloped

areas' – one of the highlights of the recruitment literature and
the aspiration of every one applying to be a DO – 'may make it
undesirable that an officer should be accompanied by his wife
and family'.[14] The acute housing shortage in East and Central
Africa in the 1950s was blamed for the regulation that no cadet
could take his wife and family out without prior permission from
the governor, and such permission would not be given in the first
six months. In Tanganyika permission would not be given until
a cadet had passed his law and language examinations, probably
towards the end of his second year. West Africa was even stricter.
A blanket embargo existed: 'Except in the case of senior officers,
all officers must obtain permission from the government on each
occasion for their wives to accompany them or join them.' One
more regulation remained in force to the end: 'Women officers
may be, and in general are, required to resign on marriage.' A
further caution on the lack of suitable education facilities for children and the thinly spread medical care available, in addition to
warnings about the high cost of living in Africa, were calculated
to make the ADO think further, and then think yet again, about
the wisdom of getting married … for a few years yet.

In Nigeria cadets were for a time in the 1930s required to sign
a subsidiary contract that they would not marry during their
first three years of service.[15] This, it was argued, was to allow
the Secretariat to make its dispositions on the posting of officers
without being constrained by whether a station had accommodation fit for a wife or whether a married ADO could be expected
to undertake all the touring required in that division. The fear
of resentment about the possible influence that being married
might bring to bear on a DO getting a 'better' station while
another (bachelor) DO was sent out to a bush station, or that of
marriage entitling a man to superior accommodation while his
bachelor colleague had to move to a worse house, was a constant
worry over postings, though, if the truth be told, more in the
perception than in the practice. In Tanganyika after the war, if
a DO married a woman already resident in the country and the
wedding took place in Tanganyika, the DO would have to pay
his wife's passage home when they went on their first leave.[16] For
many years no married DO was ever allowed to be posted to the
Northern Frontier District, thought by many to be the plum posting for DOs and an essential part of their training for service in
Kenya. R. Wainwright asked for his requisite stint in the north

to coincide with the year when his wife Bridget would be preoc-
cupied in England with the new baby.[17] When K. Blackburne,
who had enjoyed his five years in Nigeria in the 1930s, decided
to get married, he applied for one of two vacancies announced in
Cyprus, since he was worried that his bride, with a permanent
stiff leg, might slip on the bush paths when they were out on tour.
This was accepted, but within a fortnight of sailing he was told
he was being sent to Palestine, to take the place of a DO whom
the CO had discovered was a Jew who had changed his name by
deed-poll.[18]

Although the 'immoral relations' Crewe Circulars of 1909 on
concubinage[19] were withdrawn in 1934, 'sleeping dictionaries',
as the colonial vocabulary had it, continued to be part of some
DOs' *ménage* right up to the war, and now and then beyond.
Arriving in the Gold Coast in 1946, J.S. Lawson in due course
moved into the old DC's cliff-top bungalow, where he discovered
that 'a discreetly covered stair led from below the bungalow to
the master-bedroom'.[20] Trekking in Sierra Leone in 1954, H.E.
Mitchell found that 'the charming custom' of the chief sending
a young woman to the rest-house to serve the DO's pleasure
among the other 'dash' or traditional gifts of food and hospitality offered to important visitors 'had fallen into disuse, partly as
so many officers had their wives with them and partly because
improved communications caused details of the private lives of
both bachelors and married men to become common knowledge
throughout the country'.[21] Many pre-war DOs never married or
else married late. Elspeth Huxley drew a sad portrait of the PC
whom she met in Sierra Leone, still a bachelor, whose thoughts of
the comforts of matrimony in retirement gradually faded until,
finally destroyed, he bought a new car instead and planned
to drive back to England as slowly as possible.[22] E.K. Lumley
wondered whether he had got it all wrong in Tanganyika. He
waited until he had 16 years' service so that he could offer his
bride 'reasonably good conditions of life', but on their first tour
together they were posted to Kikerege, known among DOs as one
of Tanganyika's 'penal settlements' with an uninhabitable house
populated by hundreds of rats and thousands of *siafu* or soldier
ants. His wife was bitten by a tsetse fly on the first day of their
first trek.[23]

It was the Second World War that accelerated the normaliza-
tion of the young DO's life in so far as getting married and having

his wife and family out with him in Africa was concerned. Most of those who joined between 1945 and 1950 were already five years older than the standard joining age of 23.[24] Many of these ex-servicemen were already married. By virtue of their previous positions of authority during their war service, they were less likely to be amenable to some of the pre-war colonial conventions about being accompanied by their wives. In 1944 the total ban on any children accompanying their parents to West Africa was lifted. War in North Africa and in South East Asia helped develop new medicines and new attitudes to keeping healthy, which were bound to have an effect on the long-held belief that Africa, in particular West Africa, was not the place for men to expose their family to. I. Brook's experience in Western Nigeria is representative of many of the immediately post-war ADO cohorts. His Resident, who had spent his whole service on the Coast as a bachelor, found considerable difficulty 'in accepting the idea of ADOs who are married and have children', and other colleagues accused Brook and his wife of 'criminal irresponsibility' in risking having children in Warri.[25] He and Annette, who had come out from England to join her husband in Warri when she was, to the Resident's horror, already pregnant, had no better luck in their next province, where the Resident's wife 'told me peremptorily that she didn't approve of men who brought their children out to the Coast'.[26] Across in Eastern Nigeria in 1951, F. Ashworth had to wait for the arrival of a more sympathetic Resident to secure permission for his wife to join him, after getting married just a month before he took up his job. Even then Dorothy had only three days' notice to catch the ship.[27] As late as 1954 P.H. Burkinshaw was told by the chief commissioner, on his third attempt to have his wife come out from England to join him, that he could not really see why Burkinshaw needed to travel down to Freetown to meet her. 'While permission was granted, he could not resist commenting that he did not know what young women were coming to nowadays. Surely, if my wife had travelled out some two and a half thousand miles on her own she could manage the last two hundred unescorted.'[28]

Yet the arrival on the scene of this kind of older newcomer, wife and all, and the departure of the bachelor old brigade did mark the end of an era. More and more ADOs on their first to fourth tours were married. In a long enumeration of what the advent of wives among DOs (and no longer only senior officers) meant, Beverley Gartrell concluded that it not only provided 'socially legitimate sexual relationships' but also represented 'the home culture and its moral standards. Their [women's] function in this regard was to assist in the maintenance of the "dignity" seen as politically essential. They helped to maintain "civilised standards".'[29] In the 1930s matrimony had been largely regarded by colonial governors, as one DO saw it, 'in the same light as prohibition, communism and cat-worship – conditions known to prevail in certain impossible areas of the planet but unworthy of rational discussion.'[30] The belief that DOs, and unquestionably ADOs, made better DOs when they were unencumbered by matrimonial baggage was manifest in the rule, rigidly enforced in Northern Rhodesia up to the 1950s, that a cadet could not marry for his first three years. This veto was rationalized, as R. Short saw it, thus: 'It had a purpose, though it was a hard one. It was to force cadets to bury themselves in wherever they found themselves, and if they were lucky, come to love the people where they lived.'[31] There were also the practical hurdles, such as the absence of suitable accommodation for a wife in stations where the ADO was likely to serve – and to want to serve – and personal finances.[32]

It was not the post-war DOs alone who brought about the change of mind (rather than of heart) in colonial governors. The wives, too, were maybe a little older and certainly maturer after five years in wartime Britain, sometimes in war-service themselves. Why should 'roughing it in Africa' be any worse than surviving in war-battered Britain and then in a still rationed and war-stained country? As the wife of an older man but still only a cadet in rank, Carol Christian pointed to another source of stubborn refusal by the post-war generation of CS wives to take no for an answer, the wives themselves: 'Given the privations of post-war Britain, women either could not, or would not, leave their babies behind.'[33] Moving with her husband from India to Accra in 1948, Carol Pickering was sensitive to the contrast: 'Before the war few white children were ever seen on the Gold Coast', and for a European woman to give birth there was 'unheard of'.[34] Those who dared to bring their children out for the summer holidays were expected to pay the fare themselves. Nevertheless it is undeniable that, for all the initial coolness, both official and personal, encountered by married ADOs bringing their wife out on their first tour – cooler still if children came too – the war years created, according to Charles Allen, 'an altogether new model of colonial wife'.[35] Not only was she freed from many of the constraints that had inhibited women in the pre-war years, but she also had 'more positive ideas about her role, and was often determined to do as much as a woman is allowed to do in an African male society', involving herself in local women's organizations and in schools.

It must not be supposed that the changes brought about by wartime cured all the problems that a DO and his wife had to face. Some were inherent in the career. Among these was the fundamental one of what used to be known as courtship. Did the longer-than-usual bachelor DO, who would likely have married in his 20s had he been working in Britain, have sufficient time on his home leave to meet, attract and build a mutually respecting relationship with a woman which both might confidently expect to be able to withstand the strains of married life in Africa? Might the imminence of the end of a four to six months' leave be a spur to an accelerated wedding or would the happiness of meeting survive the apartness for another two or three years? How would that attractive girl, whom the DO on leave had danced with and dined and taken to the theatre, adjust to a life in the bush having none of these things, a life which he knew he loved – but what about her? As one such DO on leave from Nigeria mused as he partied with a group of girls back at Cambridge, 'which of these lovely and intelligent beauties would share my rest-house this minute? Perhaps not with me, but with anyone?!'[36] 'With glorious ignorance,' admitted A.N. Skinner of meeting, when on leave, a girl, an architectural student in London, whom he believed was destined to be the love of his life, 'I thought I could win her with long factual accounts of life in the colonies, the adventure of carrying the White Man's Burden, and the privilege of being the helpmeet of one carrying that burden.' 'Needless to say,' he concluded, 'I didn't have much success and I bear the scars to this day.'[37] In her reflections on why a woman went out to a colonial life, Joan Alexander accepts that a DO on leave who wished to get married could hardly be blamed for embroidering the truth a little: 'Did the small bungalow with a wilting garden become a palace? Did the arduous journeys into bush become comfortable safaris? Very likely!'[38] Not all that unusually, B.L. Jacobs found his stiffest opposition in the parents of his wife-to-be, who objected to her being taken off to Uganda and probably never seeing her again.[39] But as single women began to enter the civil service in

Africa, the bachelor DO was often able to meet potential wives over a longer period than just a few months' leave at home.

When the amber light turned to a happy green, the next question was when the wedding should take place. Was there still time before the DO had to return to Africa? N.C. McClintock married at the very end of his leave, and he and his wife went straight from the church to board M.V. *Aureol* in Liverpool, en route for Lagos, followed by a 1,300-mile journey by car to Bornu, stopping off en route with friends 'for Pam to meet and be inspected by'; while J. Lewis-Barned's wedding also took place on the last day of his leave, followed by a honeymoon with Ursula across France and Italy and then from Venice to Dar es Salaam.[40] Ann Davidson married her husband when he was half way through the 1948–49 Devonshire Course at Oxford and she accompanied him to the lectures – 'I shall take my own notes, which will be a help to Ron, as he found it very difficult last term.' There were no fewer than 30 cadets' wives, and she was inspired by a talk from Lady Bourdillon on the role of women in the Colonial Service: 'I felt for the first time *I* had something to contribute to the Colonial Service.' She also learned a lot from the wives of DOs on the concurrent Second Devonshire Course: 'they have poise and always look immaculate'.[41]

The problem of how women with a career at home might be able to continue with it if they wished, as a DO's wife in Africa, did not exist to anything like the degree it attained 40 years later, by which time 'dual postings' had become a headache for personnel and postings officers in the Diplomatic Service and other overseas organizations – as well as for couples in Britain trying to juggle professional and domestic priorities. In any case there was still a ban in some territories on wives being allowed to take a paid job, as June Knowles found when she applied to join a CO scheme for training women in social work but was refused when she told them that she was engaged to a DO from Kenya attending the Oxford Devonshire Course.[42] What chance, DOs wondered at some of their colleagues' wives, did they have of indulging their career in the African bush when they were, to cite actual cases, a trained ballet dancer, an opera singer or a concert pianist? A qualified doctor or a trained teacher would naturally find it easier to use her talents, but still not necessarily on the basis of paid employment. Others helped their husbands in secretarial work, in which many had been trained and for which there was a growing demand in provincial HQs, but to employ an expatriate's wife in a full-time job carried political snags which few governments wished to face. So the DO's wife's interest sometimes switched from a profession to a hobby, making a name for herself as a Guider, like Eileen Sandford in Nigeria, or as an artist, like Rosemary Hollis and Caroline Sassoon, also in Northern Nigeria, or as a writer, like Erika Berry in Nigeria and June Knowles in Kenya. The last-named nevertheless warned that this was not 'a recommended pursuit for administration wives' in Kenya and accordingly wrote her books under her maiden name, just as Mrs Buxton never revealed in her *Kenya Days* that her husband was a DC.[43] There was of course no likelihood of any wife accomplished in domestic science being unable to practise her art, be it in cookery, dressmaking, running-up curtains or whatever. Some of the most popular cookbooks in East and West Africa were written by DOs' wives. Yet few brides-to-be back in Britain escaped the feeling of 'But what am I going to do all day?'

It was the long morning alone that irked at first. Olive Champion spoke for many in her reaction to becoming a DO's wife in Mbala in 1946: 'At first I found living in tropical suburbia rather strange, and it was difficult to occupy the mornings.' Working what were known as 'Eastern Province hours', where it was hotter than elsewhere in Uganda, meant that her husband was away in the office from 7.30 to 1.30 without a break, and it was usually 3.30 before they sat down to lunch and the tedious 'morning' was over.[44] In Abuja, where the Weatherheads were the only Europeans in the 1930s (60 years later Abuja was the capital of Nigeria), Sylvia was delighted that her husband was home by 12.30 each day, for 'she found the mornings rather long'.[45] Joan Sharwood-Smith, marrying a senior DO in Minna, was dismayed when her worried husband told a policeman to shadow her whenever she left the house by herself (inside their old-fashioned, tin-roofed bungalow the temperature was well over 100°), but soon found that 'trying to elude "my" policeman was an excellent cure for boredom'.[46] Peggy Watt was warned by friends at home that marrying a Northern Nigerian DO would mean she would quickly become bored, 'confined to the house with no transport all day long and with not even a telephone', so they gave her a small handloom to occupy herself with. She quickly discovered that 'something is always cropping up and I never seem to get enough time'. Few scarves were ever produced.[47] Looking back,

The DO's wife presents the cup at a sports meeting

Elizabeth Warren's verdict on life in Azare was short and shared: 'What did I do? Memory fails – I must have kept myself busy. ... I played with my child, and was scrupulous about water, hygiene and malarial precautions. I made my own frocks, read, did a little confidential typing, cut the men's hair, and went for a walk morning and evening. ... The political situation passed me by. It was a man's world.'[48] The DO was able to immerse himself in this man's world and draw greater interest and pleasure from it than his wife probably could. 'In retrospect,' A.N. Skinner recorded at the end of his time as a DO, 'I have a strong suspicion that Pip did not think much of being a DO's wife in Nigeria.' Besides all the usual problems of accommodation and health, servants and cleanliness, language and fewer of what one had been brought up to look on as standard amenities at home, there was too, he concluded in his case, the additional problem of 'marrying a husband who already had two full-time mates, work and polo'.[49]

One of the most widely read books on the life of a DO's wife was Emily Bradley's *Dearest Priscilla*, published in 1950, with its catching subtitle of 'Letters to the Wife of a Colonial Civil Servant'. She set out to answer all those seemingly small yet personally major questions that every DO's bride-to-be was likely to be asking herself when she learned that she was off to live in Africa.

The book could also serve as an antidote to any myths that friends and family at home might anxiously circulate. Helpfully if dauntingly, a whole appendix was devoted to 31 suggested items for a wife to take out on her first tour.[50] It certainly made a less alarming list than that sent to Joan Sharwood-Smith by the wife of one of her husband's friends when they were married in 1939: 'Be sure to buy 12 cotton dresses, 6 semi-evening dresses, and a dozen of every form of underwear – and don't forget to bring mosquito boots.'[51] In 17 chapters Emily Bradley sought to set out 'all you ought to know about marrying an Empire Builder', on practical matters like servants, what to wear when, race relations, committees, children, health and living off one's pay. The chapter 'The Silent Partner' had a particular relevance to the DO's wife, with its advice that on social occasions 'one must never, never talk shop to senior administrative officers who hold the keys to transfers, promotions, leaves', and its wisdom that 'one of the most difficult lessons for a wife to learn is to know a great deal of what is going on and then forget it'.[52] Being alone was in no way the same thing as loneliness. 'To cultivate a private interest or indulge in a hobby,' such as gardening or keeping a diary, 'will make you the envy of your friends at home who can hardly remember, or perhaps have never known, the real leisure unharassed by chores.' Her conclusion was unexceptionable: 'It is whether you are happy or not that matters, to you and to your husband and to everybody in your world.'[53] If today's reader accepts the fact that this is the language of the 1940s applied to the social context of the same period, the text can be of primary importance in helping to understand the situation of the DO's wife as she headed for the double unknown, what a DO's life was and what part she would be playing in it.

If the young ADO could revel in the unexpectedness of his new life, one which he had chosen, happily prepared to devote all his time to his work, his wife had a different set of introductory experiences to handle, and, excitement apart, with an arguably different motivation. There was the voyage out, for example, not necessarily the cruise style which tourists could expect from the Castle line. In 1951 the CO was still content to put the cadets headed for East Africa in three-berth cabins, wives having to share one and husbands the other, rather than booking three twin-cabins – unless one paid the difference oneself. 'This policy,' commented one of the cadets, M. Longford, 'certainly had a detrimental effect on the way in which some of the wives settled in their new way of life.'[54] As for some of the bride's female passengers, she was likely to be exposed to grim tales and dire warnings of what to expect – and what not to expect – as a DO's wife. As Alys Reece noted in 1936, on what turned out to be a historic total of 11 years in Kenya's notoriously male NFD, 'There were plenty of people on the boat to let me know something of what lay ahead, and their versions could at no point be reconciled with the life Gerald [her husband] had described', in his courtship propaganda. 'The veteran Colonial Service wives on board had time enough to put the new girl in the picture and see to it that she did not arrive at her remote paradise with any illusions. ... Long before the voyage was finished I had to dodge them to avoid a bad attack of nerves, and some of the glory had gone out of the voyage.'[55]

Then there was the journey up-country following disembarkation, an unforgettable trip but one to be endured rather than enjoyed. For one reason or another (a local crisis, a senior's inhumanity) not every wife was met by her husband – another huge shock to an already over-shocked system. Next came the first sight of the house, yet another event replete with shock-potential. 'To Sylvia's credit,' acknowledged D. Barton on their arrival in an up-country station in Tanganyika, 'she did not burst into tears when she saw her new home. In truth, it was very bush, two round rooms 12–15 feet in diameter, joined by an enclosed verandah.'[56] 'In my first day in Kano,' wrote Noël Rowling, with her husband already gone to the office, 'I was left at 7a.m. to cope with a strange house, strange houseboys, and innumerable trunks and packing cases to be opened and the contents sorted.' She found life in Kano dull, although morning coffee, games and occasional dinner parties relieved the boredom. But she was excited by it all, 'excited by the country, excited by learning Hausa, and excited to discuss the country and his work with my husband'. Never having been a career woman (on graduating she taught only because she sought independence), she declared that she looked on her marriage as her job.[57] In northern Kenya June Knowles (true, a PC's daughter) spent her first two weeks, while her husband was out on safari, determinedly doing up their house, a one-roomed mud hut. 'I whitewashed all the walls inside and out, lined the thatched roof with fine matting to stop the dust, stained the floors green, hung some old chintz curtains on the windows, turned the piano crate into a wash stand, and even managed to construct a garage to shelter our car', all with the assistance of the tribal policemen and without tools or even nails.[58] In Kenya too, T.G. Askwith, whose courtship of a girl in Kisumu, 500 miles away from his station, was difficult enough, decided not to ask Pat what she thought of their home when they finally reached Taveta, consisting of just three rooms (one of them the DO's office) but with an unrivalled view over two cemeteries and a thousand acres of sisal. Level-voicedly she simply asked 'Are we there?'[59] Carol Pickering, coming from India, was distinctly unimpressed by the house they were allocated in Accra – 'like all its neighbours, a meat safe on stilts' because of the wire netting all round to keep out mosquitoes and other insects – but in Tanganyika Lorna Hall immediately fell in love with their first house in 1932, 'a large mud-walled guard-house, whitewashed in parts and thatched, with a cool verandah'.[60]

Seeing her home for the first time also meant for the new wife meeting the servants. Most DOs' wives coming out had been born in the inter-war years and were likely to have known how to engage with domestic staff in their grandparents' if not their parents' house, but the possibility of culture shock over having to manage household staff was often still present. But one cadet's wife, Morag Hollis, seemed more worried on the way out to Tanganyika about how she was going to cope without all the electrical gadgets to which she had been used in Scotland, than handling domestic servants.[61] For a wife to inherit her formerly bachelor husband's personal staff was a well-known hurdle for all three parties to negotiate, though a success story frequently ensued. 'Don't be upset if Ali [her husband's steward and former batman] walks out on you,' Peggy Watt was advised by another wife when she arrived in Lagos. When she repeated the warning to her husband, Leith's reply was 'If Ali goes, so do you!'[62] In Marsabit Alys Reece soon discovered that her husband's servants, whom he had had throughout his bachelor years, 'had the customary nomadic contempt for women and regarded themselves as Gerald's servants, not mine'.[63] She learned that the one thing a wife should never do in a small CS community was to criticize another person's servants. 'This would be to hit the man's master in the most sensitive part of his *amour-propre* because it is questioning his judgement of men.'[64] In Northern Rhodesia Ann Davidson soon settled into the domestic routine, commenting that 'it always surprises and pleases me when I realise how essential a woman's presence is in a house, however good the servants'.[65]

With the journey accomplished, house seen and servants met, the new wife, like her husband earlier, now had to meet the station and learn who was who in the community where she was probably going to spend the next year or so. When Eileen Sandford, never having been out of England before, reached Bauchi in 1949, her husband's first words of advice on meeting the station was 'the golden rule' never to play bridge, which he believed could so easily divide a station.[66] In a provincial HQ, the bride would, at her first formal dinner at the Residency, invariably be invited to sit on the Resident's right. It was not always easy for the younger wife who married an older DO and thus became, though maybe in her 20s while others were in their 30s or 40s, the senior lady of the station.[67]

The last, and lasting, aspect of this induction into being a DO's wife was her relationship to his work: to share in his enthusiasms and his frustrations and to act as his inspiration and his support without causing his colleagues (and their wives) ever to begin to suspect that she was either an interference in or an influence on their work and repute. Such diplomacy, never easy at any time, was even more delicate when, as was often the case, like Noël Rowling, a wife 'did quite a lot of typing in my two-fingered method and typed all the confidential reports and secret letters'.[68] ADOs probably accepted that their DO's wife inevitably knew quite a lot about them from her husband, but what had to be avoided was any impression like that of W.F.H. Newington, who felt that 'the DO's wife at Ahoada was a very strong character, who tended to interfere in the running of the Division'.[69] Posted as ADO Office in Zaria, it did not take J.H. Smith long to learn that 'one of the problems of working with the Resident was the opportunities it provided, unless one was careful, of working for his wife' – in this case 'a rather status-conscious Bostonian'.[70] It was hard for the DO's wife when she was a close friend of the wife of another officer who happened to be at the centre of a row with her husband. On the other hand, many ADOs took the sympathetic line towards their senior's wife, of 'Poor Mary, I don't know how she stands him'.

Certainly the DO's wife was a classic example of 'the incorporated wife', who in marrying a man also married a Service and was expected to perform her role in the same way as he was – with the difference that he was paid for it and she was not. In her willy-nilly capacity as the first lady of the station, it was to the DO's wife that other wives were wont to turn in moments of uncertainty or anxiety. It was she who was expected to take the lead in official functions and to advise on dress and matters of protocol. Of major support to her husband was entertaining for lunch or dinner, both socially on the station and officially for colleagues passing through on tour. The account by Ann Davidson of the first party she and her husband gave in Northern Rhodesia is a wealth of dining-room detail, recognizable by many a DO's wife but still an elaborate riot of what could be done with a handful of servants and an enthusiastic hostess.[71] But it was often pot luck as much as a party, for every officer passing through the Divisional HQ would invariably call on the DO and quite likely be asked back home for a meal. During his period as PC Northern Province in Kenya, R. Wainwright calculated that he and his wife Bridget entertained 1,142 people to lunch and 932 to dinner, and put up 355 people for overnight stays, 'all on a minute entertainment allowance'.[72] Across in Nigeria, the exasperated wife of a senior DO, Diana Bridges, listed the hospitality they had had to offer, so as to correct 'the impressions which we know some visiting parties from Home have formed, that all administrative officers live in luxury and comfort and that Residents have a large entertainment allowance'.[73] P. Dennis was among the embarrassed guests at a dinner given by the PC whose wife, known for her 'somewhat frugal attitude towards entertaining', declared that she could not understand why people complained about the cost of living in the Gold Coast when the meal they were about to eat had cost her no more than five pence a head.[74] When H. Mitchell reached his new station in Sierra Leone, 'the DC was busy, and his wife came to the public jetty to meet me' and took him home for lunch.[75] P.H. Burkinshaw, also in Sierra Leone, realized how lucky he was to have had Eileen Watson as his DO's wife: 'she took young recruits under her wing and made her own contribution to the process of their training'.[76]

Even when some stations up-country began to have a catering rest-house (CRH), a sort of mini-motel, which considerably reduced the number of guests the DO and his wife were expected to put up overnight, the DO's wife sometimes oversaw the running of it and took the brunt of travellers' comments in its complaints book, à la 'I was brought up that brains should be used in the head and not served up for breakfast'. Christmas was a challenging time, especially in the Residency. In Yola the Watts gave a dance for some 80 people in 1956, with the kitchen looking 'like a battlefield', in Leith's words, after Peggy and her cook had made 50lbs of ham, 50 meringues and trussed the turkeys. For the governor's visit she organized pre-lunch drinks for 12 DOs and their wives, followed by a pre-dinner drinks party for 130 people and dinner for another dozen. 'To an outsider,' she guessed, 'the constant round of social events must appear a waste of time. It was anything but that, for once the pleasantries were over little but "shop" was ever discussed. Few governors had gained that posting for nothing, and points could be raised over a drink and a meal which might otherwise never reach a conference table.' Her verdict was that 'wives of officers could make or mar their husbands' careers'.[77] Fresh from his London vantage point in the CO, R. Terrell came to the conclusion that successful entertaining of a husband's colleagues was looked on as a yardstick of her success as a DO's wife. 'The woman who could not entertain, could not manage a cook or steward and was not interested in gossip, did not really fit into the scene.'[78]

Beyond 'incorporation', as it were, one of the DO's wife's gifts was the speed with which she could transform any colonial house into a home. When, as often happened, she preceded him on leave or returned to the colony after he had, her artistry (or the temporary lack of it) was equally noticeable. Received by his Resident, L.T. Chubb, in Port Harcourt, K.V. Arrowsmith noticed how 'the absence of Mrs Chubb was evidenced by the barrenness of the room, which was plainly furnished with poor furniture', a single carpet, one or two *passe-partout* prints on the walls, no cushions for the chairs, and no curtains for the long French windows.[79] It was, however, a matter of unresolved debate among wives, especially mothers, whether the house should be furnished as far as possible as it would have been in Britain (the Surbiton syndrome), or whether pictures and carpets, cushion covers and curtain material might imaginatively include African paintings, colours and designs. Some wives, R. Sadlier observed in Dar es Salaam, 'especially those brought up in the country, took to life in the bush stations like a duck to water, creating beautiful homes and gardens, playing tennis and golf, going on safari or busying themselves teaching local girls to knit or sew. Others, used to urban life in Europe or America, found this existence incredibly boring and had to resort to coffee mornings or bridge parties enlivened by gin and tonics.'[80] Yet there was a mental limit to the number of coffee or bridge parties with the same people that one could continue to enjoy, and the DO's wife was aware that, with the ever-present possibility of time hanging heavy on her hands when her husband was away in the office from 7am to 3pm, what she needed above all was the ability, once the domestic supervision was over, to make her own leisure, perhaps learning the language, reading and writing, or in 'good works' such as the Red Cross and Girl Guides.

A list of what commitments DOs' wives took on at one time or another, mostly unpaid, would result in a very long and varied roll-call. In this she was in the same position as her husband had been, and learned to master, in his first tours as a bachelor ADO. For his wife the art could be of translating 'nothing to do' into 'so much to do' until her husband came home for a late lunch and they could enjoy together a game of tennis or an evening walk. Trevor and Jocelyn Kerslake felt that 'life began again at 4p.m.', with a cup of tea and a change into casual clothes for a walk or a ride, and, in Diana Bridges' routine, 'the evening walk and shooting for the pot' at five o'clock made the best moment of the day.[81] Yet narrating how well her husband was keeping in Nyasaland, because 'like most of the men out here, he is perfectly happy and is living as he would choose to live and doing the work he loves to do', Ann Davidson was right when she observed that 'it is the wives who have to *create* a life for themselves'.[82] Kathleen McCall spoke for many when she confessed that 'it was this interminable waiting for one's husband which so many of the Colonial Service wives found most trying'[83] – nearly always, of course, with no possible way of communicating a delay.

There was more than a touch of irony in the common colonial jest that the most important book of reference in the DO's wife's library was the *Staff List*, which gave every officer's salary, listed in strict order of seniority. This allowed both of them to locate the visitors in the framework of government. To know who was who in the government was of value in welcoming them and getting to know them against a subsequent meeting or a shared station in the years ahead. The CAS was a tight-knit as well as a friendly service, and during most DOs' careers they had probably met and knew by sight all but 10 per cent or so of their colleagues … whom they certainly knew by name!

But the problem of not knowing how to fill the day could pale before another problem inherent in the life of a DO and his wife:

their feelings about the continuous moves to which they were subjected. For him there was the excitement of a new job, new challenges, new opportunities to look forward to. For her there was the upheaval of packing up and moving, leaving the garden she may have proudly planted and friends made on the station, followed on arrival by the need to lengthen or shorten curtains and to work out how their belongings could fit into a smaller house or fill a larger one, in either case built to a different design. In Eastern Nigeria Cecillie Swaisland and her husband moved into ten houses on eight stations within one 18-month tour.[84] Mrs G.D. Popplewell experienced three transfers in the first six months, one of them to a one-man station (i.e. they were the sole residents) and another to Ufip, 'probably the most cut-off district' in Tanganyika, along with a ghastly safari from the hospital at Tabora carrying their new child.[85] It could be the peremptoriness and short notice given of a transfer that was as upsetting as the move itself. In 1944 Elnor Russell and her husband were posted to Bauchi and finally finished unpacking on a Tuesday. On Wednesday a note was received from the Resident, telling them they 'must leave for Azare not later than 'Saturday. We started straight off packing up again, glass, china, curtains, books and all.'[86] In Kenyan lore, one DO's wife unwittingly let the side down when she and her husband were moved into a terrible house. The governor, on tour in the area, courteously walked across to the hut to pay his respects to the new bride. 'I think the house is delightful,' she is said to have gushed, when the PC had spent months in arguing with the Secretariat that it was uninhabitable and ought to be condemned.[87]

Amid all the taxing, at times traumatic, introductions to the life of being a DO's wife, one experience remained which seemed to be as exciting as it was novel. This was accompanying one's husband out on tour, that undertaking which he seemed happy to talk about all the time and which had filled his stories about life in Africa when they had first met back home. Many safaris, as A.L.K. Liddle found in Kenya in 1957, meant leaving one's wife and family behind on the station. 'The lot of the Colonial Service wife could be very a lonely one, and quite often was. Exceptionally, if a safari was likely to be based in one centre, my family came too,' including the baby in her cot fitted into the back of his long-wheel-base Land Rover.[88] In Tanganyika what worried J.A. Golding was how his wife on their first night on tour would take to sleeping in the bush to the sound of grunting lions, but she told him next morning that she was more worried that he might wake with a start and blow both their feet off with the loaded shotgun he kept beside him.[89] W.F.H. Newington, who had declared that taking a wife out to a place like Nigeria could prove a trial for both parties, promptly took his bride out on trek within 48 hours of their arrival in station.[90] By contrast J. Lewis-Barned, married on the very last day of his leave, stayed in station most of the time to allow Ursula to settle in to station life before the upheaval of safari.[91] For Yvonne Fox in Northern Rhodesia, with four children it was out of the question to accompany her husband on tour. 'There were times,' she conceded, 'when the even tenor of our lives became a little monotonous, as I never had the opportunity of getting away on trek.'[92] Before motherhood, she had been able to immerse herself in touring in the Gold Coast. 'Though I never grew enthusiastic about early rising, I loved the excitement of the days on trek. ... The attraction of trekking in the rains lay in the fact that one tended to visit out-of-the-way places. Instead of keeping to the roads, one travelled along bush paths, passing isolated compounds and finding new country.' By the end of the trek 'I felt in a position to write a couple of volumes on "dawn"!'[93]

Understandably, going out on tour did not afford every wife all the pleasure it always seemed to hold for her husband. Violet Cragg, who spent most of her first five years trekking with her husband through half of the Northern Provinces of Nigeria well before the war, wrote a long account of her often horrifying privations, but, fortunately for the sake of possible brides-to-be, it was never published. On her first trek they were allowed 18 carriers and two rickshaw boys (this was in the late 1920s). At Baro, on the Niger, 'the hundreds of insects were so bad at night that we cannot have the lamp close enough to read or work, but I just managed to do a little knitting'.[94] After a few days, on one of which she completed a 19-mile trek, she felt 'I shall be glad to have food again that does not smell or taste of smoke.' Things got worse when she ran out of paper and could write no more. On the next tour (they were required to tour four divisions in four months, mapping and surveying), when her husband asked her to think of all the travelling allowance that was accruing, at two shillings (10p) per day, in return for all the 'unpleasantness', Violet Cragg reflected as she plodded through the rain forest that this presumably meant she could look forward to lunch at the

Trocadero and theatre afterwards.[95] When her husband rode into one village, a group of young boys screamed with fear. Yes, they explained, of course they had seen a white man before, but never a horse. Her verdict on such touring was that no one could possibly conceive what trekking meant. Providentially, Violet Cragg had by now taken up sketching.

Thirty years later, and still in Northern Nigeria, Rosemary Hollis found a greater problem with the psychological loneliness than the physical discomforts: 'I found myself alone in an alien world, abandoned in the midst of the unknown and paralysed by a feeling of fear, of vague apprehension ... not fear of anything specific but just a terrible sense of something malign working against me.'[96] Mrs Shipp in Tanganyika was glad to learn that it was not her responsibility to work out what was needed on safari. 'I soon learned not to fuss and put things out.'[97] The household staff knew best what was wanted and what was not. She reckoned that foot safari was infinitely more enjoyable than a safari by car. 'It is by far the best fun, and camping in a tent is the ideal night in the wilds. One does want to be sure of foot and good health to honestly enjoy it, and during the rains a little sun is necessary when one gets into camp to dry one's damp clothes and bedding.'[98] Mrs T. Scrivenor also preferred to tour on foot rather than lorry in Tanganyika, once one got over 'the first, agonizing stiffness'.[99] The best compensation of touring lay in sleeping outside, lying back and looking at the huge stars through the mosquito net, and the early evening, sitting outside on deck chairs, enjoying a long cool drink and having a chat with her husband back from his inspections in the village – 'the perfect moment of the day'. That was also the greatest attraction of touring for Mavis Stone in Uganda, sitting round a camp fire lit at sunset and often watching a display of local drumming and dancing.[100] For a wife, that was when touring showed what living in Africa was all about.

Health worries were often more of a strain on a wife than on her husband, especially where children were concerned. Often a medical officer would be 100 miles from a station, a hospital three times that distance. In the whole of Tanganyika in the 1930s, there was one government dentist, supported by a handful of itinerant Asian dental assistants. When Yvonne Fox needed urgent dental treatment in the northern Gold Coast, it took her 11½ hours to cover the 338-mile journey from Tamale to Kumasi, but the compensation (apart from the relief from pain) was that this, her first visit to a town in a whole year, allowed her to go shopping.[101] The dramatic suddenness of children's illnesses made the worrying all the worse. 'One day,' recorded K.G. Bradley in Northern Rhodesia, 'our baby suddenly swelled up like a little Michelin-tyre man and ran a temperature of 106° ... with no doctor within a hundred miles.'[102] Fortunately it turned out to be case of eating green mangoes, but it gave the DO and his wife such a scare that they set about clearing a landing-strip for emergencies. Marrying at the end of his second tour, K.V. Arrowsmith's wife Angela had acute pain in her stomach three weeks after arrival. Fearing appendicitis (a frequent anxiety among DOs in the bush), they made an agonizing overnight journey by launch through the creeks to Port Harcourt, where, a day later, the appendix was removed.[103] On leave, Rosemary Hollis's husband had to have lessons from a sister-tutor friend of hers at Bristol Royal Infirmary on how to give his wife a course of injections, since there would be no doctor to do this within 100 miles of the station to which they were going.[104]

The approach of home leave could be a much larger landmark in a wife's tour than in her husband's. Sometimes he could be so engrossed in the progress of a pet project that he wished he had another six months before going home. For his wife, the allure was sharper. Whatever the downside of life in Britain, it was likely to be less wearing on the spirit than trying to run a home in Africa. With more time to reflect and maybe more time to regret, for a wife family separation could be brought home more meaningfully than for her husband. In emotional as well as physical terms, the climate could, in the judgement of I. Brook, be 'benign in comparison to its effects on women'.[105] What had Emily Bradley warned in her compendium for the newcomer colonial bride? 'Your skin dries, your hair grows lank, and you will lose most of your colour. Your looks will deteriorate inevitably, but so do everyone else's, and a very short time in a temperate climate repairs all the damage.'[106] At the same time, might there not be a frisson of anxiety about how one would fit in at home after being away so long? That was certainly in Lorna Hall's mind as she approached the end of her first tour in Tanganyika: 'What will it be like in England?'[107] With mail arriving only once a month and newspapers being four to six weeks out of date, it would be hard to keep up with the interests of people at home, be it in new plays or novels, former friends, holidays abroad, clothes and fashions, the news of the day. Another tingle of leave anxiety must have been in the Longfords' minds as they determined to plan their second leave from Tanganyika so as to avoid the disaster of the first, when each mother meticulously counted up every minute they had spent with her and accused her rival of getting more than her fair share.[108]

Against this demanding life of the DO's wife up-country, it is of no surprise that a husband's posting to the Secretariat could be more enthusiastically welcomed by her than by him on their return from leave. Now, with a posting to the Secretariat, dreamed-of amenities which had been unknown up-country turned out to be not luxuries but daily fare. Gone was the need to work out how much sugar and salt, soap and lavatory paper, tinned foods, beer and spirits and soda sparklets would be needed for the next six months and order them to be sent up by rail and road from Lagos or Nairobi, always with the fear at the back of one's mind that some basic item had been forgotten and hence foregone for months to come. There would be people for her to meet, other wives and single women, opportunities to participate in picnics and parties and pantomimes, to go to the cinema or join in amateur dramatics, to go to church and to find a library with books. No more birthdays either, like Ann Davidson's in Magomero: 'Ron went off [on tour] on Monday morning and I have spoken to no-one since, and it is most unlikely that I shall until his return on Saturday.'[109] Loneliness was frequently complemented by homesickness, a condition to which the up-country DO's new wife might initially be very prone. Posted to the Secretariat, at last the wife could go shopping rather than to the market, at large stores just like at home, a long way removed from Nigeria in the 1930s when 'women could not buy clothes locally and had to bring out an adequate supply from home or have them sent by post'.[110] And, joy of joys for the long-suffering wife, to be able to have one's hair properly done – no more cutting by a valiant friend or attempts at a home perm.

Whether up-country or in the Secretariat, there still remained the frequent question of whether a wife should go home on leave before her husband, probably to see the children settle into school or to be there for their holidays, or again whether she ought not to come out again until after her husband had returned from leave, because of the uncertainty of their new accommodation and even a last-minute alteration to his posting. Such was the awful experience of T. Harris's wife as she sailed for Dar es Salaam with a six-month-old daughter, only to learn on arrival that he had been posted to the other side of the country.[111] For many wives, too, it was frequently a matter of 'the awful choice, which comes sooner or later, between husband and children, the saddest and most controversial part of the lot of the colonial officer'.[112] What is more, the need for a family to keep two households or pay boarding school fees was an extra strain on the DO's limited salary. Life apart was once more life alone, which the bachelor DO thought he had finished with. 'Annette had gone home,' wrote I. Brook in Western Nigeria, 'and the house had grown larger. The end of the day in the office had become the end of the day. In the evening the bottle came more smoothly to the hand, its neck slim and comforting.'[113] It is not hard to endorse Beverley Gartrell's conclusion on what she calls 'the enclave life of colonial wives': 'what is surprising is that so many women were able to summon the inner resources to cope with the demands and to live successful lives within the constraints of their situation.'[114] The DO's wife had certainly come a long way from that portrayed by Yvonne Fox, with her experience of being a DO's wife in the Gold Coast, Northern Rhodesia and Nigeria between 1939 and 1959, hopefully endowed with stick-by-your-man values and living up to her tongue-in-cheek prescription of 'As long as you were quiet, did not get ill, nor interfere with your husband's work, you were pretty welcome – if you kept him happy and in good form, it was worth the Government's while to have you out there.' Yet even in 1950, as Carol Christian ruefully reflected in Eastern Nigeria when her husband decided to turn down a place on the Second Devonshire Course, 'in Service terms the family continued to be something of a drawback'.[115]

The post-colonial memoir of the 1980s and beyond, written perhaps a quarter of a century after retirement, presents a far more positive image of the DO's wife and her role in the life of a DO. If there was little opportunity to exercise the prerogatives of what is today called 'the working wife' (a concept as outmoded as 'the working class' yet just as meaningful a shorthand), there was seldom a lack of interesting, worthwhile and frequently quite unusual challenges to meet and things to do. Like so many DOs in their memoirs, wives also often conclude that 'I loved every moment of the day' and 'it was an experience I would not have missed for anything'. They tend to use the descriptive term 'paradise' in their recollections more than their husbands do. Always allowing for the DO's wife who, doubtless with good enough reason, just could not wait for him to pack up and retire from Africa, the more common sentiment, despite the trials and tribulations, the problems and the pain inherent in a colonial life, follows the lines of that expressed by Anna, the wife of a Kenyan DO, P. Osborne: 'Nearly half a century later the house, the *kitetes* [mongooses], safari, and our African servants come back like old friends. Yet again I hear the smash and withdrawal of the waves [at Malindi], breaking on the silver sand.'[116] Effectively but sincerely, Noël Rowling's recollections of life as the husband of a DO in Northern Nigeria in 1933 to 1953 have recourse to a single, repeated sentence to introduce virtually every paragraph in the closing pages of her last chapter: 'I remember, I remember'.[117]

Yet might there be one significant difference in the pleasure content of service in Africa discernible in the DO's memory when set against that of his wife? While both parties could be glad to have had the experience, there is a suggestion that the women were generally happier than the men were to leave and return to life in Britain. In Heather Dalton's analysis of the experiences of some two dozen wives who had lived in the Gold Coast, carried out to right the wrong in Colonial Service memoirs of the absence of recognition of the part played by wives where 'domestic, family and social life seemed sparsely recorded', the weight of her evidence is that yes, it had been a bonus in their life but, no, they would not want to do it again.[118] Nor must one dismiss those wives who, like R. Terrell's, felt they had been snatched away from the comforts of life in London and found nothing in common with her husband's friends ('they were my colleagues but not hers'). In his sad judgement, 'I was in Africa and she could never be.'[119] For just one moment Faith Dennis thought she might after all be more important than her DO husband when a crowd started to shout 'White Man out', before one man rushed up to the car and said 'Not you, madam, White Woman stay', and turned to the noisy crowd to explain 'She be teacher'.[120] And what of those wives who married their DO husband after, following decolonization and loss of career, he had once been a DO? Were they, one wonders, glad or sad not to have had the African experience? At least we have one such DO's view: 'If only we had met in the 1950s – she would have been such a wonderful District Officer's wife.'[121]

The virtual absence of women from the mainstream accounts of the work and life of the DO in Africa until the post-colonial surge of published memoirs since the 1980s gives rise to a final reflection on the DO's career as shared by and seen by his wife. Given the new richness of memoirs by DO's wives, how few other wives have written memoirs of like calibre in situations where their husband has had, by virtue of his office, inevitably and invariably to take centre stage? Some diplomats' wives and some political/presidential wives apart, the answer is few. Certainly not the wives of home civil servants, of military officers, of professors or company chairmen, 'incorporated' as their wives frequently were. Emily Bradley was bold enough to write *Dearest Priscilla* as a sort of *vade mecum* for a DO's bride. But once she had become a wife and with a few years' seniority under the belt, it would have been well nigh impossible for her to draw up a definitive job description of a DO's wife based on what she had actually done among 'all the things that went with the job'. Reading what is today growing into a welcome, complementary mini-library of memoirs (not all published yet) by and about DO's wives – though, regrettably, not as yet enough from the children of DO families who spent their younger days in Africa, along the lines of Jean Campbell Bruce-Austin's 'Impressions of a Teenager' in the Cameroons in 1947[122] – it can be argued that what inspired them to write such graphic and informative accounts is that they were, by the nature of their husband's work, profoundly integrated into his career performance, to an extent not always encountered in other professions. It was a degree of involvement – not interference – in what he did and how he did it not easily matched in any other career. Almost uniquely, too, and unlike the majority of careers in the twenty-first century, the career of being a DO was never anything other than an exclusively male opportunity. The outcome is that our understanding of the life and work of the DO in Africa, the focus of this study, is immeasurably enhanced by this additional and critical resource of the record as seen through female eyes.

PART III. ALL CHANGE

CHAPTER 10

The District Officer and Decolonization

As imperial historians look back on the period covered
in this study of the last generations of District Officers in Africa, the inter-war cadres of 1930 onwards and
the post-war cohorts of 1946–66, and see the speed with which
a hitherto major career in government for British – and some
Commonwealth – graduates came to an end, inevitably they put
one question to that penultimate generation (1946–54) of DOs.
'When did you realize that you had embarked on a career which
would be terminated before you reached the compulsory retiring
age of 55?'

Had the question of when Africa would be independent been
put to the inter-war generations, the answer would likely have
been, 'Certainly not in my lifetime, probably not in my son's,
possibly in a hundred years', a response accompanied by a wave
of the hand over a vast swathe of underdeveloped country and
a nod towards the abysmally low levels of secondary, let alone
tertiary, education and the virtual void of Africans appointed to
any government post of control. Even the most liberal-minded
DOs would have had to concede the remoteness of anything
like early African self-government, as he was confronted with
the considered policy statements of the Secretary of State for
the Colonies on the eve of the Second World War, who made it
clear that in encouraging African colonies to stand on their own
feet, the spread of freedom would be a slow process: 'It may take

generations, or even centuries, for the peoples in some parts of the Colonial Empire to achieve self-government.'[1] That was in 1938. There could be little doubt that, up to 1939, self-government was a matter of indefinite time ahead. The DO was going to be in Africa, and needed, for many years to come.

It is when that critical question is put to the last generation of career (permanent and pensionable) DOs, those who joined in the decade following the end of the war and before the Colonial Service was ultimately reconstructed into a non-pensionable and contract Overseas Civil Service, that the answer assumes a more realistic relevance. Given that the average cadet applying in 1946–50 had behind him a university degree, as well as, in nine cases out of ten, several years of wartime service, responsibility and general alertness to the international scene, it is inconceivable that he was not only aware that Britain – and the world – was going to be a very different place after the war but that he was not also cognizant of the fact that the British Empire, which he had learned about with pride and admiration at school in the 1930s, was already eroding. The fall of Hong Kong in 1941 and of Malaya and Singapore in 1942 might be written off as primarily military defeats, but the impact in local minds and the grant of independence to India in 1947 and to Ceylon and Palestine in 1948 rendered the future direction clear to all but the wilfully blind. Over half the once-dependent empire was now independent. In the face of post-war nationalism in the colonies – the traditional American and now the new UN anti-colonialism – it could no longer be a question of 'whether' self-government, but simply of 'when', even 'how soon'. By 1947 the Colonial Office, too, the would-be DO's new master, was redefining HMG's African policy, from one of 'trusteeship' in the 1930s and then of 'partnership' in the 1940s to that of 'development' so as to 'bring forward the African territories to self-governing responsibility within the Commonwealth'. In such a programme 'the key to success lies in the development of an efficient, democratic system of local government'.[2] The classic policy of indirect rule and Native Authorities was out; democratic local government structures and councils were in. The DO was still essential, but now he had a fresh mandate, to implement the new policy at all levels. District administration was to give way to district development.

What is surprising to historians 50 years later is how few of the 1946–50 DO intakes seem either to have asked the interviewing officials in the CO, or to have been worried by any negative answer, whether they might expect a full career ahead of them in the CS. As to the CO raising the issue themselves, that was a recruiting non-starter in the CS manpower-starved 1940s. To an extent this may reflect no more than the fact that for ex-servicemen, whether their university education had been interrupted by the war or had just lapsed, the fact that they were being offered a good job there and then was what counted. Those who knew a little more about the Indian model (and many had been there during the war) realized that, while political devolution had been implemented in the 1920s and self-government accepted in 1935, independence had still not come about for another 12 years beyond that agreement. A programme of African independence would surely take longer yet. Furthermore, even if West Africa was more advanced than elsewhere in Africa in political and educated manpower terms (the first two African DOs had been appointed only in 1942, whereas India had been recruiting Indian DOs since the 1860s), in settler East and Central Africa any timetable for independence was probably going to be 25–30 years in the making, time enough to see the new DO's career out.

The DO, newly arrived in the territory, found a stronger optimism that a full career lay ahead of him than the discreet reticence of the CO interviewers. Sir John Macpherson asked one of the 1951 cadets how long a career he thought he had before him. When he replied 'A certain five years, a probable ten, and a lucky fifteen', the governor-general said, 'My boy, you have thirty years or more ahead of you. My own son is coming into the Service next year.'[3] In Uganda B.L. Jacobs recalled the chief secretary stating in 1957 (five years before independence) that it was 'inconceivable' that Uganda would become independent within the next 25 years.[4] The CO sent P. Stigger out as a DO to Tanganyika in 1958, three years before it became independent and 12 years short of the CO interviewer's estimate of 1970, while the last two cadets allocated to Nyasaland took up their appointment in 1961 (three years before independence), having attended the Overseas Service course, without the question of length of career being mentioned at all at their interviews.[5] As it happened, the African timetables became rapidly foreshortened, even after a Cabinet meeting at Chequers in 1959 concluded that East Africa would not be ready for independence until the 1970s, with Kenya not until 1975.[6] Even the United Nations took a similar view, its Trust

Territory Visiting Mission of 1954 thinking in terms of another 20 years for Tanganyika under British tutelage. So maybe this was not the time, in the late 1940s, for the new DO, keen to get on with his career after five years or so of interruption or postponement, to worry too much. After all, it looked as if there would always be other African colonies to transfer to, and after them the Pacific, should independence come earlier to his territory than expected. Even the significance of the riots in Accra in 1948 was not immediately grasped. As one DO there wrote, 'At the time nobody could have known that the 28th February would mark the beginning of a movement to end colonial rule throughout Africa.'[7] As it was, the whole of colonial Africa, all 14 territories, achieved independence between 1957 and 1968. By then, none of the post-war DOs had any more than 22 years' service to his name.

The principal question for the post-war DO is not, then, how long he expected to be a DO when he joined, but rather in what ways was his work changed by the nascent political party activity and the phased advance to independence. It was, as he was already learning, palpably more than K.G. Bradley's rather glib recruiting reassurance of 1955 that 'the objective of the nationalists has been self-government, and as that has been our objective too, there has never been any conflict of principle. Such difficulties as there have been have arisen from the question of timing.'[8] If anti-colonial nationalism rarely if ever featured as a factor in the work of the pre-war DO, it soon became, however varying in degree in different places at different times, the most conspicuous and compelling influence on his work and a fact of life which he now needed to take into careful consideration in nearly every one of his administrative decisions. To cite Bradley again, 'To the simple-minded administrator, politics are apt at first to be an irrelevant and obstructive nonsense and politicians anathema'[9] – not a recipe for a successful DO to adopt in the 1950s. He soon encountered the new political party cadres, though as it turned out 'political' trouble did not start immediately, as many of the older DOs had feared, with ex-servicemen angrily returning to their villages after not only war service in India and Burma but also having witnessed the vociferous 'Quit India' movement. 'They seemed an obvious focus for political agitation,' surmised R. Bere in Uganda, 'but actually settled down well.'[10]

But the administrative alarm-bell word 'trouble' was now linked with political discontent and impatience and no longer just taxation, corruption or lack of development. As J.H. Smith observed in the emergent political party scene of Northern Nigeria, 'politicians and parties did not so much drive the process of achieving representative government as emerge from it'.[11] The emirs and chiefs did not take the politicians all that seriously, seeing them more as a nuisance to their own role than to colonial rule. Many of the party activists were well known to or well guessed by the DO, people who had been at loggerheads with the Native Authority or blamed it for their dismissal. To quote Bere again, 'most of their followers were men with a grievance and little real stature'.[12] Sometimes they also included some of the better-educated young men who felt that their chance of merited advancement was stifled by their elders. The African aphorism of respect being given to old age (and hence wisdom in worldly matters) was often one of the first casualties of politics. At the local level, nationalism was now more and more interpreted as getting rid of the DO – after all, who else was it who always seemed to say 'no'? 'The common man knows the DO to be a valuable friend,' thought B. Nightingale of his work as one of the last DOs appointed to Northern Nigeria, 'but he also knows that the DO must be the first to go if his country is to claim before the world that it is a nation managing its own affairs.'[13] Such tensions could turn nasty for the DO at a public meeting as well as in the office. This was particularly so when political protest led to violation of peace and disobedience of the law, traditionally the responsibility of the DO. In the opinion of P. Stigger, one of the last DOs appointed to Tanganyika, TANU's aggressive growth was often helped by a combination of weak Native Authorities and a compliant DC rather than by a 'strong DC, who knew his mind and brooked no interference'.[14] Once the political parties had been constituted, the next 'political' pre-occupation of the DO – and one which was going to take up a lot of his time, even though he had had no training for it and had probably never voted in a general election at home – was the organization of elections in his district.

The relationship between the DO and the political class could operate somewhat differently at the provincial and Secretariat level. In the district the DO and the MP might not always see eye to eye over the handling of local matters in the national legislature, particularly over the 'proper' and preferred channels of communication. In the ministries, not only did a new protocol of behaviour for the DO, now an assistant secretary or higher in a ministry, have to be worked out (there would be initial head-aches over whether to address one's boss as 'Sir' or 'Minister') and scrupulously observed, but sometimes there was another source of potential friction. Many ministers had started their life in the Native Administration or local government and might well have had differences of opinion with the very DO who had now been assigned to work in his office. Sometimes this relationship worked the other way, with some ministers keen to have in their office a DO whom they had known in the pre-political party days, and liked and trusted. R. Barlow-Poole mused on the inherent contradiction when he invited two Northern Nigerian ministers to dinner and realized that one of them had been a councillor in the NA where he had been DO. 'It is a curious situation when one is used to "advising" him what to do and the "advised" suddenly becomes your Minister.'[15] Working as private secretary to a new minister in Lagos, D. Savill felt that the British and Nigerians both found this a tricky situation after years of reversed roles, but most took to it: 'we protected our charges as they covered up for our political naivety'.[16] For the most part relations between the political leaders and the DOs, now turned into ministry officials, were good. Now and again a minister blew his top or personal-ized an issue of principle and a frustrated DO failed to keep his cool. A notorious case was the outburst of the Premier of North-ern Nigeria over the Northern Cameroons plebiscite, in which he allegedly blamed his defeat on certain DOs for having persuaded the populace to postpone a UN decision on their future rather than voting to join Nigeria.

However, in the growing mood among up-country political activists, particularly in Tanganyika, for whom independence was to be equated with getting rid of the DO, the DO often had a rougher time than did his colleagues at the centre. This became manifest in the activists' policy of taking on the DO, querying his decisions and challenging his authority. M. Longford found himself the victim of a malicious letter in Lindi and then at the wrong end of an argument with a TANU MP who wanted to remove an official file classified as secret from the *boma* office and was refused.[17] In Kondoa R. Brayne found himself the target of TANU's 'unthinking political opposition', often, as it seemed, towards him *qua* DO and for no constructive purpose.[18] TANU's policy of supporting non-co-operation with the NA and local

Organizing national elections: a primary responsibility
of the District Officer from the 1950s

councils, and hence the DO, could sour the DOs' memory of their
last years of Tanganyikan service. J.A. Golding condemned their
habit of stirring up support at public meetings by inciting people
to unrest and civil disobedience. 'The constant repetition of *kupi-
gana*, literally to fight physically for independence rather than
to strive for or aim for freedom, encouraged the hot-headed to
commit acts of lawlessness', leading him to feel that many believed
their own propaganda, that the DO was trying to prevent them
from obtaining self-government.[19] TANU did not hesitate, at least
in the districts where Golding served, to use strong tactics with
their own people, holding their own courts and passing illegal
sentences on those who refused to contribute to party funds,
as well as attacking Golding publicly in the TANU newspaper
Nguromo, and demanding his removal.[20] Many DOs found it hard
to reconcile unreasonable TANU behaviour in the field with the
more level-headed leadership of its leader Julius Nyerere, and
in particular with his 1961 letter to every DO appealing to their
'sense of mission' to stay on after independence.[21]

Across in the Gold Coast, in 1952 DOs were already feeling
unsettled about their future, a sentiment that quietly grew into
one of 'being slowly squeezed to death' as they were brought
under closer control from Accra.[22] In Sierra Leone DOs like H.
Mitchell recognized that the politicians 'were jealous of the
power and influence of the DCs' and were ready to undermine
it, including their insistence on the disbandment of the Court
Messenger Force on which the PCs and DCs depended for the
efficient discharge of their duties.[23] In Nigeria, where some of the
political party opposition tactics were redirected against other
political parties – to the extent that in the north it was sometimes
said that the government party was keener to get rid of the south-
erners than the British – the political parties in the east and west
initiated a vigorous campaign of non-fraternization with DOs. If
Kenya was alone in having a full-scale (but in no way national)
rebellion on its hands with the Mau Mau uprising, nearly every
African territory could point to at least one severe riot with political undertones during the 'political party' decade of the 1950s,
with the inevitable call on the DO to be at the centre of the calm-
ing operation. Their memoirs provide ample testimony of the
personal courage called for and the sadness that administration
should have come to this.

In the Gold Coast, Nigeria, Tanganyika and elsewhere, a

further blow was struck at DOs when their historic titles were changed and the new regional or provincial heads became political appointments, leading a Tanganyikan DO to declare that 'If the administration was not to be politically impartial then most of us felt that we could not be part of it.'[24] From Tanganyika, too, came an epitaph to which DOs elsewhere might have wished to subscribe. D. Barton concluded, in the twilight years of Tanganyika's administration, that 'One thing was certain, a DC on the eve of independence could not win!'[25] For DOs in East and Central Africa, already beset by the politics of European settlers and how they affected plans for African advancement, an added impetus to any potential pessimism over the ability of the provincial administration to remain effective under political strains came through the influx of thousands of European refugees, all with their horror stories, as they fled the collapse of the administration in the Belgian Congo and headed for the coast.

In summary, despite the total absence on the Devonshire Courses of any instruction on party politics in the Africa they were being trained to work in, once in the field every DO could have identified 'politics' as the most pervasive and persistent influence on the conduct of his job in the 1950s. As 'politics' emerged, the DO found, according to J.H. Smith in Northern Nigeria, that 'the time-honoured routines of district administration consequently and increasingly took on a political flavour', a view reinforced by that of a seasoned DO in Tanganyika, that, quite simply, 'politics were part of the life-blood of one's existence'.[26] If the average DO found, as B.L. Jacobs asserted, that 'political parties were anathema to the average colonial administrator'[27] and, as J.H. Smith suggested, the typical DO was 'much too thin-skinned' over this totally new challenge to established authority,[28] nevertheless 'the political years' retain a special place, not always negative, in the career and memory of the DOs who served in Africa during the final decade of colonial administration.

To round off this examination of the DO and politics, it is interesting to see what the DO did on and felt about the literal climax, independence day itself. Few DOs who were there omit such a major historical event from their memoirs. For the DO independence was no sudden climacteric: it was the envisaged end of a process in which he still had a role to play, not a dramatic *finis* to his work and being. H. Brind was amused to learn that on the day itself in the Gold Coast he was required to wear his full-dress

Colonial Service uniform and read out to the assembled crowd the prime minister's message, with its 'numerous references to "our fierce struggle against colonialism", which must have sounded odd when read out by someone clothed in the panoply of colonial power'.[29] For M. Longford, it was a relief that this was the last occasion that he would ever have to squeeze into his Colonial Service uniform.[30] In Kaduna one DO's memory was of the acting premier of Northern Nigeria asking him to come to his house and listen to him reading the speech he had prepared. In Dar es Salaam J. Lewis-Barned, whose wife was engaged by the Celebration Office to address envelopes, could not help regretting the sight of 'barbed wire and gates going up round Government House above the low wall which had previously been sufficient', while the DO at Lindi remembered the ban on any alcohol being served during the four days of the celebrations.[31] In Entebbe R. Posnett found himself in the thick of it, being responsible with another DO, B.L. Jacobs, for organizing the independence celebrations countrywide, attended in the capital by the Duke of Kent.[32] For some DOs, like R.A. Purcell in Uganda, it was only on independence day that 'the full impact of imminent and total change' came.[33] Graphic and symbolic was the description of I.F.C. Macpherson in Dar es Salaam as he stood on the dais beside the governor at the climax of the *uhuru* ceremony: 'At midnight when the lights went off the British flag came down, we took off our colonial uniform hat, his [HE's] with plumes, and put on new hats so that when the lights came on again at the stadium we were new men.'[34]

For the DO up-country, life soon returned to its routine, but psychologically things were different. In HQ that psychology took a practical turn when, shortly before independence, secret files were destroyed where it was judged that their contents could provide more embarrassment to the political leadership than enlightenment. Writing of this weeding out process in Lagos, D. Savill described how 'We had begun to destroy certain secret files, others were sent to London, and others again set aside for the incoming British High Commissioner so that there would be some continuity in British dealings on certain matters with the independent government.'[35] In one provincial HQ a DO's wife is said to have had 'the intelligent idea of using the cardboard covers for the octagonal basis required in making a patchwork quilt'.[36]

This discussion of the effect of political party activity on the work of the DO in the 1950–60s, as profound and pervasive as it was, is not to suggest that it was politics alone that changed the nature of his work during the final decade. From 1947 onwards he was required to direct his energies into a succession of new programmes, to an extent unknown in the pre-war routine of field administration. The Second World War may be said to have killed off the Sanders of the River *modus operandi* in Africa and to have replaced it with the beginnings of a hands-on bureaucracy, even if a few DOs found themselves in 1946–50 touring villages which, because of the staff shortages caused by the war, no DO had visited for ten years or more. The abandonment in 1947 of indirect rule as the fundamental imperative of native administration coincided with the introduction of new responsibilities for the DO. Its replacement by a system of local government, somewhat slavishly based on the UK model, became the catalyst for conciliar rather than Native Authority institutions. Indeed in Southern Nigeria the DO soon lost his title and was redesignated Local Government Adviser.

At the same time as these changes were introduced, the DO learned that the central thrust of district administration was to be 'development', starting with an enthusiasm for community development and mass education and from there moving into agricultural projects such as cotton cultivation, rice growing, well-sinking and fish farming. If the inflow of funds from Britain under the 1945 Colonial Development and Welfare Act brought more professionals into the field to help out with all this 'development', the DO was nevertheless pivotal in their operation, even when the pilot schemes had settled down and District Development Teams were formalized under his chairmanship. Such was the increase of European officers involved in all these schemes, at a time when the approach of self-government might have been expected to result in fewer overseas civil servants in the territory rather than more, that critics have labelled this the period of 'the second colonial occupation'.[37] Next, the classic DO found himself steadily removed from his traditional district work and transferred to work either in the new ministries or in one of the new specialist institutions in HQ, for instance as secretary of the public service commission, the broadcasting authority, the scholarships board, and, of course, as we have already seen, the inauguration of elections at every level up to the national one. For a select group of DOs in each territory, their transfer to newly opened Institutes of Administration, with a special remit to design and teach courses for the training of African DOs, made them think back to the strengths (and the weaknesses) of the course they had attended in Britain years before. At the same time, it brought them to the heart of Africanization, that key programme in the advance towards independence and the critical token of the honesty of Britain's policy to hand over control as soon as possible.[38] Self-government was not only in the air, it was getting on to the ground. It was all change for the DO. For the DO everywhere policy-generated preparation for independence dominated the 1950s, in stages and in accelerating tempo, but with the ultimate aim always in mind. From the CO Sir Andrew Cohen's assessment of this overall policy for a decolonizing Africa was that 'In helping Africans prepare for the future, British officers are in fact working themselves out of a job. This they do with admirable cheerfulness.'[39]

As tardy as that policy to Africanize the posts of control (i.e. the DOs) was, any hope of an earlier programme was undermined by the failure of colonial governments (unlike in the Sudan, with its established *mamurs*) to build up a reservoir of experienced subordinates. In Britain these would have been recognized as the executive grade. Working as assistants to the DC in his office, they could have acted for him while he was on leave, and gradually advanced in ability and experience until, come Africanization of the DO posts, they could have held those down until such time as the new African DOs had graduated, been trained (instead of crash-trained) and come into the Service. Another negative factor in thinking about Africanizing the DO posts was the biased argument sometimes put forward by senior DOs when asked to consult the chiefs over how they would react to having an African as their DO. Framed, in Northern Nigeria for instance, in the weighted language of 'the governor wants to know whether you, as chief of this Hausa emirate, would like to have an Ibo as your DO' or again in the context of Kenya's Samburu, whose chief told C. Chenevix Trench that 'as you white men are determined to go, let me make it quite clear to you that we do not want to be ruled by a gang of Kikuyu and Luo',[40] it was not difficult for the DO to confirm to HQ that the chiefs were against African DOs. There were also cases of what might be called the perfectionist syndrome among some senior DOs, unrealistically insisting on 'no lowering of standards' and on possessing a degree as a *sine qua non*, despite the fact that, because of wartime conditions, many DOs recruited in the early 1920s and again in the late 1940s did not have BA after their name – a point not lost on nationalists. It was Margery Perham, the DOs' favourite academic, who at an Oxford conference on decolonization in 1978 entered a blunt verdict on Africanization: 'Perhaps the most serious problem of the transfer of power was due to Britain's tardiness in opening the civil service to Africans.'[41]

The present book is centred on the British DO, not on his African successor. Fortunately a few of them have begun to write their memoirs of the years of overlapping administration.[42] Allusions to how the first generation managed are also to be found in the memoirs of some of those DOs who had one of the new African DOs posted to his division. Suffice it to say that most of the newcomers quickly settled in, sometimes in a situation (and a language) as alien to them as it had been to their European predecessor first-tour ADOs. An approving comment from a Resident's wife on the very first set of Northern Nigerian ADOs to graduate from Zaria brought comfort to all: 'If their administrative work was as good as the bread and butter letters they had been taught to write to their hostesses, I was convinced they would be able to keep the country running smoothly.'[43] They did, and did it well. In one respect, however, the African DO had no wish to emulate the work and reputation of his predecessors, often to the surprise, if not the chagrin, of his expatriate seniors. Whereas to the DO of this study the essence of his work, and often the very soul of his being, was a posting up-country, with all the romantic attraction of a remote bush station and the allure of bush touring on foot or horseback, to the new African DO a district posting was, like a Secretariat posting for his predecessors, something to be avoided at all costs. J. Lawley reported that the first African DO appointed DC Gwembe, a recently promoted clerk, seemed to spend all his time moaning that he had not been posted to one of the ministries in Lusaka and 'did not hesitate to make his feelings known'.[44] In Kenya C. Chenevix Trench, a typical NFD aficionado, feared, as he contemplated the arrival of southern-born-and-bred Kenya DOs, that 'when the last British DCs had left, their African successors regarded such places as Wajir, Mandera and Moyale not as administrative centres but as punishment stations, beleaguered fortresses'.[45] In Western Nigeria I. Brook was shocked to find that he could not get his African DO, a Lagos man and a graduate of a European university, to go on tour. 'He said he had been too frightened to spend a night in the bush,' and told how 'he went down on his knees every night to pray that the British DOs would never leave Nigeria.' He was soon posted to the Secretariat in semi-disgrace, 'and made no attempt to hide his delight'.[46] Of his new African ADO in Eastern Nigeria, K. Addis noted, when he called on him in the old bush rest-house that had been given him as his quarters, that 'the bush came up to the windows, and I doubt if [he and his wife] felt easy there'. In his observation of 'odd how educated Nigerians hated it', it is his gloss that is important: 'or perhaps it is odder that we did not'.[47] For what the incredulous European DO too often overlooked was that, while the bush life and loneliness had for him a strong element of attraction, through their romance and novelty and as a welcome contrast to the pressures of his often urban upbringing, the bush was often either the place where the African DO had been brought up and had vowed to put behind him or else the place which filled the city-bred African with horror, even fear. There was also one more consideration, which the European may have missed in his evaluation. The African DO saw perfectly clearly that promotion was going to lie in being seen in the right places by the right people, not by being out of sight in the relative obscurity of district administration. In any case, as one worried African DO in training said to his supervisor, 'You have one great advantage in an urban riot or rural disturbance. How will a stone-throwing, matchet-wielding rioter know that I am the DO? Your white skin is a symbol of authority, a badge of office, which I can never wear.'

Few colonial governments gave – maybe did not have time to give – their DOs much official guidance by way of manuals or directives on their new role as DOs serving a government in the hands of elected African ministers. Instead this seems to have been done largely by word of mouth, on visits to their field staff by the governor or through pep-talks from the head of the civil service.[48] Part of this reticence may have been due to uncertainty whether an independent government would wish to retain the office of District Officer, the very model of colonial authority. Here the shadow that lay over top officials was that of what was known as 'the scaffolding theory'. Upheld by the CO, it originated in the writing of the academic Margery Perham, who in 1937 had argued that it would be inappropriate to recruit Africans into the Administrative Service because this would disappear with independence – who, as one DO cogitated, had ever heard of a DO Kent or the PC Oxon? The Administrative Service, she wrote, 'should aim at being increasingly advisory in its function. It should be regarded as the temporary scaffolding round the growing structure of native self-government. African energies should be incorporated into the structure: to build them into the scaffolding would be to create a vested interest which would make its demolition at the appropriate time very difficult.'[49] In the event, of course, despite changes in nomenclature and some areas of responsibility introduced by the nationalist governments, no African government wished to rid itself of its critical field agents and representatives. Indeed, in a country like Kenya, the postcolonial DO in the 1970s appeared to be endowed with a status and authority unknown to his predecessors.

For all the excitement of and enthusiasm for 'mission accomplished' at many levels and in particular among those DOs closely involved in the formation of the new African DO cadres, it was inevitable that the majority of DOs would be beginning to assess the impact of imminent decolonization on their career and to start giving thought to their own future. It might well be a case of living in cloud cuckoo land to expect promotions to continue in the conventional way, namely by merit modified by the factors of age and seniority. Naturally African DOs would have to be given accelerated promotion: no African DO, and no government on the threshold of independence, was going to wait the standard 12–18 years for a DO to be advanced to Senior DO or Deputy PC. In decolonizing Africa political expectations would not wait on civil service conventions. For F. Bex in Eastern Nigeria, where relationships between DOs and their political masters had been distinctly chilly in the mid-1950s, this was a factor propelling him into taking early retirement. 'The refusal of the Regional Government to increase senior officers' salaries and the promotion of Nigerian officers over my head were a blow to family finances [and] meant I could not continue in the Service.'[50] In Western Nigeria, M.C. Atkinson could not disguise his dismay when one of the new DO entrants was promoted to permanent secretary after only seven years: 'I thought I was doing well in reaching the same post in sixteen.'[51] Jennifer Cawte and her ADO husband were not pleased when they heard their new DO was to be a Nigerian cadet, 'who was an ADO here two months ago and would now be acting Senior DO, and I will be answerable to him. You can imagine our feelings.'[52] As it happened, Abubakar Mashegu went on to become Resident at the end of a mere five years' service – deservedly, in the eyes of many DOs who recognized his quality. The final straw, however, for the Cawtes and that last generation of ADOs came when they heard in 1962 that there would be no more promotion for non-Nigerian DOs and that European Residents were being asked to retire. 'We feel it is time to move on' – in the event, to the Solomon Islands.[53]

Other questions besides promotion prospects began to creep into the DO's mind. How far would the fundamental nature and responsibilities of his job be altered? To what extent would the DO's status remain? Could he expect the same degree of support from an elected government as he had enjoyed, largely unquestioned, from his new seniors in the civil service? How much political interference in his job could a DO's conscience take, especially over appointments, a change that seemed to be inevitable as patronage spread its wings? Would the DO's reputation for neutrality and impartiality and honest (however unpalatable) opinion be respected by his political masters, with the growing credo of 'those who are not publicly for us must be privately against us'? These were some of the professional queries the DO began to put to himself when he addressed the problem of his own situation in confronting the ultimate personal question of the DO and decolonization, 'Where do I go from here? And when do I go?'

In West Africa, which was politically further along the road to independence than East or Central Africa, DOs began to face up to the hitherto undreamed of challenge, what would they do when they no longer wanted (or were no longer wanted) to continue in their chosen career of DO. At the back of the minds of many lay an expectation that they could, of course, always move on to territories where DOs would still be required for some time and were indeed still being actively recruited: East and Central Africa first, 'where', to quote a DO's view in 1958, 'whatever the pace of political advance in the territories on the West Coast, one always had the impression that [they] were the last bastions of empire',[54] and maybe the High Commission Territories; and then, when they perhaps became independent in say another ten years or so, there would surely for many years to come be vacancies in the Pacific territories and Hong Kong. Maybe a career as a DO could just be eked out. Yet such a transfer might turn out to be nothing more than a short-term one. H. Brind was one of these doubters, deciding not to take up the offer of a transfer to another colony when the Gold Coast became independent, 'mainly because I did not want to find myself in a colony which might become independent in a few years' time, leaving me to seek another career at a less favourable age and possibly with greater family commitments.'[55] In the Colonial Office Sir Charles Jeffries famously minuted how he foresaw 'a depressing picture of the future of the Colonial Service as a series of transfers of officers from one untenable post to another slightly more tenable, until in the end the Administrator of Tristan Da Cunha would remain as the sole inheritor of past glories: in short, a kind of "tontine" '.[56]

Searching for a career back in the UK was another possibility – perhaps the Commonwealth Relations Office, which would surely need people with African experience to staff their High Commissions in the new African countries? Maybe it was better not to think of competing in the UK job market: ten years administering the Northern Frontier District in Kenya or being District Officer i/c Niger Division was unlikely to impress a company board in search of qualifications and experience, even if they knew where the NFD was or what a DO did. The reflections of J. Millard in 1958, now in Bechuanaland after transferring from Tanganyika, on the changing character of the DO's life and the problems it posed, while in no way unique, may be read as a summary of the indecision now taking hold of the DO's mind across much of Africa: 'I had reached a milestone, a cross-roads. What to do now? Where to go? What next? The Colonial Service, the war, and all the wonderful experiences and adventures of recent years were a period not completed. Ahead lay another phase, and I had a gut feeling that I should launch forth on something new while I was young enough to make a go of it. ... If one decided to attempt something new it should be done now or never.'[57]

London was not blind to the effect on the morale of its DOs that 'politics' and imminent decolonization was going to have. After all, there were the precedents of the transfer of power and the closure of the ICS in 1947 and of the Sudan Political Service in 1955. The first move came in 1954 when the Colonial Service was ended and replaced by the new corporate title of Her Majesty's Overseas Civil Service. The Colonial Administrative Service now became the Administrative Branch of HMOCS. The rationale was that the political developments in train necessitated a review of the structure of the former Colonial Service. Furthermore, its members were entitled to know what their position would be when the UK government no longer exercised control over their appointment and conditions of service. DOs were guaranteed certain conditions when their present government became independent, for example that they would be eligible for consideration for transfer to other territories within HMOCS, and that, in the event of premature retirement resulting from constitutional changes, they would receive compensation from the government of the territory concerned. Furthermore HMG would endeavour to find them alternative employment should they so desire. The White Paper of 1954 concluded with the hope that 'this evidence of real concern for the present officers of the Colonial Service and of H.M.G.'s determination to safeguard the interests of those officers will allay the doubts and anxieties which are now apparent.'[58] Some DOs looked on this statement of policy as a damp squib.[59] Many more regretted HMG's failure to proceed with the proposals for a new British Overseas Service, whose members would be directly employed by HMG for service anywhere in the Commonwealth. Such an opportunity would have been attractive to DOs keen to continue in public administration overseas and already suspicious that any compensation for loss of career was to be the responsibility of their present employer and not of HMG.

Such was the pace of political change that within two years the CO found it necessary to issue another policy document.[60] The thrust of the new policy was twofold. First, in order to meet the staffing needs of the territories approaching independence, HMG planned to draw up a list of 'people with the necessary qualifications for secondment to overseas governments ... who would be ready and available to accept this kind of career'. Should the demand reach a substantial proportion and regular employment over a number of years be on the cards, these Special List officers could come into the regular employment of HMG for service overseas. The idea of such a Special List, put forward by a delegation of officers from Nigeria who called on the CO in June 1955, differed from the earlier plan for a British Overseas Service in that it would remain within the framework of the newly established HMOCS and not be a separate service.

The second purpose of the 1956 scheme was peculiar to Nigeria, where all four governments were facing the alarming prospect of officers, notably DOs, turning their back on the 1954 HMOCS structure and its six promises on terms of service, and leaving Nigeria as soon as they could in accordance with the provision for compensation. In Nigeria, where morale among the DOs had been dropping steadily for some years and many DOs, particularly in the Eastern Region, felt that, as K. Barnes expressed it, increasingly uncompetitive salaries and their uncertain future in an independent country outweighed the interest and responsibility of the job,[61] they were now assured that, instead of the 1954 arrangement that the Nigerian government would be responsible for paying their entitlement, pensions and compensation payments would be paid to them by the UK government and reclaimed from the employing government. Officers who joined the new Special List would be expected to serve HMG up to the age of 50, 'in any post to which they might be assigned from time to time',[62] a condition which generated discussion among some DOs of whether they could really contemplate years in the UK Ministry of Agriculture and Fisheries or working for the Coal Board. HMG included one further offer in order to win over Nigeria's hesitant DOs. If an officer who joined the Special List should remain unemployed through no fault of his own, HMG would continue to pay him his salary for up to five years while efforts were made to find him a job. The 1956 White Paper ended by stressing that, while for the present its provisions applied only to officers in the Nigerian government, they might in future be extended to other territories should HMG consider that such a concession justifiable. As it turned out, the Special List concept was never applied outside Nigeria.

More than that, it hardly took off even in Nigeria. Out of the 2,000 officers eligible to join the new Special List, fewer than 400 applied. As self-government approached, DOs became vilified in the press and doubts began to grow among them whether it was worth staying on at all. As M.C. Atkinson saw it, the nationalist attacks 'varied between two extremes, at one time accusing those expatriates who took their compensation terms and pensions of leaving them in the lurch, and at others asserting that there could be not true self-government until all top posts were filled by Nigerians'.[63] So the CO went back to the drawing board and HMG issued a new White Paper in 1958, the third to deal with the consequences of decolonization on the career of serving DOs within the space of just four years.[64] The offer of employment under HMG in any work of their choosing had not caught the imagination of DOs. The offer of compensation for loss of office seemed to undermine rather than sustain the staff position, for often it attracted not the older DOs in their 40s but those with 10–15 years' service, still under 40, the very DOs whom the Nigerian governments were anxious to retain for some years to come. Conscious of the conditions of compensation, the White Paper created yet another Special List, 'B' (the original was now restyled 'A'). In return for DOs being required to give at least a year's notice of any intention to retire, they were offered an interest-free advance of 90 per cent of their eventual entitlement to lump-sum compensation, along with further financial inducements related to the age and length of service, factors which conditioned the amount of compensation for which they were eligible. This was known as 'freezing' the sum once the optimum timing was reached rather than allowing it to decline annually thereafter. Such a 'Pay to Stay' rather than the original 'Pay to Go' approach had been in the mind of A.T. Weatherhead in Kaduna, and he had put it to the CO official charged with arresting the exodus of DOs after the non-starter Special List 'A'.[65] This was Sir John Martin, who described his role in his tricky mission as that of 'trouble shooting in Nigeria', following what he saw as the inadequate response to nomination to join the first scheme.[66] He identified three areas of dissatisfaction among Nigeria's demoralized DOs: (i) 'political' difficulties, not only political interference and the declining promotion prospects but also a feeling that the DO 'is being squeezed out and is in danger of prostituting his personal or professional integrity by service to an inefficient and corrupt regime'; (ii) the effect of the lump compensation scheme and the importance of getting out earlier rather than later, while the going was good in the UK job market; and (iii) dissatisfaction with the present emoluments and the fear of the Nigerian government defaulting on its promise to pay compensation and pensions.[67]

An important and so far largely unexplored source for further research into the compensation schemes for loss of career and premature retirement which has not yet been explored is the records of the various Senior Civil Service Associations and the pressures they were able to exert both on the government and on the Colonial Office.[68] Although Special List 'B' was a success when set beside the aborted Special List 'A' – after all, it gave the DO much of what he wanted: to stay on in the country and in the job he had grown to love, rather than being at the beck and call of HMG for assignment to a post he knew nothing about – the staffing position in Nigeria's DO cadres continued to be dire. In 1959, a year after its introduction, a quarter of the established posts in Western Nigeria's administration were unfilled, with the figure rising in Eastern Nigeria to 40 per cent. In the north, 161 out of the 221 approved posts were still held by expatriate DOs.[69] Among DOs in the north, it was rumoured that a phrase commonly heard was 'Only saints or sinners will stay on'.[70] What is remarkable in Northern Nigeria is how many DOs (in whichever category) did stay on, willingly and wantedly, for at least five years after independence in 1960. Some were still there into the 1970s, though only a few in divisional posts. Many African presidents and prime ministers went out of their way to pay tribute on independence day or in their memoirs to the DOs and others who had contributed to the well being and development of the country. Imaginatively Julius Nyerere invited a group of ex-Tanganyikan DOs to return to the country at the time of its tenth anniversary of *uhuru* and revisit their old districts to see what progress had been made.

With the DO having now made up his mind whether to stay or to go (and when), there remains one more major aspect of his life to illustrate. What did the DO do after he returned prematurely, typically in his 30s or 40s instead of at the regulatory age of 55? Research into this final period of the life and work of the DO, into what has been labelled 'second careers', has only just begun.[71] Yet the kind of employment the DO secured on his return to Britain constitutes an important and the ultimate part of charting his career and experiences.

Decolonization meant that the CO was no longer able to look after its own, as it had strenuously sought to do in the White Papers of 1956 and 1958, often against opposition from other Whitehall departments. In 1966, even before the granting of independence to the last of its African territories, it closed its doors and merged with the Commonwealth Relations Office into a single Commonwealth Office. A further amalgamation took place in 1968, when the Foreign and Commonwealth Office was formed. The responsibilities for the remnant HMOCS personnel moved to the FCO's

Overseas Territories Division and then to the new Overseas Development Administration (ODA). Before it closed, however, the CO, ever caring of its Colonial Service staff, was instrumental in setting up an office in London to help retiring DOs and other CS officers to set about finding further employment. The Overseas Service Resettlement Bureau (OSRB) was an extension of the Re-employment Bureau opened in 1957 for retiring civil servants from Malaya, which became independent in the same year as the first of the African colonies, the Gold Coast. In no way did every DO find re-employment through the services of the OSRB, nor were DOs obliged to register with it. While some complained about its work, such as D.G.P. Taylor, a former DO in Tanganyika,[72] others were grateful for the help they received, perhaps none more so than T. Gardner who, on his way home from Northern Rhodesia in 1964, found a cable waiting for him when the ship berthed at Port Said, informing him of a vacancy as Deputy Treasurer of Cambridge University. Eventually promoted to University Treasurer, he reckoned on his retirement in 1983 that those five years as Deputy were the happiest days of his life next to his three years as a DO in Fort Jameson.[73]

The OSRB was able to feed many DOs into what was for them the fresh fields of business and commerce, in particular on the personnel side, where their previous human relations experience as a DO proved a useful resource. The Bureau's director, M. Molohan, formerly a DO in Tanganyika, wisely warned applicants that DOs were 'an unknown commodity on the job market' and advised that 'one should not have an inflated opinion of oneself'.[74] Other DOs found help in resettlement from their Oxford or Cambridge Appointments Boards. P. Dennis expressed his relief and surprise at this courtesy when he left the Gold Coast in 1956: 'I thought they would think they had finished with me when they had paved my way into the Colonial Service,' 18 years earlier.[75] Throughout the 1960s the largest number of applications to the OSRB were from DOs. It closed in 1978, and when its books are opened in the Public Record Office (normally this would be after 30 years) the final picture of the DO in his 'second career' will become available.

Pending the opening of the OSRB files – and obviously they are so full of personal details that they could be held back for a further period, if made accessible at all – two research projects, one in 1983–86 and the other in 2001–2, have provided important preliminary statistics. Out of the approximately 600 DOs who took part in the first one organized by the Oxford Development Records Project, 14 per cent secured a job in commerce or business while 12 per cent remained in employment in another Commonwealth country. Charity and voluntary work accounted for another 7 per cent, 6 per cent became school teachers and 5 per cent were taken into university/college administration. Four per cent each went into the Foreign and Commonwealth Office, local government and university teaching, and 5 per cent each went into the church, law, the Ministry of Overseas Development and the Ministry of Defence (principally security). Others found employment in UN agencies, the World Bank and consultancy. At least six DOs from Africa were elected to parliament, two of them becoming ministers.[76] A preliminary report on the second project was completed in 2002.[77] Its findings elaborate on the former, with more categories of employment identified, but tend to follow the same pattern. The 'second careers' field is rich in promise for further research.

The FCO presented the prematurely retiring DO with a problem. Many had hoped for a lateral transfer into the Commonwealth Relations Office. Who better equipped, as they saw it, to help man all the posts in the new British High Commissions opening up in Africa than those who already knew something about Africa, its political dynamics and its politicians? True, they might, as Joan Alexander saw it from the inside (her husband was on the staff of a High Commission in Africa), have first to learn to live with a regime 'as strange as a can-can girl learning ballet',[78] but the DO was nothing if not versatile and adaptable. But the amalgamated FCO was having none of it. If the DO wanted to join, he would have to take the same entrance exam as anyone else, with a concession on the age limit. *En revanche*, as it were, the British High Commission staff did not always make a good impression on the DOs still working in Africa as they arrived to open up the new High Commissions. In Uganda, for instance, no less than three DOs (two of whom later joined the FCO) were highly critical, both of how they 'looked askance at the old hands' and of their deviousness and pussy-footing attitude towards local conventions.[79] Word soon got around that, to quote an unnamed governor's son as he contemplated his career options, the FCO wished to distance itself from former DOs. However, an examination of the *Foreign Office Lists* reveals that in fact a substantial number of DOs were accepted into the Diplomatic Service, some of them ending up as ambassadors or high commissioners. The occasions when a DO was posted back to 'his' old country were often real success stories, at least in local eyes. Several ended up in Government House, not on their original CAS track but as administrator of an independent island (New Hebrides, Montserrat, Seychelles, etc.), appointed from within the ranks of the FCO.

One final thought on the yet-to-be explored record of second careers. Who, looking around their colleagues in the 1950s, would ever have guessed that in the years ahead he would be able to point to no less than three former DOs as members of the Queen's household: Lord Luce (Kenya) as Lord Chamberlain, Sir Roger du Boulay (Northern Nigeria) as Vice-Marshal of the Diplomatic Corps, and the Reverend M. Mann (Eastern Nigeria) as Dean of Windsor?

The DO successfully brought, besides his experience, to his search for a second career those qualities which the CO had so carefully identified when they interviewed him for the CAS ten to 20 years earlier. They included the ability to put his hand to any task imposed on him regardless of the fact that he had never been trained for it, determination and dedication, an interest in human relations, and a capacity for getting on with a job without supervision. Such characteristics of versatility, responsibility and reliability were to stand him in as good a stead in his second career as they had in his first. Among all the multifarious jobs that DOs undertook in their second careers, one outcome stands forth as of supreme importance to the whole story of the life and work of the DO, and the very inspiration of this present study. This is the decision of so many DOs to write their memoirs, sometimes as books written for their children who might not otherwise know what a DO was or did, and sometimes as recalled primary evidence for historians keen to learn about colonial administration from the last generation of DOs. This time there is no successor to hand over to. Hence the imperative of the DOs setting down what they knew, writing, as it were, their own handing-over notes, and recording their memories. No one else will ever be able to do it. The history of the last DOs who served in Africa must not be allowed to die with them.

CHAPTER 11

Looking Back: The Image and the Memory of the DO

L ooking back is almost as inseparable an element in a career as the company pension. It is rare for any career memoir to omit a final chapter reviewing what has been achieved and reflecting on what opportunities were missed as well as those moments never to be forgotten. Indeed, in memoirs where a service composes the writer's principal locus (the Diplomatic Service, one of the armed forces, the Colonial Service), not to conclude with such a curtain fall might be looked on as no conclusion at all. In the same way that many DO memoirs open with the young cadet's speculation on what lay ahead as he sailed from Liverpool to Lagos, so do many of them close with the senior officer's reflections on his career as he sailed home from Dar es Salaam or Takoradi in retirement after ten to 30 years in African service.

At the same time, the modern DO's memoir is associated with what is arguably a unique difference from other current genres of service memoirs. In the case of the DO in Africa, his memoirs and his analysis of his life and work there are overwhelmingly written by the last generation of African DOs, those who retired in the 1960s. Their contribution thus has, willy-nilly, a finality, sometimes an obituary element to it. There can be no further new memoirs of the British DO in Africa other than those written by the swiftly dwindling last generation. The British DO in Africa

has no ongoing successors. Africa's colonial territories have all
been independent for more than 35 years. The Colonial Office
closed in 1966. The permanent and pensionable Colonial Service
was abolished in 1954 and its follow-on HMOCS came to an end
in 1997. In May 1999 these two overseas civil services (the only
ones to be officially designated as a Crown Service, bearing the
prefix Her/His Majesty's) were laid to rest at Westminster Abbey
in the presence of the Queen.

This chapter looks back on a service that no longer exists.
After the present generation of sexagenarians there can be no
more memoirs of the British DO in Africa because there are no
more British DOs in Africa. To a degree the marked readiness
of this last generation of DOs to write their memoirs may well
have been motivated by the realization that they were just that,
the final generation. Many have felt that it is incumbent on them
to record – 'for posterity' or 'for the family' – a job and a way
of life – 'how it really was' – which others would otherwise not
know about save by hearsay and which nobody else will ever
experience again. Robin Wainwright was direct in prefacing his
unpublished memoir with a declaration that he had compiled
it 'to record for my grandchildren the small parts played in our
colonial history', just as Yvonne Fox, wife of a DO who served in
both West and Central Africa up to the mid-1950s, pointed out
that her memoirs (also unpublished) had been written 'for the
amusement of our children and their families, and to help our
great-grandchildren get the colonial record into focus'.[1] No pre-
war memorialist ever needed to dedicate his or her memoir to
their children or grandchildren so that they would know what
a DO's life and work were, because there was every chance that
those offspring might well join the CAS themselves. Not so those
who came in after 1950 and soon learned that there would be
no career for their scions to follow in. It now became necessary
to explain what was once obvious. A. Stuart rationalized his
memoirs thus, 'All these things did happen. Their improbability
springs as much as anything else from the fact that the British
colonial experience is today as dead as a dodo. That period is over
and will never recur. Few understand it.'[2]

Welcoming half a century ago the autobiography of Sir Philip
Mitchell, as an addition to the number, 'none too considerable, of
the personal records of administrative life in the Colonies', Lord
Hailey emphasized that 'it is in such records that we look to find

those intimate accounts of service as District Officer which can be so attractive in their revelation of the human relationship underlying the official discharge of official duties.'[3] In a way, then, looking back in the case of the DO in Africa is linked to a certain looking forward, to the time when the very last DO has gone and only the personal memoir remains as the testament of who the DO was and what he did, of what he thought he was doing and why he did it, all those intimate concerns which no official records can ever bring to life.

The significance of looking back is conditioned by who is looking back and from what point of view. The essence of the present study has been on how the DO recorded and reflected on his career. In this final chapter the retrospective view is set beside a number of other major viewpoints. Beside the self-projection of his identity there is the received image of his role interpreted by various groups of people with whom the DO came in touch in the performance of his work. For instance, what did his own departmental colleagues think of the DO, the agricultural, police, education officers etc., as they worked together in the same district? What about the views of the private sector working in the same division, the settlers, commercial agents and missionaries? What was the image of the DO within the Colonial Office, to an extent his once-removed employer and certainly the one who appointed him and promoted him, but which was staffed by a completely different service and often as innocent of the Wajir way of life as the DO was of the Whitehall *modus operandi*? What kind of impression of the DO was taken back by the investigative journalist as he (sometimes she) began to visit 'emergent Africa' and learn what colonial rule really meant on the ground rather than in the lobbies and White Papers of Westminster? Again, how did academics, especially imperial (soon to be restyled Commonwealth) historians, react to their meeting up with the DO – sometimes their former student – as they undertook their field research? And what of the critics of empire, seemingly determined in the late and post-colonial period to condemn DOs even before they had ever met one? Finally, and potentially the most relevant and revealing of them all in evaluating the received image of the DO, how did 'the African' look on the DO? This critical question needs to be unpacked into the sub-question of 'Which African?' Is it the view of the nationalist politician or the traditional chief? The Western-educated elite or an

NA or government employee, especially those on the DO's staff, like clerks and messengers? The peasant farmer in the bush or a transhumant pastoralist in the plains? Or that of the DO's successor, the African District Officer? Finally, the search for the identity and the image of the DO might be extended to, as it were, his afterlife. What did his new employers think of the DO 'retread' as he embarked on his second career, often in the British job market, after years of a very different career, with all the advantages as well as the disadvantages of the first in his baggage? Not all the sources for probing the image of the DO can be explored here, but a brief discussion of some of them may open up ideas of where further research might profitably be directed towards the understanding of the life and work of the DO in Africa.

The DO as seen by his colleagues

While the relationship between the DO and his departmental colleagues was not as formalized as it was in the government of India, where the DO in the exclusive Indian Civil Service was known as 'The Heaven Born', by virtue of his office as the colonial government's principal agent in the field (and sometimes by the transferred role of the DO's wife as 'the First Lady' in the station), the DO was inevitably No. 1 among all the government staff in the division. In short – and it was a maxim found in many of the local languages – the DO *was* the government and the government *was* the DO. This was so regardless of the sometimes smarting fact that the DO might be just a few years down from the university and still very much on the learning curve, and literally (in length of service) junior to an older engineer or police officer. In strict indirect-rule areas like the emirates of Northern Nigeria, no professional officer could meet the emir to discuss a matter of policy without being accompanied and introduced by the DO. The occasional tension this gave rise to was generally reduced through social pressures and the continuing need for harmony in a small community, but it emerged into prominence in the capital when ministries were created. To the indignation and fury of many a chief engineer or chief education officer, not only did he lose his role as the top officer in the ministry but the new post of permanent secretary almost invariably went to an administrative officer, with most of the assistant secretaries being DOs and not drawn from the professional cadres. When District Development Teams became the fashion at the beginning of the 1950s, the chairman was invariably the DO, regardless of his likely lack of seniority vis-à-vis some professional officers on the team. The argument was advanced that among so many experts he alone had the capacity to remain neutral.

Looking back on his time in the Northern Rhodesian administration, T. Gardner admitted that jealousies frequently existed between departmental officers and the DO. 'The role of the Provincial Administration as, so to speak, *primus inter pares*, may have been resented because members of specified departments felt that their own expertise was not always sufficiently regarded when collective decisions were taken.'[4] Up-country, the allocation of housing on a station, a sensitive item especially when a married officer was in the frame, was the DO's responsibility and, as glad as he would have been to be rid of it, the way he handled it could certainly colour the opinion of the DO by others. In Nigeria the question of the relationship between professional officers and DOs had long exercised the mind and the minute writing of the governor in Lagos. There was never any doubt in HE's mind that someone had to be responsible for overall politics in a province or a district and that such co-ordination must be in the hands of the DO, even to the extent that, to quote from the famous Clifford Minute of 1922, 'a DO in charge of a division occupies within the area under his administrative charge a position as nearly analogous to that of a Resident in his province as the relative dignity and importance of the two offices render possible'.[5] There was certainly room for offence to be taken by those who were determined to take it.

Memoirs by DOs so far outweigh those from departmental officers. In neither case do they indulge in sustained vituperative comments on colleagues, unlike the cut-and-thrust of many political memoirs. Where criticism is made it is as often of an officer in the writer's own service (administration, agriculture, etc.) rather than of a departmental officer by a DO or vice versa. A rare outburst came from the Canadian wife of a Public Works Department engineer in Somaliland, Margaret Laurence, who simply could not stand the British DO and his womenfolk: 'I found the sahib-type English so detestable that I always imagined that if ever I wrote a book about Somaliland it would give me tremendous joy to deliver a withering blast of invective in their direction.'[6] In the end she did not, feeling that it 'would be something obscene and pointless, like mutilating a corpse'. Nevertheless the criticism she did allow herself was severe enough, condemning officials as being 'motivated by a brutally strong belief in their own superiority ... so desperately uncertain of their own worth and their ability to cope within their own societies that they were forced to seek some kind of mastery in a place where all the cards were stacked in their favour'. One can begin to understand why, at least in Nigeria, the administration and the PWD were said to be never the best of friends.[7]

Nor is there a lot of evidence of DOs in their memoirs criticizing other DOs. Where this does occur, it is nearly always of a junior criticizing his senior, rarely the other way round.[8] Often the accused is left nameless, yet immediately recognizable to the cognoscenti. DOs did share a strong *esprit de corps* and, apart from the occasional nuanced post-prandial incident, deprecating another DO was not common, beyond the way junior DOs happily grumbled to each other about the shortcoming of their seniors.

Not literally colleagues, rather fellow-expatriates (Dutch or Italian too), the image of the DO in the eyes of missionaries and the commercial community deserves more attention than it has received to date. The European settlers in East and Central Africa were historically no friend of the DO, with their opposite views of what the policy of trusteeship meant and what was in the best interests of the African. Lewis Gann's comment on how relations deteriorated into a 'pitched battle' over the issue of the Central African Federation, with the settlers and copper-mining community ranged against 'upper-class civil servants with Oxford accents and Thirds from Balliol [posing as] the Africans' chosen champions' is suggestive.[9] In Kenya, of course, the socio-educational background of settlers was often similar – on occasion superior – to that of the DOs, but even without that area of potential antagonism their view of the DO and his interpretation of the paramountcy of African interests was by no means consistently comfortable. It is doubtful whether, at least until the Mau Mau emergency, either party was convinced that they were on the same side. As for missionaries, the typical DO seems to have looked on Catholic priests, many of them from Ireland, more favourably than on Protestant and evangelical missionaries, often from America and Denmark as well as Britain. As for commercial agents, the Edwardian values of looking on trade and those engaged in it as socially inferior may have prevailed among some DOs had they ever been pressed for a view, yet in the close community of a small station any such divisive atti-tude was carefully concealed. DOs knew they could rely on the commercial managers to take a full part in maintaining the well being of the station. One of the few written comments are the memoirs of J. Maslen, a British American Tobacco employee since the 1930s, who not only dedicated his memoir 'To the Bush DO' but also paid him this tribute: 'A DO was expected to combine the wisdom of Solomon, the patience of Job, and the state-craft and resourcefulness of Metternich, and above all a keen sense of humour without which he was a doomed man. Mostly they passed with flying colours.'[10]

The image of the DO in Whitehall

The fact that the CAS was not part of the CO staff, though the latter was responsible for its recruitment and oversaw its terms of service, promotion and transfers, was always at the back of the mind of CO officials. In the course of several committees set up between 1900 and 1950 to consider the amalgamation of the CO and the CS along the lines of the FO and the Diplomatic Service, with regular interchange and cross-postings, this historic 'two services' attitude remained a major stumbling block. From the 1930s a few assistant principals began to be seconded to colonial administrations to spend a year or two working as a DO. One or two DOs were regularly seconded to Whitehall to see how the CO handled its business, though they were always kept away from policy files dealing with their territory. Both seconded parties were known as 'beachcombers'. As long as Sir Ralph Furse, the father of the modern Colonial Service, was involved in the recruitment of DOs (and it was a record period, in one capacity or another from 1910 to 1950), and as long as Sir Charles Jeffries was responsible for the CAS (again, for over 20 years), there was no question about the dedication of the CO's missionary efforts to promote the image of the DO as the symbol of all that was best in British youth. It was in Furse's time that the CAS overtook the ICS as the No. 1 choice of British graduates in search of a career overseas in a Crown Service.

Jeffries, who spent 40 years in the CO and ended as under-secretary, was the first head of the Colonial Service Department in the new (1930) Personnel Division. He once half-endorsed the epigram that the Colonial Service was the only profession of the inter-war world where one could live the life of a country gentleman on the salary of a civil servant.[11] He applauded Furse's highly selective method of selection for appointing DOs, 'inasmuch as they have been hand-picked for their jobs, their average of ability and character is probably above the normal' and had no time for the person who 'is just looking for a job'.[12] It was fitting that when *Corona*, the Colonial Service journal, published its final issue in 1962, one of the *valete* pieces should have been written by Jeffries. Entitled 'The Colonial Service in Perspective', in it Jeffries spoke enthusiastically 'as one who was outside it but intimately connected with it'.[13]

Furse, who was immensely respected by DOs, was known by them as their leading friend at court, the man who championed their cause and whose vision of their work and character was a proud inspiration to them. The chief attractions of the CAS were, he stoutly argued, cast in a spiritual image rather than a practical one: 'the challenge to adventure, the urge to prove himself in the face of hardship and risk to health, of loneliness and not infrequently danger; the chance of dedicating himself to the service of his fellow men, and of responsibility at an early age on a scale which life at home could scarcely ever offer; the pride of belonging to a great service elevated to a mighty and beneficent task.'[14] One criticism he allowed himself of his recognized role as 'the father of the modern Colonial Service', as he mused in 1943 towards the end of his reign in Whitehall on what reforms would be needed in `the training of new DOs after the war, was, 'Might it not be worth while to try and teach our future administrators more about the artistic and spiritual background of the people amongst whom they are to live?'[15]

If this was an image approved in London and welcomed by the aspirant DO, it was a very different story in Whitehall in the 1960s, when the Fursean DOs sought in their dozens to offer their talents to the Commonwealth Relations Office as independence in Africa brought their career to a close. To the DO's disbelief, he was given to understand that in Whitehall's opinion the last thing the independent states would want would be to see a former colonial civil servant on the staff of the new British High Commission.[16] Fortunately for all concerned, many DOs refused to be put off by such a negative response, and were in due course accepted by the new FCO. In terms of looking back, the memoirs of diplomats who started life as DOs often offer valuable comparative perspectives on the two services.[17] What still eludes historians is the reverse view of the FCO, as employer, on the calibre of those former DOs whom they did appoint, many of whom went on to reach the top as ambassadors or high commissioners.

Top Whitehall mandarins who worked at the United Nations as Britain's representative, like Sir Alan Burns and Sir Andrew Cohen (the latter with a profound insider's knowledge of both the CO and the CS), had their own view of the proper worth of the DO. Burns, as UK representative on the Trusteeship Council of the UN, had no doubt about the CAS's 'high tradition of integrity' and maintained that DOs had 'identified themselves with the interests of the people for whom they worked to a degree that is seldom appreciated.'[18] Nevertheless he did not shrink from penning a thought-provoking catalogue of the DO's shortcomings, prefaced by the admission that 'they made many mistakes, as all men do'.[19] Sir Andrew Cohen once defined the proverbial commitment of the DO to his area in a telling way: 'In Nigeria ... if one talked about a Northerner or an Easterner or a Westerner, one did not necessarily mean a Hausa or an Ibo or a Yoruba. One might equally mean a member of the Northern, Eastern or Western Service.'[20]

When it came to Whitehall versus the colonial government, there was never any doubt in the DO's mind that his loyalty lay, unequivocally and totally, to what was in, as he saw it, the best interests of his territory and not of the CO. As Burns commented, 'British civil servants in dependent territories almost invariably adopt the point of view of the local inhabitants', even to the point of embarrassing the Colonial Office in their resistance to what they saw as misguided policies and on occasion willing to resign rather than comply.[21] A senior DO in Northern Nigeria in the 1950s confirmed and extended this basic principle of where a DO's loyalty lay when he spoke of the 'age-old tradition of our service that a DO would stand up for his own people, right or wrong, against all comers'.[22] Such loyalty was summed up by a senior DO in Uganda who in the 1930s was struck by how 'a surprisingly large part of the DO's energies was devoted to fighting higher authority on [his people's] behalf. The interests of the British government rarely came into the reckoning.'[23]

The DO as seen by outside visitors

It would have been virtually impossible for any non-government
visitor to colonial Africa to have gone up-country without getting
in touch with the DO. The era of undercover investigative jour-
nalism had not yet made its entry. Indeed, for reasons of protocol, background-briefing introductions and, before the war, basic
board and lodging, to call on the DO could be as much a matter
of survival as of courtesy. It was not really until the mid-1950s
that Africa, rapidly politicizing and with self-government in the
air, brought the media tourist and the Africa correspondent on
to the scene as they visited Africa to see for themselves. Some,
like Derek Ingram, Patrick Keatley, Bill Kirkman, Colin Legum
and David Williams, went on to make a reputation as leading
commentators and respected interpreters of the African scene.

At least three early commentators published well-observed
and widely read travelogues. Negley Farson accomplished his
epic coast-to-coast drive across Africa in 1939, being one of the
very few pre-war visiting journalists to identify themselves with
colonial Africa. Inevitably he was in regular contact with DOs,
not all of whom emerged unscathed from his observations. His
first impression of Tanganyika was that there were too many officials, 'among them too many young men who spend most of their
working moments *being* "gentlemen" '.[24] He pointed out the planters' opinion that the DOs 'although almost notoriously honest,
are obsolete. These good people still regard an honest, impartial
administration over the natives as their foremost, and practically
sole objective', and any thought of an economic policy was notice-
ably absent among colonial administrators.[25] Farson emphasized
his disdain for the DO in his role as a gentleman: 'This sahib-
complex is one of the most dangerous characteristics ... it carries
with it the *being* a gentleman, the odious inhibition that somehow
business men are unclean.' Nevertheless among the DOs 'there
were some splendid men, and the tone of the Service was friendship, even love' for their African subjects – 'do not minimize that'.[26]
He was much impressed by the DOs working in Uganda, who, he
felt, 'unimpeded by white settlers' demands', had constructed 'an
administrative laboratory in which they have made their work a
model for the rest of Africa'.[27] One of his conclusions on the art of
being a successful DO is of particular interest: 'You must be an
actor to handle Africans. And the histrionic abilities of my host

made me blink with shame. Such a deliberate pose. ... The DO put on a performance that was better than Emlyn Williams.'[28]

Another blockbuster journalist (his account extended to 960 pages) who in 1952–53 travelled 40,000 miles criss-crossing Africa and visited over 100 towns, was the American John Gunther. Apart from his shock ('I blinked, I could not believe my eyes') at discovering that 'half the guests at a Government House dinner were African and that the Governor-General had an African lady on his right as a matter of course',[29] he was less interested in describing DOs than his British predecessor a dozen years before. In Northern Nigeria, however, he collected a number of 'DO tidbits', not only that 'DOs have on occasion formed relationships with African women – the beautiful Fulanis – and sometimes even marry them', but also a few legends, such as the hoary (and pan-African?) one about a DO who, on learning that a riot was in progress outside his office and the crowd was massing for an attack, said to his messenger, without looking up from his desk, ' "Tell them to go home. In this area we do not have riots on Wednesdays. Let them come on a Saturday if they wish, when I have more time." '[30]

While Elspeth Huxley was an author and not a journalist, and a long-term resident of East Africa and not a visitor, whose intimate knowledge of Kenya earned wide respect, her first visit to West Africa in 1952 resulted in a travelogue in which she observed the DO at work in a setting fresh from the one she knew so intimately. In West Africa she found that the post-war 'modern young [DOs] seem, as a rule, alert, enthusiastic, intelligent and possessed of charming manners of a rather formal kind. ... As a whole they drink little and often only beer. They marry young and have babies, which destroys their single-mindedness but improves their health. ... They do not live as close to Africans as their predecessors did.' She concluded that 'in some ways they know more than did men of an earlier generation, but when their time is up they will understand less, for they are more insulated from the people by family life and better living, and different motives bring them here'.[31] Meeting D. MacBride, one of the old school of DO in Nigeria, she saw in him 'a bachelor who understands comfort, with perfect servants, perfect manners, a good table, French bread, a love of tradition. He would be more at home, you feel, in a university Common Room, or in the now extinct kind of parsonage with useful daughters and cricketing sons.'[32] Meeting Northern Nigerian dignitaries in a DO's house, she was at once sensitive to the differences in attitude of DOs in Nigeria towards the local people. ' "Dirt and dignity" is how [they] describe the North, half-mocking their own affection for it. "Sweat and swank" described the South.'[33] In one of her last publications, Elspeth Huxley looked back on almost a century of 'her Kenya' in a series of mini-portraits, many of them on the series of DOs who made – and were in turn made by – the NFD, those 'great men of the North' like H.B. Sharpe, T. Miles, V. Glenday, G. Reece and R.G. Turnbull.[34] Elsewhere, in a discussion of DOs as belonging to a *corps d'élite*, she nevertheless conceded that 'it was all very old-fashioned, Sanders-of-the-River like, and today seems either incredible or absurd.'[35] It was here, too, that Elspeth Huxley dismissed the much-quoted remark of the Spanish writer G. Santayana, that 'never had the world known such a just, sweet and boyish master' as the DO, as 'over-glamourizing' the Colonial Service, while 'the word "boyish" strikes a chill to modern hearts'. She preferred to see DOs as men selected for the standard middle-class virtues of integrity, discipline, loyalty, sobriety, and the schoolboy ideals of team spirit and all-roundedness, qualities often tempered, however, by 'a conventional outlook, a lack of imagination, and a tendency to let sleeping dogs lie'.[36] Sadly, by the time latter-day observant travel writers like Paul Theroux and Bill Bryson turned their perceptive eyes on Africa, the British DO was no longer part of the scene.

Lone researchers, predominantly a post-war phenomenon apart from the pioneering Margery Perham, soon to become the authority on colonial administration and administrators,[37] and a handful of anthropologists, reinforced from the late 1950s by American Ph.D. researchers and, from the 1960s, by the US Peace Corps and British Voluntary Service Overseas, were no less consistently – though not always so happily – in touch with the DO of the area in which they operated. Anthropologists did not always see eye to eye with the DO, who in extreme cases suspected they were likely to stir up trouble among 'his' people. J.G. Liebenow acknowledged his debt to the DO Newala when he was doing his fieldwork in Tanganyika in the mid-1950s for the offer of a vacant house, 'a gesture which I am convinced was calculated to frighten me away from the district'.[38] Visitors from the outside could find the DO often paternalistic, sometimes pompous, and generally proprietorial of 'his' people in 'his' district – in brief, the well-known 'squirearchical' syndrome of the DO in Africa. One ADO in Northern Nigeria remembered being sent out at the double during a Sunday pre-prandial gin and tonic session by his DO who had suddenly heard a car changing gear as it climbed the hill to his house, with the furious command of 'Go and see who the hell that is entering my district without my permission.' It turned out to be a stray trans-African traveller. Arguably such an attitude of possessiveness could at times be as much a virtue as a vice.

The academics' view of the DO

This look-back takes into account some of the changing themes and fashions in imperial historiography during the post-war years in so far as the DO is featured. Though no defence of the colonial administrator, Jan Morris's *Pax Britannica* trilogy of empire (1968–78) was widely popular and, in R. Winks's estimation, came 'at a time when many younger British scholars appeared to be writing from a sense of shame' as 'a necessary corrective'.[39] Where Morris did refer to DOs, her picture was, in the eyes of P. Mullins, formerly a DO in the Gold Coast and Nyasaland and then joining the BBC for his 'second career', 'bathetic in the extreme ... portrayed as a figure from another era'.[40] Later Morris came to a characteristically unblimpish judgement on the generic DO when giving her strong support to the project for a new British Empire and Commonwealth Museum in Bristol. The British Empire, she declared, 'brought out the best and the worst in people, and it certainly brought out the most energetic. ... It was a colossal historical undertaking executed, for the most part, by young people ... it had all the flair and failing of youth.'[41] That the public interest in the history of the Empire is still there is not at issue. Indeed, to the countless books on it published since its dissolution have been added television and radio programmes, the most recent carrying titles like 'The British Empire in Colour', 'When the Flags Came Down' and Niall Ferguson's 'Empire', all within the space of six months in 2002. Attention here is directed not to such spectacular surveys but to some of those who remembered the DO.

Here the leading academic was, by common consent, Margery Perham. From a lifetime of studying colonial administration and meeting DOs in the field as well as at Oxford seminars and conferences, the DO never ceased to feature in her authoritative writings – including her authentic DO-centred novel, *Major Dane's Garden*. If she was, as the psychologist Kathryn Tidrick affirms, 'a leading lay admirer of the Colonial Service',[42] to some DOs she represented a colonial governor *manquée*. In her first critique of colonial administration, she saw the DO under indirect rule as 'the power behind the throne',[43] a role recast by some as, perhaps more accurately, 'the whisper behind the throne'. A quarter of a century later, in her BBC Reith Lectures, Perham elaborated on the classic definition of the daunting list of qualities required in the DO, set out in the definitive 1930 report on the Colonial Service by Warren Fisher. To 'vision, high ideals of service, fearless devotion to duty born of a sense of responsibility, tolerance and, above all, team spirit',[44] she added two more virtues she had recognized among the DOs she met, 'courage and physical prowess'.[45] Her field diaries, replete with notes on the DO as she saw him, provided her with the retrospective impression that 'the great majority of the men I knew revelled in their work. ... It was certainly a man's job. It could take all he had to give, with every faculty employed at the stretch. ... He could be relied upon to be humane, uncorrupt, diligent, even when left alone quite unsupervised in the outer regions of a very testing continent.'[46] But at the same time, she saw him as being 'too British to activate an intimate social relationship with Africans'. But her overall assessment is unqualified: 'If the Colonial Service was not a task for the genius, the marvel is that it attracted so many men of high standards of character and education.' In her opinion, 'the office of District Commissioner should stand out in history as one of the supreme types developed by Britain to meet a special demand'.[47]

Close academic adherents of Margery Perham overseas were the prolific historians P. Duignan and L.H. Gann and the enthusiastic disciple R. Heussler, all of them – significantly – American scholars. Among the works of the first two, it is enough in the context here to indicate the telling titles *The Rulers of British Africa* (1978) and *Burden of Empire* (1968). The work of Heussler, 'a shrewd and not uncritical observer', in the opinion of the governor-general of Nigeria,[48] deserves particular mention, for his *Yesterday's Rulers* (1963) may be said to have pioneered the academic study of the non-ICS DO. With several books on the DO to his credit, two judgements are enough to indicate the tenor of his research: 'The DO's perspective was broad; perhaps no one else was in so good

a position to take a locality's pulse. And few general practitioners in human history were as active and powerful in the whole
sweep of community life as DOs were.' Furthermore 'the legacy
that will endure longest is the personal one. ... More than the
characteristics of colonial rule, the personal achievements and
services of individual officers are remembered.'[49] Yet all this has
to be qualified by the American Heussler: 'My regard for these
men does not remove the fact that I salute their *accomplishments*
more than their *aims*.'[50]

W.M. Macmillan, who had given the CO a wake-up call over
its Caribbean colonies in his timely *Warning for the West Indies*
(1936), set aside a whole chapter in his next book on the Empire
for an examination of the Colonial Service, 'The Rulers of British
Africa'. For him the DO was 'the likeliest person' to know the
details of African policy in detail, 'any peculiar wishes or preju-
dices of the people, and the effect on them of instructions from the
centre'.[51] Despite his situation as 'the lowest rank in the administrative hierarchy', for Macmillan the DO was incontrovertibly the
person 'on which the efficacy of the whole most of all depends'.
Such endorsement was quickly followed by qualification. Even
the most junior of DOs was still 'one of a very tiny ruling caste,
living a life apart, seldom answered back in his private any
more than in his public capacity'. What the Service needed was
a greater readiness 'to laugh at itself and the fallibility of authority'.[52] He believed that some of the best DOs were those who, too
rare in a CAS career, had been 'compelled by the free criticism
of their equals to think out and justify in detail every step they
might be called on to take'.[53]

Throughout the 1970s and 1980s the tone of historians writing about the Empire continued to be sharp and unsympathetic,
often devoid of any serious attempt to understand – or want to
understand – the real nature of the DO and his work. Unsurprisingly this deliberate refusal to accept that there were two sides
to the colonial coin and that much-vaunted academic objectivity
required that both should be considered, caused intense frustration and fury among former DOs, now retired as members of
their Overseas Service Pensioners' Association (OSPA), and their
morale was shaken by the failure of some academics to want to
see all sides in setting the record straight. The tide did not begin
to turn until the last decade of the century, with the appearance
of studies like those by Lawrence James (1994), with his verdict

on Britain that 'few empires have equipped their subjects with the intellectual wherewithal to overthrow their rulers. None has been survived by so much affection and moral respect'; and by Trevor Royle, with his hailing the end of empire in Africa as an episode of which Britain can be proud, and his conviction that 'the British empire in Africa was not just the wicked, grasping and rapacious institution derided by the croakers in the immediate aftermath of its demise, nor was it simply a force for universal good, a great adventure which benefited anyone concerned in its execution', but 'somewhere in between'.[54]

The imperial look-back of the 1990s had come a long way from the strident and self-flagellatory, guilt-searching, breast-beaters of the 1970s. Balance had returned to the historical debate and it had now become possible for historians to look at the work of the DO with objectivity rather than instant and unthinking odium. For all his reservations on British policy in Kenya, primarily during the Mau Mau revolt, the historian J.M. Lonsdale has acknowledged that the reputation of the DO in Africa, having moved from a proud one in history and then to a defensive one, has 'in the 1990s benefited from respect for an ability to get things done in the Third World with more tangible benefit, more willing co-operation from its peoples, and only a fraction of resources that make possible some of the colossal cock-ups of today'.[55] By 2003 Niall Ferguson, one of the new voices presenting Britain's imperial story to a TV audience of millions, had no qualms in concluding, without any hint of qualification, that in the end empire had been 'a good thing'.[56]

Academics who visited Africa on sustained fieldwork had a personal view of the DO, given the proximity in which they often co-existed for months at a time. One went so far as to undertake a profound socio-statistical analysis of the Gold Coast DOs between 1920 and 1939, in which she examined 'their intellectual back-grounds, their collective value systems, and their behavioural patterns'.[57] Another, Kathryn Tidrick, subjected a number of DOs to an exploration of the effect of imperial rule on the character of the colonial Englishman, among them those DOs who found among the Maasai of the Great Rift Valley 'a Colonial Service paradise', represented in its 'tradition of preternaturally forceful DOs' who enjoyed all the autonomy they liked.[58] Focusing on inter-war Kenya, Bruce Berman was critical of the role played by the administration in Kenya's political economy, describing the inter-war DOs as 'autocratic and paternalistic', and endorsing Norman Leys' (no admirer of Kenya's provincial administration) condemnation that 'the basis of government in a reserve is that every wish of the DO is law'.[59] His highly critical chapter 'The Bureaucratic Dialectic' is a substantial, if densely written, anatomy of the DO in Kenya, with numerous references to his make-up and role, in particular of the legacy of his public school and Oxbridge upbringing. He criticizes what he calls the DO's sense of 'pastoral nostalgia', 'based on a romanticised image of agrarian society (notably the English village of some ill-defined golden age) as the repository of communal virtues'.[60]

Not all academics have been so charitable as some of those quoted above, least of all those teaching and writing in the 1970s and 1980s, when DO-baiting seemed so to predominate in the less-informed literature that ex-DOs humorously coined a Hobbesian pastiche of the Empire as 'nasty, brutish and in shorts' and mischievously thought of designing a tie with a 'WI' motif, denoting 'Wicked Imperialist'. On the whole it would seem that the academics who rarely left their classrooms for field work, and regrettably never encountered a DO, were less convincing in their description and definition of the DO's role in Africa than those who had undertaken field research and had at least seen the DO in action and the lie of the land for themselves. If the image of the inter-war DOs was sometimes that of 'ignorant, gin-swigging, unshaven remittance men of whom Britain was well rid',[61] who had taken jobs in Africa because they could not get ones at home, irascible, authoritarian, besotted with black mistresses and yet more of the bottle, puffed-up pooh-bahs who promoted the mystique that they were lords of all they surveyed, in the post-colonial age the DO sunk for a while to being less a figure of fun and more of an Aunt Sally for a younger generation born too late ever to have met a DO while he was still a DO. I. Brook, a DO in Western Nigeria, recounted this kind of imagery in his meeting with a Harvard anthropologist in the early 1950s. 'The thing that had struck him the most, he said, was that none of the administrators he had met remotely resembled the popular idea of a British DC. He had felt chastened, he went on, that he, as an intellectual, had so completely accepted the popular American image of a British DO as a large whisky-swilling red-necked man who walked about in riding breeches, with a hunting crop in his hand, beating hell out of Africans.'[62] Those he had met, he went on, 'had all been men with a great deal more knowledge of African problems and customs than the academics who lectured on the subject. How come, he wanted to know, did the legend bear so little resemblance to the reality?'

As the symbol of colonial rule, the DO became for a while as much a dirty word in the demonology of empire in post-imperial Britain as he had now and then been in the last years of colonial rule in Africa. Malcolm Muggeridge had no compunction in bitingly portraying DOs as 'permanently adolescent prefects in grown-up dress, who would put up with discomfort and sometimes danger from a sense of duty, finding their reward in the social eminence accorded them and in the ribbons and stars which they were permitted to pin on their persons.'[63] For all its clearly tongue-in-cheek mockery of the DO (this time by a DO from Tanganyika, possessed of what one of his superiors called 'a deplorably exaggerated sense of humour'), A.T. Culwick's comments made in 1963 on the conduct of the DO in Africa and his preoccupation with 'the code of a gentleman' and the credo that 'successful administrators depended on concealing the facts' contain a lot of the easy criticism that was to swell in volume in the immediate post-colonial decades.[64]

As we have seen, the tide began to turn in the 1990s. Since then not only has the DO begun to be seen by academics in a better light, especially, as Lonsdale pointed out,[65] when the condition of Africans in 2000 is compared to that of 1960, but also positive advances have been made in the study of his own history and pride restored to his demonized service. No longer, as was sometimes the case during his search for a second career in the 1960s and 1970s, was it necessary for a DO instinctively to play down his recent past. Writing of his role as a local government consultant with a Danish aid agency, H.J.B. Allen, formerly a DO in Uganda, observed how 'I knew that my Nordic colleagues were embarrassed that their team should contain an ex-imperialist, so I maintained a discreet silence about my murky past', until his Nordic team-mates witnessed the exuberant warmth of welcome extended to Norris when the team undertook a project in Uganda.[66] Too many critics, both academics and those with more excuse, have fallen into the intellectual trap of trying to view, and then judge, the past by the present. As George MacDonald Fraser warned the younger generation as they sought to put forward their explanations of the Second World War, wanting to see it in their terms and keen that it should conform with their notions, 'You must try to see it in its own terms and values if you are to have any inkling of it.'[67]

The latest exemplar of imperial history scholarship, *The Oxford History of the British Empire*, confirms the argument of this section that the DO may expect to share in the more balanced assessment of empire which has characterized the past decade. DOs were, in J.W. Cell's concluding sentence, 'often passionately committed to the success of the independent countries they left behind', an observation matched by Judith Brown's verdict that 'at the time of independence, departing British colonial officials hoped that their enduring legacy would be that of the rule of law and of democratic procedures and institutions which they left behind', and her conclusion that the British Empire 'still arouses immense curiosity and at times passion, though there is perhaps less incentive to draw up moral balance sheets and to portray it in stark terms of praise and blame than there once was.'[68]

The DO in the African mind and memory

Potentially the most significant mode of investigation, yet in practical terms the most elusive, to look at the DO from the bottom upwards, i.e. how Africans saw him, remains (and is now likely to remain forever) a huge missed opportunity of scholarship. With the end of colonial rule approaching its 50th anniversary and with most of those who experienced it at first-hand now dead, we shall never know the primary evidential answer to the fundamental and final question in the appraisal of colonial rule in Africa: how did 'they' see 'us'? In the event this has to be a question of the *quot homines* format. Leaving aside the existence of a DO's individual relationships and often his personal friendships, the underlying thrust of the question of 'how did Africans see the DO?' needs to be immediately reformulated into 'which Africans?'

First, there is the broad category of the rural peasantry, those hunters and gatherers and nomads among whom the DO spent many (and generally the most happily remembered) years and where he felt that the essence of his work and the summit of his achievements lay. What they thought of their DOs and how the image lives on in the post-colonial memory is either fading away from folk memory or is almost impossible to gauge other than

impressionistically 40 or 50 years after the last DO left. Heussler's
message in 1968, that 'the vital subject of how the Africans felt
[was] an eminently researchable' topic,[69] could expect no priority
among all the more exciting research projects in the immediate
aftermath of independence, least of all by African scholars and
the new historians for whom there was neither hurry nor imperative to revisit the colonial era. Sadly, with so little done in this
field, today any research into how Africans saw the DO would
have to depend more and more on a generation of informants
who are themselves too young ever to have met a DO and whose
parents were not always literate enough to have any evidence to
rely on other than their experience and memory. Yet what tales
could have been told, especially when one takes account of the
fact that in much of Africa the 'stranger' was a consistent element
in folk tales and proverbial lore. Tantalizing glimpses of this
'village' image of the DO can still be gained here and there by
listening to elders' gossip or the reminiscences of former government messengers and policemen told under the moon or round
the village fire in the evening, and, from time to time, at second-
or third-hand from the student sons and daughters of that older
generation. It is likely to be the DO who was a 'character', the
eccentric or larger-than-life DO rather than the run-of-the-mill
one, who captured the local memory. Stories may well be heard
about Bwana X who compelled his uncomprehending carriers
to stop a small ball which he hit towards them with a cut-down
tree trunk or about Mr Y who used to run round the town walls
every day, with his horse following, or of Bwana Z who always
opened the village meeting with a selection from his repertoire of
juggling tricks. A significant clue to the district image of the DO
can be found in the revealing nicknames earned by many DOs.
Even in the 1950s, DOs of the 1920s and sometimes earlier were
identified by their vernacular nicknames, for instance 'Mr Easy
Dozy', 'Mr Chat-Chat-Chat' or 'Mr Scorpion', *Bwana Kiboko* ('Mr
Whip') or, for his developmental enthusiasms, 'Prince of the Pit
Latrine'. Physical features and behavioural traits also lent themselves as ready identity tags, like 'The One with a Third Eye' (he
wore a monocle) or 'The Owner of an Ostrich', kept as a pet.

A second category of Africans whose memory of the DO
could be of intense interest is the local rulers, the emirs and chiefs
both traditional and appointed. Once again this is a more or less
silent source.[70] Yet here was a group of Africans who interacted

with their DOs in a particularly close and regular fashion and whose views on the DO would have been of unique value. From the other end, as it were, we have A.T. Weatherhead's perceptive reflection after a lifetime working in the emirates of Northern Nigeria: 'For their part, [the emirs] found us on the whole unpredictable, uncertain of temper, impossible about what they considered unimportant and tolerant when they were not prepared to budge an inch.'[71]

Thirdly, the search could be directed towards two of the newest African arrivals in the DO's life, the nationalist politicians and the educated elite. In the case of the latter, the evidence is strong of an initial antipathy between the Western-educated, often mission-schooled African and the DO, unused as the latter was to his decisions being questioned or his motives queried. Perhaps the educated youth broke the DO's golden-age mould of what 'real' Africa and Africans should be in his Arcadian or squirearchical image. 'We had an easier relationship with chiefs, headmen and messengers/tribal policemen than we did with the emerging elite,' J.R. Johnson noted from his post-war Kenyan experience.[72] A Tanganyikan DO, T.J. Tawney, saw it similarly: 'In general the less educated people were, the greater the mutual affection and respect, but the further away from urban centres, the easier and more rewarding the relationship.' It was often a sad story how the DO commonly (but not always, of course) snubbed or ignored the educated elite, saved to an extent when the pendulum swung dramatically the other way and, in the late colonial period, Africanization became the order of the day and many DOs became immediately involved in and dedicated to working with educated Africans who were going to take up senior governmental positions, including that of DO. J.H. Smith noted how much easier in the last years of colonial rule it was 'for those of us who belonged to the time of transition, had a stake in the Nigerian future, and wanted to know Nigerians as fellow human beings rather than just as pleasant people one administered'.[73] Here is at least one chance to gain access to how the DO was seen by at least one surviving segment of the African population, for many of yesterday's first African DOs have now retired and are in a fine position to write their memoirs of what it was like to have served 'under two masters', in the same way as their British counterparts have done. Historians of the DO in Africa must hope that memoirs like those by, for instance, J.O. Udoji, A.

Adebayo and M. Maciel, will be but the forerunners of others.[74]

In the case of nationalist politicians, the memoir and speech are a rich source of evidence of their image of the DO denied to the researcher investigating that image among the rural peasantry and the chiefs. This is not surprising, for vilification of the DO was an easy and obvious weapon in nationalist oratory, where getting rid of the alleged obstructiveness of DOs was an integral item in the demand for independence. African politicians have, like politicians everywhere, not been shy in writing their memoirs or collecting their speeches for publication. Nnamdi Azikiwe, the leading Nigerian nationalist of the 1950s and a sturdy critic of colonial administration, sponsored plenty of anti-DO column inches in the fiery Zik press, but in his self-selected anthology of his speeches his principal assault was on his old sparring partner, the governor of Nigeria, Sir Arthur Richards. His castigation of CO policy included the personal shaft of how 'it seems to be dedicated to "the gospel according to the man on the spot", whose word is law and whose maladministration often entitles him to be kicked upstairs with a GCMG or a peerage as his reward'.[75] It was another top Nigerian nationalist, Chief Obafemi Awolowo, who coined the phrase that made its mark in the anti-colonial lexicon, referring to 'the petty autocracy' of DOs.[76] The epithet was echoed in Kwame Nkrumah's accusation in the Gold Coast that 'Before my party came into office the DCs were actually the little governors of the rural areas.' 'I knew,' he went on, 'by travelling through the country that many of those officers were hated by the people … a law unto themselves.' Because DOs represented colonialism in practice, Nkrumah concluded that 'their presence was harmful to the country'.[77]

In Central Africa, too, the 'little tin god' imagery of the DO was also promoted as a gibe. Rationalizing the Africanization of the provincial administration, Kenneth Kaunda explained in an address to PCs and DOs in 1968 that their predecessors' systems 'had a terribly bad element in it – it embraced far too much power for any human being to have without turning him into a small and cowardly little god on earth'.[78] Premier Awolowo was tireless in his condemnation of the DO. The chapter 'Bones of Contention' in his memoir opens with the accusation that 'the most meritless Chief is pampered *ad nauseam*' by the DO, 'who at the same time shows some unfriendliness towards educated politicians.' Fortunately that 'myth about [the DO's] omniscience and omnipotence' was fast on the way out 'thanks to the agency of lawyers and public letter-writers'.[79] In Northern Nigeria, too, the chiefs were accused of collaboration with the DO under what was sometimes disdainfully alleged to be an Anglo-Fulani compact. Awolowo rounded off his tirade against DOs with the comment that the DO was 'a source of annoyance to the people. He is aloof, suspicious of the educated classes, and treats their political aspirations with contempt. The DO is arrogant.'[80]

In Northern Nigeria the Premier, Sir Ahmadu Bello, in whose domain the relationship between nationalists and the DOs was palpably calmer (though in no way free from friction), if only because some of his senior party members argued that the first priority for removal was the fellow Nigerian yet alien Ibos rather than the much simpler to remove British administrator, accepted that pre-war DOs varied a great deal: some were very helpful but some 'thought too much of their own position to think properly of others'. Fundamentally he preferred the earlier generation of DOs to the post-war cohorts: 'the earlier ones were friends and teachers, the latter ones – many of them but by no means all – were not'.[81] Perhaps the most quoted nationalist politician's comment was that made by the prime minister of Nigeria on independence day, when he spoke of 'the British officers whom we have known, first as masters, and then as leaders, and finally as partners, but always as friends' – this from the man who had severely criticized the Northern Nigerian administration in the legislative council in 1949 and pointed to the waste of resources in recruiting 36 ADOs that year at a time when the peoples were 'crying for development'.[82] Further up the west coast, the president of Sierra Leone, Siaka Stevens, recalled how, at the end of family prayers, his father used to add 'And save us, O Lord, from the trouble of the DC', adding that not only was the DC held in dread all over the country but he had now joined the pantheon of children's hobgoblins and bogey-men.[83] TANU's constant spats with the DOs have already been documented.

The final groups identified here (further sub-categorization is of course possible in all the groups isolated above) have tended to be overlooked when it comes to the memory of the DO in the African mind. They comprised the three kinds of Africans who were, in one way or another, members of the DO's personal staff and hence closer to him at work than any other Africans. Once more, regrettably, their memories have not been a source tapped by researchers. The categories envisaged are the DO's office clerks; the DO's messengers, orderlies and in some areas interpreters; and the DO's domestic staff. A senior police officer in Botswana recalled in 2000 his unflattering image of the Bechuanaland DO when a young constable in the 1960s: 'They only drank, and did as little as they could so that they were less noticed in Mafeking for their inadequacies.'[84] Clerical staff were, like the Goans in Kenya and the Sierra Leoneans and Gold Coasters in Northern Nigeria, often as much foreigners in the country as the DO was. Whether this made it easier or harder for them to record their impressions is arguable, but none can yet equal Mervyn Maciel's valuable memoir, with its wealth of pen-sketches of DOs under whom he worked.[85] As for the DO's domestic staff, if only the DO featured in their memory one-tenth of the times they do in his, what rich data the social as well as the imperial historian would have at his disposal, for verily 'no man is a hero to his valet'.

With so many opportunities missed to flesh out the image of the DO in the African mind, attention may be drawn to the original data which has emerged from a recent research project undertaken for the Overseas Service Pensioners' Association.[86] Even though, under the circumstances, this is still 'our' view of how 'they' saw us and not the ultimate one of how they actually saw us, compensatory data can be informative. 'They treated us with friendly incomprehension,' felt B. Loach of his time in up-country Northern Rhodesia. From his experience of district work in Uganda, J.P. Twining wondered how the British would feel if they were 'ruled by demi-gods from Mars'. At the end of 20 years in the Kenyan administration, G. Ellerton's guess at how the Africans viewed the DO was 'sometimes, I suspect, with utter bewilderment', a view elaborated on by M. Macgregor's response from Northern Rhodesia: 'mutual disbelief'. J.A.R. Forster's verdict from the Gold Coast's last 12 years of colonial rule was that 'we were respected for most of the time; tolerated as sometimes rather strange individuals; and sometimes genuinely liked'. In B.L. Jacobs' opinion, the DOs were looked on more kindly than they merited. In Uganda D. Brown's reply was moderated to 'acceptance. … We were there, we were a fact of life.' P.H. Jones in Kenya had no doubt that the pre-war peasantry believed that the taxes they paid went straight into the DO's pocket. From Nigeria R.F. Bendy's summary of touring was that 'in a bush village the arrival of the DO was rather like the arrival of a touring music hall'. The DO, wrote another respondent, was probably looked on as 'well-meaning, if slightly comical', an opinion echoed by A.P. Smith derived from his Nigerian experience: 'they thought us slightly mad but were glad to take advantage of our sense of fair play and honesty'.

Others took the line that the African's natural courtesy and tolerance, and maybe his cultural upbringing of telling those in authority only what they wanted to hear, concealed his instinctive dislike of the DO as ruler. 'Many of us overestimated the respect in which we thought we were held,' warned J.H.F. Bown from Northern Rhodesia. 'The Africans were very good at being polite but saw through a lot of our thoughts.' In Tanganyika in the 1950s M.H. Dorey felt 'throughout my service that those Africans who worked closely with us ... were able to distinguish between good and bad officers'. 'The large number of people,' he went on, 'who came to us with their problems showed that they trusted us and knew they would get a fair hearing.' In the end he reckoned that 'Many thought us a bit of a nuisance, as we tried to persuade them to send their children to school, prevent erosion, pay tax, etc., preferring to be left alone.' S. Delmege's view followed a similar track, seeing the Africans' reactions as 'the same as the attitude of any underlings (whether at school, in the army, or in the old Lord of the Manor situation): they are decent, doing a reasonable job – but I wish they would get off our backs, we could do it just as well ourselves.' Another Tanganyikan DO, W.J. Warrell-Bowring, took a different line, observing how Africans 'essentially hedonists, thought we were mad to work so hard'. Others have pointed to the fact that, had the DO been as unpopular, feared or hated as nationalist oratory sometimes depicted him, it would have been too easy to eliminate him. In the event, once the initial years of 'pacification' were past, remarkably few DOs were assaulted or assassinated, though some died in the course of duty or through illness.

Generally goodwill, the lack of personal animosity, and the remarkable uncaring sense of personal security (especially when compared to what they found on their return to Britain) all featured in the DO's consideration of how Africans looked on him in their midst. G.C. Guy's conclusion was that in general the DO was 'treated with respect and some affection'. 'Many were admired and well-loved personally, but not as representatives of the system' was a thoughtful judgement.

Switching the scene momentarily from Africa back to the UK, there was truth too in the contemporary retrospective assessment hinted at by M.H. Shaw, that DOs were respected a great deal more by the Africans than by people in Britain today.

The DO looks back on the DO

DOs' memoirs almost invariably close by looking back on their careers. In most cases they conclude on a note of pleasure, pride and even privilege as they contemplate their work in Africa. Few look back in disillusionment, fewer still in anger. Those who do bid their career farewell in partial disappointment tend to do so as they contemplate the colonial aftermath and nostalgically compare the continent's contemporary woes with what they feel were the happier days when they were DOs. If they reflect with a hint of pessimism on the post-colonial present, they remain positively satisfied with its colonial past and what they believe they achieved in their job as a DO.

Assessing his work in pre-war Nigeria, A.E. Cook was of the opinion that being a DO was 'a job which can be learnt only doing it and for which the essential qualifications are common-sense and integrity'. Cook closed his memoir with a call for patriotic pride redolent of pre-war Britain: 'I hope that one day you will be as proud of your Colonial Service as you are of the Royal Navy,' though he stressed how difficult he always found it when people said to him 'But what do you do?', too often meeting with the assumption that a DO in Nigeria was some sort of military officer from Nicaragua, or with an enquiry whether you had come across his/her uncle Ted somewhere in East Africa.[87] A decade later J. Morley on his first leave encountered a similar confusion of identity, when at a party a girl asked him what he did. When he said he was a DO in Northern Nigeria, she said 'Tea-planting, I presume?'[88] A similar misconception, this time in the mind of the future wife of a DO, befell Rosemary Hollis when her hostess told her that she had invited to dinner a rather special person for her to meet, a District Officer on leave. 'In my ignorance I imagined a mere lump of brainless masculinity, talking only of shooting lions. How wrong I was! Our first conversational exchange was to hum together the slow movement of the Bach Double Violin Concerto. I was to discover soon that most of the Service was composed of equally civilized men.'[89] G. Billing was also impressed at the end of his 30 years as a DO in Northern Rhodesia by the diversity of his colleagues' gifts: 'one might be a good shot and keen on hunting; another might be a stern disciplinarian and markedly efficient; another might have an unusual sense of humour and raise laughs all round.'[90] M. Varvill's service in Nigeria covered both the pre- and the post-war years, and what struck him was the vast difference in the DO's work between the 1930s and the 1950s. 'In the earlier years we had little concern for the grand issues of imperial policy,' he noted. 'We were too busy to trouble with such things – an unbuilt bridge, an unbuilt dispensary, a school without a playing field, tax evaders and odd court decisions were what mattered. ... The halcyon days between the two world wars were never to return. They were years when the young bush administrator could involve himself in the affairs of the territory with little regard to what was happening elsewhere. ... Although the outlook was limited, his job was supremely worthwhile.'[91] To P. Dennis in the Gold Coast, the DO's work was as much about learning as teaching: 'We were supposedly in an educative role, but I am quite sure I learned more than I ever taught anybody' are the closing words of his memoir, while at the end of his challenging years in Sierra Leone H. Mitchell felt that 'I added cubits to my stature.'[92]

In his enraptured recollection of what turned out to be a very abbreviated career as a DO in Uganda because of ill health, the future Lord Tweedsmuir produced a recipe that would have won endorsement from many DOs fortunate enough to have had a full career to look back on: 'To be twenty-two, to be strong, and to be in Africa. There was nothing else that the world had to offer that I would have exchanged for that life.'[93] That initial falling in love with the place and the work also exercised its magic on J. Gutch and his fellow cadets: 'I think we all acquired an affection for the very differing parts of the Gold Coast to which we had been assigned. Yet what I was able to see of other districts never destroyed my affection for Ho.'[94] For some DOs, indeed, the meaning of feeling 'homesick' took on a reverse locational meaning: home was now away.

In keeping with the times, the post-war DO appears to be far more articulate about the Service than perhaps his predecessors had ever felt the need to be. Looking back on his career in Northern Rhodesia, R. Short believed that under the leadership of Sir Arthur Benson, 'the spirit of the provincial administration equalled that of a first-class regiment at the height of condition. ... [It] was a band of brothers, and every DC had friends everywhere he had served in the territory and among every class. There was no snobbishness, no patronage, and the post sought after was the "field".' But, he claimed, with a change of governor 'a more narrow, calculating, negative era began, and the spirit of the service began to change and wither'.[95] R. Oakley also identified a strong sense of *esprit de corps* among DOs: 'I never once heard a [DO] run down the work of another.'[96] The Australian W.R. Crocker, who in the 1930s did not fit into every senior officer's idea of what an ADO should be, dismissed many of his colleagues as 'careerists' and lambasted his seniors in a section of his frank memoir unmistakably titled 'Inferiorities in the Quality of Administration'.[97] Thirty years on and in the same territory J.H. Smith came to a more balanced view of the Service: 'There was plenty wrong with it ... it could have been so much better, but it might have been very much worse.'[98] M. Milne's valuable comment on the CAS as he found it in Eastern Nigeria – 'We obeyed the accepted usages of the Service: we were encouraged, at whatever level we served, to say what we thought, but we did what we were told' – can be set beside I. Brook's reflection on the other bank of the River Niger: 'The Colonial Service is a disciplined one. You can make your protest but when it is overruled you just accept the decision and get on with something else.'[99]

Of course there was a downside to a life as a DO, more often of a personal rather than a professional nature. These disadvantages are not concealed in DOs' memoirs, particularly over matters like the frequency of transfers and sometimes the distortion and deprivation of family life. One thinks of I. Mackinson's dampener on the happiness of his years in Northern Rhodesia – 'in spite of disease, absences, children away, often danger' – and of H.J.B. Allen's alliterative trilogy of 'discomforts, disappointments and disease' in Uganda. Despite the fact that both his father and his father-in-law had been DOs in Uganda, S. Delmege conceded that on his retirement in 1959 from Kenya 'being back in the UK brought many advantages to my family – young and old'. But when the DO looks back on being a DO, it is overwhelmingly the plus side of his life that predominates. 'One forgets the hard times,' R. Short reflected, 'and remembers the best of it. But wives don't always agree.' A large element in that reconstruction, sometimes openly expressed and sometimes unconsciously hinted at, is the 'romance' of being a DO, particularly of being an ADO. Always allowing for the 5 per cent who were unsociable – or were made miserable by their seniors[100] – on their first tour, DOs tend to look back on their first bush station as a time of immense and unrepeatable happiness, when all they could hope for was that they might be blessed by remaining there for the rest of their days. W. Bazley in Uganda represented this cadet emotion when he described how 'the first district to which an officer is appointed possesses for him almost poetic overtones', a sentiment echoed by M.W. Norris's emphasis on 'the initial, first district emotion'.[101] The emotion was easily carried through to one's memoirs written many years later. 'First impressions leave lasting indentations,' wrote A.T. Clark. 'The *tabula rasa* that is the very junior officer's mind will never lose the tracings of his first job.'[102] So strong was the pull of that first posting that incidents have been known of officers wishing to perpetuate their memory of it even after their death, one by leaving a sum of money to 'his' Pokot for the benefit of the people and another requesting that should he die on duty he might be buried in 'his' Yola. The DO's wife Peggy Watt spoke for many DOs when on leaving Nigeria she closed her narrative with 'we sailed away with no small part of our hearts remaining in Nigeria'.[103] K.G. Bradley's evocation, too, of the Africa of all our yesterdays remains a trigger in the mind of many DOs back in a sudden shower in the middle of a dry English summer: 'But oh! The smell of Africa after the first rain! So pungent, so sweet!'[104]

The final quotation on looking back on the DO's life comes not from a DO but from one who for over 20 years taught DOs at Cambridge and ran the DOs' annual summer school there on African administration. At the close of a symposium on the District Officer in the age of decolonization and his role as 'the man in the middle', Professor Ronald Robinson acknowledged that he had found among DOs 'a tremendous amount of idealism, but they don't like admitting it – too boy-scoutish. But the fact is, surely nobody would be so foolish as to take his wife and family out in the bush as a career, for the greater part of his working life, without being an idealist and a Utopian!'[105]

The DO looks back on the DO 40–50 years later

The bulk of the evidence supporting this study of the DO between 1932 and 1966 has been drawn from memoirs compiled from personal documentation while the DO was still in work and supplemented by stimulated recollections before being, for the most part, published not too long after his retirement. The events were still fresh in his mind, the excitement still recurring as he moved into a second career and often found reasons to compare it unfavourably with his first. This section considers how the DO saw his work some 40 to 50 years later, after he had retired not only from his first but often his second career. The original evidence that follows is derived from the documentation from some 250 DOs collected, in an attempt at retrospective reflection, to establish and to analyse what might be called the 'Colonial Service mind'.[106]

On the selection of the CAS, there is no doubt that from the 1930s up to at least the mid-1950s, to become a DO was a well-respected job among British (and some Commonwealth) graduates, offering responsibility at an early age and the chance to see one's work coming to fruition, all in a setting that was at once adventurous and attractive in its novelty. Despite the human tendency to view yesterday's questions through the Third World prism of today, with its idiom of 'wanting to help others less fortunate' and 'helping Africans to govern themselves', there did exist in the mind, if not so prominently in the vocabulary, of the young DO an understanding that to improve the lot of Africans would inspire much of the work of the DO. A general sense of achievement in being accepted for government service was enhanced by the realization that the Colonial Service, unlike its sister services in India and the Sudan, was the only one to bear the prefix of 'His/Her Majesty's'.

In handling the questions of 'where did we go wrong?' the bulk of DOs' responses (qualified now and again by a staunch 'if we did!') focus on the tardiness, almost unforgivable in retrospect, in introducing any schemes to offer Africans the chance to gain experience in a subordinate administrative rank or schemes designed to train Africans to become DOs. When such innovations eventually materialized, many former DOs describe their involvement in training their successors as the most rewarding of their latter-day assignments. Against this bonus, many DOs felt that the introduction of political parties, national elections and a ministerial system of government spelled the end of the job of DO as they had learned and loved it. Some felt that, while the objective of independence was unarguable, the timetable was so fore-

shortened that there simply was not enough time for the complex
checks and balances of Westminster democracy (the only pattern
on offer by the British) to put down roots, acquire understanding and earn respect and support. 'We were right not to oppose
independence but we still left too early' is a frequent paradoxical
comment in this context. While some DOs pointed to the poverty
of personal relationships with the Western-educated African
elite, many were at pains vigorously to refute the sometimes
retrospectively voiced pan-continental accusation that 'Yes, you
gave us roads and schools and hospitals – but did you give us our
hearts?' On the whole, there are still echoes in the evidence of the
long-standing charge that while the DO's relations with peasants
and princes were easy and often good, in the districts he found
himself uncomfortable in the presence of educated Africans, at
least until the transition years leading into independence.

Perhaps the most interesting self-revelations of how the DO
long after retirement recalled his work came when he sought
to compare his second (and often third) career with his time as
a DO. G.C. Guy, who had started as a DO in Sierra Leone, was
satisfied that he 'could have wished for no other career nor any
better way to spend one's life', so that when it came to subsequent
employment this came out badly, principally because there was,
by comparison, 'so little scope for initiative'. For A.G. Ditcham the
ultimate difference lay in the fact that whereas one had chosen
the CAS as a career, the next time round one was simply looking
for a job: 'After a career, a job is a pain.' Comparing his work as
a DO in Tanganyika with his later job as general secretary of a
major UK charity, S. Hardwick was one of those struck by 'the
lack of those wide responsibilities in being in charge of a district'.
A few, like J.E. Blunden, who took up his second job after 29 years
as a DO in Northern Rhodesia, wondered how far the big fish/
little pond syndrome coloured the assessment of a second career.
There was strong support for the kind of view expressed by K.P.
Shaw, who was a DO in Kenya from 1949 to 1963, that it was a
'privilege' to have been a DO, 'doing a well-worthwhile job, often
in trying and difficult circumstances'. From Nyasaland, J.N.E.
Watson remembered his career 'with affection', and in retrospect
'would have chose no other'. Becoming a solicitor after serving
as a DO in Nyasaland, G.W.S. Bowry gave his successive careers
a different rating. At the end of 26 years in his second career he
felt 'I would rather have had 26 years in Nyasaland and none as a

lawyer.' T.R.W. Longmore, on the other hand, perceived a distinct similarity between his work as a DO listening to complainants in Northern Nigeria and his later job as a solicitor: 'In the beginning I found myself dealing with the simpler sons of Sussex much as I would have dealt with Audu from the Kano bush – only to be brought up short when I realized this time I had to charm them into paying the bill for my services.' For E.B.S. Alton, who spent 12 years as a DO in the Gold Coast before making his second career in the Home Civil Service, his second career was 'more challenging intellectually but much less fun. ... And results were much slower.' While some DOs have stressed that one advantage of their second career was that it was far more family-friendly, Alton made the compelling comment that as a DO 'one's family was a large part of living and of one's work, a factor totally absent in the Home Civil Service'.

In his look-back after a career shift from the CAS in the High Commission Territories to the Diplomatic Service, J. Hennessy enjoyed them both but felt 'overall it was probably more constructive and satisfying to be doing things myself rather than reporting what others were doing'. J.R. Johnson, who also joined the Diplomatic Service after starting life as a DO in Kenya, felt 'there was less independence of thought and action in the early career stage', while D. Joy, who was a DO in Northern Rhodesia for 14 years before entering the FCO, was aware that he had now switched from the 'doing' to 'watching and reporting'. M.H. Shaw, from Tanganyika, put his finger on a difference between the CAS and the Diplomatic Service which a number of such transferred DOs hinted at: 'You never get under the skin of another country in the same way we did [as a DO].' Another DO, C.A.K. Cullimore in Tanganyika, who took the DO/FCO route via a spell in commerce (ICI), reckoned that 'in breadth of direct responsibility my three years in the provincial administration spoiled me for life'. F. Kennedy, who also made the transition into a third career from CAS to FCO via big business, reflected that although he looked back on his days as a DO in Eastern Nigeria with great fondness, 'I have always been grateful that those days were numbered' and frankly came to the conclusion that 'if I had had to forfeit one of the three I would choose to give up the Colonial Service.'

To compare a second career with a first career has one built-in fallacy in it, particularly in the case of those having been DOs. This is the assumption that in both cases the person is the same age. For the DO, as has been argued earlier, to be young was of the essence and for a younger man, as J. Hennessy declared, 'the Colonial Service undoubtedly had the edge'. D.L. Mathews' verdict from Tanganyika was the same: 'to be a DC in a remote part of Africa – that must be the No.1 job ever, especially for a young man', a view shared by his colleague D. Connelly, who declared that one's youth coloured much of the remembered glamour. R.T. Kerslake, who left Nigeria in 1946 to join Guinness, thought the same: 'Any job, after that of a N. Nigerian ADO, was bound to be something of an anti-climax.' A one-word image remains in J.M. Golds' mind for ever as he looked back on five years spent in the NFD: 'Wonderful!'

Twenty years later, N.F. Cooke, who had spent nearly 30 years in the provincial administration in Nigeria, felt that 'a senior position in personnel at Courtaulds was in no way comparable to that I had held in Nigeria [Senior Resident]'. Several DOs commented on how they inevitably linked the man-management problems of their second career directly with their experience as a DO. Some found the transition from provincial office to college administration familiar enough and not too traumatic, such as J.G. Davies and T.J. Barty. As an administrator at the University of Nottingham, R.J. Graham 'used to tell the Board of the Faculty of Medicine that dealing with Native Authorities and Local Councils in Nigeria had really trained me well for dealing with academics and consultants', while R.J. Purdy recognized in dealing with the governing body of the public school of which he became bursar how valuable his experience of handling an obdurate emirate council had been. As Secretary of Imperial College, London, J.H. Smith 'found academics *en masse* far more difficult and far less co-operative than the most difficult and least co-operative people I ever dealt with overseas. "Ah", they would comment, "we don't just do anything you say – and you can't call up the navy to force us to obey."'

Overall, what emerges from this survey of more than 200 DOs' look-backs in 2000 to the 1950s and 1960s is a level of enthusiasm for their first careers – remembered 'with great affection and nostalgia' as a 'worthwhile experience that I would not have missed for all the world' – not always found so incontrovertibly in other Service careers, civil or military, and rarely in business. Where else, D.G.P. Taylor wondered, could one enjoy 'being a magistrate, architect and accountant all in the course of one morning?' P.H. Jones modified his enthusiasm with a compelling caveat: 'I still believe that the job of a DO was the best in the world – if not perhaps for one's wife.' Setting it beside a second career, R.B.S. Purdy argued that to be a DO was a 'vocation, whereas in England one just had a job'.

Two more post-colonial conundrums remain to be analysed one day. In the first decade or so after the end of the career DO in Africa, talk was sometimes heard in clubs and common rooms speculating on what had happened to the kind of young graduate who had once been the mainstay of the DO, now that the DO no longer was. Where did he make his career these days? Probably not in the FCO or the Home Civil Service. Some saw the big oil companies, leading multinational firms, the City and overseas banking as the gainers, attracting 'the upper Second with a Blue' which so often characterized the DO entrants. A few years later others began to point to NGOs like Oxfam or Save the Children and the VSO, volunteers who took on the new troubles of Africa, with a commitment to help those in dire need. Such volunteers often displayed the courage that DOs had sometimes required, and as time went by they seemed to take over from the DO as the repository of intimate knowledge about a district and the person to whom outsiders would first turn for briefing. Yet there was one huge difference: a DO was for life, the NGO worker was generally geared to a two- or three-year appointment.

As for the legacy of British administration as exemplified in the performance of the DO in Africa, we are undoubtedly too near to the event for any ultimate objective judgement to be entered. As a temporary stop-gap answer, one might propose the claim of the English language to priority.[107] No final verdict can be handed down while any of those involved are still alive, be they rulers or ruled. At the most, it has been argued, we shall have to wait until the British Empire of the nineteenth and twentieth centuries is as far removed from the moment of judgement in Africa as the Roman Empire is from us in Britain today. Only then, the analogy continues, can the total legacy be assessed. Both empires were far and deep in their reach, and over the *longue durée* often beneficial in their legacy of material things like roads and viaducts and public buildings, as well as the less tangible but equally influential benefits like law and language. Neither was faultless in the eyes of those who experienced or who administered the empires. Time must be a compelling factor in the objective evaluation of any historical legacy. But this time, unlike 1,600 years ago, one difference will distinguish the arguments on the respective interpretations of empires and their lasting legacies. This is the substantial archive already available to future historians on the Colonial Administrative Service. Imagine the fresh insights, the unexpected revelations and the new avenues of enquiry that today's historians would gain on the practice and personnel of the Roman administration of Britain were they to have access to the memoirs, diaries, letters, reports and correspondence of governors and civil administrators to the same extent as tomorrow's historians will have access to on the life and work of the DO in Africa.

Looking back by keeping in touch

Given the vigour of the retrospective belief that 'my time spent as a DO was the best years of my life' and the sense of camaraderie and *esprit de corps* which existed among DOs in each territory, together with P. Dennis's observation from his experience as a DC in the Gold Coast in the 1950s that 'a happy thing about the latter colonial days was the formation of life-long friendships', it was hardly to be expected that the end of being a DO would equally mean the end of former DOs wishing to create opportunities to meet from time to time and keep in touch, so as to recall and reflect on their first career – often their first love. One such organization was already in place when the Colonial Office closed in 1966. This was the Corona Club, best described – if somewhat grandiosely, given its limited function and facilities – as the Colonial Service's social club.[108] At least it provided a club tie, which, in the absence of a Colonial Service tie (there were, of course, territorial Administrative Service ties), tended to take its place as a bonding symbol. Founded in 1900 on the initiative of the Secretary of State for the Colonies, Joseph Chamberlain, the club was brought to realization through an annual white-tie and decorations dinner in London presided over by his successors at a top table of the gubernatorial elite, but by the end of the 1960s this formal event had begun to mutate into an informal cocktail party. The occasion still provided a unique opportunity for reunion and reminiscence, much welcomed by DOs and others. Yet its days were clearly numbered, and the Corona Club finally came to an end in 2000. To the joy of its members, the Overseas Service

Pensioners' Association agreed to sponsor an annual luncheon instead, and this continues to be held every May. According to its revised objectives OSPA, which had been founded in 1964 primarily to give advice and assistance to members over pension queries and problems, has now extended its declared interests to promoting the study of the work and history of HMOCS and being a guardian of its good name and reputation, assuming a role as a focal point for the former members of HMOCS. Once again, a new tie has become the sign of Colonial Service inclusivity.

Apart from these two CS organizations, former DOs often took a leading role in the creation of a new opportunity for keeping in touch after independence, both with one another and with visitors from the African country where they had once served. This led to the setting up of territorial friendship societies, motivated by a desire to maintain old personal relationships and make new ones by promoting meetings, social events, one-day conferences and a newsletter. Typical of these friendship societies are the Britain–Nigeria Association, now past its 40th year and founded on the initiative of a former DO, I. Stanbrook; the Britain–Tanzania Society; the Northern Rhodesia Reunion Association; the Uganda Kobs, etc. At any of their functions a gathering of ex-DOs can be guaranteed. In some instances, DOs from a territory also formed their own reunion clubs (subsequently widened to all who served there), for example the Kenya Administration, the Tanganyikan Reunion, the Northern Region, Western Region and Eastern Region of Nigeria Associations, all keeping going up to at least the year 2000.[109] Wider-based London organizations like the Royal Commonwealth Society and the Royal African Society have traditionally numbered many DOs among their members.

Another route for DOs wishing to keep in touch with each other has been the colonial records retrieval projects. Here the principal scheme was that of the Oxford Colonial Records Project (1965–72) which set out first to collect the private papers (memoirs, diaries, letters, reports) of DOs and other members of the CS, and then in its second phase (1977–84) as the Oxford Development Records Project, to research and hold conferences on selected aspects of the work of the CS.[110] A major spin-off from this archival enterprise was the outstanding programme of oral interviews, mostly of DOs, undertaken by Charles Allen and Helen Fry for the BBC Radio 4 series 'Tales from the Dark Continent', broadcast in 1979 and later published as a book under the same title. In the mid-1990s an active oral history programme was initiated by the British Empire and Commonwealth Museum at Bristol under the direction of Mary Ingoldby.[111] A parallel revival of interest in the history of the CS has been evidenced by the output of memoirs published since the 1980s by DOs (and their wives).[112] The academic view is now growing that in terms of research value colonial memoirs can often be advanced from secondary sources to the status of primary documentation.

Apart from all these opportunities and encouragements for the DO to keep in contact and to contribute to the building up of a Colonial Service archive, five historic gatherings of DOs have taken place during the last quarter of a century. The most memorable occasion was the 'Service of Commemoration and Thanksgiving to mark the end of Her Majesty's Overseas Civil Service, the Centenary of the Corona Club and the Golden Jubilee of Corona Worldwide', held at Westminster Abbey in the presence of the Queen in May 1999. A history of the Colonial Service from the first issue of Colonial Regulations in 1837 to its closure with the handover of Hong Kong to China in 1997 was published to coincide with this occasion.[113] In 1966, when the Colonial Office came to an end, the Queen had already unveiled a plaque in the Abbey dedicated to 'All Those Who Served the Crown in the Colonial Territories', with its inscription of 'Whosoever will be chief among you let him be your servant'.[114] Another reunion of DOs, this time emphatically a working one, took place in Africa in 1980, when the British government's election monitoring team to oversee the transition of Southern Rhodesia to the new Zimbabwe included over 50 former DOs from Britain (along with a number of British local government officials) who had had extensive experience of organizing and supervising political party elections during the 1950s and 1960s. On the academic/research side, some 100 DOs took part in the symposium held at St Antony's College, Oxford, in 1978 on the DO in the age of decolonization, while a similar number attended the symposium on the CS in retrospect held at the Institute of Historical Research in the University of London in 1999.[115] Since then the Institute of Commonwealth Studies has organized a series of seminars in co-operation with OSPA under the general rubric of 'The History of the Colonial Service – Unfinished Business', which have again brought DOs together. The last sizeable gathering of former DOs was for the official opening of the British Empire and Commonwealth Museum at Bristol by the Princess Royal in 2002.

By now the DO was, it seems, learning happily to laugh at himself in a way he perhaps could not have done in his district 40 years before. At the 1978 Oxford symposium he heard one of the leading academic speakers good humouredly mocking the largely DO audience as essentially a collection of museum pieces (recalling how Sir Gawain Bell, the last colonial governor of Northern Nigeria, used to tell how an Oxford tutor in the 1980s introduced one of his students in African history with the advice 'look carefully, this is the last colonial governor you'll ever set eyes on in your life'), while at a Bristol meeting in 2000 a student was heard to whisper to a friend about one of the somewhat ageing ex-DO speakers, 'you mean that old buffer used to keep the peace among the Maasai?' One other comment, redolent of the image of the DO in today's public mind, appeared in the obituary of a former DO who served in Tanganyika from 1947 to 1962 in the very week that the final draft of this book was completed. As a DO, A.H.S. Linton 'did all the things a man of his type, a solitary European in a rural African world was expected to do: learning Swahili, climbing Kilimanjaro, exploring the Serengeti National Park and building as close a relationship with the Maasai as anyone outside the tribe could hope to build.'[116]

Without a doubt the DO is reclaiming his place in the serious literature on the history and administration of Britain's colonial territories. Infinitely more has been written about and by the DO in Africa since the 1960s than was ever written in the whole of the colonial period. Besides the unique resources of the Public Record Office (now renamed the National Archives), the private papers deposited in the Rhodes House Library at Oxford, along with further records in the Royal Commonwealth Society collection now housed in the University Library at Cambridge and in the BECM at Bristol, together represent an archive of resources utterly non-existent during the period when to be a DO in Africa was still an ongoing career.

Yet for all this rich archival documentation and the extensive data now available on the DO in Africa, who he was and what he did, there remains one further source that many readers will continue to turn to for the popular image of the DO in Africa. Leaving the primary sources to the scholarly-minded researcher, the man and woman in the street are likely to go on, as they have done since Sanders of the River came on the scene in 1911, reading the colonial novel for the 'best' and most comfortably accessible image of the DO in Africa. Africans too young ever to have known a DO in their life have a fine opportunity to recoup today in the novels of writers like Achebe, Ngugi, Aluko and Ulasi. Britons, who showed more indifference than interest in their African colonies and may perhaps have now and then come across an ageing ex-DO in Sussex or Cheltenham, are equally fortunate to have the character of the DO in Africa enshrined in the writings of an extensive list of British novelists. This literature is likely to continue to offer to the general public a primary and potentially persuasive perspective on the image and identity of the DO in Africa for a long time ahead. Besides his unique story in fact, which has been the theme of this study of the DO in Africa, he has earned a permanent niche in fiction, by British and African novelists alike.[117]

Notes

Introduction

[1] Philip Mason, *The Men Who Ruled India, II. The Guardians*, 1954, Introduction, p 13.

[2] Charles Allen, *Plain Tales from the Raj*, 1975; *Tales from the Dark Continent*, 1979; *Tales from the South China Seas*, 1983.

[3] L.H. Gann and P. Duignan, *The Rulers of British Africa, 1870–1914*, 1978.

[4] Douglas and Marcelle V. Brown (eds), *Looking Back on the Uganda Protectorate: Recollections of District Officers*, 1996.

Chapter 1. The CAS: Chronology and Context

[1] *The Colonial Office List*, 1946, p 243.

[2] *Ibid.*, 1952, p 124.

[3] Quoted in A.H.M. Kirk-Greene, *On Crown Service*, 1999, p 13.

[4] For a complete calendar, see Kirk-Greene, *On Crown Service*, p 35.

[5] Based on Gann and Duignan, *The Rulers of British Africa, 1870–1914*, p 292.

[6] Based on Lord Hailey, *An African Survey*, 1938, p 226.

[7] Sir Charles Jeffries, *Whitehall and the Colonial Service*, 1972, p 48.

[8] Cmd. 3554, 1930.

[9] Sir Charles Jeffries, *The Colonial Empire and its Civil Service*, 1938, p 55.

[10] For examples of the patronage system at work in CS interviews, see

A.H.M. Kirk-Greene, 'Not Quite a Gentleman', *The English Historical Review*, cxvii, 472 (2002), pp 622–33.

11 Reproduced in A.H.M. Kirk-Greene, *This is Northern Nigeria*, 1955, p 80.

12 A.H.M. Kirk-Greene, 'The British Colonial Service and the Dominions Selection Scheme of 1923', *Canadian Journal of African Studies*, 15, 11 (1981), pp 33–54.

13 Statistics taken from PRO CO877/16/2, 1943.

14 W.R. Crocker, *Nigeria: A Critique of British Colonial Administration*, 1936. See also his autobiography, *Travelling Back*, 1981.

15 J.C. Cairns, *Bush and Boma*, 1959; W. Bazley, *Bunyoro: A Tropical Paradise*, 1993.

16 For example, from Nigeria alone, M.S. Kisch, *Letters and Sketches from Northern Nigeria*, 1910; Langa Langa, *Up Against It in Nigeria*, 1922; A.C.G. Hastings, *Nigerian Days*, 1925; F. Hives, *JuJu and Justice in Nigeria*, 1930; E.F.G. Haig, *Nigerian Sketches*, 1931.

17 'Sanders of the River', *New Society*, 10 November 1977, pp 308–9. Sanders of the River was the eponymous hero of nearly a dozen adventure novels written by Edgar Wallace between *c*.1910 and 1930. Posted as a turn-of-the-century District Officer in Southern Nigeria, Sanders rapidly came to represent in the mind of the British public the typical colonial administrator – resolute, resourceful and self-reliant, the very stereotype of the lone up-country DO in Africa. So widespread and well known did the figure of Sanders become throughout interwar Britain that even in the 1950s it was sufficient for the tabloid press to use the symbolic shorthand 'Sanders of the River: Still the Best Job for British Boys' (cf. *Sunday Express*, 25 February 1951) for readers immediately to grasp that what was at stake was a career in the Colonial Administrative Service.

18 A.H.M. Kirk-Greene, introduction to Charles Allen (ed), *Tales from the Dark Continent*, 1979, p xv. For a comment on the problem of the so-called 'Fifteeners' (DOs recruited in 1915) see Crocker, *Nigeria*, pp 199ff.

19 Crocker, *Nigeria*, p 20.

20 Covenant of the League of Nations, Article 22.

21 Sir Frederick Lugard, *Political Memoranda: Instructions to Political Officers*, 1906, rev. 1919, first public edition 1970; Lugard, *The Dual Mandate in British Tropical Africa*, 1922; Sir Donald Cameron, *The Principles of Native Administration and their Application*, 1934; despatch by the Secretary of State for the Colonies to the Governors of the African Territories, dated 25 February 1947. The last two documents are reproduced in A.H.M. Kirk-Greene, *The Principles of Native Administration in Nigeria*, 1965, pp 193–225, 238–48.

22 Lugard, *Political Memoranda*, Memo ix, para 44.

23 Memorandum enclosed with the circular issued by the Secretary, Northern Provinces, dated 23 November 1928 and distributed to all DOs. It is reproduced in full in Kirk-Greene, *The Principles of Native Administration*, pp 189ff.

24 Sir Bryan Sharwood-Smith, *But Always as Friends: Northern Nigeria and the Cameroons 1921–1957*, 1969, p 63.

25 Jeffries, *The Colonial Empire*, p 134.

26 J.H. Smith, *Colonial Cadet in Nigeria*, 1968, p 108.

27 R.E. Robinson, 'Why Indirect Rule has been replaced by Local Government in the Nomenclature of British Native Administration', *Journal of African Administration*, 2 (1950), pp 12–15; A. Creech Jones, 'The Place of African Local Administration in Colonial Policy', *Journal of African Administration*, 1, 1 (1949), pp 3–5.

28 Local Government despatch, note 21 , para 14.

Chapter 2. Towards a Colonial Service Career

1 Personal communication from B.H. Brackenbury.

2 In this chapter, unless otherwise indicated, the source for the quotations from named DOs' recollections is the research project 'Towards a Retrospective Record' which I conducted, with the co-operation of members of the Overseas Service Pensioners' Association in 2002. For a list of the DOs quoted, showing territory and date of joining the CAS, see Bibliography, I. Memoirs (Unpublished), (c) OSPA Research Projects (v).

3 R. Brayne, 'Memoirs of Tanganyika', unpublished memoir, p 159.

4 *Appointments Handbook* (Confidential), Colonial Office, 1948, p 13.

5 Strictly speaking, Baddeley was OAG and Patterson Chief Commissioner.

6 K.G. Bradley, *Once a District Officer*, 1966, p 4.

7 R. Heussler, *Yesterday's Rulers*, 1963, p 164.

8 R. Heussler, 'The Legacy of British Colonialism: The Colonial Service', *South Atlantic Quarterly*, 60, 3 (1961), p 306.

9 Nile Gardiner, 'Sentinels of Empire: The British Colonial Administrative Service 1919–1954', unpublished Ph.D. thesis, Yale, 1998, Chapter 3. Interestingly, Gardiner reveals that Heussler's original title for his study was 'Gentlemen Rulers' (p 130). The present author takes this opportunity to say that it was a privilege to have worked with Dr Gardiner on his thesis (soon to be published, one hopes) and the extensive quotations here are taken with gratitude from his assiduously collected data.

10 See tables of DOs' school provenance, 1926–56, in Kirk-Greene, *Britain's Imperial Administrators 1858–1966*, 2000, p 137, and for 1919–60 in Gardiner, 'Sentinels of Empire', p 175.

[11] Letter from D.G.P. Taylor, quoted in Gardiner, 'Sentinels of Empire', p 199.

[12] Letter from A. Forrest, quoted *ibid.*, p 222.

[13] Sir Ralph Furse papers, RHL MSS.Br.Emp.s.415, Box 4, f.4, item 6.

[14] A.H.M. Kirk-Greene, *The Sudan Political Service: A Preliminary Profile*, 1982, Tables I and II.

[15] Personal files are not retained in the PRO.

[16] See Bibliography, I. Memoirs (unpublished), (c) OSPA Research Projects (i). These forms, some 1,900 in all, form the basis of the tables compiled by Gardiner, 'Sentinels of Empire', pp 275–335. See Table 13.

[17] One other notable pre-war exception to this general lack of intimate contact with serving CAS officers was Ifor L. Evans of St John's College, Cambridge, who in 1929 visited West Africa to see at first hand what the products of the new (1926) Tropical African Service course would be doing in the field. A copy of his report on Nigeria and the Gold Coast is privately held.

[18] Between 1920 and 1960, over half the CAS intake came from Oxford and Cambridge, with the former slightly in the lead. See Gardiner, 'Sentinels of Empire', pp 226–7, and A.H.M. Kirk-Greene, 'A Tale of Two Universities', *Oxford*, xlvi, 2 (1994), pp 71–5.

[19] Cf. Jeffrey Richards (ed), *Imperialism and Juvenile Literature*, 1989.

[20] Reproduced in J. Lewis-Barned, *A Fanfare of Trumpets*, 1993, p 3.

[21] R.D. Furse, *Aucuparius: Recollections of a Recruiting Officer*, 1962, p 275.

[22] Furse papers, RHL, Box 4, f.4.

[23] D. Lambert, 'Back to Kenya'; C. Minter, 'From KAR to Administration', in J.R. Johnson (ed), *Colony to Nation: British Administrators in Kenya, 1940–1963*, 2002, pp 19, 21.

[24] A.T. Clark, 'Good Second Class', unpublished memoir, p 113.

[25] D.O. Savill, 'Colonial Service', RHL MSS.Afr.s.1038, p 1.

[26] OSPA Research Project (i) computed in Gardiner, 'Sentinels of Empire', p 91.

[27] F. Ashworth, in R. Anderson (ed), *Palm Wine and Leopard's Whiskers: Reminiscences of Eastern Nigeria*, 1999, p 32.

[28] Reproduced in C. Jeffries, *Partners for Progress: The Men and Women of the Colonial Service*, 1949, pp 17–19. Among those present was R. Posnett, allocated to Uganda. See his *The Scent of Eucalyptus*, 2001, pp 13–14.

[29] *Appointments in His Majesty's Colonial Service*; Part iv, 'General Conditions of Service', CSR1, 1952, p 2.

[30] T.G. Askwith, *Getting My Knees Brown*, 1996, p 24.

[31] *Ibid.*, p 89.

32 Sir Kenneth Blackburne, *Lasting Legacy*, 1976, p xiii.

33 T. Gavaghan, *Of Lions and Dung Beetles*, 1999, p 20.

34 Letter quoted in Gardiner, 'Sentinels of Empire', p 104. Gardiner is one of the few scholars to have paid close attention to motivation.

35 *Ibid.*, p 119.

36 OSPA Research Projects (i) and (v).

37 Johnson (ed), *Colony to Nation*, p viii.

38 R. Hyam, *Empire and Sexuality: The British Experience*, 1990, p 1.

39 For a discussion, see R. Hyam, 'Concubinage and the Colonial Service: The Crewe Circular (1909)', *Journal of Imperial and Commonwealth History*, xiv, 3 (1986), pp 170–86.

40 Hyam, *Empire and Sexuality*, p 1.

41 Copy privately held (there are several versions, all claiming to be the original).

42 C.S.R.I. (Colonial Service Recruitment), 1952.

43 J.A. Golding, *Colonialism: The Golden Years*, 1987, p 107.

44 Smith, *Colonial Cadet in Nigeria*, p 5.

45 J.S. Lawson, 'West African Service', unpublished memoir, p 6.

46 R.E. Wainwright, 'Memoirs', RHL MSS.Br.Emp.s.524, p 130.

47 W.F.H. Newington, 'West Coast Memories', RHL MSS.Afr.s.1983, p 43.

48 Askwith, *Getting My Knees Brown*, p 23.

49 This pamphlet was issued as C.S.R.I. (see note 42), followed by the year of updating. After 1954 the code became O.C.S. (Overseas Civil Service). Before the war, it was known as *Colonial Appointments*.

50 Cmd. 8553.

51 K.G. Bradley, *The Diary of a District Officer*, 1943, Foreword, p v.

52 Bradley, *The Colonial Service as a Career*, 1950, p 7.

53 A. Forward, *You Have Been Allocated Uganda*, 1999, p 5.

54 This warning goes back to at least the 1921 edition of the CO's *Colonial Appointments*, Misc. No. 96, p 26.

55 From a DO's personal papers, unattributable.

56 Some of these are from the testimonials quoted, under privileged access, in Heussler, *Yesterday's Rulers*, p 75. He comments on the high number of allusions to appearances and mannerisms.

57 *Appointments in HM Colonial Service*, 1953, p 13.

58 Quoted, without attribution, in A.H.M. Kirk-Greene, 'The Colonial Service Mind', *Overseas Pensioner*, 85 (2003), p 16.

59 *Appointments Handbook*, p 4.

60 Ann Davidson, *The Real Paradise: Memories of Africa, 1950–1963*, 1993, p 6.

61 *Appointments Handbook*, pp 13–15.

[62] Furse, *Aucuparius*, Chapter 10.

[63] *Ibid.*, p 228.

[64] Heussler, *Yesterday's Rulers*, p 201.

[65] Bradley, *Once a District Officer*, pp 27–8.

[66] *Ibid.*, p 29.

[67] Kirk-Greene, *On Crown Service*, p 98.

[68] Unattributed.

[69] Personal file of R.J. Graham (privately held). A photograph of another such telegram appears in Forward, *You Have Been Allocated Uganda*, p 9.

Chapter 3. Training for the Colonial Service

[1] Gann and Duignan, *The Rulers of British Africa 1870–1914*, p 292.

[2] A.F.B. Bridges, *So We Used To Do*, 1990, p 1.

[3] Sir Alan Burns, *Colonial Civil Servant*, 1949, p 302. See also W. Golant, *Image of Empire: The Early History of the Imperial Institute*, 1984.

[4] See R. Symonds, *Oxford and Empire: The Last Lost Cause?*, 1986, Chapter 10.

[5] R.G. Syme, 'The Wanderings of a Misfit', RHL MSS.Afr.s.1722, p 9.

[6] P. Dennis, *Goodbye to Pith Helmets*, 2000, p 14.

[7] Reproduced in the Devonshire Committee report, *Post-War Training for the Colonial Service*, Col. No. 198, 1946, pp 20–44.

[8] Col. No. 198, p 33.

[9] *Ibid.*, p 24.

[10] *Ibid.*, p 27.

[11] *Ibid.*, p 28.

[12] Nuffield Foundation, *Report on a Visit to Nigeria*, 1946, p 3. This important report of 1946 compares interestingly with the unpublished report (1929) of Ifor L. Evans of St John's College, Cambridge, similarly familiarizing himself with the work of the DO *in situ* in Nigeria as a guide to how the universities might best help in their new responsibility for CAS training.

[13] *Ibid.*, pp 10, 66.

[14] *Ibid.*, p 13.

[15] Col. No. 198, p 7.

[16] In this chapter, unless otherwise indicated, the comments of named DOs about the Devonshire training courses are taken from the written responses to my research project, 'Colonial Service Training', carried out with the collaboration of members of the Overseas Service Pensioners' Association. For a list of the DOs quoted, showing territory and date of joining, see Bibliography, I. Memoirs, (c) OSPA Research Project (iii), 2000.

[17] B.L. Jacobs, 'Going Backwards', unpublished memoir, p 329.

[18] I. Brook, *The One-Eyed Man is King*, 1966, p 147.

[19] A. Stuart, *Of Cargoes, Colonies and Kings*, 2001, p 5.

[20] Brook, *One-Eyed Man*, p 148.

[21] Personal file of R.J. Graham (privately held).

[22] P. Mullins, *Retreat from Africa*, 1992, p 5.

[23] G. Winstanley, *Under Two Flags in Africa*, 2000, p 8.

[24] R. Sadleir, *Tanzania: Journey to Republic*, 1999, p 55.

[25] *Ibid.*, p 59.

[26] D. Bates, in C. Allen, *Tales from the Dark Continent*, 1979, p 41.

[27] R. Wainwright, memoirs, RHL MSS.Br.Emp.s.524, p 16.

[28] L.C. Giles, 'The University and the Colonial Service', *Oxford*, 1949, pp 1–8.

[29] For a summary, see ' "Candidates Are Expected" … Examiner's Report', *Overseas Pensioner*, 82 (2001), pp 35–9.

[30] R.T. Kerslake, *Time and the Hour*, 1997, p 16.

[31] Smith, *Colonial Cadet in Nigeria*, p 5.

[32] M. Varvill, 'A Cadet's Progress', RHL MSS.Afr.s.2093.

[33] J. Cooke, *One White Man in Black Africa*, 1991, p 6.

[34] T. Harris, *Donkey's Gratitude*, 1992, p 11.

[35] J. Russell, *Kenya, Beyond the Marich Pass: A District Officer's Story*, 1994, p 90.

[36] Stuart, *Of Cargoes, Colonies and Kings*, p 4.

[37] K. Addis, in Anderson (ed), *Palm Wine and Leopard's Whiskers*, p 250.

[38] S.S. Richardson, *No Weariness*, 2001, p 185.

[39] Sir Gawain Bell, *Shadows on the Sand*, 1983, p 16. See also K.P. Maddocks, *Of No Fixed Abode*, 1988, p 4.

[40] G.L. Stephenson, 'Nigerian and Other Days', RHL MSS.Afr.s.1833, p 36.

[41] H.H. Marshall, *Like Father, Like Son*, 1980, p 77.

[42] J. Morley, *Colonial Postscript: Diary of a District Officer, 1935–1956*, 1992, p 21.

[43] B. Nightingale, *Seven Rivers to Cross*, 1996, p 36.

[44] Varvill, memoirs, p 7.

[45] Blackburne, *Lasting Legacy*, p 11. In the event, Goldie turned out to be the great-uncle of his future wife.

[46] A.H.M. Kirk-Greene, *The Transfer of Power in Africa: The Colonial Administrator in the Age of Decolonization*, 1978, pp 12–14. See also pp 104, 158–9.

[47] Bazley, *Bunyoro*, p 5. Cf. Note 14.

[48] S. White, *Dan Bana: The Memoirs of a Nigerian Official*, 1966, p 14.

49   M. Milne, *No Telephone to Heaven*, 1999, p 225.
50   A.H.M. Kirk-Greene, 'Public Administration and the Colonial Administrator', *Public Administration and Development*, 19 (1999), pp 19, 513. For a North American's view on the Devonshire Courses, see B. Berman, *Control and Crisis in Colonial Kenya*, 1990, p 103.
51   Henrika Kuklick, *The Imperial Bureaucrat: The Colonial Administrative Service in the Gold Coast 1920–1939*, 1979, p 26.
52   Dennis, *Goodbye to Pith Helmets*, p 16.
53   The proceedings of both conferences were privately printed for those who had attended, under the title *Oxford University, Summer School on Administration*.
54   See G. Cartland, 'Retrospect', *Journal of Administration Overseas*, 1 (1974), pp 269–72.
55   An anthology from *Corona* appeared in 2001, under the title of *Glimpses of Empire* (ed A.H.M. Kirk-Greene). *Journal of African Administration*, has continued although under a succession of titles and sponsors. Its current title is *Public Administration and Development*.
56   Kirk-Greene, *Glimpses of Empire*, p xi.
57   Russell, *Kenya*, pp 14–15.
58   Col. No. 198, p 38.
59   Golding, *Colonialism: The Golden Years*, p 155.
60   A.H.M. Kirk-Greene, 'The Tropics and Ten the Turl', *Oxford*, 52, 1 (2000), pp 13–18, from which many of the following illustrations and quotations are drawn. See also K. Addis, 'Helps and Hindrances for Cadets' in Anderson (ed), *Palm Wine and Leopard's Whiskers*, pp 278–9.
61   Stuart, *Of Cargoes, Colonies and Kings*, p 6.
62   Cf. C. Meek, quoted in Allen, *Tales*, p 42.
63   Wainwright, memoirs, RHL MSS.Br.Emp.s.524, p 20.
64   A satirical poem on a tropical outfitters' establishment at work is to be found in K. Dewar and K.J. Bryant, *In Lighter Africa*, n.d., p 23.
65   G.D. Popplewell, 'Random Recollections of a District Commissioner', RHL MSS.Afr.s.2156, p 6.
66   J.S. Lawson, 'West African Service', memoir (privately held), p 21.
67   The intrepid journalist William Boot, bound for Ishmaelia, in Evelyn Waugh's *Scoop* (1938).
68   K.V. Arrowsmith, *Bush Paths*, 1991, p 47.

Chapter 4. First Tour

1   Blackburne, *Lasting Legacy*, p 2.
2   R. Terrell, *West African Interlude*, 1988, p 27.
3   Mullins, *Retreat from Africa*, p 21.

4   J. and M. Wild, *Uganda Long Ago*, 2002, p 3.
5   Lewis-Barned, *A Fanfare of Trumpets*, pp 3–6.
6   R.N. Barlow-Poole in A.T. Clark (ed), *Was It Only Yesterday? The Last Generation of Nigeria's Turawa*, 2002, p 207, and personal information.
7   Bradley, *The Diary of a District Officer*, p 168.
8   Christine Fitz-Henry, 'African Dust', RHL MSS.Afr.s.367, p 3.
9   Allen, *Tales from the Dark Continent*, p 45.
10 R. Short, *African Sunset*, 1973, p 29.
11 O. Knowles, 'A Posting for a Non-Cricketer' in Johnson (ed), *Colony to Nation*, p 176.
12 G.L. Aitchison in Clark (ed), *Was It Only Yesterday?*, p 299.
13 D.O. Savill, memoirs, RHL MSS.Afr.s.1038, p 33. See also his 'Colonial Service' memoir, 1993, Chapter 3 (privately held).
14 A. Sillery, 'Working Backwards', RHL MSS.Afr.r.207, p 42.
15 R. Wainwright, memoirs, RHL MSS.Br.Emp.s.524, p 24.
16 *Ibid.*, p 30.
17 *Ibid.*, p 43.
18 G. Billing, 'Crest of the Wave', RHL MSS.Afr.s.1763, p 2.
19 In a protectorate the title was Chief Secretary.
20 D. Barton, 'A Medal for Ndabisi', RHL MSS.Afr.s.1777, p 21.
21 J. Cooke, *One White Man in Black Africa*, 1991, p 7.
22 Smith, *Colonial Cadet in Nigeria*, p 6.
23 Brook, *The One-Eyed Man is King*, pp 78–80.
24 Noël Rowling, *Nigerian Memoirs*, 1982, p 8.
25 Allen, *Tales*, p 61.
26 Morley, *Colonial Postscript*, p 22.
27 Yvonne Fox, 'The Years Between', RHL MSS.Afr.s.2084, p 18.
28 G.L. Stephenson, 'Nigerian and Other Days', RHL MSS.Afr.s.1883, p 40.
29 Allen, *Tales*, p 46.
30 J.B. Carson, *Sun, Sand and Safari*, 1937, p 16.
31 Allen, *Tales*, p 46.
32 Lady Scrivenor, 'Reminiscences as Wife of a Colonial Administrator', RHL MSS.Br.Emp.r.5, p 2.
33 Mrs G.W.I. Shipp, 'Safari', RHL MSS.Afr.s.424, p 3.
34 Popplewell, 'Random Recollections of a District Commissioner', p 6.
35 Allen, *Tales*, p 50.
36 J.H. Vaughan and A.H.M. Kirk-Greene, *The Diary of Hamman Yaji*, 1995, p 146.
37 P. Sanders, *The Last of the Queen's Men*, 2000, p 3.
38 Popplewell, 'Random Recollections of a District Commissioner', p

14.

[39] Maddocks, *Of No Fixed Abode*, pp 8–9.

[40] Cooke, *One White Man*, pp 11–12.

[41] Syme, 'The Wanderings of a Misfit', p 11.

[42] Brook, *The One-Eyed Man is King*, p 153.

[43] Allen, *Tales*, p 58.

[44] D. Bates, *A Fly-Switch from the Sultan*, 1961, p 18.

[45] Z.E. Kingdon, 'Posted in Tanganyika', RHL MSS.Afr.s.2255. p 3.

[46] H. Brind, *Lying Abroad*, 1999, p 25.

[47] K.L. Hunter, memoirs, RHL MSS.Afr.s.1942, p 4.

[48] J. Smyth, in Anderson (ed), *Palm Wine and Leopard's Whiskers*, p 398.

[49] Arrowsmith, *Bush Paths*, p 1.

[50] T. Mayhew, 'Bwana DC', RHL MSS.Afr.s.1837, p 31.

[51] P.D. McEntee, 'Something for the Record', RHL MSS.Br.Emp.s.544, p 66.

[52] *Ibid.*, p 73.

[53] Golding, *Colonialism: The Golden Years*, p 112.

[54] Quoted in Kirk-Greene, *The Transfer of Power*, p 176.

[55] J. Moxon, 'Plumes in My Haversack', RHL MSS.Afr.s.2055, vii, p 1.

[56] R.O. Hennings, *African Morning*, 1951, p 33.

[57] J.S. Smith, 'The Last Time', RHL MSS.Afr.s.1986, p 69.

[58] Stephenson, 'Nigerian and Other Days', RHL MSS.Afr.s.1833, p 45. David le Breton was amazed in Tanganyika to find that one of his DOs ran his entire administration with just two files, 'Letters In' and 'Letters Out' – letter to *The Times*, 29 December 2001.

[59] Cf. N.F. Cooke, 'Empire in Decline: A Personal Experience', unpublished memoir, p 8.

[60] F.W. Carpenter, 'African Patchwork', RHL MSS.Afr.s.1710, p 22.

[61] Sadleir, *Tanzania: Journey to Republic*, p 129.

[62] Maddocks, *Of No Fixed Abode*, p 64.

[63] Bazley, *Bunyoro*, pp 39, 260. Humorously, D.O. Savill in Nigeria wondered whether his DO ever forgave his cadet for his presumption in usurping the sacred initials of rank!

[64] Elizabeth Watkins, *Jomo's Jailor: The Life of Leslie Whitehouse*, 1993, p 131.

[65] Respectively, C.G. Mackenzie, J.G. Lenox-Conyngham and R.L. Payne, on all of whom see the memoirs by K. Johnson, R.W.H. du Boulay and D. Russell in Clark (ed), *Was It Only Yesterday?*, Chapter 22; J.H. Carrow; and W.A.C. Cockburn, on whom see M.C. Atkinson (ed), *Nigerian Tales of the Colonial Era*, n.d. (privately circulated), pp 3–6, and the various adventures of 'Rustybuckle' narrated in *The Nigerian Field*, 42 (1977), pp 36–8; 1978, pp 43, 128ff. For other 'characters'

see Allen, *Tales*, p 10, and, on the celebrated C.C. Lilley in the Gold Coast, see Sir John Gutch, *Colonial Servant*, 1987, pp 19–20.

66   Mullins, *Retreat from Africa*, p 8.

67   Brook, *The One-Eyed Man is King*, p 101.

68   C. Chenevix Trench, *Men Who Ruled Kenya: The Kenya Administration 1892–1963*, 1993, p 127.

69   Anne Goldsmith, *Gentle Warrior*, 2001.

70   Gavaghan, *Of Lions and Dung Beetles*, pp 83ff.

71   Turnbull dominates C. Chenevix Trench's autobiography, *The Desert's Dusty Face*, 1964, as well as Chapter 7 of Allen's *Tales*. A biography is currently in hand, by C.A. Baker. Alys, Reece's wife, wrote an account of their days in the NFD in *To My Wife: Fifty Camels*, 1963.

72   Chenevix Trench, *Men Who Ruled Kenya*, pp 136–7.

73   Besides those quoted above, among the other NFD memoirs not yet open are those of T.H.R. Cashmore.

74   For a good description, see Marshall, *Like Father, Like Son*, p 68.

75   Mullins, *Retreat from Africa*, pp 51–2. One of the most detailed descriptions is that by R.T. Kerslake, of the DO's house at Numan, in his *Time and the Hour*, 1997, pp 240–2.

76   Allen, *Tales*, p 160.

77   Russell, *Kenya, Beyond the Marich Pass*, p 20.

78   The Lokoja house is described in Clark (ed), *Was It Only Yesterday?*, p 29. The prefabricated house lived in by the ADO in Bida in 1955 was that shown in the photograph on p 198 of Constance Larymore's *A Resident's Wife in Nigeria*, 1908.

79   Brook, *The One-Eyed Man is King*, p 301.

80   McEntee, 'Something for the Record', p 75.

81   Cooke, *One White Man*, p 12.

82   Shipp, 'Safari', p 2.

83   I.F. Macpherson, 'Aspects of Crown Service', p 13 (unpublished memoir).

84   T. Gardner, *My First Eighty Years*, 1998, pp 51–2.

85   E.K. Lumley, *Forgotten Mandate: A British District Officer in Tanganyika*, 1976, p 35.

86   Bazley, *Bunyoro*, p 69.

87   Carson, *Sun, Sand and Safari*, p 19.

88   H. Phillips, *From Obscurity to Bright Dawn*, 1998, p 8.

89   Gavaghan, *Of Lions and Dung Beetles*, p 31.

90   M. Longford, *The Flags Changed at Midnight*, 2001, p 384.

91   Arrowsmith, *Bush Paths*, p 39.

92   Askwith, *Getting My Knees Brown*, pp 41–2.

93   *Ibid.*, pp 44, 47.

[94] Macpherson, 'Aspects of Crown Service', pp 11–12.

[95] Terrell, *West African Interlude*, p 76.

[96] Allen, *Tales*, p 52.

[97] J.S. Lawson, 'West African Service', memoir (privately held), p 11.

[98] Arrowsmith, *Bush Paths*, p 7.

[99] Blair, *Juju and Justice*, pp 75–6.

[100] For a 1952 account, see Longford, *The Flags Changed at Midnight*, p 92.

[101] M.C. Atkinson, *An African Life: Tales of a Colonial Officer*, 1992, p 35. See also V.K. Johnson, 'Autumn Leaves' (privately published), p 57.

[102] Longford, *The Flags Changed at Midnight*, p 24.

[103] Askwith, *Getting My Knees Brown*, p 54.

[104] Bazley, *Bunyoro*, pp 12–14. See also Smith, *Colonial Cadet in Nigeria*, p 12, on his being presented to the very grand Emir of Kano.

[105] R. Wollocombe, *A Passage from India*, 1988, pp 253–4.

[106] Forward, *You Have Been Allocated Uganda*, p 28.

[107] Dennis, *Goodbye to Pith Helmets*, p 20.

[108] Famously in Nigeria the Clifford Minute of 1922 and its successors (reproduced in Kirk-Greene, *The Principles of Native Administration in Nigeria*, pp 174ff).

[109] P.L. Burkinshaw, *Alarms and Excursions*, 1991, p 65.

[110] M. Varvill, 'A Cadet's Progress', RHL MSS.Afr.s.2093, p 7.

[111] A. Peet, 'First Safari', in Johnson (ed), *Colony to Nation*, p 151.

[112] K. Johnson, in Clark (ed), *Was It Only Yesterday?*, p 222.

[113] R.L. Findlay, memoirs, RHL MSS.Afr.r.170, p 6.

[114] Forward, *You Have Been Allocated Uganda*, p 38.

[115] R. Posnett, *The Scent of Eucalyptus*, 2001, pp 30–3.

[116] Barton, 'A Medal for Ndabisi', pp 32, 45.

[117] D.T.M. Birks, memoirs, RHL MSS.Afr.s.1071, p 33.

[118] R. Bere, *A Cuckoo's Parting Cry*, 1990, p 45.

[119] Lawson, 'West African Service', pp 4–5.

[120] Bazley, *Bunyoro*, p 234.

[121] Stephenson, 'Nigerian and Other Days', p 54.

[122] Kingdon, 'Posted in Tanganyika', p 5. See also D. O'Hagan's account of Kenya in 1931, in Johnson (ed), *Colony to Nation*, pp 2–3.

[123] H. Franklin, *The Flag-Wagger*, 1974, p 37.

[124] W. Bazley has a good account of a *baraza* in Uganda in his memoir *Bunyoro*, pp 30–3, and again, reflectively, at pp 66–7.

[125] Lawson, 'West African Service', p 17.

[126] J. Stacpoole, memoirs, RHL MSS.Afr.s.678, p 52.

[127] Brook, *The One-Eyed Man is King*, p 117.

128 J.H. Clive, 'A Cure for Insomnia', RHL MSS.Afr.s.678, p 52.
129 Varvill, 'A Cadet's Progress', p 7.
130 Arrowsmith, *Bush Paths*, p 2.
131 Kerslake, *Time and the Hour*, p 29. See also Morley, *Colonial Postscript*, pp 29ff.
132 H.P. Elliott, 'Memoirs of Colonial Administrative Service in Nigeria', RHL MSS.Afr.s.1838, p 5.
133 Brook, *The One-Eyed Man is King*, pp 86–8.
134 Sir Donald Cameron, *My Tanganyika Service and Some Nigeria*, 1939, p 270.
135 Forward, *You Have Been Allocated Uganda*, pp 56–8.
136 Nightingale, *Seven Rivers to Cross*, p 46.
137 Anderson (ed), *Palm Wine and Leopard's Whiskers*, p 41. Unusually, the junior A.T. Clark spent three consecutive tours in Bauchi.
138 See Newington, 'West Coast Memories', p 2 (privately held); Varvill, 'A Cadet's Progress', p 140; Forward, *You Have Been Allocated Uganda*, p 38; Wainwright, memoirs, p 42.
139 Gutch, *Colonial Servant*, p 13.
140 *Post-War Training for the Colonial Service*, 1946, Col. No. 198, p 29.
141 Johnson, 'Autumn Leaves', p 54.
142 J. Pollok-Morris, 'Glimpses of a First Tour' in Anderson, *Leopard's Whiskers*, pp 404–7.
143 Mullins, *Retreat from Africa*, p 36.
144 Hennings, *African Morning*, p 66.
145 M.W. Norris, 'Experience in the Overseas Civil Service', RHL MSS. Afr.s.2025, p 12.
146 Johnson, *Colony to Nation*, p 22.
147 Sadleir, *Tanzania: Journey to Republic*, p 93.
148 Wainwright, memoirs, p 55.
149 McEntee, 'Something for the Record', p 92.
150 This was commented on in the Nuffield Foundation's visit to Nigeria (*Report*, 1946, pp 22, 33).
151 Maddocks, *Of No Fixed Abode*, p 25.
152 Kingdon, 'Posted in Tanganyika', p 19.
153 Lord Tweedsmuir, *Always a Countryman*, p 163.
154 Brind, *Lying Abroad*, p 26.
155 Norris, 'Experience in the Overseas Civil Service', pp 9, 15.
156 Chenevix Trench, *The Desert's Dusty Face*, p 2.
157 P. Johnson, 'First Post', in Johnson (ed), *Colony to Nation*, p 17.
158 Hennings, *African Morning*, p 145n.
159 C. Baker, in Kirk-Greene, *The Transfer of Power*, p 174.

[160] Milne, *No Telephone to Heaven*, p 48.
[161] Winstanley, *Under Two Flags in Africa*, p 52.
[162] Sillery, 'Working Backwards', p 67.
[163] McEntee, 'Something for the Record', p 77.
[164] Phillips, *From Obscurity*, p 12.
[165] Bradley, *Once a District Officer*, p 6.

Chapter 5. The Day's Work: In Station

[1] Newington, 'West Coast Memories', p 10.
[2] Morley, *Colonial Postscript*, p 27.
[3] Sillery, 'Working Backwards', p 57.
[4] Brook, *The One-Eyed Man is King*, p 148.
[5] Longford, *The Flags Changed at Midnight*, p 126.
[6] Clive, 'A Cure for Insomnia', p 178.
[7] Hennings, *African Morning*, p 192.
[8] Mullins, *Retreat from Africa*, p 45.
[9] P. Stigger, in Kirk-Greene (ed), *The Transfer of Power*, p 151 n.7.
[10] Watkins, *Jomo's Jailor*, p 48.
[11] Golding, *Colonialism: The Golden Years*, p 160.
[12] Maddocks, *Of No Fixed Abode*, p 57.
[13] Quoted in White, *Dan Bana*, p 239.
[14] Gavaghan, *Of Lions and Dung Beetles*, p 109.
[15] Terrell, *West African Interlude*, p 108.
[16] Varvill, 'A Cadet's Progress', p 143.
[17] Crocker, *Nigeria: A Critique of British Colonial Administration*.
[18] H. Brind, *Lying Abroad*, 1999, p 41. The station referred to was Buem-Krachi, in the north-east of the Gold Coast.
[19] Anderson (ed), *Palm Wine and Leopard's Whiskers*, p 233.
[20] J.G. Liebenow, *Colonial Rule and Political Development in Tanzania*, 1971, pp 148–9.
[21] Lugard, *Political Memoranda*, Memo 1, para. 14.
[22] Mullins, *Retreat from Africa*, p 56.
[23] P. Dempster, 'A Young Man's Job', in Johnson (ed), *Colony to Nation*, p 62.
[24] W. Bazley, *Bunyoro*, p 129.
[25] Unattributed.
[26] H.P. Elliott, 'Memoirs of Colonial Administrative Service in Nigeria', p 71.
[27] J. Millard, *Never a Dull Moment*, 1996, p 192ff.
[28] The origin of the phrase is described in C. Chenevix Trench, *The Desert's Dusty Face*, pp 4–5. In parts of Northern Rhodesia it was

known as the 'bull bag'; see Eugenia Herbert, *Twilight on the Zambezi*, 2002, p 40.

29 Russell, *Kenya, Beyond the Marich Pass*, pp 25–6.

30 M. Maciel, 'Goans and Administration', in Johnson (ed), *Colony to Nation*, p 111.

31 Dennis, *Goodbye to Pith Helmets*, p 68.

32 For the autobiography of one of the most distinguished of them, see M. Maciel, *Bwana Karani*, 1985.

33 Harris, *Donkey's Gratitude*, p 21.

34 Kerslake, *Time and the Hour*, p 27.

35 Short, *African Sunset*.

36 Herbert, *Twilight on the Zambezi*, p 13.

37 Sadleir, *Tanzania: Journey to Republic*, p 79.

38 Cairns, *Bush and Boma*, pp 1–2.

39 *Ibid.*, p 68.

40 White, *Dan Bana*, p 205. On the NFD version, see Chenevix Trench, *The Desert's Dusty Face*, p 5.

41 Mullins, *Retreat from Africa*, p 61.

42 Berman, *Control and Crisis in Colonial Kenya*, p 317.

43 J. Blair, *Juju and Justice*, p 88.

44 Bradley, *Once a District Officer*, p 70.

45 E.K. Lumley, *Forgotten Mandate*, 1976, p 70.

46 Bradley, *The Diary of a District Officer*, pp 54–5.

47 Arrowsmith, *Bush Paths*, p 94.

48 Sadleir, *Tanzania: Journey to Republic*, p 143.

49 O. Knowles, 'Multiple Duties at Malindi', in Johnson (ed), *Colony to Nation*, p 40.

50 Golding, *Colonialism: The Golden Years*, p 149.

51 Maddocks, *Of No Fixed Abode*, pp 67–8.

52 K. Addis in Anderson (ed), *Palm Wine and Leopard's Whiskers*, p 15.

53 P. Johnston, memoir, RHL MSS.Afr.s.1887, I.

54 Lumley, *Forgotten Mandate*, p 46.

55 Chenevix Trench, *The Desert's Dusty Face*, p 91.

56 A typical account of 'complaints' in the DO's office is given in Cairns, *Bush and Boma*, pp 5–6.

57 Bradley, *Once a District Officer*, p 75.

58 Brook, *The One-Eyed Man is King*, p 259.

59 Atkinson, *An African Interlude*, p 14.

60 Johnson, *Colony to Nation*, p 44.

61 Arrowsmith, *Bush Paths*, p 61.

62 Varvill, 'A Cadet's Progress', p 109.

[63] The case described in Short, *African Sunset*, p 199, hints at the problem – and one solution.

[64] Golding, *Colonialism: The Golden Years*, p 119.

[65] Cooke, *One White Man in Black Africa*, p 30.

[66] Atkinson, *An African Life*, p 12.

[67] *Ibid.*, pp 24–5.

[68] *Ibid.*, p 30.

[69] Quoted in Herbert, *Twilight*, p 39 (DO unnamed).

[70] N.C. McClintock, *Kingdoms in the Sand and Sun*, 1992, p 12.

[71] G. Allen, 'Whence Few Come Out', RHL MSS.Afr.s.1687, p 99.

[72] Johnson, *Colony to Nation*, p 14.

[73] Brook, *The One-Eyed Man is King*, p 93.

[74] Johnson (ed), *Colony To Nation*, pp 65–7. See also Anthony Merifield, 'Kenya Elections', *ibid.*, pp 220ff.

[75] K. Addis, 'Voters and Rioters', in Anderson (ed), *Palm Wine and Leopard's Whiskers*, pp 248ff.

[76] Bridges, *So We Used To Do*, p 179.

[77] Clark (ed), *Was It Only Yesterday?*, pp 49, 261.

[78] Cf. Joan Sharwood-Smith, *Diary of a Colonial Wife*, 1992, pp 34–6.

[79] Newington, 'West Coast Memories', pp 35ff.

[80] Millard, *Never a Dull Moment*, pp 74–7.

[81] Johnson, *Colony to Nation*, p 9.

[82] Clark (ed), *Was It Only Yesterday?*, p 302.

[83] Maddocks, *Of No Fixed Abode*, p 34.

[84] Carson, *Sun, Sand and Safari*, p 123.

[85] R. Wainwright, memoirs, p 45.

[86] Kingdon, 'Posted in Tanganyika', p 150.

[87] While it was the exception rather than the rule for a governor to be appointed to the territory where he had been a DO, such up-country tours allowed him to recapture his own days on tour as a DO wherever they had been.

[88] Lewis-Barned, *A Fanfare of Trumpets*, pp 109–10.

[89] J. Brayne-Baker, 'I Liked It Out There', RHL MSS.Afr.s.1926/4, p 43.

[90] Harris, *Donkey's Gratitude*, pp 221–2.

[91] Gavaghan, *Of Lions and Dung Beetles*, pp 199–200.

[92] Johnson, *Colony to Nation*, p 11.

[93] Stuart, *Of Cargoes, Colonies and Kings*, p 41.

[94] Wainwright, memoirs, p 161.

[95] J.R. Johnston, 'Bits and Pieces', RHL MSS.Afr.s.1270, p 14.

[96] Johnston, *ibid.*, pp 5–6: Arrowsmith, *Bush Paths*, p 171.

[97] Typically a whole chapter, for instance in Sir Bryan Sharwood-Smith,

But Always as Friends, Chapter 19.

[98] Johnson, *Colony to Nation*, p 118.

[99] Chenevix Trench, *The Desert's Dusty Face*, pp 79–80.

[100] Smith, *Colonial Cadet in Nigeria*, pp 101–5.

[101] Watkins, *Jomo's Jailor*, p 123.

[102] Clark (ed), *Was It Only Yesterday?*, p 326. Cf. R.C.B. Gray's enthusiastic description of the Mbali club in D. and M. Brown (eds), *Looking Back on the Uganda Protectorate*, p 9.

[103] Arrowsmith, *Bush Paths*, p 20.

[104] Sir Andrew Cohen, *British Policy in Changing Africa*, 1959, p 74.

[105] Bazley, *Tropical Paradise*, p 77.

Chapter 6. The Day's Work: On Tour

[1] Lord Tweedsmuir, *Always a Countryman*, p 177.

[2] Hennings, *African Morning*, p 129.

[3] Barton, 'A Medal for Ndabisi', p 80.

[4] Stacpoole, memoirs, 18/19 August 1959.

[5] Chenevix Trench, *The Desert's Dusty Face*, p 19. See also p 61.

[6] Lugard, *Political Memoranda*, I, p 12.

[7] Hastings, *Nigerian Days*, p 153.

[8] Short, *African Sunset*, p 42.

[9] R.L. Findlay, memoirs, RHL MSS.Afr.r.170, p 6.

[10] Longford, *The Flags Changed at Midnight*, p 336.

[11] Lewis-Barned, *A Fanfare of Trumpets*, p 17.

[12] Brayne, 'Memoirs of Tanganyika', p 27.

[13] Birks, memoirs, III, pp 4–6.

[14] E. Gordon, in Johnson (ed), *Colony to Nation*, p 55.

[15] D. and M. Brown (eds), *Looking Back on the Uganda Protectorate*, p 24.

[16] Bradley, *Once a District Officer*, p 92.

[17] Lugard, *Political Memoranda*, I, p 12.

[18] *Ibid.*, and II, p 39.

[19] Anderson (ed), *Palm Wine and Leopard's Whiskers*, p 132.

[20] Blair, *Juju and Justice*, p 110. See also p 132.

[21] Terrell, *West African Interlude*, p 66.

[22] P. Thirsk, 'Bush Touring', in Anderson (ed), *Palm Wine and Leopard's Whiskers*, p 76.

[23] Cf. Hennings, *African Morning*, Chapter 9, for a tax safari among the Suk.

[24] Atkinson, *An African Life*, p 18.

[25] Johnson (ed), *Colony to Nation*, p 21.

[26] Morley, *Colonial Postscript*, p 87.

27   Arrowsmith, *Bush Paths*, p 145.
28   Burkinshaw, *Alarms and Excursions*, p 105.
29   Hennings, *African Morning*, pp 157, 160.
30   Dennis, *Goodbye to Pith Helmets*, p 57.
31   Harris, *Donkey's Gratitude*, p 117.
32   Bazley, *Bunyoro*, p 36.
33   Carson, *Sun, Sand and Safari*, p 21.
34   Brind, *Lying Abroad*, p 30.
35   Blair, *Juju and Justice*, p 134.
36   Lumley, *Forgotten Mandate*, p 139.
37   McClintock, *Kingdoms in the Sand and Sun*, pp 16ff.
38   Carson, *Sun, Sand and Safari*, p 30.
39   Hennings, *African Morning*, p 44.
40   White, *Dan Bana*, p 45.
41   Gardner, *My First Eighty Years*, p 54.
42   Anderson (ed), *Palm Wine and Leopard's Whiskers*, p 80.
43   *Ibid.* p 95.
44   R.A. Dick, memoirs, RHL MSS.Afr.s.952, p 6.
45   Quoted in Herbert, *Twilight on the Zambezi*, p 17.
46   M. Varvill, 'Cadet's Progress', p 7.
47   Russell, *Kenya, Beyond the Marich Pass*, p 60.
48   Smith, *Colonial Cadet in Nigeria*, p 13. Interesting timetables for a day
      on trek are given for Tanganyika, by A. Sillery, 'Working Backwards',
      p 11, and for the very different Eastern Nigeria by J.S. Smith, 'The
      Last Time', RHL MSS.Afr.s.1986, p 45.
49   White, *Dan Bana*, p 74. See Cooke, *One White Man in Africa*, pp 113–14,
      for how his carriers negotiated an even better rate.
50   Bates, *A Fly-Switch from the Sultan*, p 21.
51   D. and M. Brown (eds), *Looking Back on the Uganda Protectorate*, pp
      158ff.
52   Short, *African Sunset*, pp 143–4.
53   Morley, *Colonial Postscript*, p 35. On the hazards of the pit latrine, see
      Posnett, *The Scent of Eucalyptus*, p 54.
54   Stuart, *Of Cargoes, Colonies and Kings*, p 41.
55   Smith, 'The Last Time', p 15.
56   Bere, *A Cuckoo's Parting Cry*, p 76.
57   R.F. Bendy, OSPA Research Project (v), Another respondent drew a
      similar analogy, with the appearance of a touring troupe in a medi-
      aeval English village.
58   Jacobs, 'Going Backwards', p 115.
59   J. Cleave, 'First Posting', in D. and M. Brown (eds), *Looking Back on the*

Uganda Protectorate, p 85.

[60]　*Ibid.*, p 25.

[61]　F.W. Carpenter, 'African Patchwork', RHL MSS.Afr.s.1710, p 15.

[62]　Wollocombe, *A Passage from India*, p 256.

[63]　Sillery, 'Working Backwards', p 55.

[64]　Askwith, *Getting My Knees Brown*, p 153.

[65]　Chenevix Trench, *The Desert's Dusty Face*, p 25.

[66]　Bradley, *The Diary of a District Officer*, p 135.

[67]　Askwith, *Getting My Knees Brown*, p 121. Cf. Bradley, *The Diary of a District Officer*, p 40.

[68]　Burkinshaw, *Alarms and Excursions*, p 75.

[69]　Gavaghan, *Of Lions and Dung Beetles*, p 99.

[70]　Bradley, *The Diary of a District Officer*, p 39.

[71]　Golding, *Colonialism: The Golden Years*, p 121.

[72]　Lumley, *Forgotten Mandate*, p 67.

[73]　Smith, *Colonial Cadet in Nigeria*, pp 117–98.

[74]　Anderson (ed), *Palm Wine and Leopard's Whiskers*, p 84.

[75]　R. Heussler, *British Tanganyika: An Essay and Documentation on District Administration*, 1971, pp 69–137.

[76]　Lewis-Barned, *A Fanfare of Trumpets*, p 34. The point is underscored by a glance at the large amount of space allocated to touring in the composite Service memoirs of recent vintage, e.g. those edited by D. and M. Brown (1996), R. Anderson (1999), J. Johnson (2002) and A.T. Clark (2002).

[77]　A.H.M. Kirk-Greene, *Nationalism and Arcadianism in the Sudan*, 1993, p 26.

[78]　Lord Tweedsmuir, *Always a Countryman*, p 191.

[79]　McClintock, *Kingdoms in the Sand and Sun*, p 26.

[80]　White, *Dan Bana*, p 248.

Chapter 7. The Day's Work: The Secretariat

[1]　Blair, *Juju and Justice*, p 115 and Chapter 11, passim.

[2]　Olive Champion, *Journey of a Lifetime*, 1994, p 52.

[3]　R. Heussler, *The British in Northern Nigeria*, 1968, p 88.

[4]　Jeffries, *The Colonial Empire and its Civil Service*, p 129.

[5]　Harris, *Donkey's Gratitude*, p 40.

[6]　Golding, *Colonialism: The Golden Years*, pp 131ff.

[7]　*Ibid.*, p 179.

[8]　Gutch, *Colonial Servant*, p 39.

[9]　Kerslake, *Time and the Hour*, p 262.

[10]　Mullins, *Retreat from Africa*, p 33.

11 J. O'Regan, *From Empire to Commonwealth*, 1994, p 114.
12 Milne, *No Telephone to Heaven*, p 372.
13 Chenevix Trench, *Men Who Ruled Kenya*, p 198.
14 Milne, *No Telephone to Heaven*, pp 294ff.
15 Askwith, *Getting My Knees Brown*, p 215.
16 F.R.J. Williams, 'Colonial Administration in Uganda' (privately held).
17 Posnett, *The Scent of Eucalyptus*, p 106.
18 W.L. Bell, 'Central Government and the Secretariat', in, D. and M. Brown (eds), *Looking Back on the Uganda Protectorate*, p 109.
19 P. Thirsk, 'Life as a Private Secretary', in Anderson (ed), *Palm Wine and Leopard's Whiskers*, p 306. See also R.J. Graham, *ibid.*, pp 310–16; Owen Griffith's several reminiscences of being PS to Sir Andrew Cohen in D. and M. Brown (eds), *Looking Back on the Uganda Protectorate*, passim; M. Longford, *The Flags Changed at Midnight*, Chapter 5, on being PS to Sir Edward Twining; N. Skinner, *Burden Assumed*, 1985, pp 75ff.
20 Mayhew, 'Bwana DC', p 60.
21 Johnson, 'Autumn Leaves', p 87.
22 Millard, *Never a Dull Moment*, p 61.
23 Longford, *The Flags Changed at Midnight*, p 184.
24 H.P. Elliott, 'Memoirs of Colonial Administrative Service in Nigeria', RHL MSS.Afr.s.1838, p 44.
25 Sir Rex Niven, *Nigerian Kaleidoscope*, 1982, p 145.
26 Milne, *No Telephone to Heaven*, p 179.
27 Franklin, *The Flag-Wagger*, p 149.
28 Sanders, *The Last of the Queen's Men*, p 24.
29 P. Gordon, 'The Old Secretariat', in Johnson (ed), *Colony to Nation*, p 73.
30 Wainwright, memoirs, p 71.
31 Blackburne, *Lasting Legacy*, p 14.
32 Sadleir, *Tanzania: Journey to Republic*, p 154.
33 H. Walker, 'A Stint in the Secretariat', in Johnson (ed), *Colony to Nation*, p 77.
34 D. Brown, 'In the Secretariat, 1956–57', in D. and M. Brown (eds), *Looking Back on the Uganda Protectorate*, pp 120–1.
35 Johnson (ed), *Colony to Nation*, pp 73–4.
36 Barton, 'A Medal for Ndabisi', p 21.
37 Sadleir, *Tanzania: Journey to Republic*, p 149.
38 Longford, *The Flags Changed at Midnight*, p 147.
39 Askwith, *Getting My Knees Brown*, p 84. One is reminded of the altercation in one Secretariat car park over an empty parking space,

when the new assistant secretary challenged his boss with 'Shall we proceed by seniority or the rule of the road?' – Mullins, *Retreat from Africa*, p 81.

[40]   Johnson (ed), *Colony to Nation*, p 78.

[41]   Phillips, *From Obscurity to Bright Dawn*, p 33.

[42]   Niven, *Nigerian Kaleidoscope*, p 112.

[43]   The Royal Wajir Yacht Club, founded by F. Jennings, DC Wajir, in the 1930s, was set in the middle of the country in Kenya's NFD, 250 miles away from the sea and was – in all ways – *sui generis*.

[44]   Savill, 'Colonial Service', p 73.

[45]   Findlay, memoirs, p 1.

[46]   Brind, *Lying Abroad*, p 31. P.H. Burkinshaw, writing from his experience in post-war Sierra Leone, also sought to set out both sides of the bush v. Secretariat debate, concluding that while he personally preferred 'the freedom of the bushwhacker', he appreciated DOs' reasoning, particularly if they had a wife and family, of the more ordered and amenable life attaching to a Secretariat posting – *Alarms and Excursions*, p 88.

[47]   Champion, *Journey of a Lifetime*, pp 76, 92.

[48]   Savill, 'Colonial Service', p 85.

[49]   Askwith, *Getting My Knees Brown*, p 83.

[50]   Gutch, *Colonial Servant*, p 44. Cf. the problem of socializing as seen by Mullins, *Retreat from Africa*, p 100.

[51]   Sadleir, *Tanzania: Journey to Republic*, p 157.

[52]   McEntee, 'Something for the Record', p 95.

Chapter 8. After the Day's Work

[1]   Lumley, *Forgotten Mandate*, p 13.

[2]   Milne, *No Telephone to Heaven*, p 62.

[3]   Kerslake, *Time and the Hour*, p 206.

[4]   Longford, *The Flags Changed at Midnight*, pp 315, 377.

[5]   Harris, *Donkey's Gratitude*, p 300.

[6]   D. and M. Brown (eds), *Looking Back on the Uganda Protectorate*, Chapter 7; Anderson (ed), *Palm Wine and Leopard's Whiskers*, Chapter 22; Clark (ed), *Was It Only Yesterday?*, Chapter 24.

[7]   Allen, *Tales from the Dark Continent*, p 90.

[8]   Forward, *You Have Been Allocated Uganda*, p 102.

[9]   R.G. Syme, Memoirs, RHL MSS.Afr.s.1722, p 23. On fishing as a DO's leisure pursuit in West Africa, see R. Somerset, 'Fishing in the Onitsha Province' in Anderson (ed), *Palm Wine and Leopard's Whiskers*, pp 338–42, and I.F. Gunn, *With a Rod in Four Continents*, 1981, pp 29ff.

[10]   Bates, *A Fly-Switch from the Sultan*, p 33.

[11] Brook, *The One-Eyed Man is King*, p 116.
[12] Bazley, *Bunyoro*, p 130.
[13] Lewis-Barned, *A Fanfare of Trumpets*, p 27.
[14] Cairns, *Bush and Boma*, pp 32–3.
[15] Kerslake, *Time and the Hour*, p 245.
[16] Smith, 'The Last Time', p 70.
[17] Atkinson, *An African Life*, p 82.
[18] Bazley, *Bunyoro*, p 118.
[19] Bridges, *So We Used To Do*, p 35.
[20] Kerslake, *Time and the Hour*, p 192.
[21] Phillips, *From Obscurity to Bright Dawn*, p 62; M. Fairlie, *No Time Like the Past*, 1992, p 243.
[22] On such cricket tournaments, see Wollocombe, *A Passage from India*, p 310.
[23] Stuart, *Of Cargoes, Colonies and Kings*, p 36; Posnett, *The Scent of Eucalyptus*, Chapter 5.
[24] Bere, *A Cuckoo's Parting Cry*, Chapter 21.
[25] Anderson (ed), *Palm Wine and Leopard's Whiskers*, pp 346ff.
[26] On the tragedy of one such Loitokitok expedition, see R. Brayne, 'Memoirs of Tanganyika' (privately held), pp 128ff.
[27] Blair, *Juju and Justice*, p 221.
[28] Posnett, *The Scent of Eucalyptus*, p 50.
[29] Popplewell, 'Random Recollections of a District Commissioner', p 22.
[30] Marshall, *Like Father, Like Son*, p 126.
[31] Milne, *No Telephone to Heaven*, p 77.
[32] For a preliminary collection and commentary, see A.H.M. Kirk-Greene, 'For Better or for Verse', *Overseas Pensioner*, 72 (1996), pp 47–50; 75 (1998), pp 33–8.
[33] Norris, 'Experience in the Overseas Civil Service', p 9.
[34] Wainwright, memoirs, pp 41, 175.
[35] A.C. Russell, *Gold Coast to Ghana*, 1996, pp 142–3.
[36] Morley, *Colonial Postscript*, pp 98–9.
[37] Posnett, *The Scent of Eucalyptus*, p 37; Sadleir, *Tanzania: Journey to Republic*, p 107.
[38] R.H. Wright, *Then the Wind Changed in Africa* (ed R. Pearce), 1992, p 112.
[39] Smith, 'The Last Time', pp 102–3.
[40] Wollocombe, *A Passage from India*, pp 250, 315; W.F.H. Newington, 'West Coast Memories', p 20.
[41] Clark (ed), *Was It Only Yesterday?*, pp 232–4. For an account of polo in Northern Nigeria, see T.R.W. Longmore, *ibid.*, pp 234–6.

[42] Quoted in Atkinson, *An African Life*, p 83.

[43] Lumley, *Forgotten Mandate*, p 119.

[44] Russell, *Gold Coast*, p 54. Cf. Atkinson, *An African Life*, p 82.

[45] H. Mitchell, *Remote Corners: A Sierra Leone Memoir*, 2002, p 92.

[46] Niven, *Nigerian Kaleidoscope*, p 132.

[47] Gutch, *Colonial Servant*, p 56.

[48] Heather Dalton, *The Gold Coast: The Wives' Experience*, RHL ODRP Report No. 15, 1985, p 1.

Chapter 9. Through Female Eyes

[1] Negley Farson, *Behind God's Back*, 1940, p 296.

[2] Clark (ed), *Was It Only Yesterday?*, p 133. One of his contributors, G. Blackburne-Kane, noted of his Resident's welcome when he arrived in Sokoto in 1949, aged 23: 'If I'd known you were going to be accompanied by a wife, I wouldn't have accepted you' (p 253).

[3] Niven, *Nigerian Kaleidoscope*, p 62.

[4] For a history of the Colonial Nursing Service, founded in 1896, and in 1966 renamed Queen Elizabeth's Overseas Nursing Service, see H.P. Dickson, *The Badge of Britannia*, 1990. See also Pat Holden, *Nursing Sisters in Nigeria, Uganda, Tanganyika*, RHL ODRP Report No. 17, 1985.

[5] For accounts of this experience, see the memoirs of Jennifer Cawte at the end of the 1950s, *From Kaduna to Kirakira*, 2000, as a PA and later a DO's wife in Northern Nigeria; of J. and M. Wild in Uganda at the beginning of the decade, *Uganda Long Ago*, 2002; and of Vivienne Bell in Northern Rhodesia in the 1950s, *Blown by the Wind of Change*, 1986.

[6] Gavaghan, *Of Lions and Dung Beetles*, p 139.

[7] The leading source on WAOs is Pat Holden, *Women Administrative Officers in Colonial Africa*, RHL ODRP Report No. 5, 1985. See also the autobiographical accounts by Elizabeth Purdy (Sharp) and Jill Whitfield in Clark (ed), *Was It Only Yesterday?*, pp 248ff.

[8] Larymore, *A Resident's Wife in Nigeria*; Laura Boyle, *Diary of a Colonial Officer's Wife*, 1968.

[9] Joan Alexander, *Voices and Echoes*, 1983, p 7. See also Joanna Trollope, *Britannia's Daughters*, 1983, Chapter 7, for DOs' wives.

[10] Hilary Callan and Shirley Ardener (eds), *The Incorporated Wife*, 1984, p 3. See also the chapters 'Colonial Wives: Villains or Victims?' by Beverley Gartrell and, 'Memsahibs in Colonial Malaya' by Janice Brownfoot.

[11] Helen Callaway, *Gender, Culture and Empire*, 1987, pp 3–4.

[12] Diana Bridges, 'Black and White Notes', RHL MSS.Afr.s.1634, p i.

[13] Golding, *Colonialism: The Golden Years*, p 146; Clark (ed), *Was It Only*

Yesterday?, Chapter 13.
14 *Appointments in His Majesty's Colonial Service*, Pt. IV, General Conditions of Service, CSR1 1952, para. 11. Those conditions were still in force in the 1955 edition.
15 Stephenson, 'Nigerian and Other Days', p 49.
16 J. Ainley, *Pink Stripes and Obedient Servants*, 2001, p 180.
17 Wainwright, memoirs, p 81.
18 Blackburne, *Lasting Legacy*, pp 15–16.
19 See Chapter 2, p 32. Hyam's Chapter 2 is titled 'Chastity and the Colonial Service'.
20 Lawson, 'West African Service' (privately held), p 5. Cf. Allen, *Tales from the Dark Continent*, p 14.
21 Mitchell, *Remote Corners: A Sierra Leone Memoir*, p 72.
22 Elspeth Huxley, *Four Guineas*, 1954, p 62.
23 Lumley, *Forgotten Mandate*, pp 113ff.
24 Compare Tables 2a and 2b in the computation of the ODRP's 1986 'HMOCS Data Project' by N. Gardiner, 'Sentinels of Empire', Yale University unpublished Ph.D. thesis, 1998.
25 Brook, *The One-Eyed Man is King*, pp 93–4.
26 *Ibid.*, p 121.
27 Dorothy Ashworth, 'ADO's Madam', in Anderson (ed), *Palm Wine and Leopard's Whiskers*, pp 19–23.
28 Burkinshaw, *Alarms and Excursions*, p 90.
29 Beverly Gartrell, 'Colonial Wives: Villains or Victims?', in Callan and Ardener (ed), *The Incorporated Wife*, pp 168–9.
30 Haig, *Nigerian Sketches*, p 27.
31 Short, *African Sunset*, p 33.
32 Cf. Allen, *Tales*, p 110, and Chapter 8, 'The DO's Wife and the Governor's Lady'.
33 Carol Christian, 'Elderly Cadet', in Anderson (ed), *Palm Wine and Leopard's Whiskers*, p 29.
34 Carol Pickering, 'The Gold Coast Remembered', RHL MSS.Afr. s.2092, p 15.
35 Allen, *Tales*, p 128.
36 Carpenter, 'African Patchwork', p 18.
37 A.N. Skinner, *Burden at Sunset*, 1996, p 89.
38 Alexander, *Voices and Echoes*, p 6.
39 B.L. Jacobs, 'Going Backwards' (privately held), p 162.
40 McClintock, *Kingdoms in the Sand and Sun*, p 62; Lewis-Barned, *A Fanfare of Trumpets*, p 52.
41 Ann Davidson, *The Real Paradise: Memories of Africa, 1950–1963*, 1993, pp 7–10.

[42] Cecillie Swaisland (ed), *A World of Memories*, Women's Corona Society, 2000, p 89.

[43] Watkins, *Jomo's Jailor*, 1993, p 35n. On Eileen Sandford's work, see Clark (ed), *Was It Only Yesterday?*, pp 133–8. Rosemary Hollis's memoir, *A Scorpion for Tea*, 1973, is enriched by her own illustrations.

[44] Champion, *Journey of a Lifetime*, p 40.

[45] A.T. Weatherhead, 'Possessors of Power', RHL MSS.Afr.s.232, p 79.

[46] Sharwood-Smith, *Diary of a Colonial Wife*, p 14.

[47] Peggy Watt, *There is Only One Nigeria*, 1985, p 55.

[48] Elizabeth Warren, in Clark (ed), *Was It Only Yesterday?*, pp 140–1.

[49] Skinner, *Burden at Sunset*, pp 183–4.

[50] Emily Bradley, *Dearest Priscilla*, 1950, pp 238–9.

[51] Sharwood-Smith, *Diary of a Colonial Wife*, p 4.

[52] Bradley, *Dearest Priscilla*, pp 114, 119.

[53] *Ibid.* pp 92–3.

[54] Longford, *The Flags Changed at Midnight*, p 2.

[55] Reece, *To My Wife: Fifty Camels*, pp 15ff.

[56] Barton, 'A Medal for Ndabisi', p 26.

[57] Rowling, *Nigerian Memories*, pp 11–14.

[58] Watkins, *Jomo's Jailor*, pp 157–8.

[59] Askwith, *Getting My Knees Brown*, p 108.

[60] Carol Pickering, 'Gold Coast Remembered', p 9; Lorna Hall, 'A Bushwife's Progress', RHL MSS.Afr.s.1834, p 1.

[61] Longford, *The Flags Changed at Midnight*, p 13.

[62] Watt, *There is Only One Nigeria*, p 24.

[63] Reece, *To My Wife: Fifty Camels*, p 92.

[64] *Ibid.* p 107.

[65] Davidson, *The Real Paradise*, p 126.

[66] Clark (ed), *Was It Only Yesterday?*, p 133.

[67] Cf. Sharwood-Smith, *Diary of a Colonial Wife*, p 27.

[68] Rowling, *Nigerian Memories*, p 32.

[69] Newington, 'West Coast Memories', p 11.

[70] Smith, *Colonial Cadet in Nigeria*, p 58.

[71] Davidson, *The Real Paradise*, p 88.

[72] Wainwright, memoirs, p 212.

[73] Diana Bridges, ' Black and White Notes', p 46.

[74] Dennis, *Goodbye to Pith Helmets*, p 61.

[75] Mitchell, *Remote Corners: A Sierra Leone Memoir*, p 134.

[76] Burkinshaw, *Alarms and Excursions*, p 86.

[77] Watt, *There is Only One Nigeria*, pp 119, 155.

[78]   Terrell, *West African Interlude*, p 43.

[79]   Arrowsmith, *Bush Paths*, p 2.

[80]   Sadleir, *Tanzania: Journey to Republic*, pp 147–8.

[81]   Kerslake, *Time and the Hour*, 1997, p 246; Diana Bridges, memoirs, p 15. See also Arrowsmith, *Bush Paths*, p 124, for their afternoon routine.

[82]   Davidson, *The Real Paradise*, p 77.

[83]   Alexander, *Voices and Echoes*, p 66.

[84]   Cecillie Swaisland, memoirs, RHL MSS.Afr.s.1855, p 12.

[85]   Popplewell, 'Random Recollections of a District Commissioner', pp 42, 55.

[86]   Elnor Russell, *Bush Life*, 1978, p 123.

[87]   Wainwright, memoirs, p 158.

[88]   Johnson (ed), *From Colony to Nation*, p 160.

[89]   Golding, *Colonialism: The Golden Years*, p 150.

[90]   Newington, 'West Coast Memories', p 21.

[91]   Lewis-Barned, *A Fanfare of Trumpets*, p 64.

[92]   Yvonne Fox, 'The Years Between', RHL MSS.Afr.s.2084, p 35.

[93]   *Ibid.*, pp 145–7.

[94]   Violet Cragg, memoirs, RHL MSS.Afr.s.1588, I, pp 18ff.

[95]   *Ibid.*, pp 44ff.

[96]   Hollis, *A Scorpion For Tea*, p 45 and Chapter 6, passim.

[97]   Shipp, 'Safari', p 4.

[98]   *Ibid.*, p 28.

[99]   Scrivenor, 'Reminiscences as the Wife of a Colonial Administrator', p 3.

[100] Allen, *Tales from the Dark Continent*, p 120.

[101] Fox, 'The Years Between', II, p 158.

[102] Bradley, *Once a District Officer*, p 70.

[103] Arrowsmith, *Bush Paths*, p 104.

[104] Hollis, *A Scorpion for Tea*, p 142.

[105] Brook, *The One-Eyed Man is King*, p 141. Emily Bradley was not far off the mark when she cautioned DOs' brides that there were two reasons why they might dislike their new life: health and the effect of the climate on children – *Dearest Priscilla*, p 215.

[106] Bradley, *Dearest Priscilla*, p 40.

[107] Hall, 'A Bushwife's Progress', p 18.

[108] Longford, *The Flags Changed at Midnight*, p 358.

[109] Davidson, *The Real Paradise*, p 141.

[110] Niven, *Nigerian Kaleidoscope*, p 113.

[111] Harris, *Donkey's Gratitude*, p 365. A similar shock awaited Noël Rowling, who on landing in Lagos was met not by her husband but by a

friend, to tell her that he had been sent to Bornu, 600 miles away, the previous day … but would be back quite soon! – *Nigerian Memories*, p 54.

112　Quoted in Allen, *Tales*, p 123.

113　Brook, *The One-Eyed Man is King*, p 284.

114　Beverley Gartrell, in Callan and Ardener (eds), *The Incorporated Wife*, p 182.

115　Fox, 'The Years Between', II, p 66; Carol Christian, in Anderson (ed), *Palm Wine and Leopard's Whiskers*, p 29. In labelling her Chapter 4 'Women and Children Last', Joan Alexander considers the title sums up the absolute dedication which DOs brought to their job, giving it 'priority over all other considerations' – Alexander, *Voices and Echoes*, p 38.

116　Anna Osborne, in Johnson (ed), *Colony to Nation*, p 158.

117　Rowling, *Nigerian Memories*, pp 79–80.

118　Heather Dalton, *The Gold Coast, The Wives' Experience*, RHL ODRP Report No. 15, 1985, pp 1, 59. In terms of DOs' wives' views, this survey was valuably followed up by the Women's Corona Society millennium survey *A World of Memories*, 2000, containing the memoirs of many wives from Africa, notably complemented in the narratives collected by Joan Alexander, *Voices and Echoes*, Chapters 1 to 8, and Joanna Trollope, *Britannia's Daughters*, especially Chapter 6.

119　Terrell, *West African Interlude*, pp 102–3.

120　Dennis, *Goodbye to Pith Helmets*, p 171.

121　Forward, *You Have Been Allocated Uganda*, acknowledgements.

122　Anderson (ed), *Palm Wine and Leopard's Whiskers*, pp 195ff (her name, Campbell, wrongly appears as Clare in the text – communication from her DO husband, J.A. Jones). Among childhood reminiscences, one recalls the stoic remark made by Alys Reece's nine-year-old daughter when she left her at boarding school in Aberdeen, 'But Mummy, I don't even know the language', quoted in Alexander, *Voices and Echoes*, p 25.

Chapter 10. The District Officer and Decolonization

1　Speech by Malcolm Macdonald in the House of Commons, 7 September 1938.

2　Secretary of State's despatch, 25 February 1947, para. 1.

3　Smith, *Colonial Cadet in Nigeria*, pp 6–7.

4　D. and M. Brown (eds), *Looking Back on the Uganda Protectorate*, p 58.

5　Kirk-Greene (ed), *The Transfer of Power*, pp 140, 155, 157.

6　Sir Michael Blundell, *So Rough a Wind*, 1964, p 262.

7　Dennis, *Goodbye to Pith Helmets*, p 5.

8   K.G. Bradley, *A Career in the Oversea Civil Service*, 1955, p 58.

9   *Ibid.*, p 55.

10 Bere, *A Cuckoo's Parting Cry*, p 220.

11 Clark (ed), *Was It Only Yesterday?*, p 200.

12 Bere, *A Cuckoo's Parting Cry*, p 220.

13 Nightingale, *Seven Rivers to Cross*, p 68.

14 Kirk-Greene, *Transfer of Power*, pp 144–5. Parts VI and VII, on 'The DO as the Man in the Middle', focus largely on the DO in the context of nationalist politics.

15 *Ibid.*, p 86.

16 Savill, 'Colonial Service', pp 106–7, 135–6.

17 Longford, *The Flags Changed at Midnight*, p 24.

18 R. Brayne, 'Memories of Tanganyika' (privately held), p 99.

19 Golding, *Colonialism: The Golden Years*, pp 177, 207.

20 *Ibid.*, pp 212, 198.

21 The prime minister's letter is reproduced in Lewis-Barned, *A Fanfare of Trumpets*, pp 113–15.

22 Dennis, *Goodbye to Pith Helmets*, p 174.

23 Mitchell, *Remote Corners*, p 57. In Northern Rhodesia R. Short dedicated his *African Sunset*, 1973, to the District Messengers, whom he felt the colonial government had let down. His memoir presents a very negative view of political party activism as a threat to everything the colonial administration stood for.

24 Harris, *Donkey's Gratitude*, p 382.

25 Barton, 'A Medal for Ndabisi', p 114.

26 Clark (ed), *Was It Only Yesterday?*, p 200; P.H. Johnston, in Kirk-Greene, *Transfer of Power*, p 161.

27 Jacobs, 'Going Backwards' (privately held), p 332.

28 Smith, *Colonial Cadet in Nigeria*, p 18.

29 Brind, *Lying Abroad*, p 44.

30 Longford, *The Flags Changed at Midnight*, p 416.

31 Lewis-Barned, *A Fanfare of Trumpets*, pp 98, 99; Longford, *The Flags Changed at Midnight*, p 416.

32 Posnett, *The Scent of Eucalyptus*, pp 106–7. An important organizer at more than a dozen independence day celebrations was Colonel Eric Hefford, who described himself as 'a willing midwife always on hand to help with the birth of a new country'. See his obituary in the *Daily Telegraph*, 29 September 1995.

33 D. and M. Brown (eds), *Looking Back on the Uganda Protectorate*, pp 266–7.

34 I.F.C. Macpherson, 'Aspects of Crown Service' (privately held), pp 14–15.

[35] Savill, 'Colonial Service', p 117.

[36] Watt, *There is Only One Nigeria*, p 161.

[37] D.A. Low and J.M. Lonsdale, *History of East Africa*, Vol. III, 1976, pp 12ff.

[38] A major origin source for the study of those Africanization and Administrative Service programmes is E. Burr (ed), *Localization and Public Service Training*, ODRP Report No. 4, 1985.

[39] Cohen, *British Policy in Changing Africa*, p 76.

[40] Chenevix Trench, *The Desert's Dusty Face*, p 227. In the same context, one recalls Rudyard Kipling's short story 'The Head of the District', in which a Pathan leader turns on the DC when the latter informs him that the new DC will be an Indian, with the searing reaction 'Has the Government gone mad to send a black Bengali dog to us? Am I to pay service to such a one?'

[41] In Kirk-Greene, *The Transfer of Power*, p 14.

[42] For example, J.O. Udoji, *Under Three Masters: Memoirs of an African Administrator*, 1995, and, in a semi-fictional form, A. Adebayo, *I Am Directed*, 1991.

[43] Watt, *There is Only One Nigeria*, p 189.

[44] J. Lawley, 'When Northern Rhodesia Became Zambia' (privately held), p 8.

[45] Chenevix Trench, *The Desert's Dusty Face*, p 294.

[46] Brook, *The One-Eyed Man is King*, p 306.

[47] Anderson (ed), *Palm Wine and Leopard's Whiskers*, p 15.

[48] See, for example, the incidents narrated in Kirk-Greene, *Transfer of Power*, pp 13, 65 (Kirk-Greene) and 158 (Baker).

[49] Margery Perham, *Native Administration in Nigeria*, 1937, p 361.

[50] Anderson (ed), *Palm Wine and Leopard's Whiskers*, p 304.

[51] Atkinson, *An African Life*, p 76.

[52] Cawte, *From Kaduna to Kirakira*, p 138.

[53] *Ibid.*, p 153.

[54] Mitchell, *Remote Corners*, p 213.

[55] Brind, *Lying Abroad*, p 55.

[56] Jeffries, *Whitehall and the Colonial Service*, p 57.

[57] Millard, *Never a Dull Moment*, p 202.

[58] *Reorganisation of the Colonial Service*, Col. No. 306, 1954, paras. 6 and 11.

[59] Typical was the reaction of J. O'Regan, who had started his career as a DO in Ceylon and ended up in Nigeria – see *From Empire to Commonwealth: Reflections of a Career in Britain's Overseas Service*, 1994, p 104 and Chapter 10.

[60] HMOCS, *Statement of Policy Regarding Organization*, Cmd. 9768, 1956.

61   K. Barnes, *Polio and Me*, 1998, p 20.

62   *Statement of Policy*, 1956, para. 7 (iv).

63   Atkinson, *An African Life*, p 118.

64   HMOCS, *Statement of Policy Regarding Overseas Officers Serving in Nigeria*, Cmnd. 497, 1958.

65   Weatherhead, 'Possessors of Power', pp 263–4.

66   M. Jackson, *A Scottish Life: Sir John Martin*, 1999, p 220. See also *The Times*, leader, 7 August 1958.

67   *Ibid.*, pp 226ff. For a detailed revelation of the stops and starts in Whitehall of those three White Papers (1954, 1956 and 1958) dealing with the DOs' premature retirement and compensation schemes, see Jeffries, *Whitehall and the Colonial Service*, Chapters 5–8.

68   Cf Gavaghan, *Of Lions and Dung Beetles*, pp 278ff. See also R. Rathbone, 'The Colonial Service and the Transfer of Power in Ghana' in J.H. Smith (ed), *Administering Empire*, 1999, pp 149ff.

69   K. Younger, *The Public Service in New States*, 1960, pp 25, 107.

70   Watt, *There is Only One Nigeria*, p 149.

71   A.H.M. Kirk-Greene, 'Decolonization: The Ultimate Diaspora', *Journal of Contemporary History*, 36 (2001), pp 133–51.

72   *Overseas Pensioner*, 81 (2001), p 51.

73   Gardner, *My First Eighty Years*, pp 140–1.

74   Golding, *Colonialism: The Golden Years*, p 229.

75   Dennis, *Goodbye to Pith Helmets*, p 196.

76   A statistical analysis of these forms now deposited in Rhodes House Library (as yet uncatalogued) appears in N. Gardiner's unpublished thesis, 'Sentinels of Empire', p 353.

77   A.H.M. Kirk-Greene, 'What Became of Us?', *Overseas Pensioner*, 84 (2002), pp 30–4. The forms are destined for deposit in Rhodes House Library, Oxford.

78   Alexander, *Voices and Echoes*, 1983, p 3.

79   Stuart, *Of Cargoes, Colonies and Kings*, p 82; Posnett, *The Scent of Eucalyptus*, p 111; Forward, *You Have Been Allocated Uganda*, p 151.

Chapter 11. Looking Back: The Image and the Memory of the DO

1   Wainwright, memoirs, p i; Fox, 'The Years Between', p i.

2   Stuart, *Of Cargoes, Colonies and Kings*, p x.

3   Sir Philip Mitchell, *African Afterthoughts*, 1954, Foreword, p xi.

4   Gardner, *My First Eighty Years*, p 53.

5   The Clifford Minute, published in the *Nigeria Gazette*, 2 March 1926. Sir Hugh Clifford's inflexible tone was modified by his successor, Sir Donald Cameron, and again reviewed by another governor, Sir Arthur Richards. See Kirk-Greene, *The Principles of Native*

Administration in Nigeria, p 19 and passim.

6   Margaret Laurence, *The Prophet's Camel Bell*, 1963, pp 205ff.

7   Smith, *Colonial Cadet in Nigeria*, p 96.

8   In *The Flags Changed at Midnight*, M. Longford is outspoken about some of his fellow officers, e.g. pp 134, 276–8, 373, 422.

9   L.H. Gann, *A History of Northern Rhodesia*, II, 1969, p 240.

10   J. Maslen, *Beating about the Nigerian Bush*, 1994, p 38.

11   Sir Charles Jeffries, *Partners for Progress: The Men and Women of the Colonial Service*, 1949, p 101.

12   *Ibid.*, pp 189, 193.

13   Sir Charles Jeffries, 'The Colonial Service in Perspective', *Corona*, December 1962, pp 450–4.

14   Furse, *Aucuparius*, p 221.

15   *Ibid.*, p 303.

16   J. Garner, *The Commonwealth Office, 1925–1968*, 1978, pp 363, 406.

17   For instance, Brind, *Lying Abroad*; Posnett, *The Scent of Eucalyptus*; Stuart, *Of Cargoes, Colonies and Kings*; and from a colonial and not diplomatic viewpoint, A.T. Clark, 'Chalk and Cheese? The Colonial and Diplomatic Services', in J.H. Smith (ed), *Administering Empire*, 1994, pp 49–60. Interestingly one top diplomat, Sir Ivone Kirkpatrick, was quoted as saying that the same three qualities were essential in both the Foreign and the Colonial Services: 'intellectual curiosity, catholic tastes, and humanism' – Sadleir, *Tanzania: Journey to Republic*, p 53.

18   Burns, *In Defence of Colonies*, p 46.

19   *Ibid.*, p 36.

20   Cohen, *British Policy in Changing Africa*, p 76.

21   Burns, *In Defence of Colonies*, p 301.

22   McClintock, *Kingdoms in the Sand and Sun*, p 103.

23   Bere, *A Cuckoo's Parting Cry*, p 45.

24   Farson, *Behind God's Back*, p 139.

25   *Ibid.*, pp 147–8.

26   *Ibid.*, pp 149–51.

27   *Ibid.*, p 269.

28   *Ibid.*, p 201.

29   John Gunther, *Inside Africa*, 1955, p 734.

30   *Ibid.*, p 768.

31   Elspeth Huxley, *Four Guineas*, p 14. For her biography, see Christine Nicholls, *Elspeth Huxley*, 2002.

32   *Ibid.*, p 248.

33   *Ibid.*, p 219. Writing a decade later, a Southern Nigerian DO echoed Huxley's dichotomy by pointing out, 'There was a calm about the

North, an easy rhythm and confidence strange to anyone who had served only among the varied and restless people of the South' – Brook, *The One-Eyed Man is King*, p 264.

[34] Elspeth Huxley, *Out in the Midday Sun: My Kenya*, 1995, p 177.

[35] Elspeth Huxley, Introduction to Franklin, *The Flag-Wagger*, p x.

[36] Quoted in Dick Hobson, 'Northern Rhodesia in the 1930s', unpublished memoir (privately held), p 4.

[37] Her travel diaries of the years 1929–32 in Africa abound in portraits of the countless DOs she met. See Margery Perham, *African Apprenticeship*, 1974, *East African Journey*, 1976, and *West African Passage*, 1983.

[38] J.G. Liebenow, *Colonial Rule and Political Development in Tanganyika*, 1971, p xii.

[39] R. Winks (ed), *Oxford History of the British Empire*, V, 1999, p 657. The trilogy is *Heaven's Command*, 1973; *Pax Britannica*, 1968; *Farewell the Trumpets*, 1978.

[40] Mullins, *Retreat from Africa*, pp 102ff.

[41] Jan Morris, 'Now that the Sun is Setting', *The Times*, 9 November 1995.

[42] Kathryn Tidrick, *Empire and the English Character*, 1992, p 145.

[43] Perham, *Native Administration in Nigeria*, p 331.

[44] *Committee on the System of Appointment in the Colonial Services* (Warren Fisher), Cmd 3554, 1930, p 23.

[45] Margery Perham, *The Colonial Reckoning*, 1961, p 124.

[46] *Ibid.*, pp 126, 125. On the published field diaries, see note 37.

[47] *Ibid.*, pp 128, 125.

[48] Sir John MacPherson, Foreword to R. Heussler, *Yesterday's Rulers*, 1963, p xiii.

[49] Heussler, *The British in Northern Nigeria*, p 7; *Yesterday's Rulers*, p 217. He also wrote *British Tanganyika*, 1971, and a two-volume history of the Malayan civil service, *British Rule in Malaya 1867–1942*, 1981, and *Completing a Stewardship*, 1983.

[50] Heussler, *Yesterday's Rulers*, p xxv.

[51] W.M. Macmillan, *Africa Emergent*, 1938, p 193.

[52] *Ibid.*, pp 196–7.

[53] *Ibid.*, p 200.

[54] Lawrence James, *The Rise and Fall of the British Empire*, 1994, p 629; Trevor Royle, *Winds of Change: The End of the Empire in Africa*, 1996, p 283. See also R. Neillands, *A Fighting Retreat: The British Empire, 1947–1997*, 1996.

[55] J.M. Lonsdale, Foreword to Gavaghan, *Of Lions and Dung Beetles*, p 9.

56   N. Ferguson, *Empire: How Britain Made the Modern World*, 2003, pp 358ff.
57   Kuklick, *The Imperial Bureaucrat*, p xi.
58   Tidrick, *Empire and the English Character*, pp 172ff.
59   Berman, *Control and Crisis in Colonial Kenya*, pp 57, 61n.37.
60   *Ibid.*, p 106.
61   White, *Dan Bana*, p xv.
62   Brook, *The One-Eyed Man is King*, p 175.
63   Quoted by A. Chenevix Trench, Foreword to C. Chenevix Trench, *The Desert's Dusty Face*, p ii.
64   A.T. Culwick, *Britannia Waives the Rules*, 1963, pp 12ff.
65   Lonsdale, Foreword to Gavaghan, *Of Lions and Dung Beetles*, p 9.
66   D. and M. Brown (eds), *Looking Back on the Uganda Protectorate*, p 321.
67   G. MacDonald Fraser, *Quartered Safe Out Here*, 1992, p xviii.
68   Judith Brown and W.R. Louis (eds), *The Oxford History of the British Empire*, 1999, pp 253, 705, 711.
69   Heussler, *The British in Northern Nigeria*, p 7.
70   A partial exception is R. East, transl., *Akiga's Story*, 1939, Chapter 8.
71   Weatherhead, 'Possessors of Power' (privately held), p 284.
72   In this chapter, where no separate reference is given for remarks attributed to named DOs, the source is 'The Colonial Service Mind' – see Bibliography, Memoirs, I. unpublished (c) MS contributions, OSPA Research Project (v).
73   Smith, *Colonial Cadet in Nigeria*, p 113.
74   Udoji, *Under Three Masters*; Adebayo, *I Am Directed*; Maciel, *Bwana Karani*.
75   Nnamdi Azikiwe, *Zik*, 1961, p 155.
76   Chief Obafemi Awolowo, *Awo*, 1960, p 43.
77   K. Nkrumah, *Ghana: An Autobiography*, 1959, p 125.
78   K. Kaunda, *State of the Nation*, 1988, I, pp 219–20.
79   Awolowo, *Awo*, pp 45, 92.
80   *Ibid.*, p 108.
81   Sir Ahmadu Bello, *My Life*, 1962, p 6.
82   Sir Abubakar Tafawa Balewa, *Mr Prime Minister*, 1964, pp 49, 205.
83   Siaka Stevens, *What Life Has Taught Me*, 1984, p 32.
84   Fay Pearson, 'Isaac Motsusi', unpublished ms, 2002, p 5.
85   Maciel, *Bwana Karani*.
86   See *Overseas Pensioner*, 85 (2003), pp 15–21. See also Note 72.
87   Cook, 'District Officer', pp i–ii.
88   Morley, *Colonial Postscript*, p 79.
89   Hollis, *A Scorpion for Tea*, p 11.

90 G. Billing, 'Crest of the Wave', RHL MSS.Afr.s.1763, p 32.

91 Varvill, 'A Cadet's Progress', pp 4, 52.

92 Dennis, *Goodbye to Pith Helmets*, p 203; Mitchell, *Remote Corners*, p 248.

93 Lord Tweedsmuir, *Always a Countryman*, p 192.

94 Gutch, *Colonial Servant*, p 28.

95 Short, *African Sunset*, p 184.

96 R.R. Oakley, *Treks and Palavers*, 1938, p 287.

97 Crocker, *Nigeria: A Critique of British Colonial Administration*, pp 235–47.

98 Smith, *Colonial Cadet in Nigeria*, p i.

99 Milne, *No Telephone to Heaven*, p 404; Brook, *The One-Eyed Man is King*, p 258.

100 One Resident in Northern Nigeria was a notorious 'bully': see G.L. Aitchison in Clark (ed), *Was It Only Yesterday?*, p 300.

101 Bazley, *Bunyoro*, p vii; Norris, 'Experience in the Overseas Civil Service, p 15.

102 Clark, *Was It Only Yesterday?*, p 253.

103 Watt, *There is Only One Nigeria*, p 197.

104 Bradley, *The Diary of a District Officer*, p 170. Cf. Sadleir, *Tanzania: Journey to Republic*, p 108.

105 Kirk-Greene (ed), *The Transfer of Power*, p 181.

106 See note 86.

107 For R.G. Turnbull's famous alternatives to the claim, see C. Chenevix Trench, *Men Who Ruled Kenya*, p 108.

108 For short history, see Kirk-Greene, *The Corona Club 1900–1990*, 1990.

109 A glance at the announcement pages of the twice-yearly *Overseas Pensioner* magazine gives an idea of the more than a score of associations and reunions which still meet at least once a year.

110 See Clare Brown (ed), *Manuscript Collections in Rhodes House Library, Oxford*, 1996, p v, for a list of ODRP's 21 major research reports. This is now the leading archive of primary unpublished Colonial Service documentation in the world, with over 10,000 items catalogued to date.

111 See their catalogue *Voices and Echoes*, 1999, especially the entries under 'District Officer'.

112 A major work of reference will be Terry Barringer's forthcoming annotated checklist of Colonial Service personal memoirs.

113 Kirk-Greene, *On Crown Service*.

114 The Queen's special message to the Colonial Service on her accession to the throne, often overlooked by CS historians, is valuably reproduced in Anderson (ed), *Palm Wine and Leopard's Whiskers*, pp 428–9.

[115] See the proceedings in Kirk-Greene (ed), *The Transfer of Power*, and Smith (ed), *Administering Empire*.

[116] *The Times*, 27 June 2003, p 39.

[117] See A.H.M. Kirk-Greene, 'The Colonial Service in the Novel', in Smith (ed), *Administering Empire*, p 44; and A.H.M Kirk-Greene, 'Sanders of the River', *New Society*, 10 November 1977. A checklist of such novels is to be found in the Bibliography, Section III (d).

Bibliography

I.   MEMOIRS (unpublished)

a.   Ms memoirs in Rhodes House Library, Oxford

b.   Ms memoirs privately held

c.   Ms contributions, OSPA Research Projects (RHL Oxford)

II.   MEMOIRS (published)

a.   Books

b.   Collective memoirs

III.   GENERAL WORKS

a.   Books

b.   Articles and chapters

c.   Official publications

d.   Novels

I. MEMOIRS (unpublished)

a. Ms memoirs in Rhodes House Library, Oxford

Allen, G., 'Whence Few Came Out', MSS.Afr.s.1687

Balmer, P.H., memoirs, MSS.Afr.s.1895

Barton, D., 'A Medal for Ndabisi', MSS.Afr.s.1777

Bevan Jones, D.G., memoirs, MSS.Afr.r.123

Billing, G., 'Crest of the Wave', MSS.Afr.s.1763

Birks, D.T.M., memoirs, MSS.Afr.s.1071

Brayne-Baker, J., 'I Liked it Out There', MSS.Afr.s.1926

Bridges, Diana, 'Black and White Notes', MSS.Afr.s.1634

Bushwhacker, 'Reminiscences of a Nigerian Administrator', MSS. Afr.r.177

Carpenter, F.W., 'African Patchwork', MSS.Afr.s.1710

Clive, J.H., 'A Cure for Insomnia', MSS.Afr.s.678

Cook, A.E., 'District Officer', MSS.Afr.s.1924

Cragg, Violet, memoirs, MSS.Afr.s.1588

Denny, S.R., memoirs, MSS.Afr.s.2039

Dick, R.A., memoirs, MSS.Afr.s.952

Elliott, H.P., 'Memoirs of Colonial Administrative Service in Nigeria', MSS.Afr.s.1838

Findlay, R.L., memoirs, MSS.Afr.r.170

Fitz-Henry, Christine, 'African Dust', MSS.Afr.s.367, 2

Fox, Yvonne, 'The Years Between', MSS.Afr.s.2084

Hall, Lorna, 'A Bushwife's Progress', MSS.Afr.s.1834

Hunter, K.L., memoirs, MSS.Afr.s.1942

Johnston, J.R., 'Bits and Pieces', MSS.Afr.s.1270

Johnston, P., 'Service in Tanganyika', MSS.Afr.s.1887

Kingdon, Z.E., 'Posted in Tanganyika', MSS.Afr.s.2255

McEntee, P.D., 'Something for the Record', MSS.Br.Emp.s.544

Mayhew, T., 'Bwana DC', MSS.Afr.s.1837

Moxon, J., 'Plumes in My Haversack', MSS.Afr.s.2055

Newington, W.F.H., 'West Coast Memories', MSS.Afr.s.1983

Norris, M.W., 'Experience in the Overseas Civil Service', MSS.Afr. s.2025

Pickering, Carol, 'The Gold Coast Remembered', MSS.Afr.s.2092

Popplewell, G.D., 'Random Recollections of a District Commissioner', MSS.Afr.s.2156

Savill, D.O., 'memoirs', MSS.Afr.s.1038 and s.2165

Scrivenor, Lady, 'Reminiscences as the Wife of a Colonial

Administrator', MSS.Br.Emp.r.5

Shipp, Mrs G.W.I., 'Safari', MSS.Afr.s.424

Sillery, A., 'Working Backwards', MSS.Afr.r.207

Smith, J.S., 'The Last Time', MSS.Afr.s.1986

Stacpoole, J., memoirs, MSS.Afr.s.2272

Stephenson, G.L., 'Nigerian and Other Days', MSS.Afr.s.1833

Swaisland, Cecillie, memoirs, MSS.Afr.s.1855

Syme, R.G., 'The Wanderings of a Misfit', MSS.Afr.s.1722

Varvill, M., 'A Cadet's Progress', MSS.Afr.s.2093

Wainwright, R.E., memoirs, MSS.Br.Emp.s.524

Weatherhead, A.T., 'But Always as Friends', MSS.Afr.s.232 (also titled 'Possessors of Power')

Note: The Royal Commonwealth Society's collection of unpublished memoirs (*Catalogue*, 1975) is now held in the University Library, Cambridge. Rhodes House Library, Oxford, holds transcripts of oral history interviews undertaken by the OCRP in 1969–72. For a listing of those undertaken by the British Empire and Commonwealth Museum, Bristol, see their catalogue *Voices and Echoes*, 1999. The National Library recorded some interviews under its Scottish Decolonization Project.

b. Ms memoirs privately held

Brayne, R., 'Memoirs of Tanganyika'

Carr, F.B., 'Remembrances: Nigeria'

Cashmore, T.H.R., 'Kenya Days'

Clark, A.T., 'Good Second Class'

Cooke, N.F., 'Empire in Decline: A Personal Experience'

Davies, F., memoir

Evans, Ifor L., 'Notes of a West African Journey'

Hobson, R., 'Northern Rhodesia in the 1930s' (V. Brelsford's autobiographical notes)

Jacobs, B.L., 'Going Backwards'

Johnson, V.K., 'Autumn Leaves'

Lawley, J., 'When Northern Rhodesia Became Zambia'

Lawson, J.S., 'West African Service'

Macpherson, I.F., 'Aspects of Crown Service'

Savill, D.O., 'Colonial Service'

Sealy-King, L., 'Our African Experiences'

Tanner, R.E.S. and K.A. Kjerland, 'Paranoia in the Colonial

Administrative Service'
Thorp, J.K.R., 'The Glittering Lake'
Williams, F.D.K., 'Third Tour'
Williams, F.R.J., 'Colonial Administration in Uganda'

Attention is also drawn to the important unpublished Ph.D. thesis by Nile Gardiner, 'Sentinels of Empire: The British Colonial Administrative Service, 1919–1954', Yale University, 1998.

Note: Since the research into these privately held memoirs was undertaken, several have been deposited in Rhodes House Library (e.g. Brayne, Jacobs, Johnson, Savill), though they have not yet all been catalogued or allocated a shelf number.

c. Ms contributions, OSPA Research Projects (RHL Oxford)

Five major research projects have been undertaken by the author with the co-operation of members of OSPA. These are:

(i) HMOCS Data Project, 1983–86
This material, some 1,900 forms in all, has been analysed in detailed tables by N. Gardiner, 'Sentinels of Empire: the British Colonial Administrative Service 1919–1954', Ph.D. thesis, Yale University, 1998, pp 275–335.

(ii) 'For Better of for Verse', 1996–97
The project, collecting copies of verse written by members of the Colonial Service, was discussed in *The Overseas Pensioner*, 72 (1996), pp 47–50; 75 (1998), pp 33–8.

(iii) 'Candidates Are Expected to Answer…', 2000–1
The project, collecting memoirs of the Colonial Service Training Courses at Oxford, Cambridge and London, was discussed in *The Overseas Pensioner*, 80 (2000), pp 41–3; 82 (2001), pp 35–9.

(iv) 'What Became of Us? (Second Careers)' 2001–2. The material, some 600 forms, provides information about which of the 35 identified occupations were taken up by officers who retired prematurely from the Colonial Service. The project, the first part of 'Towards a Retrospective Record', was discussed in *The Overseas Pensioner*, 83 (2002), p 12; 84 (2002), pp 30–4.

(v) 'The Colonial Service Mind', 2001–2
The written contributions for the second part of 'Towards a Retrospective Record', some 500 memoirs, focused on seven questions about motivation, thoughts on work, and the CS career in retrospect. The project was discussed in *The Overseas Pensioner*, 85 (2003), pp 15–21.

The complete documentation for all five projects is destined for deposit in Rhodes House Library in 2005.

The names of DOs, showing their original territory and date of joining, whose memoirs from Research Project (iii) are quoted in Chapter 3, and those quoted from Research Project (v) in Chapters 2 and 11, are listed below:

Project (iii)

D. Connelly (Tang. 54)

N. Goldie Scot (G.C. 47)

R.J. Graham (Nig. 54)

R.A. Hill (N. Rhod. 49)

B.L. Jacobs (Ug. 47)

J.A. Jones (Nig. 46)

F. Kennedy (Nig. 53)

D.E. Nicoll-Griffith (K. 52)

J.P.L. Scott (S.L.)

R.E.N. Smith (Nyas.)

J.H.D. Stapleton (Nig. 35)

Project (v)

H.J.B. Allen (Ug. 55)

E.B.S. Alton (G.C. 46)

K.V. Arrowsmith (Nig. 49)

M.C. Atkinson (Nig. 38)

J.H. Banforth (S.L. 50)

R.N. Barlow-Poole (Nig. 47)

K.J. Barnes (Nig. 54)

T.J.R. Barty (Ug. 49)

D. Barton (Tang. 52)

W.L. Bell (Ug. 46)

R.A. Hill (N. Rhod. 49)

B.L. Jacobs (Ug. 47)

J.R. Johnson (K. 55)

P.H. Jones (K. 49)

D. Joy (N. Rhod. 56)

F. Kennedy (Nig. 53)

R.T. Kerslake (Nig. 37)

J.C. Lawley (N. Rhod. 60)

J. Lennard (G.C. 42)

B. Loach (N. Rhod. 58)

R.F. Bendy (Nig. 47)

J.E. Blunden (N. Rhod. 44)

T.F. Bolter (Nig. 46)

P.O. Bowcock (N. Rhod. 55)

J.H.F. Bown (N. Rhod. 55)

G.W.S. Bowry (Nyas. 46)

B.H. Brackenbury (Nig. 46)

R.B. Brayne (Tang. 48)

T.G. Brierly (Tang 50)

J. Brock (G.C. 51)

D. Brown (Ug. 51)

R.A. Campbell (N. Rhod. 60)

D. Connelly (Tang. 54)

N.F. Cooke (Nig. 38)

C.W.B. Costeloe (G.C. 44)

C.A.K. Cullimore (Tang. 58)

J. Dalzell (K. 54)

J.G. Davies (Nig. 42)

S. Delmege (K. 47)

P. Dennis (G.C. 46)

A.G. Ditcham (Nig. 48)

M.H. Dorey (Tang. 50)

J.S. Duthie (G.C. 46)

B.F. Eberlie (Tang. 57)

G. Ellerton (K. 45)

A.G. Eyre (Nig. 42)

J.A.R. Forster (G.C. 45)

D. Frost (N. Rhod. 47)

T. Gavaghan (K. 43)

D. Glendenning (N. Rhod. 56)

J.M. Golds (K. 53)

T.R.W. Longmore (Nig. 48)

M. Macgregor (N. Rhod. 53)

I. Mackinson (N. Rhod. 52)

A.E. MacRobert (Ug. 52)

D.L. Mathews (Tang. 56)

P.N. Mawhood (Tang. 49)

J.C.A. Mousley (N. Rhod. 51)

D.E. Nicoll-Griffith (K. 52)

F.A. Peet (K. 49)

I.W.D. Peterson (K. 52)

R.B.S. Purdy (Nyas. 52)

R.J. Purdy (Nig. 39)

C.G.C. Rawlins (G.C. 46)

B.A.F. Read (Bech. 57)

P.A.P. Robertson (Tang. 36)

D.O. Savill (Nig. 49)

E.N. Scott (K. 53)

K.P. Shaw (K. 49)

M.H. Shaw (Tang. 59)

R. Short (N. Rhod. 50)

A.P. Smith (Nig. 42)

J.H. Smith (Nig. 51)

J.R. Smith (Tang. 55)

J.H.D. Stapleton (Nig. 35)

T.J. Tawney (Tang. 58)

D.G.P. Taylor (Tang. 58)

J.P. Twining (Ug. 53)

P.H.M. Vischer (Nig. 47)

W.J. Warrell-Bowring (Som. 47)

J.N.E. Watson (Nyas. 48)

D.D. Yonge (Tang. 48)

R.J. Graham (Nig. 54)

G.C. Guy (S.L. 51)

S. Hardwick (Tang. 57)

M.R. Harris (Nyas. 48)

J. Hennessy (Basuto. 48)

II. MEMOIRS (published)

a. Books

Adebayo, Augustine, *White Man in Black Skin*, 1981
——, *I Am Directed*, 1991
Ainley, J., *Pink Stripes and Obedient Servants*, 2001
Arrowsmith, K.V., *Bush Paths*, 1991
Askwith, T.G., *Getting My Knees Brown*, 1996
Atkinson, M.C., *An African Interlude: Tales of a Colonial Officer*, 1992
——, *Nigerian Tales of the Colonial Era*, n.d.
——, *More Nigerian Tales of the Colonial Era*, n.d.
——, *Yet More Nigerian Tales of the Colonial Era*
Awolowo, Chief O., *Awo*, 1960
Barnes, K., *Polio and Me*, 1998
Bates, D., *A Fly-Switch from the Sultan*, 1961
Bazley, W., *Bunyoro: A Tropical Paradise*, 1993
Bell, Sir Gawain, *Shadows in the Sand*, 1983
——, *An Imperial Twilight*, 1989
Bell, Vivienne, *Blown by the Wind of Change*, 1986
Bello, Sir Ahmadu, *My Life*, 1962
Bere, R., *A Cuckoo's Parting Cry*, 1990
Berry, Erick, *Mad Dogs and Englishmen*, 1941
Blackburne, Sir Kenneth, *Lasting Legacy*, 1976
Blair, J.M., *Juju and Justice*, 1991
Boyle, Laura, *Diary of a Colonial Officer's Wife*, 1968
Bradley, K.G., *The Diary of a District Officer*, 1947
——, *Once a District Officer*, 1966
Bridges, A.F.B., *So We Used To Do*, 1990
Brind, H., *Lying Abroad*, 1999
Brook, I., *The One-Eyed Man is King*, 1966
Burkinshaw, P.L. *Alarms and Excursions*, 1991

Burns, Sir Alan, *Colonial Civil Servant*, 1949

Cairns, J.C., *Bush and Boma*, 1959

Cameron, Sir Donald, *My Tanganyika Service and Some Nigeria*, 1939

Carson, S.B., *Sun, Sand and Safari*, 1937

Carter, T.D., *The Northern Rhodesia Record*, 1992

Cawte, Jennifer, *From Kaduna to Kirakira*, 2000

Champion, Olive, *Journey of a Lifetime*, 1994

Chenevix Trench, C., *The Desert's Dusty Face*, 1964

——, *Men Who Ruled Kenya: The Kenya Administration, 1892–1963*, 1993

Cooke, J., *One White Man in Black Africa*, 1991

Crocker, W.R., *Nigeria: A Critique of British Colonial Administration*, 1936

——, *Travelling Back*, 1981

Davidson, Ann, *The Real Paradise: Memories of Africa, 1950–1963*, 1993

Dennis, P., *Goodbye to Pith Helmets*, 2000

Fairlie, M., *No Time Like the Past*, 1992

Forward, A., *You Have Been Allocated Uganda*, 1999

Franklin, H., *The Flag-Wagger*, 1974

Furse, Sir Ralph, *Aucuparius: Recollection of a Recruiting Officer*, 1962

Gardner, T., *My First Eighty Years*, 1998

Gavaghan, T., *Of Lions and Dung Beetles*, 1999

Golding, J.A. *Colonialism: The Golden Years*, 1987

Goldsmith, Anne, *Gentle Warrior*, 2001

Greenhall, E.C., *Kaunda's Gaoler*, 2001

Gunn, I.F., *With a Rod in Four Continents*, 1981

Gutch, Sir John, *Colonial Servant*, 1987

Haig, E.F.G., *Nigerian Sketches*, 1931

Harris, T., *Donkey's Gratitude*, 1992

Hastings, A.C.G., *Nigerian Days*, 1925

Hennings, R.O., *African Morning*, 1951

Hives, F., *Juju and Justice in Nigeria*, 1930

——, *Justice in the Jungle*, 1933

Hollis, Rosemary, *A Scorpion for Tea*, 1973

Huxley, Elspeth, *Out in the Midday Sun: My Kenya*, 1995

Jackson, M., *A Scottish Life: Sir John Martin*, 1999

Jeffries, Sir Charles, *Whitehall and the Colonial Service*, 1972

Kerslake, R.T., *Time and the Hour*, 1997

Kisch, M.S., *Letters and Sketches from Northern Nigeria*, 1910
Langa Langa, *Up Against it in Nigeria*, 1922
Larymore, Constance, *A Resident's Wife in Nigeria*, 1908
Laurence, Margaret, *The Prophet's Camel Bell*, 1963
Leith-Ross, Sylvia, *Stepping-Stones: Memoirs of Colonial Nigeria, 1907–1960*, 1983
Lewis-Barned, J., *A Fanfare of Trumpets*, 1993
Longford, M., *The Flags Changed at Midnight*, 2002
Lumley, E.K., *Forgotten Mandate: A British District Officer in Tanganyika*, 1976
McClintock, N.C., *Kingdoms in the Sand and Sun*, 1992
Maciel, M., *Bwana Karani*, 1985
Maddocks, K.P., *Of No Fixed Abode*, 1988
Maiden, R.L., *The Nasarawa Gate*, 1952
Marshall, H.H., *Like Father, Like Son*, 1980
Maslen, J., *Beating About the Nigerian Bush*, 1994
Millard, J., *Never a Dull Moment*, 1996
Milne, M.H., *No Telephone to Heaven*, 1999
Mitchell, H., *Remote Corners: A Sierra Leone Memoir*, 2002
Mitchell, Sir Philip, *African Afterthoughts*, 1954
Morley, J., *Colonial Postscript: Diary of a District Officer 1935–1956*, 1992
Mullins, P., *Retreat from Africa*, 1992
Nightingale, B., *Seven Rivers to Cross*, 1996
Niven, Sir Rex, *Nigerian Kaleidoscope*, 1982
Nkrumah, K., *Ghana; An Autobiography*, 1959
Oakley, R.R., *Treks and Palavers*, 1938
O'Regan, J., *From Empire to Commonwealth: Reflections of a Career in Britain's Overseas Service*, 1994
Parkinson, Sir Cosmo, *The Colonial Office from Within*, 1947
Perham, Margery, *African Apprenticeship*, 1974
——, *East African Journey*, 1976
——, *West African Passage*, 1983
Phillips, H., *From Obscurity to Bright Dawn*, 1998
Posnett, R., *The Scent of Eucalyptus*, 2001
Postlethwaite, *I Look Back*, 1947
Reece, Alys, *To My Wife: Fifty Camels*, 1963
Richardson, S.S., *No Weariness*, 2001
Robertson, Sir James, *Transition in Africa*, 1974
Rowling, Noël, *Nigerian Memories*, 1982
Russell, A.C., *Gold Coast to Ghana*, 1996

Russell, Elnor, *Bush Life*, 1978

Russell, J., *Kenya, Beyond the Marich Pass: A District Officer's Story*, 1994

Sadleir, R., *Tanzania: Journey to Republic*, 1999

Sanders, P., *The Last of the Queen's Men*, 2000

Sharwood-Smith, Sir Bryan, *But Always as Friends: Northern Nigeria and the Cameroons 1921–1957*, 1969

Sharwood-Smith, Joan, *Diary of a Colonial Wife*, 1992

Short, R., *African Sunset*, 1973

Smith, J.H., *Colonial Cadet in Nigeria*, 1968

Skinner, A.N. *Burden Assumed*, 1985

——, *Burden at Sunset*, 1996

Stevens, Siaka, *What Life Has Taught Me*, 1984

Stuart, A., *Of Cargoes, Colonies and Kings*, 2001

Terrell, R., *West African Interlude*, 1988

Tweedsmuir, Lord, *Always a Countryman*, 1953

Udoji, J., *Under Three Masters: Memoirs of an African Administrator*, 1995

Watkins, Elizabeth, *Jomo's Jailor: The Life of Leslie Whitehouse*, 1993

——, *Oscar from Africa*, 1995

Watt, Peggy, *There is Only One Nigeria*, 1985

White, S., *Dan Bana: The Memoirs of a Nigerian Official*, 1966

Wild, J. and M., *Uganda Long Ago*, 2002

Winstanley, G., *Under Two Flags in Africa*, 2000

Wollocombe, R., *A Passage from India*, 1988

Wright, R., *'Strewth, So Help Me God*, 1994

Wright, R.H., *Then the Wind Changed in Africa*, ed R. Pearce, 1992

b. Collective memoirs

A recent addition to the literature of DOs' memoirs has been the volume of territorial collective memoirs, each bringing together some 50 or so memoirs of officers (overwhelmingly DOs) who served in a given territory between 1940 and independence. So far four volumes feature in this composite genre of memoirs along with two comparable collective sources.

1. D. and M. Brown (eds), *Looking Back on the Uganda Protectorate: Recollections of District Officers*, 1996

2. R. Anderson (ed), *Palm Wine and Leopard's Whiskers: Reminiscences of Eastern Nigeria*, 1999

3. J.R. Johnson (ed), *Colony to Nation: British Administrators in Kenya, 1940–1963*, 2002
4. A.T. Clark (ed), *Was It Only Yesterday? The Last Generation of Nigeria's Turawa* [N. Nigeria], 2002
5. A.H.M. Kirk-Greene (ed), *The Transfer of Power in Africa: The Colonial Administrator in the Age of Decolonization*, 1979
6. Charles Allen (ed), *Tales from the Dark Continent*, 1979

A further seven volumes fall into a similar collective category of memoirs but with a remit wider than that of the DO in Africa alone:

1. Joan Alexander, *Voices and Echoes*, 1983
2. Joanna Trollope, *Britannia's Daughters*, 1983
3. Pat Holden (ed), *Women Administrative Officers in Colonial Africa, 1944–1960*, ODRP Report No. 5, 1985, RHL MSS.Afr. s.1799
4. E. Burr (ed), *Localization and Public Service Training*, ODRP Report No. 4, 1985, MSS.Br.Emp.s.478
5. Heather Dalton (ed), *The Gold Coast: The Wives' Experience*, RHL ODRP Report No. 15, 1985, MSS.Afr.s.1985
6. Heather Dalton (ed), *The Experience of Colonial Governors' Wives*, 1989, RHL MSS.Br.Emp.s.529
7. Cecillie Swaisland (ed), *A World of Memories*, Women's Corona Society, 2000

A major work of reference will be Terry Barringer's forthcoming annotated bibliography of published Colonial Service memoirs, most of them of DOs.

III. GENERAL WORKS

a. Books

Allison, P., *Life in the White Man's Grave*, 1988
Azikiwe, Dr. N., *Zik*, 1961
Berman, B., *Control and Crisis in Colonial Kenya*, 1990
Blundell, Sir Richard, *So Rough A Wind*, 1964
Bradley, Emily, *Dearest Priscilla*, 1950
Bradley, K.G., *The Colonial Service as a Career*, 1950
——, *A Career in the Oversea Civil Service*, 1955

Brown, Judith M. and W.R. Louis (eds), *The Oxford History of the British Empire*, IV, 1999

Burns, Sir Alan, *In Defence of Colonies*, 1957

Callan, Hilary, and Shirley Ardener (eds), *The Incorporated Wife*, 1984

Callaway, Helen, *Gender, Culture and Empire*, 1987

Cameron, Sir Donald, *The Principles of Native Administration and their Application*, 1934

Cohen, Sir Andrew, *British Policy in Changing Africa*, 1959

Culwick, A.T., *Britannia Waives the Rules*, 1963

Dewar, K. and K.J. Bryant, *In Lighter Africa*, n.d.

Dickson, H.P., *The Badge of Britannia*, 1990

Farson, Negley, *Behind God's Back*, 1940

Ferguson, Niall, *Empire: How Britain Made the Modern World*, 2003

Gann, L.H., *A History of Northern Rhodesia*, 1969

Gann, L.H. and P. Duignan, *The Rulers of British Africa 1870–1914*, 1978

Garner, J., *The Commonwealth Office, 1925–1968*, 1978

Gill, A., *Ruling Passions: Sex, Race and Empire*, 1995

Golant, W., *Image of Empire: The Early History of the Imperial Institute*, 1984

Goldsworthy, D., *Colonial Issues in British Politics 1945–1961*, 1971

Gunther, J., *Inside Africa*, 1955

Hailey, Lord, *An African Survey*, 1938

Herbert, Eugenia, *Twilight on the Zambezi*, 2002

Heussler, R., *Yesterday's Rulers*, 1963

——, *The British in Northern Nigeria*, 1968

——, *British Tanganyika: An Essay and Documents on District Administration*, 1971

Huxley, Elspeth, *Four Guineas*, 1954

Hyam, R., *Empire and Sexuality: The British Experience*, 1990

James, Lawrence, *The Rise and Fall of the British Empire*, 1994

Jeffries, Sir Charles, *The Colonial Empire and its Civil Service*, 1938

——, *Partners for Progress: The Men and Women of the Colonial Service*, 1949

——, *Proud Record*, 1962

Kaunda, K., *State of the Nation*, I, 1986

Kirk-Greene, A.H.M., *The Principles of Native Administration in Nigeria*, 1965

——, *The Sudan Political Service: A Preliminary Profile*, 1982

——, *The Corona Club, 1900–1990*, 1990

——, *A Biographical Dictionary of the British Colonial Service 1939–1966*, 1991

——, *Nationalism and Arcadianism in the Sudan*, 1993

——, *On Crown Service*, 1999

——, *Britain's Imperial Administrators 1858–1966*, 2000

Kuklick, Henrika, *The Imperial Bureaucrat: The Colonial Administrative Service in the Gold Coast 1920–1939*, 1979

Lane, C., *The Ruling Passion*, 1995

Lee, J.M., *Colonial Development and Good Government*, 1967

Liebenow, J.G., *Colonial Rule and Political Development in Tanzania*, 1971

Low, D.A. and J.M. Lonsdale, *The History of East Africa*, Vol. III, 1976

Lugard, Sir Frederick, *Political Memoranda: Instructions to Political Officers*, (1919), 1970

——, *The Dual Mandate in British Tropical Africa*, 1922

Macmillan, W.M., *Africa Emergent*, 1938

Mason, P., *The Men Who Ruled India, II; The Guardians*, 1954

Morris, J., *Pax Britannica*, 1968

——, *Heaven's Command*, 1973

——, *Farewell the Trumpets*, 1978

Neillands, R., *A Fighting Retreat: The British Empire 1947–1997*, 1996

Pearce, R.D., *The Turning Point in Africa: British Colonial Policy 1938–1948*, 1982

Perham, Margery, *Native Administration in Nigeria*, 1937

——, *The Colonial Reckoning*, 1961

Roberts, A. (ed), *The Colonial Moment in Africa*, 1990

Royle, T., *Winds of Change: the End of the Empire in Africa*, 1996

Smith, J.H. (ed), *Administering Empire: the British Colonial Service in Retrospect*, 1999

Swaisland, Cecillie, *Forty Years of Service: the Women's Corona Society*, 1992

Symonds, R., *The British and Their Successors*, 1966

——, *Oxford and Empire: The Last Lost Cause?*, 1986

Tafawa Balewa, Sir Abubakar, *Mr Prime Minister*, 1964

Tidrick, Kathryn, *Empire and the English Character*, 1992

Vaughan, J.H. and A.H.M. Kirk-Greene, *The Diary of Hamman Yaji*, 1995

Winks, R. (ed), *The Oxford History of the British Empire*, V, 1999

Younger, K., *The Public Service in New States*, 1960

b. Articles and chapters

Cartland, G., 'Retrospect,' *Journal of Administration Overseas*, 1 (1974), pp 269–72

Creech Jones, A. 'The Colonial Service', in W.A. Robson (ed), *The British Civil Servant*, 1937, pp 231–50

——, 'The Place of African Local Administration in Colonial Policy', *Journal of African Administration*, 1, 1 (1949), p 35

——, 'Founding A Link', *Corona*, December 1962, pp 464–6

Gartrell, Beverley, 'Colonial Wives: Villains or Victims?' in Hilary Callan and Shirley Ardener (eds), *The Incorporated Wife*, 1984, pp 165–85

Giles, L.C., 'The University and the Colonial Service: The Colonial Service as a Career', *Oxford*, 1949, pp 1–8

Heussler, R., 'The Legacy of British Colonialism: The Colonial Service', *South Atlantic Quarterly*, 60 (1961), p 3

Hyam, R., 'Concubinage and the Colonial Service: The Crewe Circular (1909)', *Journal of Imperial and Commonwealth History*, xiv, 3 (1986), pp 170–86

Jeffries, Sir Charles, 'The Colonial Service in Perspective', *Corona*, December 1962, pp 450–4

Kirk-Greene, A.H.M., 'The British Colonial Service and the Dominions Selection Scheme', *Canadian Journal of African Studies*, 15, 11 (1981), pp 33–54

——, 'Imperial Administration and the Athletic Imperative: the Case of the District Officer in Africa', in W.J. Baker and J.A. Mangan (eds), *Sport in Africa*, 1987, pp 81–113

——, 'A Tale of Two Universities', *Oxford*, xlvi, 2 (1994), pp 71–5

——, 'Public Administration and the Colonial Administrator', *Public Administration and Development*, 19 (1999), pp 507–19

——, 'The Colonial Service in the Novel', in J.H. Smith (ed), *Administering Empire*, 1999, pp 19–48

——, 'The Tropics and Ten the Turl', *Oxford*, lii, 1 (2000), pp 13–18

——, 'Decolonization: The Ultimate Diaspora', *Journal of Contemporary History*, 36 (2001), pp 135–51

——, 'Not Quite a Gentleman', *English Historical Review*, cxvii, 472 (2002), pp 622–33

——, 'The Colonial Service Mind', *Overseas Pensioner*, 2003, pp 15–21

Laski, H., 'The Colonial Civil Service', *Political Quarterly*, 4, 1938

Lonsdale, J.M., 'British Colonial Officials and the Kikuyu People', in J.H. Smith (ed), *Administering Empire*, pp 95–102

McCleery, H.H., 'The Overseas Service Course at Cambridge', *Cambridge Review*, October 1966, pp 29–30

Poynton, Sir Hilton, 'Speculation in Church House', *Corona*, December 1962, pp 456–64

Rathbone, R., 'The Colonial Service and the Transfer of Power in Ghana', in J.H. Smith (ed), *Administering Empire*, 1999, pp 149–66

Robinson, R.E., 'Why Indirect Rule has been Replaced by Local Government in the Nomenclature of British Native Administration', *Journal of African Administration*, 2 (1950), pp 12–15

Rowe, E.G., 'Aucuparius Aftermath: the Overseas Services Courses', *Oxford*, 23, 2 (1970), pp 70–84

Thomas, A.B., 'The Development of the Overseas Civil Service', *Public Administration*, 35 (1958), pp 319–33

Note: Because of the appearance of an anthology from *Corona*, the Colonial Service house magazine (1949–62), *Glimpses of Empire*, 2001 and *More Glimpses of Empire* (in press), both edited by A.H.M. Kirk-Greene, DO articles in *Corona* have not been cited other than those in the special farewell issue of December 1962.

c. Official publications

The Administrative Officer in Tanganyika Today and Tomorrow (1957)

Appointments Handbook, 1948 (CO, confidential)

Appointments in Her Majesty's Colonial Service, CSRI, 1953

Appointments in Her Majesty's Oversea Civil Service, OCSI, 1955

A Career in the Administrative Service in Northern Rhodesia (1956?)

The Colonial Administrative Service List (3rd edition), 1937, Col. No. 137

Colonial Appointments, Misc. No. 96, 1921

Colonial Office: Appointments Handbook (confidential), 1948

Colonial Office Conference, 1930, Summary of Proceedings, Cmd. 3628

The Colonial Office List, 1947–1966 (annual)

Colonial Regulations, Col. No. 322, 1956

The Colonial Territories, 1948–1949, Cmd. 7715, 1951–52, Cmd 8553

Committee on the System of Appointment in the Colonial Office and the Colonial Services (Warren Fisher), Cmd. 3554, 1930

The Dominion and Colonial Office List, 1932–1940
First Devonshire Course, Oxford University Committee for Colonial Studies, 1953
Information Regarding the Colonial Administrative Service, CSR2, 1935
Life and Duties of an Administrative Officer in Kenya, 1958
Native Administration and Political Development in British Tropical Africa (Hailey), 1942, (CO, confidential)
Nigeria: Northern Provinces Office Guide, 1932
Post-war Opportunities in the Colonial Service, RDW6, 1945
Sokoto Emirate Notes on Procedure, n.d.

White Papers on post-war restructuring of Colonial Service/ HMOCS:

Col. No. 197, *Organization of the Colonial Service*, 1946
Col. No. 198, *Post-War Training for the Colonial Service*, 1946
Col. No. 209, *Civil Services in British West Africa* (Harragin), 1947
Col. No. 222, *Civil Services of Northern Rhodesia and Nyasaland* (Fitzgerald), 1948
Col. No. 223, *Civil Services of Kenya, Uganda, Tanganyika and Zanzibar* (Holmes), 1948
Col. No. 306, *Reorganisation of the Colonial Service*, 1954
Cmd. 9768, *Her Majesty's Oversea Civil Service: Statement of Policy Regarding Organization*, 1956
Cmnd. 497, *HMOCS: Statement of Policy Regarding Overseas Officers Serving in Nigeria*, 1958
Cmnd. 1193, *Service with Overseas Governments*, 1960
Cmnd. 1308, *Technical Assistance from the UK for Overseas Development*, 1961
Cmnd. 1698, *Technical Co-operation*, 1962
Cmnd. 1740, *Recruitment for Service Overseas: Future Policy*, 1963
Cmnd. 2099, *Policy on the Recommendations* [above], 1963

See also the Nuffield Foundation, *Report on a Visit to Nigeria*, 1946, and the following volumes in the *British Documents on the End of Empire* series for excerpts from official documents involving Colonial Service matters:

Ashton, S.R. and S. E. Stockwell (eds), *Imperial Policy and Colonial Practice 1925–1945*, 1996

Goldsworthy, D. (ed), *The Conservative Government and the End of Empire 1951–1957*, 1994

Hyam, R. (ed), *The Labour Government and the End of Empire 1945–1951*, 1992

Hyam, R., and W.R. Louis, *The Conservative Government and the End of Empire 1957–1964*, 2000

d. Novels

Achebe, Chinua, *Things Fall Apart*, 1958

——, *Arrow of God*, 1964

Adebayo, Augustine, *I Am Directed*, 1991

Aluko, T.M., *One Man, One Matchet*, 1964

Barnard, Jane, *Black Mistress*, 1957

Bates, D., *A Fly Switch from the Sultan*, 1961

——, *The Shell at My Ear*, 1961

——, *The Mango and the Palm*, 1962

Berry, Erick, *Mad Dogs and Englishmen*, 1941

Best, H. *A Rumour of Drums*, 1962

Brook, I., *Jimmy Riddle*, 1961

——, *The Black List*, 1962

Cary, Joyce, *An American Visitor*, 1933

——, *The African Witch*, 1936

——, *Mister Johnson*, 1939

——, *Aissa Saved*, 1949

——, *Cock Jarvis*, 1974

Christian, Carol, *Into Strange Country*, 1959

Dickenson, P., *Tefuga*, 1986

Dobson, K., *Mail Train*, 1946

——, *The Inescapable Wilderness*, 1953

——, *District Commissioner*, 1954

——, *Colour Blind*, 1955

Fowler, W., *Karama*, 1962

Garaghan, T., *Corridors of Wire*, 1994

Gerrard, F., *The Return of Sanders of the River*, 1938

——, *Justice of Sanders*, 1951

Gordimer, Nadine, *A Guest of Honour*, 1951

Greene, Graham, *The Human Factor*, 1978

Hanley, Gerald, *The Consul at Sunset*, 1951

Hargreaves, Elizabeth, *Handful of Silver*, 1954

Hastings, A.C.G., *Gone Native*, 1923

——, *Jane's Way*, 1936

Hives, F., *Juju and Justice in Nigeria*, 1930

——, *Justice in the Jungle*, 1933

Huxley, Elspeth, *Murder at Government House*, 1937

——, *Murder on Safari*, 1938

——, *The African Poison Murders*, 1939

——, *The Walled City*, 1948

——, *A Thing to Love*, 1954

Kittermaster, M., *The District Officer*, 1957

——, *Katakala*, 1957

Le Carré, J., *Smiley's People*, 1979

——, *A Small Town in Germany*, 1991

Lovatt Smith, D., *My Enemy, My Friend*, 2000

Makasa, Kapasa, *Bwana District Commissioner*, 1989

Monserrat, Nicholas, *The Tribe That Lost its Head*, 1956

——, *Richer Than All His Tribe*, 1968

Ngugi wa Thiongo, *Weep Not Child*, 1964

——, *A Grain of Wheat*, 1967

Ogunyemi, M., *The D.O.*, 1987

Perham, Margery, *Major Dane's Garden*, 1926

Raven, Simon, *The Feathers of Death*, 1959

Ruark, Robert, *Something of Violence*, 1955

——, *Uhuru*, 1962

Taafe, M., *The Dark Glass*, 1963

Ulasi, Adaora Lily, *Many Thing You No Understand*, 1970

——, *Many Thing Begin for Change*, 1971

——, *The Man from Sagamu*, 1978

Vasanji, M.G., *The Book of Secrets*, 1994

Wallace, Edgar, *Sanders of the River*, 1911

——, *The People of the River*, 1912

——, *Bosambo of the River*, 1914

——, *Bones*, 1915

——, *The Keepers of the King's Peace*, 1917

——, *Lieutenant Bones*, 1919

——, *Sandi the King-Maker*, 1923

——, *Bones of the River*, 1923

——, *Bones in London*, 1924

——, *Sanders*, 1926

——, *Again Sanders*, 1928

Index

Numbers in *italics* refer to illustrations.